Perspectives in American History

No. 29
THE OPENING OF TEXAS
TO FOREIGN SETTLEMENT 1801-1821

THE OPENING OF TEXAS TO FOREIGN SETTLEMENT, 1801–1821

By

MATTIE ALICE AUSTIN HATCHER, M.A.
Archivist of the University of Texas

PORCUPINE PRESS

Philadelphia 1976

First edition 1927
(Austin: University of Texas Bulletin
No. 2714, 1927)

Reprinted 1976 by
PORCUPINE PRESS, INC.
Philadelphia, Pennsylvania 19107

Library of Congress Cataloging in Publication Data

Hatcher, Mattie Alice Austin.
    The opening of Texas to foreign settlement, 1801-1821.

    (Perspectives in American History ; no. 29)
    Reprint of the 1927 1st. ed. published by the University, Austin, Tex., which was issued as no. 2714 of the University of Texas Bulletin.
    Bibliography: p.
    1. Texas—History—To 1846. I. Title.
II. Series: Perspectives in American history (Philadelphia) ; no. 29.
F389.H36   1976   976.4'02   76-7430
ISBN 0-87991-353-3

Manufactured in the United States of America

CONTENTS

	PAGE
Introduction.—The Background in Louisiana and Texas, 1763–1801	7
Chapter I.—Admisison of Vassals from Louisiana, 1801–1803	60
Chapter II.—Decision for a Buffer against the United States, 1804–1805	70
Chapter III.—Establishment of *Villas* and Disagreement over Management of Immigrants, 1806–1807	102
Chapter IV.—Ambition of Napoleon and Precautions of the Commandant-General, 1808	127
Chapter V.—Instructions for Closing the Door to Immigration from Foreign Territory, 1809	147
Chapter VI.—Opposition of Active Enemies, Headstrong Subordinates, and Rebellious Vassals, 1810	182
Chapter VII.—Preliminary Testing of Nations and Principles, 1811–1812	207
Chapter VIII.—Temporary Triumph of Progressive Royalists, 1813–1814	233
Chapter IX.—Final Preparation for a Successful Colony, 1814–1821	234
Appendix	293

MAPS AND ILLUSTRATIONS

1. Sketch of Villa de Palafox 201–202

The following maps will be found after page 368

2. Texas, 1805–1812. Adapted from Puelles' Map of 1807
3. Plan of San Fernando de Béxar
4. Texas, 1801. Adapted from Puelles' Map of 1807
5. Texas after 1821, showing Austins' Colony

The benefits of education and of useful knowledge, generally diffused through a community, are essential to the preservation of a free government.
                                Sam Houston

Cultivated mind is the guardian genius of democracy. . . . It is the only dictator that freemen acknowledge and the only security that freemen desire.
                            Mirabeau B. Lamar

PREFACE

As yet, no detailed history of Texas for the early years of the nineteenth century has been written. Consequently, the writer has been compelled to act as a pioneer in the special field chosen and, therefore, has been obliged to work out many related questions which had a determining influence upon the development of a liberal colonization system by the Spaniards in their vain efforts to place an effective barrier against the irresistible tide of American immigration to the West. As a result, it has been necessary to enter into great detail in setting forth the many facts discovered so that justice may be done to all the formative influences involved. In dealing with this great mass of details, it is not possible that all mistakes have been avoided. Nevertheless, the writer will feel amply repaid if she has succeeded in showing that, during these years, Texas—at first absolutely closed to foreigners—was considered the most vital point in the Spanish Dominions of America; that by 1820 all royalists who understood the situation had come to believe that colonization was the one thing needed to make the much coveted province safe against attack; and that by 1821 the liberals were prepared to welcome foreigners, even the Anglo-Saxons, who had established the principles of freedom in 1776 and who had demonstrated their ability to hold every region into which they had penetrated—if by this means Texas could be developed. If at times the enormity of the task has been somewhat appalling, an adequate compensation has been derived from the pleasure of discovery, lasting from the moment Daniel Boone's petition for entry into Texas first attracted attention to the subject until the documents showing the final determination of the authorities to find some apparently safe means of colonizing this important territory and the decree opening the Spanish Dominions to foreigners had been discovered. Besides, the generous response of all those to whom appeals for aid were presented gave additional encouragement. Among those deserving especial mention are Dr. Eugene C. Barker, Professor of American History in the University of Texas, who has given valuable criticism and has made helpful suggestions for the arrangement of materials, and Miss Lilia Mary Casis, Professor of Romance Languages of the University of Texas, who has given encouragement and advice and assisted in the translation of difficult and obscure passages from the Spanish. Thanks are also due to Miss Hilda Norman for aid in translating certain French documents. Among those who helped by securing documents lacking from the collections available at Austin, Dr. H. E. Bolton, Professor of American History in the University of California; Dr. H. I. Priestley, Professor of Mexican History in the same institution; Mr. E. W. Winkler, Librarian at the University of Texas; Dr. W. E. Dunn, formerly Associate Professor of Latin-American History, and Dr. Charles W. Hackett, Professor of Latin-American History at the same institution, have been especially kind.

THE OPENING OF TEXAS TO FOREIGN SETTLEMENT, 1801–1821

INTRODUCTION

Historians have assigned but little importance to the story of the frontier province of Texas for the first quarter of the nineteenth century. In the main, they have neglected its economic and diplomatic history and have confined their attention to the military defenses undertaken by the Spaniards against certain relatively unimportant "filibusters" and against the possibility of aggression from the United States government—intent upon securing Texas as a part of the Louisiana Purchase. As a consequence of this undue emphasis, little has been written of the efforts of the Spaniards to place an effective barrier against the advance guards of the westward-bound Americans who began to reach Texas in considerable numbers early in the nineteenth century; of their attitude towards the Indians who then lived within the province and towards others who soon sought entry into its jealously guarded precincts; of their later successful efforts to defeat the plans of Napoleon for gaining control in the Spanish Dominions of America and especially of Texas, "the key to the whole"; and of their final plans for peopling and developing the important region—so long practically given over to the wild Indian tribes.

For instance, Bancroft, probably the most reliable historian who has dealt with this period, states that, through the introduction of troops and colonists into Texas, Spain put forth unusual efforts to interpose a powerful buffer on the Mexican frontier to prevent the encroachments which she believed her neighbor in North America would make as soon as the latter secured possession of Louisiana. But, although he gives some account of the military operations of the times, he fails to discuss the equally important colonization plans carried out in conjunction therewith. He merely notes the failure of a project for the transportation of families from Spain to Texas in 1804 under the direction of Pedro Grimarest, who was scheduled to become commandant-general of the proposed Eastern Interior Provinces;[1] and then adds the statement that other settlers introduced as a buffer against the United States effected no expansion of the community. In his footnotes, he barely mentions a few of the other plans undertaken at this time for the settlement of Texas; while to some of the important projects considered he makes no reference whatever. In the end, he dismisses the result of all colonization during this period with the terse remark that none met with success. Other historians either fail to convey even a hint of this phase of the subject, or give only an imperfect account of the movement.

---

[1]The Provincias Internas, as originally created by the decree of August 22, 1776, included the frontier provinces of the two Californias, New Mexico, Sinaloa, Nueva Viscaya, Coahuila, and Texas. They were under the control of a commandant-general, Theodore de Croix, who was responsible to the king but practically independent of the viceroy of Mexico. This *régime*, with slight modifications, continued until 1785, when the authority of the viceroy was practically restored because a new viceroy, Conde de Gálvez, formerly governor of Louisiana, was familiar with conditions on the frontier. At this time, the Interior Provinces were divided into three military districts, one of them, under command of Juan de Ugalde, including Coahuila, Nuevo León, Nuevo Santander, and Texas. Upon the death of Gálvez, in 1786, the commandant-general became once more independent of the viceroy. However in March, 1787, the power of the new viceroy was declared to be identical with that of his predecessor. On December 3 of the same year, the three military districts mentioned above were consolidated into two commandancies general designated as the Eastern and the Western Interior Provinces, the former including Nuevo León and Nuevo Santander, Coahuila, and Texas. The viceroy exercised a limited jurisdiction over the region until March 11, 1788, when viceregal power was fully restored. In 1793, the two commandancies were again reunited into one, independent of the viceroy—the two Californias, Nuevo León, and Nuevo Santander being detached and placed under the command of military governors who were subordinate to the viceroy. This system continued until the beginning of the period under discussion. Bolton, Hebert E., *Guide to Materials for the History of the United States in the Principal Archives of Mexico*, 75–76.

However, recent investigation in the Spanish sources has proved that the colonizing activities of the period were vastly more than the feeble reaction against foreign aggression of the periods more familiar to the student of Texas history. In fact the records show that, although the Spaniards were unable to induce any considerable number of native immigrants to settle in the wilds of Texas and attempt to subdue the Indians, there was a splendid effort towards developing the country by the settlement of vassals from Louisiana and Mexico; that a very creditable beginning was made; that lack of resources, differences of opinion among authorities, and a combination of enemies soon brought a temporary lull, followed immediately thereafter by renewed activity; and that, while most of the material gains were finally lost altogether, the way was at last prepared for its development by the North Americans.

The period of Anglo-American colonization cannot, therefore, be understood without a knowledge of the events of those years, since it was during this time that practically all the foundations for future development were laid, the diverse plans of the Spanish authorities united, and their feeble hopes of defending and developing the region hardened into a firm purpose. Indeed, by their determined stand at the beginning of the century, they postponed the loss of Texas for some years; though at the same time they unwittingly prepared an ideal soil for the planting of Austin's colony of nominal Spanish vassals, but, in reality, of true liberty-loving, home-seeking American frontiersmen who—due largely to the triumph of the movement for independence—were to change the whole history of Texas.

However, before describing Spain's effort to colonize Texas between the years 1801 and 1821, it will be necessary, first, to trace the policy previously developed in Louisiana where the problem of stemming the tide of American immigration into Spanish territory—hitherto jealously closed to all foreigners[2]—had first presented itself. By the Treaty of 1763,

---

[2]For Spain's exclusion policy see Appendix 1.

Spain secured possession of Louisiana; and, almost immediately, she was besieged by English, Irish, French, Dutch, German, and American colonizers, who, anxious to secure lands, desired to introduce settlers into the rich but undeveloped region. Instinctively sensing the danger from the Anglo-Saxons, who up to this time had been kept safely beyond the Alleghany Mountains, the local authorities protested vigorously against such a step. But higher authorities, with Charles III at their head, realized the necessity for developing the country and favored the adoption of the proposed policy. The struggle between the liberal and exclusive policies here indicated will now be traced.

THE LOUISIANA BACKGROUND, 1763–1801

Immigration into Lower Louisiana, 1763–1768.—Among the first immigrants to arrive in Louisiana after the Treaty of 1763 had converted it from French to Spanish territory, were a number of Acadians who, as early at 1755, had temporarily taken refuge in Maryland. Between January and May, 1765, about six hundred and fifty of these unfortunate people arrived at New Orleans and, later, were sent to form the settlements of Attakapas and Opelousas; while in the spring of 1766, two hundred and sixteen others arrived and received permission to settle on both sides of the German Coast[3] as far up as Point Coupé. That these hapless refugees should have been received, was natural, but the admission of the representatives of the very nation that had driven them from their former homes was likewise considered. These applicants, however, were not in sympathy with the English government.

The reports which the Acadians made in regard to their new homes reached the ears of Henry Jernigham, an

---

[3]The German Coast embraced the parishes of St. Charles and St. John. It was settled in 1723 by some two hundred and fifty Germans who had been sent to Law's concession in Arkansas and who were granted lands on the Mississippi as a compensation for their losses due to the failure of Law's financial schemes. Fortier, Alceé, *History of Louisiana*, I, 70.

Englishman living in Maryland. He at once opened up a correspondence with the governor of Louisiana and dispatched an agent to New Orleans to make arrangements for the reception of a large number of English Catholics who were discontented because of their treatment by the colonial government and who, therefore, desired to follow their former neighbors and friends. The agent was kindly received and assisted in exploring the country as far north as the new trading post just established at St. Louis. The governor believed that this movement would lead to the settlement of the country by a people hostile to the English government. He even believed that a "torrent" of immigration would flow in, not only from Maryland, but also from neighboring territories.[4] But a careful search of the records of the *Archivo General de Indias* has failed to disclose any evidence of a general movement of English towards Louisiana. Indeed, everything seems to indicate that the plan was never carried out. Nevertheless, the correspondence and the report of the agent must have spread abroad information in regard to the advantages offered immigrants in Louisiana.

Beginning of settlement in Upper Louisiana, 1767.—Spain was slow to grasp the opportunity offered her on the upper Mississippi by the cession of Louisiana. Indeed, beyond permitting the establishment of the trading post of St. Louis, encouraging the exploration just mentioned, and allowing a number of French families to locate at St. Genevieve, she made no great effort to hold that portion of the country until after 1767, when she established two forts at the mouth of the Missouri River to prevent the English from penetrating into the adjacent region westward, which abounded in valuable fur-bearing animals.[5]

Admission of Acadians, Canadians, Italians, Spaniards, and Germans, 1777–1783.—In 1777, the lieutenant-governor of Louisiana received instructions to offer aid,

---

[4]Documents contributed by James A. Robertson, *The American Historical Review*, XVI, 319–327.
[5]Houck, Louis, *The Spanish Régime in Missouri*, I, xvii.

from a fund set apart for the increase of population, the
development of commerce, and the cultivation of friendly
relations with the Indians, to such Acadians as still lived
among the English but who now desired to take refuge
among the Spaniards. In reply, he promised to make every
effort to attract the Acadians and discussed the ease with
which the French Canadians, who were Catholics, could be
induced to follow the example of certain of their countrymen who had recently come to St. Louis "to escape the direst
poverty and the grossest oppression." The king approved
this suggestion and also gave orders for the admission of
Spaniards, Italians, and Germans. To insure an enthusiastic response to this invitation, the lieutenant-governor
offered to reputable immigrants, houses, lands, provisions,
and tools, on condition that they take the oath of allegiance
to the Spanish government. A few poor families, who had
to be supported for a season, settled at Attakapas and
Opelousas and a considerable number of Acadians came back
from France, founded the new settlement of Feliciana, and
located near Plaquemines and at various other points in
Lower Louisiana.[6] In 1783, upon the proposal of Conde de
Aranda, it was decided to try to secure in France Acadian
families for the purpose of cultivating the soil of Louisiana.[7]
However, because of the expense involved, only a few
families were actually brought over. Thus failed a plan
which Aranda hoped would be the first step in the
erection of an impassable barrier against the advance
of the Americans; for it was in this same year that he

---

[6]Conde de Gálvez to Marqués de Sonora, March 22, 1786, in *Archivo Géneral de Indias*, Sevilla, Santo Domingo, 86–6–15, March 22, 1786, and Miró to Marqués de Sonora, June 11, 1787, in *ibid.*, Sto. Dom., 86–6–8, May 15, 1788–October 20, 1788, Transcripts of the University of Texas. For the sake of brevity, this collection will appear in sub-sequent notes as *A. G. I. S.*, with the proper designation of *Audencia* of Mexico, Guadalaxara, Cuba, *Indiferente General*, or Santo Domingo, Louisiana, and Florida, appearing as Mex., Guad., Cub., *Indif.*, or Sto. Dom., La., and Fla. as the case may be.

[7]Morales to the King, June 30, 1799, in *A. G. I. S.* Sto. Dom., 86–7–17, May 8, 1797–June 9, 1799.

warned Charles III that the American nation, then but a pigmy, would one day become a giant and would threaten the very existence of the Spanish Dominions of America.[8] The warning seems to have fallen upon deaf ears, for the king soon took steps favorable to the Americans.

Opening wedge for the entry of English and American Protestants, 1786.—By a royal order, dated April 5, 1786, the king granted temporary asylum in Louisiana to certain Americans and to such British royalists as had remained there after the peace of 1783, permitting them to locate wherever they might choose.[9] As a result, a large number settled at Natchez, while fifty-nine other English and American families located in the vicinity.[10] In the order providing for the protection of the English, the king announced that he had under consideration a plan for admitting other foreigners into the territory and for sending out Irish priests to convert such of them as were Protestants. All colonists were required to be Catholics since a royal order of 1786 forbade the admission to Louisiana of any person who could not prove beyond a doubt that he was a Catholic. Even those professing this faith but who were unwilling to take the oath of allegiance or could not prove good characters, were to be excluded. But now, without awaiting instructions—which the king declared were being drawn up—Diego Gardoquí, Minister from Spain to the United States, began to issue passports to foreign families who wished to share in the promised advantages.

Upon receiving an appeal for aid from New Orleans, after the disastrous fire of 1788, he sent one hundred and thirty persons from New York and Philadelphia. Among the number were four negroes and seventy-nine whites who were absolutely destitute. He paid their transportation expenses,

---

[8]Coxe, William, *L'Espagne Sous la Maison de Bourbon*, VI, 45–54.

[9]Zepedes to Marqués de Sonora, August 12, 1786, *A. G. I. S.* Sto. Dom., 86–6–15, August 22, 1786.

[10]Zepedes to Las Casas, June 20, 1790, *A. G. I. S.* Sto. Dom., 86–6–13, June 20, 1790–August 14, 1790, and Miró to Marqués de Sonora, February 1, 1787, *A. G. I. S.* Sto Dom., February 1, 1797.

but upon their arrival, the local government was compelled to support them for a year and to furnish stock and tools.[11] Estevan Miró, who was governor of Louisiana at the time, objected to this step, claiming that the government had been able to contract for families who were able to support themselves and who asked only for lands. He feared that Gardoquí's procedure would inspire thousands of indigent residents of Ohio and Kentucky to move into Spanish territory.[12] Nevertheless, he felt compelled to receive all applicants—even non-Catholics—but stipulated that, in future, they should pay their own transportation and consider themselves as temporary settlers until the king should fix the conditions under which they were to be received as vassals.[13] Many of these immigrants were men of means; and, disliking this uncertainty, immediately applied for citizenship; while a number of colonizers, several of whom were Irish, offered their services in filling the country with settlers.

Irish colonizers, 1787–1789.—Among these colonizers was Bryan Browin or Bruin, a Virginian, who had spent some time in New Orleans. In 1787, he asked to be allowed to bring in twelve wealthy Irish families. He declared that the applicants in question desired to immigrate because they had heard of the liberal laws and beneficent government in Louisiana. He inquired particularly as to the amount of land that could be secured at Baton Rouge. Miró favored the plan, more especially because the applicants offered to bring at their own expenses their household goods, their slaves, and such tools as might be necessary for clearing and cultivating plantations. This was in line with the condition for admission imposed by the supreme government, whch stipulated that no foreigner could be received who did not, of his own free will, present himself and

---

[11]Miró to Marqués de Sonora, June 28, 1786, *A. G. I. S.* Sto. Dom., 86–6–15, June 28, 1786.

[12]Miró to Váldez, January 8, 1788, *A. G. I. S.* Sto Dom., 86–6–8, Miró to Gardoquí, September 30, 1788, *ibid.*

[13]Zepedes to Las Casas, June 20, 2790, *ibid.*

swear allegiance to the king. To such persons, lands were to be granted in proportion to the number in the various families. No settler was to be molested on account of his religion, but Catholics alone were to be allowed public worship. The immigrants were to be required to bear arms in defense of the province only in case of invasion by the enemy. No inducements were to be offered save lands, protection, and kind treatment. They might bring with them property of all kinds but, in case they later exported it, they were to pay a duty of five per cent.[14] Miró liked the idea of economizing the public funds and believed that the possession of property would insure good behavior, as it was usually the people who had nothing to lose who stirred up trouble. He therefore gave permission for the settlement of the families in question at the points indicated and named a plot twenty by forty *arpents*[15] as the amount to be distributed to each family, promising an addition of an equal amount as soon as the first plot had been cleared and cultivated. He permitted them to introduce their stock, etc., upon the payment of the required six per

---

[14]Martin, Francis Xavier, *History of Louisiana*, 253–254. The plan for religious tolerance is well illustrated by a dispatch from Miró to the Spanish government, dated June 3, 1789, as a result of the call for military assistance presented by a commissary of the Spanish Inquisition. After arresting the objectionable priest and placing him on an outbound vessel, Miró made the following statement: "His Majesty has instructed me to encourage an increase of population, admitting the people living on the banks of the rivers that empty into the Ohio. . . . They were invited with the promise that they would not be disturbed on matters of religion, although the only mode of public worship was to be the Catholic. The mere name of the inquisition of New Orleans would not only suffice to restrain the immigration already beginning to take place, but might cause those who have recently immigrated to withdraw. I even fear that in spite of the fact that I have ordered Father Sedella to leave the country the case may become known and have fatal results." Wortham, Louis J., *History of Texas*, 55–56.

[15]According to Violette, the *arpent* was used for both surface and linear measurement among the French and as a unit of surface measurement is varied from five-sixths to seven-eighths of an English acre. *History of Missouri*, 58.

cent but suggested that this be remitted in the future so that immigration might be encouraged. However, he issued a warning against the introduction of any goods for subsequent sale and objected particularly to sugar and brandy, since they were contraband goods. It is not possible to ascertain whether or not any of these applicants actually entered, but the Irish continued to be interested in the settlement of Louisiana.

Later in the same year, William Fitzgerald, who had secured recommendations from Gardoquí, was allowed an advance of one thousand *pesos* for the payment of the transportation of thirty families who desired to come to Louisiana from New York. He likewise expected the government to reward him for his services. The intendant of Louisiana, who at this time had charge of colonization, recommended that these requests be granted lest the petitioner might direct his settlers to Ohio.[16] But no evidence has been found concerning the execution of this plan.

Among other Irishmen interested in colonizing Louisiana may be named William Butler. Having secured a recommendation from Gardoquí he asked to be allowed to introduce forty-six families from the extreme eastern portion of the United States, the government paying for their transportation. Miró refused this because immigrants could be secured on better terms. Thereupon, Butler signified his willingness to introduce one hundred and fifty-four persons of the original number who were willing to pay their own expenses. It is probable that a considerable number came, since those responding were to be allowed to introduce their goods free of duty.[17]

Another Irishman, Augustin Macarty, who had retired from the French army, desired to share in the commercial advantages of the decree of January 22, 1782, and "to aid in the defense of Louisiana." He, therefore, offered his help in inducing two or three thousand discontented Irish Catho-

---

[16]Navarro to Váldez, October 19, 1787, *A. G. I. S.* Sto. Dom., 87–1–21.

[17]Butler to Miró, June 28, 1789, and Miró to Váldez, July 31, 1789, *ibid.*

lics, located at various points in the United States, to settle in that province. He asked that his colonists be given the same privileges as those granted the Acadians and that Gardoquí be instructed to furnish money and vessels for their transportation. He also requested that a tract of land be given to each head of a family and that the tools needed for clearing and cultivating the ground be furnished. Miró was delighted with the proposition, because he favored the old plan of admitting Catholics only. He believed, too, that the proposed settlers would be able to defend the province and he had no fear of receiving those who were willing to renounce their allegiance to the United States.[18] It is impossible, from the records available, to estimate the number of immigrants introduced by any *one* or even by *all* the Irishmen interested in colonization at this time, since only incomplete census reports can be found. Martin declares that few or no settlers immigrated to Louisiana from Ireland[19] but this, of course, does not preclude the possibility of a heavy Irish immigration from the United States. In the meantime, other colonizers of different nationalities presented themselves.

French colonizers, D'Arges, 1787.—Pierre Wouves D'Arges, who believed that it would be exceedingly easy to induce a large number of Kentuckians to move to Louisiana, presented himself in August, 1787, and secured permission to introduce one thousand five hundred and eighty-two families on condition that they should receive lands and be allowed to worship according to their own beliefs.[20] However, because of his insistence upon free commerce between Kentucky and Louisiana—a concession which seemed implied in his contract—he incurred the displeasure of Gardoquí, who wished all efforts confined to the introduction of families; of Miró, who feared the results of religious

---

[18]Miró to Marqués de Sonora, August 15, 1789, *A. G. I. S.* Sto. Dom., 86–6–16, August 14–16, 1789.

[19]*History of Louisiana*, 254.

[20]Miró to Váldez, October 20, 1788, *A. G. I. S.* Sto. Dom., 86–6–8, May 15, 1788–October 20, 1788, and Miró to Váldez, April 11, 1789, *A. G. I. S.* Sto. Dom., 86–6–17, October 14, 1787–April 11, 1789.

toleration, and of James Wilkinson, who had colonization and commercial schemes of his own.[21] Miró even tried to persuade D'Arges that he could serve Spain best by assuming command of a post to be established at the mouth of the Ohio river, so that he might be the better able to induce immigration from *Illinois,* since the mere publication of the order granting a concession to Wilkinson would attract a great number of settlers from Kentucky.[22] As a result, D'Arges was unable to accomplish anything decisive, although it is quite possible that some families came in through his influence.[23] As he was outgeneraled by Wilkinson, an examination of the latters' colonization plans for Louisiana are necessary. However, another American preceded Wilkinson in the field and demands prior consideration.

American colonizer, Morgan, 1788.—In September, 1788, Gardoquí arranged with Colonel George Morgan, of New Jersey, to select a location upon the west bank of the Mississippi suitable for a colony of sober, industrious farmers and mechanics. Morgan induced several gentlemen farmers, traders, workmen, etc., to aid him in exploring the country and in convincing the people of the United States of the advantages to be secured by a transfer to Spanish territory. A number of prominent French royalists of Illinois promised to join the colony with their families as soon as it should be established. Morgan, who had previously served as United States Indian agent, wisely secured the good will of the red men by paying the expenses of a delegation which accompanied him. Along the circuitous route he traveled, he secured promises from numerous Germans of Pennsylvania—many of whom were Catholics—to join his colony when established, while ten of them at once joined the exploring party. Morgan continued his journey through

---

[21]Miró to D'Arges, August 13, 1788, *A. G. I. S.* Sto. Dom., 86–6–8, August 12–21, 1788.

[22]Miró to D'Arges, March 4, 1789, *A. G. I. S.* Sto. Dom., 86–6–17, March 4–15, 1789.

[23]Miró to Váldez, January 8, 1788, *A. G. I. S.* Sto. Dom., 86–6–8, January 8, 1788.

Kentucky and, in spite of Wilkinson's commercial schemes and of the opposition of British agents, he secured many enthusiastic followers by promising them religious freedom and commercial advantages "such as they had never dreamed of before."

After examining the country, he chose a point of land on the west bank of the Mississippi opposite the mouth of the Ohio as "the most important spot in His Majesty's North American dominions, both in a military and a commercial view." He suggested that this place be made an *entrepôt* for the trade of Kentucky and all the future American settlements of the Ohio, thus rendering the navigation of the Mississippi perfectly unnecessary or indifferent to the United States. He predicted that the new subjects would soon be sufficient in number and possess enough capital to transact all the business of the country, and suggested that trial by jury and legislation on purely local matters be allowed—subject, of course, to the approval of the king. Without waiting for these recommendations to be acted upon, he established the town of New Madrid and laid out tracts of three hundred and twenty acres each for three hundred and fifty prospective heads of families. To those with him and to others who were expected to join him he immediately granted lands. They were required to take the oath of allegiance and to promise to pay the sum of forty-eight Mexican *pesos*, with interest on deferred payments. He believed that a shiftless set of colonists would enter if lands were granted absolutely free. He also wrote to the inhabitants of Fort Pitt inviting them to join him. He feared that Miró's extreme anxiety to be considered "the first proposer and promoter of the settlements opposite the mouth of the Ohio," his opposition to religious toleration, and his subservience to Wilkinson would retard the execution of the plans dscribed.[24]

And, true to expectation, Miró did oppose a part of Morgan's plans. He objected to the sale of lands and defended the schedule upon which the king had allowed free grants.

[24]Houck, *The Spanish Régime in Missouri*, I, 286–300.

This provided for a minimum donation of twenty-four *arpents* to families containing two or three workmen, four hundred *arpents* in case there were between three and ten able bodied men, six hundred for those having from ten to fifteen, and eight hundred when there were more than fifteen men. Wilkinson did all in his power to handicap Morgans' work, declaring the plan dangerous and unbefitting the crown. Miró finally approved the proposal to sell to families from Fort Pitt three hundred and twenty acres each, and recommended an increase in case the grantees were able to bring negroes with them or to hire help. He promised not to interfere in matters of religion but insisted that Catholics alone should hold public worship. To strengthen the Catholics he proposed to establish a number of forts and churches. He permitted immigrants to bring into the country free of duty goods bought with the proceeds of the sale of their property in the United States. He required them to take the oath of allegiance and bind themselves to bear arms in defense of the crown. He rejected the recommendations for trial by jury and legislation on local matters, but confirmed the grants of three hundred and twenty acres already made.[25]

In spite of fair promises, Miró managed to embarrass Morgan by placing a military commandant of his own choosing at New Madrid and granting to Wilkinson permission to encourage the entry of such Kentucky families as desired to immigrate to the Spanish Dominions by granting the privilege of introducing their goods free of duty while all others were to be required to pay a duty of fifteen per cent. Wilkinson's immigrants, likewise, were to be undisturbed in their private worship and to be given free lands. Miró himself believed that, as a result of these

---

[25]Morgan to Miró, May 23 and 24, 1780, *A. G. I. S.* Sto. Dom., 86–6–17, September 1, 1788–June 12, 1789, and McCully, Dodge, and others to Miró, April 14, 1789, *A. G. I. S. Sto. Dom.*, 86–6–17, October 4, 1788–May 20, 1789.

concessions, both banks of the Mississippi would soon be settled.²⁶

Becaue of these handicaps Morgan failed to accomplish any striking results; but Houck pays tribute to his efforts by declaring that he was "the first person to set in motion the stream of American immigration into Spanish Dominions." His success was attributed to the gift of lands and exemption from taxation. As a result it was but a few years until "the American population almost equaled the French population."²⁷

Wilkinson's plans, 1788.—When Wilkinson first visited Louisiana, he discovered that colonization projects occupied the mind of Gardoquí and he determined to make use of this knowledge for his own "personal emolument" or for the "interest of his fellow citizens." With this in mind he asked Gardoquí for six thousand acres of land and presented to the government a colonization plan whose main outlines can be gathered from the decision thereon. It provided that all Kentuckians desiring to settle in Spanish territory should be received, whether coming of their own initiative or upon the solicitation of Wilkinson. They were to be required to bring their families, property, and stock and were to be allowed the enjoyment of whatever religious faith they might profess, though there was to be no public worship except in Catholic churches ministered to by Irish priests. All property introduced was to be exempt from duty. This, of course, favored Wilkinson to the detriment of D'Arges. But instructions were given that the latter should not be abandoned. However, Miró was instructed to wean him from the idea of bringing immigrants by the assurance that the government would reward him as his conduct might warrant.²⁸

In September, 1789, Wilkinson advised Miró to abandon, for the time-being, the idea of annexing Kentucky, but to

---

²⁶Miró to D'Arges, March 4, 1789, *A. G. I. S.* Sto. Dom., 86–6–17, March 4–15, 1789.

²⁷Houck, *Tre Spanish Régime in Missouri,* I. xxi.

²⁸"Decision of the Council of State on Wilkinson's First Memorial," William R. Shepherd (contributor), *American Historical Review,* IX, 749–750.

do his best to encourage Kentuckians and other Westerners to emigrate to Louisiana, for the purpose of building up a strong pro-Spanish party among the Americans and, at the same time, to encourage the separation of the West from the United States. The West, once independent of the United States, said he, would ally itself with Spain rather than with any other power. This arrangement, he declared, would be advantageous to Spain, since under the control of Spain, the Americans of the West would serve as a barrier against the advance of Great Britain and of the United States. He recommended that emigration be given the preference over all other plans for detaching the West, because it could be carried on without peril to individuals and without disturbing the amicable relations between Spain and the United States. He believed that if Louisiana became populous the misgivings excited by the settlements on the Ohio would disappear and the Spanish government would then be able to change its policy as it saw fit. He thought that the existing regulations for the admission of immigrants were very favorable, but wished them modified to meet the approval of prominent men of Virginia, who might desire as much as three thousand acres because they owned anywhere from one hundred to three hundred slaves and had been accustomed to large grants since the first settlement of North America. He insisted that no person should be received who did not bring with him visible property and who did not give ample evidence of good character. He wished each immigrant to be compelled to take the oath of allegiance and to be left free in regard to his private religious beliefs.[29] As Wilkinson was more intent upon his commercial and separation schemes than upon immigration, he could not have introduced any large number of settlers. Nevertheless, he had been able to handicap D'Arges and Morgan who soon became discouraged and abandoned the field to a colonizer from still another nation.

---

[29]*Ibid.*, 751–764.

Pennsylvania Dutch colonizer, Paulus, 1788.—Upon the suggestion of Morgan and Gardoquí, Pedro Paulus, an obscure inn-keeper of Philadelphia, and a member of the militia of Pennsylvania, offered to bring in three thousand Dutch and German families from the region lying to the north of Kentucky. He did so believing that the government would reimburse him for his labors by a gift of land, would pay the transportation expenses of such immigrants as he might secure, and would grant each of them six hundred *arpents* of land. In addition, he asked that his settlers be granted religious toleration, be furnished an English and German speaking minister, be permitted to exercise local self-government, be exempt from military service save in defense of the country, and be allowed to plant tobacco, to establish manufactories, and to export flour.[30] As in Morgan's case, Miró opposed the granting of large quantities of land, on the grounds that the system had been unsuccessful in the United States and that the granting of virtual independence would inevitably lead the settlers to revolt from the Spanish Dominions. However, he consented to the introduction of one thousand families who were to be given lands. Paulus, himself, was to be rewarded by the bestowal of military rank. He accepted these conditions; but whether or not he ever brought into Louisiana more than the thirty-four persons who accompanied him at the time he presented the proposal can not now be determined. Since he held a commission from "two thousand persons who were very anxious to immigrate" it is quite possible that he introduced a considerable number.

Prussian colonizer, Baron von Steuben, 1788.—But not all those favored by Gardoquí were able to secure from superior authorities the necessary approval of their colonization plans. According to Fortier,[31] Gardoquí "accepted the proposition of Baron von Steuben to settle on the banks of

---

[30]Petition of Paulus, December 12, 1788, and Miró to Váldez, March 15, 1789, *A. G. I. S.* Sto. Dom., 86–6–17, December 8, 1788–March 6, 1789.

[31]*History of Louisiana*, II, 128.

the Mississippi and form a colony of persons who had lately been in the army," but the Spanish government refused its approval. From the detailed information given by Frederick Kapp, Steuben's biographer, a full account of the plan is secured. In 1788, Baron von Steuben, who had rendered such valiant service to the United States in the achievement of independence, applied to Gardoquí for permission "to plant a colony, partly agricultural, partly military, within the Dominions of the king of Spain in order to secure the ruler of Spain against an invasion of his neighbors and to grant to the American settlers on the western Alleghanies a free outlet for their produce." Kapp summarizes the plan as follows:

1. Baron Steuben engages to plant a colony of farmers and artificers, not exceeding the number of four thousand two hundred persons, within the Spanish province of Louisiana.

2. For this purpose a concession of two hundred thousand acres of land, in such place as, in military view and relation to the principles of the project may be hereafter agreed upon, is made to the said Baron Steuben and his associates.

3. As a further encouragement the Spanish government allows to each person, a farmer or artificer, brought to locate himself in good faith within the said tract, the sum of one hundred Spanish dollars as a bounty.

4. Baron Steuben and his associates will, to every such settler, make conveyance in fee of two hundred and thirty acres of good and arable land within the concession aforesaid, free of all expenses such as may arise upon the writing of the deed.

5. The settlers for the said tracts will be drawn from the United States, or other foreign countries, and no person now a Spanish subject will be taken from his present settlement to make a part of this.

6. On the part of the government it will be agreed that the inhabitants of this tract be allowed to possess and exercise such mode of religious worship as they may think proper, and that no penalty, forfeiture, disqualification, etc., be incurred by any difference in faith or practice from those established within His Catholic Majesty's dominions.

7. The laws of the United States relative to the tenure, transfer, or descent of property will be granted to the inhabitants of the said tract, and they will be allowed to institute such process, offices, and courts touching these subjects as may be proper and necessary; provided only, that this will be done at their expense

and without charge to the government; and provided further, that in all cases when the parties in suit on these subjects signify their consent and desire to have decision according to the Spanish laws, it will be granted them.

8. In all other respects, the said subjects will be entirely, and without qualification, subject to the Spanish laws and usages. This part of the colony will be formed into a militia and liable to military service within the province when any exigency of government may require it.

9. In addition to this colony the baron will engage to raise a corps of eight hundred men to be formed into four battalions, three of musketry and one of riflemen. This corps will in all respects be subject to the discipline and service of His Catholic Majesty's troops, save only that in questions of property and religion, the privileges granted to the other part of the colony will be extended to this also.

10. The power of nominating all officers of the regular corps will be exclusively within the general thereof, and when approved by the king, commissions will be issued to them accordingly, and vacancies supplied in the same manner.

11. The same bounty will be given to the soldiers as to the farmers and artificers.

12. Such colonies and recruits as may be engaged in Germany, will be paid and provided at the king's expense, from the day of their enlistments or engagements, respectively, and for the purpose of safe and easy transportation, it will be agreed between the courts of Madrid and Versailles, that they be allowed a free and unmolested passage from St. Esprit in France to Carthagena in Spain, where they are to embark in royal vessels for New Orleans in Louisiana.

Kapp continues:

Steuben presented this plan to Diego Gardoqui, who dispatched it to Madrid; but it does not appear that the court engaged in any negotiations about it. Its rejection is too natural when we consider the absolute form of government in Spain. It could not suit them that one of their colonies should be more free than the rest, and if not the thorough appreciation of the case, at least the instinct of self-preservation taught the Spanish ministry, that admitting American laws even on a small scale, would by and by have opened and subjected the entire colony to the American pioneers, as has been subsequently shown in the case of Texas.

It is nevertheless interesting to examine the motives of Steubens' plan. They show us the statesman and soldier who anticipates the future and tries to found a building on materials loose in themselves, but grand in the hands of a political talent, the execution of which was only delayed and reserved to the succeeding generation. It is at the same time gratifying to observe that Steuben understood perfectly the secret of the growth of this rising American empire in the self-government of the commonwealth; a principle more antagonistic to the prerogatives of the Spanish autocrat could not be found.

As in the following year Steuben's prospects cleared up and the favorable settlement of his claims became certain, he gave up the idea of removing to the far West, and devoted his whole attention to the cultivation of his own lands in Oneida County.[32]

After the failure of this plan, the last considered during the reign of Charles III, the patron of colonization in Louisiana, several years passed before other colonizers appeared.

French colonizers, Tardiveau, Maison Rouge, Delassus, and Dubuc, 1792–1795.—In 1792, Bartholomew Tardiveau, who for fifteen years had lived in the United States, laid before the Spanish government his plans for establishing a numerous population on the west bank of the Mississippi as a means of developing the country, opposing the rapid expansion of the Americans in the West, and of "erecting a barrier between this bold people and the Spanish possessions," especially in Missouri and New Mexico. He suggested that a large part of the necessary men could be secured in the United States. However, he advised only a limited number of this class of immigrants be received as it was essential to the preservation of the Spanish Dominions of America to keep them in the minority because of their inventive genius and their tendency to assume the reins of government. He drew attention to the fact that conditions in France and in the Low Countries presented the most favorable opportunities for procuring a sufficient number of settlers from those regions to erect an effective barrier against the United States. He declared that certain French emigrants who had left their native country because of political conditions there, who had later settled on the Ohio, and who were constantly in danger of Indian attacks, and

---

[32]Kapp, Frederick, *Life of William Frederick von Steuben*, 687–689.

displeased at "the innumerable snares and rogueries of which they had been the victims from the moment when they had struck America" would adopt with enthusiasm "the idea of settling near the Illinois river." He reported that he had received a communication from a friend who was acting upon the instruction of the French company, asking if he could arrange for the reception of these colonists and for those who were to come from Europe. They desired lands and were willing to pay for them. The leaders, likewise, proposed to pay their own expenses and to advance money for such families as needed assistance, Tardiveau proposed to go to France, *via* New Orleans and Philadelphia, for the purpose of arranging all necessary details. He expected also to visit Savoy, the Swiss Cantons, Germany, Flanders, Holland, and, finally, "all countries where Frenchmen were found assembled." He engaged to secure those who by their condition, fortune, standing, and influence were capable of contributing to the attainment of the proposed plan. He estimated the number who might be obtained at between two and three hundred thousand, unless they should be forced to take up their residence in the United States because of the failure of the Spaniards to push the proposed plan. He asked that the expense of this voyage be paid and that he be given certain commercial concessions. In his final recommendation he suggested that the matter be kept a secret until everything was ready for the execution of the plan.[33] But due to a new revolution in France, Tardiveau was compelled to change his plans and to make an agreement with Duhault Delassus and Pedro Audrain by which they bound themselves to establish flour mills near St. Genevieve and to introduce one hundred families from Galliopolis, which had been founded by exiled French royalists. This new settlement was to be given the name of Nueva Bourbon, as a compliment to royalists and as a warning to those who had followed the fortunes of the

---

[33]Tardiveau to Aranda, July 17, 1792, Houck, *The Spanish Régime in Missouri,* II, 359–368.

revolutionary party. In regard to this plan, Baron de Carondelet, the new governor of Louisiana, who was particularly partial to the French, said:

> The importance of the matter, the necessity for speedy decision, the numberless advantages which it represents, the well-known character of the commissioners, their ability and fortunes, the impossibility of consulting the captain-general about it, and the absence of any risk resulting to the royal treasury—these seemed to me sufficient reasons for concluding the transaction, in the manner which is made clear in the contract. M. Audrain having set out on the 22d for Philadelphia, from which city he will go to collect the families from Galliopolis and bring them down by way of the Ohio to New Madrid, Messrs. Lassus and Tardiveau returned up the Mississippi in order to wait for those people and conduct them to the new settlement. It is evident that this scattered seed will produce a hundred fold for the state. From the brief relation which accompanies this . . . in behalf of the inhabitants of Galliopolis, it is evident that they are persons of education and good standing, and desirable [as colonists]. The poor who remain among them will follow the leading families, who will advance the necessary funds for the first settlement. The prosperity and tranquility which they will enjoy under the mild government of Spain; their relation with all the principal emigrants from France; the publicity which the removal of all these people from Galliopolis to Spanish territory cannot fail to occasion; the certainty that they will find immediate market for their wheat, by means of the contract which has been made with Messrs. Lassus, Audrain, and Tardiveau; the interest which these gentlemen (who now are in possession of a considerable fortune) have in increasing the cultivation and settlement of these lands on the Missouri and Mississippi; the similarity of religion, language, and customs between the old colonists and the new; the resentment of the latter against the Americans, who have not fulfilled any of the promises that they made to them; all these things promise us that the enormous immigration which thus far has flowed to the American territory of the North will be directed to the Spanish territory. And the latter will have this additional advantage, that those vast regions of Illinois, hitherto undefended and almost abandoned, on account of their distance at five hundred leagues from the capital, will be peopled with French royalists, who will maintain resentment against the Americans for their unfair proceedings, and will continue against the English of Canada that opposition and rivalry which is innate in the

The Opening of Texas to Foreign Settlement 29

French nation—forming a considerable barrier against both nations, on the Missouri as well as on the Mississippi.[34]

As a result of Carondelet's policies here outlined a number of other French royalists were granted lands.

The principal one of these was Maison Rouge, a French Marquís, who offered to bring down from the banks of the Ohio thirty farmers who were anxious to form a settlement on the Ouachita, where they hoped to raise wheat and manufacture flour. A contract was soon entered into between Maison Rouge and the local authorities.[35] In addition to the gift of land, the governor promised to pay to every family, consisting of at least two members, two hundred *pesos*, to those consisting of four laborers, four hundred *pesos*, etc., in proportion to the number of laborers. The immigrants were to be furnished provisions and a guide for the trip from New Madrid to Ouachita. The smallest amount of land to be granted was four hundred acres. One of the provisions of the contract required that the emigrants should be permitted to bring with them indentured European servants, who, after the expiration of their term of service, should be entitled to a grant of land.[36]

The project of inducing French royalists to migrate to Louisiana continued to be a favorite one with the Baron, and, with a view of promoting it, extensive grants of land were made. A grant was made to James Ceran Delassus de St. Vrain, who had lost his fortune during the French revolution. He had been compelled to abandon his native country and seek refuge in Louisiana. Here he had earned the good will of Carondelet by assisting him to defeat the plans of Gênet against the Spanish dominions on the Mississippi.

---

[34]Carondelet to Gardoquí, April 26, 1793, Houck, *The Spanish Régime in Missouri*, II, 376–377; and *American State Papers, Public Lands*, II, 520–521, 660, and III, 342.

[35]Morales ot the King, June 30, 1797, *A. G. I. S.* Sto. Dom., 86–7–17, May 8, 1797–July 9, 1797.

[36]Report of the Committee on Land Claims in Louisiana, *American State Papers, Public Lands*, IV, 51 and 431–434, and V, 442–443.

Delassus's grant contained ten thousand square *arpents*, and he proposed to repay the government for this concession by discovering and working lead mines. He, therefore, did not obligate himself to make any settlements.[37]

Julien Dubuc had already formed certain settlements on the frontier of the province on lands which he had purchased from the Indians. He had also discovered and worked several lead mines. Carondelet now rewarded him by a grant of six leagues of land on the west bank of the Mississippi.[38] The census reports available for this period show that a heavy French immigration took place, but nothing has been found to indicate which of the colonizers named deserved the credit for the movement.

Indian immigrants.—The immigration movement toward the Spanish Dominions was not confined to the whites. According to Morales, Intendent of Louisiana, certain Indian tribes in the United States, angered by the terms of the Jay Treaty, began to show their dislike for the United States even before any posts had been delivered or any steps taken to run the boundary line fixed by its terms. One hundred and seventy Cherokees applied to the commandant of New Madrid asking for lands; while the chief of the Alabamas, in the name of three hundred and ninety-four of his tribe, applied to the governor at New Orleans for a similar concession. He declared that practically his entire nation would follow. He testified that he did not wish to live close to the Americans or to be separated from his friends, the Spaniards, who had never harmed the red man. In response to his appeal, the governor distributed a large number of presents among the petitioners and gave them permisison to settle near Opelousas. Other nations also appeared at New Orleans and seemed inclined to follow the example of the Alabamas in case the Americans should offend them in any way. The arrangement was not entirely to the liking of Morales who did not desire to incur the expense connected

---

[37]Martin, *History of Louisiana*, 268.

[38]*Ibid.* See also *American State Papers, Public Lands*, II, 675. and VIII, 387.

The Opening of Texas to Foreign Settlement 31

with these frequent and prolonged visits. However, he consoled himself with the thought that should the Spaniards of Louisiana have any trouble with the Americans, they would find useful allies in the Indians.[39] With these Indians the Spaniards hoped to form a buffer against the further advance of the American government.

Dutch colonizers, Bastrop and Fooey, 1797–1798.—The governor was really anxious to secure as many friends as possible who could be depended upon to aid the Spaniards in case trouble with the United States should arise. He therefore conceived the idea of attracting numbers of Germans and Dutch. First in importance among the Dutch who offered their services to the governor of Louisiana may be mentioned Baron de Bastrop. But before giving an account of his work, it will be well to mention one of his countrymen who was at this time interested in colonization.

Benjamin Fooey, a Spanish interpreter, was authorized in 1798 to form a Dutch or German settlement near Campo Esperanza, not far from Memphis, in what is now Arkansas.[40] No information has been found to indicate that he took any steps to carry out his plan. But Bastrop made greater progress.

Felipe Enrique Neri, Baron de Bastrop, it is said, had fled from Holland in 1795 to escape the invading French army and had taken refuge in Louisiana. There he had taken the oath of allegiance and was offered by Carondelet a grant as a reward for the establishment of a colony on the Ouachita river which was to serve as a barrier against the Americans who had secured possession of Natchez and who were eager for the gold and silver mines in the Spanish territory, especially in the Ouachita region, which lay next in their pathway. Carondelet favored the plan of giving lands to all settlers introduced into Lower Louisiana since, in spite of the fact that Upper Louisiana was being rapidly settled without special concessions, the climate of Lower Louisiana

---

[39]Morales to Ulloa, March 31, 1797, *A. G. I. S.* Sto. Dom., 87–1–24, March 1, 1797.

[40]Houck, *The Spanish Régime in Louisiana*, II, 114.

was such that attractive inducements were necessary to secure immigrants. He therefore felt justified in offering to pay the transportation expenses of such persons as Bastrop could manage to secure in the United States and to support them for six months after their arrival. Bastrop himself insisted that no large grants be made to immigrants for fear that negroes would be introduced and the cultivation of indigo undertaken by rival *empresarios* and his own plans for cultivation of wheat in sufficient quantities to supply the flour mills he expected to erect be defeated. He wished also to export the flour thus manufactured after the needs of the province had been supplied. Upon receipt of a promise from Carondelet that these privileges would be granted and that he would receive twelve square leagues of land on the Ouachita, Baron de Bastrop departed for the United States for settlers.[41] But before he arrived again at New Orleans with ninety-nine persons whom he had induced to join him—the only immigrants he was ever able to locate—Moses Austin, who had been an importer in Philadelphia, a shot and button manufacturer in Richmond, and a miner and merchant of Austinville, Virginia, had decided to settle in Upper Louisiana.

American colonizer, Austin, 1797.—In 1797, finding that his mines in Virginia were less productive than he had expected and obtaining information from a man who had visited the lead mines near St. Genevieve, Upper Louisiana, that prospects were good in that region, Moses Austin determined to investigate.[42] The following interesting description of his journey and the success of his mission is furnished by Schoolcraft:

> Here [at Austinville] he formed a design of migrating into upper Louisiana—a country which he foresaw must at no remote

---

[41]Morales to Bastrop, June 16, 1797, *A. G. I. S.* Sto. Dom., 86–7–12, May 8, 1797–July 7, 1799.

[42]Wooten, Dudley (ed.), *A Comprehensive History of Texas, 1688–1897*, I, 440–441.

period fall within the limits of the United States, and which presented to his sanguine imagination the most flattering prospective as well as immediate advantages. He began his first journey to this country in the autumn of 1797,[43] being then in his thirty-first year, and, performing the entire journey on horseback, reached St. Louis in the ensuing winter. This was an arduous and hazardous journey, and at that early period, before the vast country west of the Ohio had been opened to emigration, was looked upon as an extraordinary feat of hardihood. Indian hostility, though ostensibly terminated by the Treaty of Greenville a few years before, was still to be dreaded, and an unprotected traveler passing through the Indian territories ran an imminent risk both of property and life. . . .

The little intercourse subsisting between Louisiana and the American States, partly owing to a dread of Republican principles, from which it has ever been a leading point, in the policy of Spain, to defend her trans-Atlantic colonies, precluded Mr. Austin almost wholly from the customary advantage of introductory letters; and, indeed, he placed his chief reliance for success upon his own personal address—a qualification which he possessed in no ordinary degree. He knew the weakness of the Spanish character, and resolved to profit by this. I have it from his own lips, that when he came near St. Louis, where the commandant, who was generally called the Governor, resided, he thought it necessary to enter the town with as large a retinue and as much parade as possible. He led the way himself, on the best horse he could muster, clothed in a long blue mantel lined with scarlet and embroidered with lace, and rode through the principal streets, where the governor resided, followed by his servants, guides, and others. So extraordinary a cavalcade in a place so little frequented by strangers, and at such a season of the year, could not fail, as he had supposed, to attract the particular attention of the local authorities, and the Governor sent an orderly to enquire his character and rank. Being answered, he soon returned with an invitation for himself and suite to take up their residence at his house, observing at the same time, in the most polite manner and with characteristic deference to the rank of his guests, that there was no other house in town that could afford him suitable accommodations during his stay. The favorable impression created by his entrée, which Mr. Austin, in after life, related to his friends with inimitable glee, led on to his ultimate success. He was recommended to the authorities at St. Genevieve, where it seems that the Indians of the upper province then resided, who approved his design to settle in the country—ordered an escort of soldiers,

---

[43]December, 1796.

under command of a national officer, to attend him on his visit to the mines—and forwarded his petition for a grant of land to the Governor-General at New Orleans, accompanied with the strongest recommendations. This petition was drawn up by the government secretary, to whom Mr. Austin had not, however, intimated the quantity he asked for, and he once observed to me that it gave him some surprise on reading it to find that *twelve leagues square* had been demanded. One-twelfth of this quantity was granted *en franc allien*, the crown reserving no other right or dues but those of fealty and liege homage; but it was stipulated on the part of Mr. Austin in an agreement with the intendent, to introduce certain improvements in the process of mining, together with some connected branches of manufacture, which were accordingly introduced.[44]

On January 27, 1797, François Valle, Commandant at St. Genevieve, engaged to grant lands to Austin and to thirty families of farmers and artisans whom Austin planned to induce to join him in establishing the new settlement. The newcomers were to be given lands in proportion to the size of their families, their means, and their ability to aid in the development of the country. In addition, they were promised the privilege of locating wherever they might choose.[45] Whether or not any of these families save a small number of Austin's family and friends ever settled can not be determined from the records on hand; but, on March 15 of the same year, Carondelet granted to Austin a league of land embracing the lead mines at "Mine A Burton."[46] In July, 1797, Austin applied for a passport to Martínez de Yrujo who had replaced Gardoquí as minister from Spain to the United States, and, after considerable difficulty, he managed to secure the coveted document. Armed with this, he removed his family from Virginia to the new grant, reaching there in September.[47] Before his arrival, however,

---

[44]Schoolcraft, Henry Rowe, *Travels in the Central Portions of the Mississippi Valley*, 241–243. *Cf.* Austin's "Journal," *American Historical Review*, V, 518–542.

[45]Affidavit by Valle, Austin Papers.

[46]*American State Papers, Public Lands*, III, 671.

[47]Wooten (ed.), *A Comprehensive History of Texas, 1685–1897*, I, 440–441.

the feeling against the English and the Americans, who were hostile to Spain's ally, France, had become very strong, and it will be necessary to trace its effects upon Bastrop's colony and then upon the general history of colonization in Louisiana.

Suspension of Bastrop's contract.—On June 20, 1797, Governor Carondelet had entered into a formal contract with Bastrop for the introduction of families, but Carondelet was soon replaced by Manuel Gayoso. The situation was immediately changed; for the new governor objected strenuously to the introduction of Protestants and suspected that, in defiance of the stipulations of his contract, Bastrop was introducing English and Americans whose fidelity to the Catholic religion and the Spanish king were merely feigned. Besides, the contract did not meet with the approval of the intendant of the province. He objected, in the first place, because it provided for the expenditure of a considerable sum from the depleted treasury for the transportation of these families from New Madrid to the new settlement and for their maintenance for some time after their location; and, principally, he said, "it would never be an advantage to increase the number of English and Americans, and other Protestants—imbued, perhaps, with the maxims of liberty which had caused so much revolution and to place them nearer Mexico, even though it might be desirable to increase the population of Ouachita."[48] As a result, the governor ordered the suspension of Bastrop's contract until the matter could be passed upon by the king. This amounted to nullification; for Bastrop was never able to secure favorable action, in spite of the fact that he promised to secure his families direct from Europe and to receive none who might have been "contaminated" by even the briefest residence in the United States. Indeed, when later considering Bastrop's claims, especially in regard to the sale of a portion of the lands in question, Charles IV, who was under the domination

---

[48]*American State Papers, Public Lands*, II, 678; III, 682, 683; VIII; and Morales to King, June 30, 1797, *A. G. I. S.* Sto. Dom., 86–7–17, June 20, 1796–July 9, 1799.

of Manuel Godoy, forbade the granting of any more lands in Louisiana to Americans.[49] This feeling against Americans—and, indeed, against all foreigners—had already been embodied in the laws of Louisiana as the following instructions of the governor to the commandants of posts will indicate:

1. [Commandants] are forbidden to grant lands to a new settler coming from another post where he has obtained a grant. Such a one must buy land or obtain a grant from the governor.

2. If a settler be a foreigner, unmarried and without either slaves, money, or other property, no grant is to be made him until he shall have remained four years in the post, demeaning himself well in some honest and useful occupation.

3. Mechanics are to be protected, but no land is to be granted to them until they shall have acquired some property, and a residence of three years in the exercise of their trade.

4. No grant of land is to be made to any unmarried emigrant who has neither trade nor property until after a residence of four years, during which time he must have been employed in the culture of the ground.

5. But, if after a residence of two years such a person should marry the daughter of an honest farmer, with his consent and be by him recommended, a grant of land may be made to him.

6. Liberty of conscience is not to be extended beyond the first generation; the children of emigrants must be Catholics; and emigrants not agreeing to this must not be admitted, but removed even when they bring property with them. This is to be explained to settlers who do not profess the Catholic religion.

7. In upper Louisiana, no settler is to be admitted who is not a farmer or mechanic.

8. It is expressly recommended to commandants to watch that no preacher of any religion but the Catholic comes into the province.

9. To every married immigrant of the above description, two hundred *arpents* may be granted with the addition of fifty for every child he brings.

10. If he brings negroes, twenty additional *arpents* are to be granted him for each; but in no case are more than eight hundred *arpents* to be granted an emigrant.

11. No land is to be granted to a trader.

---

[49]Undated petition of Bastrop (1799?), *A. G. I. S.* Sto. Dom.. 86–7–17.

The Opening of Texas to Foreign Settlement 37

12. Immediately on the arrival of a settler, the oath of allegiance is to be administered to him. If he has a wife, proof is to be demanded of their marriage; and, if they bring any property, they are to be required to declare what part belongs to either of them; and they are to be informed that the discovery of any wilful falsehood in this declaration will incur the forfeiture of the land granted them, and the improvements made thereon.
13. Without proof of a lawful marriage, or of absolute ownership of negroes, no grant is to be made for a wife or negroes.
14. The grant is to be forfeited, if a settlement be not made within the year, or one-tenth part of the land put in cultivation within two.
15. No grantee is to be allowed to sell his land until he has produced three crops on a tenth part of it, but in case of death it may pass to an heir in the province, but not to one without, unless he come and settle it.
16. If the grantee owes debts in the province, the proceeds of the first four crops are to be applied to their discharge, in preference to that of debts abroad. If, before the third crop is made, it becomes necessary to evict the grantee on account of his bad conduct, the land shall be given to the young man and woman residing within one mile of it, whose good conduct may show them to be the most deserving of it; and the decision is to be made by an assembly of notable planters, presided by the commandant.
17. Emigrants are to settle contiguous to old establishments, without leaving any vacant land—that the people may then more easily protect each other, in case of an invasion by the Indians; and that the administration of justice and a compliance with police regulations may be facilitated.[50]

Several points here set forth deserve especial attention. The old antipathy against foreign traders is shown and the religious toleration previously granted Protestants was practically withdrawn. Such mechanics and agriculturists as were willing to take the oath of allegiance to the Spanish government were still to be subjected to several years of

---

[50]Martin, *History of Louisiana*, 276–277. In October of this same year the intendant was charged with the entire responsibility of granting lands in Louisiana and thereupon issued regulations governing titles to same. *American State Papers, Public Lands*, III, 488–496.

probation before lands could be granted them while the possession of property and the duty of actual settlement and cultivation of the lands was made obligatory.[51]

Eleventh-hour plans.—Immigration into Louisiana was not completely checked by the hostility evinced against the Americans. At the court of Spain projects for settling the province were still favorably received. For instance, in July, 1799, a favorable decision was rendered upon the colonization petition of the Spanish minister at Philadelphia.[52] However, no evidence has been found that the petitioner took any steps to introduce families.

The local authorities may also have granted lands to certain Americans, who, like Daniel Boone, manifested a strong feeling against their native country. According to Violette, Boone was granted ten thousand acres by De Lassus in return for bringing into Upper Louisiana one hundred and fifty families from Virginia and Kentucky, but through failure to secure the necessary legal documents, he was never able to obtain the confirmation of his grant.[53] However, the only record found containing a mention of a grant to Boone recites that, on December 26, 1799, he was promised one thousand *arpents* by Trudeau.[54] In this no mention of the families to be brought in is made.

From the records it is clear that many Americans located in Louisiana prior to its sale to the United States; but no definite figures can be given, as the census reports are fragmentary. However, Viles, who made a careful study of the population of Missouri before 1804, estimates that the increase of white population at New Madrid after 1797 was considerable; that St. Genevieve grew steadily between 1795 and 1800; that Cape Girardeau increased in a fairly constant ratio between 1799 and 1803—fully two hundred per cent; and that St. Louis added to her population practically

---

[51]———? to Urquijo, July 9, 1799, *A. G. I. S.* Sto. Dom., 86–7–17, May 8, 1797–July 9, 1797.

[52]Trans., U. of T.

[53]*History of Missouri*, 64.

[54]*American State Papers, Public Lands*, III, 332.

one hundred persons, each year between 1796 and 1800. From actual statistics it is known that by 1800 the population of Upper Louisiana amounted to four thousand nine hundred and forty-nine and that Lower Louisiana, in spite of its unfavorable climate, had increased from twelve thousand five hundred in 1769 to approximately twenty-seven thousand in 1798, when the tide of immigration had reached its height. All authorities agree that this increase represented for the most part an immigration of Americans.[55]

Between 1763 and 1801, when, over the protest of Spain, Napoleon sold Louisiana to the United States, the American frontiersmen, in their irresistible march to the westward, had pushed their advance lines to the Mississippi river. This had come about, as has been shown, in spite of the exclusive policy of Spain and in the face of the warnings of the local Spanish officials of Louisiana, through the liberal policy of Charles III and the eagerness of his minister to the United States to erect in the region a buffer against the further advance of Spain's potential enemies, the Americans. In pursuance of this unusual policy, a great number of foreigners had been admitted—Englishmen, Irishmen, Frenchmen, Dutchmen, and even Americans who (for the most part) were mistakenly believed to be displeased with the government of the United States or at least somewhat indifferent to the claims of citizenship in that country. By the beginning of the nineteenth century, the American settlers had demonstrated their ability to wrest the country from the Indians, to clear the forests, and to cultivate the new-made fields. The buffer desired by the Spaniards had become, in the hands of the enemy, a dangerous opening wedge. Additional Americans were pushing closely behind and the pioneers were again almost ready to move forward, this time just across the Sabine to the virgin fields of Texas,

---

[55]Viles, Jonas, "Population and Extent of Settlement in Missouri before 1804," in *Missouri Historical Review*, V, 197, 199, 204, and 207; Houck, *The Spanish Régime in Missouri*, II, 414; and Martin, *History of Louisiana*, 206, 240, and 300.

now a second line of defense for the Spaniards dispossessed
of Louisiana. News of the wonderful beauty and fertility
of the new country had been carried across the Sabine by
adventurous traders who had often crossed into the forbidden
territory; but no inkling of the liberal treatment
granted foreigners in Louisiana had reached the ears of the
local authorities in Texas, where the old exclusion policy
was still nominally in full force, although the wave of immigration
was beginning to cast over the frontier the hardiest
of those borne upon its crest. Many of these newcomers,
because of their residence in Louisiana, were Spanish vassals
and, therefore, had a claim upon the bounty of the
nation. But their claims were not readily acknowledged
either by the new king, Charles IV, or by the local authorities
in Texas. In fact, all had become more cautious.
To understand the colonization problem in its new setting,
one must keep in mind Spain's inherent distrust of foreigners
which had, indeed, been reluctantly and with unhappy
results abandoned in Louisiana and remember especially her
fear of France, England, and the United States who in 1795,
because of the clashing of national interests, were all in a
position seriously to threaten her commercial and territorial
supremacy in Texas. It will be necessary to examine a little
more closely into the causes for the fear of foreigners that
had begun to manifest itself in Louisiana at the end of the
seventeenth century.

THE TEXAS BACKGROUND, 1795–1801

Naturally, distrust of foreign powers varied with the activities of her rivals both in Europe and America. For instance, as the fortunes of war in Europe had inclined now toward France and now toward England, Spain, who was the helpless victim of the two contestants, had frequently changed front in an effort to cast in her fortunes with the winning side. In 1793, she had declared war against France, with the avowed purpose of preventing the spread of revolutionary ideas, and immediately thereafter had granted special privileges to English vessels in return for promised aid. But, suddenly reversing her policy, in 1795 she had concluded an offensive and defensive alliance with her late enemy; and the two had then turned their united strength against the English. Therefore, in an effort to forestall possible retaliatory measures against her North American possessions, Spain had repeated the order which forbade the entry of any foreigner into Texas,[1] and placed a detachment at the frontier *pueblo* of Nacogdoches with instructions to enforce this ruling and to learn, through the friendly Indians of the rigion, of any hostile movement that might be planned.[2] Quite naturally, she charged all Spanish officials in America to be on the alert to avoid surprise.

Pedro de Nava, Commandant-General of the Interior Provinces, who, at this time, was directly responsible for the defense of Texas, determined to maintain his headquarters at Chihuahua, since, from that point, he could guard Texas as well as New Mexico, Sonora, and California, which were also under his jurisdiction. Personally, he did not anticipate an attack upon Texas, believing that the province

---

[1]Neve to Cabello, May 17, 1784, Béxar to Archives. The Béxar Archives have furnished practically all the documents used in this study. From this point forward reference will be to this collection unless otherwise indicated.

[2]Branciforte to Duque de la Alcudía, July 3, 1795, *A. G. I. S., legajo* 4, No. 7, March 25, 1795–October 23, 1795.

was not sufficiently rich to arouse cupidity or to promise an adequate indemnity for the expense involved in an invasion. Nevertheless, he thought it possible that the English might seize upon Louisiana and then attempt to occupy Texas as a part of the conquered territory. As to the first part of the scheme, he showed himself a true prophet; for, as soon as war was actually under way in Europe, England began to lay plans for drawing away the Indians of Louisiana from their allegiance to the Spanish king. Reports therefore soon reached De Nava's ears that the enemy had conferred upon a certain Mr. Bowles, of Virginia, the title of lieutenant-colonel, with the pay of a general, and that they were furnishing him with an *aide-de-camp*, a Frenchman, and with an English secretary, who could speak French and Spanish. He heard, too, that Bowles intended to arm the Indians under his command, to raise rebellions among the tribes nearest to the Spanish settlements, and then to attack these tribes one after another, so that he might introduce colonists favorable to the English. Following his previous lines of reasoning, De Nava thought it possible that, after Bowles had done his work in Louisiana and the Floridas, he would attack the weak settlements of Texas and then lead these Indians also to renounce their allegiance. Hence, he called upon all those responsible for the defense of Texas to make every effort to prevent this calamity and to investigate every suspicious move in Louisiana.[3]

But while Spain, from time to time, viewed the French and English with hatred, indifference, or comparative friendliness, she had consistently looked upon the Americans

---

[3]De Nava to the Governor of Texas, November 20, 1799. For an interesting account of Bowles, see *The American Historical Review*, VI, 708–709. For the efforts of the Spaniards of Louisiana to capture Bowles, see Casa Calvo to Someruelos, June 15, 1801, in *A. G. I. S.* Sto. Dom., La. y Fla., 88–7–27, June 15, 1801. For probable reasons for failure, see Morál to the Governor of Texas, March 25, 1800. Bowles was finally captured and ended his days in a Spanish dungeon. Cox, I. J., *The West Florida Controversy, 1798–1813*, pp. 140–141.

with suspicion since 1783 when they assumed their place among the nations, even though certain of the Americans had been admitted into Louisiana. Conde de Gálvez had even allayed suspicion by declaring that the United States would scarcely undertake a war of conquest against Spain and by prophesying that, even though the latter country should abandon her purely defensive policy, the vast expanse of vacant territory lying between the settlements of the two nations would preclude any great danger to the Spanish colonies.[4] But the struggle over the boundary question and the demand for the opening of the Mississippi to American commerce had increased the general feeling of distrust, and the supreme government had soon considered a plan for erecting a buffer against American growth at Spain's expense by the use of friendly Indian tribes.[5] In addition, the treaty of 1795, which sharply defined the limits of American possessions, had brought to certain far-seeing Spaniards in Louisiana a full realization of the necessity of reinforcing the population along the western bank of the Mississippi as a buffer against the advance of their "ambitious and too adjacent neighbors," in whom they had observed "a propensity for hunting and a strong penchant for exploring nearby territory, and for settling arbitrarily wherever their fancy might dictate without any legal formality whatever."[6] Immediately thereafter, the threats of war between the United States and France and rumors of the intrigues of certain Americans for the seizure of territory along the Mexican frontier had still further aroused the suspicions of the Spanish government. Using these reports as a pretext, Spain, for a time, had refused to deliver the frontier posts in accordance with the provisions of the treaty of 1795, and had made ready to fortify her territory against attack.

[4]Conde de Gálvez to Gálvez, February 6, 1784, in *A. G. I. S.* Mex., 96–2–12, September 23, 1778–August 23, 1784.
[5]Yoakum, Henderson, *History of Texas*, I, 104–105.
[6]Recommendation for formation of a barrier through colonization in Louisiana, June 11, 1797, in *A. G. I. S.* Sto. Dom., La. and Fla., 86–7–17, May 8, 1797–July 9, 1797.

This distrust was kept alive, as time passed, by constant rumors of retaliatory movements from the United States—both by individuals and by the government. The dislike of the Spaniards for their rapidly growing neighbor is illustrated by an order issued by the viceroy of Mexico in July, 1795. Declaring that he had been informed that the United States was planning to send emissaries to Mexico to insure a revolution, he gave instructions for the exclusion of all Americans as well as of all other foreigners and of all suspicious characters whatsoever.[7] On August 27, 1796, the commandant-general forbade, under penalty of imprisonment, the entry of any foreigner into that province, or even the admission of citizens of Louisiana unless they could present satisfactory passports. In this case, he singled out the Americans as especially objectionable because of their hostility to France.[8]

Apprehensions of a combined English and American attack upon the scattered settlements of Texas during the continuance of the war in Europe, brought out warning after warning to guard against surprise in Texas.[9] The fear of England's participation reached a climax during the first year of Miranda's intrigues against the Spanish dominions of America and gradually subsided until peace was finally made with England in 1802, leaving Spain free, for a brief season, to concentrate her anxiety upon the United States.

In this struggle between Spain and her changing enemies in Europe and her natural rival in America for the possession of Texas, the Indians were the determining factor. To understand Spain's inability to deal with the Indians is, therefore, important.

Policy of conciliation.—Upon first entering Texas the buffer-building Spaniards, at that time desirous of erecting

---

[7]Branciforte to the Governor of Nuevo Santander, July 10, 1795.
[8]De Nava to the Governor of Texas, August 27, 1796.
[9]Branciforte to the Prince of the Peace, May 27, 1796, in *A. G. I. S.*, *legajo* 5, No. 64, April 29, 1796–May 27, 1796; and *legajo* 18, No. 23, July 17, 1797–September 5, 1797.

a barrier against the advance of the French, had tried to christianize the Indians and to introduce among them the customs of civilized life. To this end, fearing that the priests, unaided, could not control the savages, they had established missions under the protection of *presidios* which were calculated to inspire awe in the minds of the savages. Later they had also founded a civilian settlement in the hope that the residents would furnish a stimulating example to their wards. These measures failed to produce the desired results, and the authorities next laid especial stress upon the military features of the system in an effort to control the unruly tribes that had defeated their earlier plans. But, again, no practical results had followed, owing chiefly, perhaps, to the lack of men and funds for adequate warfare against the offenders. So following the example of the English[10] and the French, the Spaniards, while still clinging to all the unsuccessful measures mentioned, began to place their chief reliance upon the policy in favor at the beginning of the nineteenth century, that of trying to hold the Indians to their promised allegiance through the systematic distribution of presents and the granting of special trade privileges.[11]

---

[10]Robertson, James A., *Louisiana under Spain, France, and the United States*, I, 103–104. *Cf.* De Nava to the Governor of Louisiana, March 26, 1809.

[11]The system had been introduced into Mexico by De Croix, De Nava to the Prince of the Peace, September 5, 1797, *A. G. I. S.*, *legajo* 18, No. 3. The situation is graphically described by a Spanish officer on the frontier. In warning the viceroy, he said: "It is true, Sir, that the French have all the Indians of this province under their influence due to the presents they make of powder, vermillion, guns, beads, and other articles appreciated by the Indians—and the royal treasury of France pays this. Besides they have other goods to sell and we do not. And even though we had them we would have to sell them at the cost price plus the excessive freight and the Indians would pay us little attention. The French pay them so much honor that even prominent persons among them marry the Indian women and are not looked down upon because of it. The French reap their greatest harvest by pleasing the Indians. If any band of Indians goes over to visit the commandant at Natchitoches, he gives them the things they like best and that, too, at the expense of the royal

This was done in the hope that the Indians would be so attached to Spain as to aid in defeating the commercial and territorial ambitions of all comers. In pursuance of this system, frequent visits were made to the ostensibly friendly Indians for the purpose of holding their good will and of learning whether or not bids for their support had been made by foreigners. In addition, presents were periodically made to forestall or destroy the effects of any possible adverse influence. This plan, too, had failed. And, at the opening of the nineteenth century, the Indian problem was even more complicated than it had been at the beginning of the Spanish occupation. For, after these efforts of so many years, the Spanish settlers were not safe from the depredations of the very Indians they had tried to befriend.

Even the mission Indians were unmanageable, often deserting the missions to hunt and fish so as to support themselves. Those who had not been under the influence of the priests were still more treacherous. One tribe would make war upon another and then beg aid from their "friends, the Spaniards." Whether or not aid were given mattered little. The unfortunate and reluctant referees were almost sure to be attacked by one contestant or the other. Again, the Indians would commit depredations merely for the sake of plunder, frequently falling upon a detachment of soldiers, carrying supplies from one point to another and making away with everything in sight; or worse still, venturing

---

treasury. You do not see a Cadodachos, Nacogdoches, San Pedro, or Texas Indian who does not have a looking glass, an embroidered belt, showy buckles, and breech-clouts. And in the winter season the French give them blankets, powder, and balls. The Indians say 'The Spaniards deliver good talks but the French deliver good talks *and the goods*.' The French make presents of ornamented hats, red coats and ruffled shirts to the captains and, at the mission of Nacogdoches, I saw many articles that cried aloud to me 'French, French.' So great is the friendship the Indians have for their benefactors that they would sacrifice their lives to please them. I also hear an echo of the prodigality of the French in the great increase of troops and settlers on the frontier." Barrios y Jauregui to Revillagigedo, November 8, 1751, *Historia*, 547, pp. 157–159.

under the very walls of the *presidios* to steal the mounts of the soldiers, so that escape with the loot was laughably easy. They robbed and often murdered settlers who ventured out to round up wild stock needed for actual subsistence—and all this without fear of effective punishment. Sometimes, indeed, soldiers were sent in pursuit but only in rare cases were the offenders overtaken; and, in rarer cases still, were they punished for their excesses. As a rule the punishment went the other way. For instance, after a catastrophe, the Spanish authorities usually ordered a careful investigation into the cause of the trouble, often claiming that some one must have "offended" the Indians and thus "provoked" hostilities; and the only result of the investigation would be an order to owners of stock to keep a closer watch over their property so that the temptation to attack would be lessened.[12] An idea of the hopelessness of the situation may be gathered from a letter written in May, 1798, by Manuel Muñoz to Antonio Cordero, Governor of Coahuila, one of the most experienced Indian fighters at that time on the frontier. In reply to a letter giving information of the excesses of the Comanches in Coahuila and of the measures adopted to secure indemnification for injuries, Muñoz advised caution, insisting that in each case the motive for attack should be ascertained. He urged that tactful measures be taken so that the whole country might not be laid waste, since the authorities—and especially those in Texas—were in no condition to prevent continuous attacks from this warlike nation whose members were exceedingly numerous and brave, and, likewise, thoroughly familiar with the country. The Comanches, he pointed out, were allied with other tribes of the North who would be glad of an excuse for entering the conflict. Previous experience, he maintained, had proved that the Spaniards had all to lose and nothing to gain by putting their cause to the test of arms, since no sufficient force for effective warfare was available. He admitted that the Spaniards had always been compelled to endure insults from the Indians and

---

[12]De Nava to the Governor of Texas, July 23, 1798.

prophesied that they would have to submit to them as long as a single red man remained. In support of this belief, he showed that both active warfare and continued conciliation had failed to have any real effect in bringing them to terms and that such plans for peace as had been tried and such weak attempts at warfare as had been made had merely given the enemy a true appreciation of the weakness of the Spaniards.[13] In speaking of this same case, De Nava suggested that the captains of such parties of Comanches and Northern Indians as might come to Béxar should be reprimanded for the excesses of their people and encouraged to return stolen horses under threat of loss of presents. However, he did not wish correction to be severe because he believed the offenders were encouraged in their depredations by faithless Spaniards who were living among them and who hoped to reap a personal benefit by disposing of stolen property in Louisiana or even in the United States.[14]

The difficulties already enumerated were enough to appall the most resolute; but the worst features of the situation have not been shown. Additional tribes, who had been under the influence of foreigners, were constantly applying for admission into Texas; and the authorities, not daring to refuse them entry definitely and finally, were soon confronted with still greater danger. For example, in July, 1800, José Miguel del Moral, Commandant of Nacogdoches, wrote Juan Bautista Elguezabal who had succeeded Muñoz as governor of Texas, reporting the receipt of a communication from Valentin Layssard, commander at Rapides, Louisiana, proposing to settle the Choctaws of that province in Texas. Moral vigorously opposed the plan, pointing out that the Indians of Texas would object to sharing benefits with the tribes of other regions; and asserting that the proposed immigrants were under the influence of the English, that they were allied with other Louisiana tribes, and, therefore, that they would naturally be hostile to the Indians of Texas. He even feared that fatal results would follow

---

[13]Muñoz to Cordero, May 29, 1798.
[14]De Nava to the Governor of Texas, May 29, 1798.

their admission. In addition, he explained that the Choctàws would trade in Louisiana, especially in Rapides—where they could buy to advantage—and that, consequently, Texas would receive no benefits whatever from their entry.[15] As a result of these objections, Elguezabal at once appealed to the governor of Louisiana to prevent the emigration of the Choctaws; while Moral urged Layssard to delay their departure until the final decision of the supreme authorities could be received.[16] De Nava soon rendered an unfavorable decision and Elguezabal issued an order forbidding their entry.[17] But not discouraged by this refusal Layssard at once began to lay plans for making peace between his *protéges* and the native tribes of Texas so that one objection to their immigration might be removed. He prepared an address setting forth the wisdom of following the proposed path of peace and forwarded it to José Vidal, Spanish Consul at Natchez, for delivery to the grand chief of the Choctaws.[18] As a result, the petitioners soon repeated their request; and, in spite of the fact that for years their conduct towards the Spaniards had not been above reproach, they finally received permission to settle in Texas. Upon more than one occasion they had attacked the Indians of Texas; and although the governor of Louisiana had charged his subordinates to see that the offenders were restrained, his efforts had been without practical results due to the proximity of the Americans and the English who kept the Indians supplied with powder.[19] Besides this, the Spanish authorities felt sure that contraband trade had been carried on under cover of these same Indians and that the Americans had been the chief gainers by the traffic.[20]

---

[15] Moral to Elguezabal, July 11, 1800.
[16] Moral to Elguezabal, July 27, 1800.
[17] De Nava to the Governor of Texas, August 4 and September 30, 1800.
[18] Layssard to the Great Chief of the Choctaws and other Nations, and Layssard to Vidál, September 15, 1800.
[19] De Nava to the Prince of the Peace, September 5, 1797, *A. G. I. S.* Mex., *legajo* 18, No. 22.
[20] M. de Salcedo to Elguezabal, May 2, 1803.

Commercial aggressions of foreigners.—In the summer of 1799, there occurred an incident which shows that distrust of foreigners was well founded and that some means of holding the friendship of the Indians against the lure of trade and conquest offered by the intruders was necessary. In July of that year, there appeared at the settlements of the ostensibly friendly Texas Indians, near the Neches, nine citizens of the post of Arkansas, Louisiana,[21] with a small party of Indians. At the same time, ten Louisianians and Englishmen, in company with still other Indians, went among the Tawehash and Comanches, who, at this particular moment, also posed as allies of the Spaniards. They carried goods and firearms to exchange for horses. Angered by their audacity, the Spaniards sent out from Nacogdoches an armed force to enquire into the intrusion, but because of the hostile demonstrations of some of the native tribes, it accomplished nothing, the traders merely withdrawing after their goods had been sold to advantage.

When De Nava learned of these occurrences, he interpreted them as meaning that the Indians of Texas were dissatisfied with their treatment by the Spaniards, and attributed their dissatisfaction either to the influence of the nearby Americans, the more distant English, of Canada, or the traders from Louisiana, who, as he said, were neither "French nor foreigners," as had been charged, but Spanish vassals. He thought, also, that the discontent of the Indians might be due, in part, to the fact that they were but little impressed with the military strength of the Spaniards or to the fact that the Texas traders could not meet the competition of other traders since the former were compelled to secure their supplies in Louisiana under a disadvantage. To the Texas authorities, therefore, he gave once more, the oft repeated instructions to treat the Northern tribes with the consideration which their numbers, location, and alliances demanded, in order that they might not be angered and raise complications with the Americans or with the English. He disapproved the sending out of the armed

---

[21]A post at the confluence of the Arkansas and Mississippi.

detachments against the intruders, declaring that Moral should have contented himself with threatening the native Indians with the loss of the Spanish trade and yearly presents, if they persisted in receiving the intruders. He maintained, however, that the order forbidding the entry of foreigners into Texas was to be strictly enforced so far as the English and Americans were concerned, both because Spain was at war with the English and because the laws of the country forbade the presence of any foreigner in Spanish territory.[22] Nevertheless, he advised dissimulation in carrying out the order for the exclusion of Louisianians when not supplied with proper passports. Such persons, as a rule, were really Spanish vassals, he said, and besides it was practically impossible to prevent their intrusion because of the many unsettled portions of the frontier through which they might gain an entrance unobserved. He feared that if they were angered by being refused admisison, they might incite the Indians to begin active warfare. He stressed the importance of maintaining the post of Nacogdoches as a means of holding the friendship of the Indians, by preventing the entry of foreigners among them, and of keeping open communication with Louisiana, in order that events in that province might be known. He urged the discouragement of trade in stock; but admitted that it was almost impossible to prevent the Indians from trading horses for firearms. He recognized, too, that a vigorous policy against contraband traders might anger the Indians themselves; and he therefore advised prudence, explaining that the authorities in Louisiana had been asked to aid in preventing similar incursions in the future.[23] In reply to the request for help, the Marqués de Casa Calvo, at that time, governor of Louisiana, expressed his willingness to aid in preventing contraband trade, but tried to divert suspicion from the Louisianians and to place it upon the English and the Americans, whose frontiers reached, as he said,

---

[22]*Recopilación de Leyes de los Reynos de las Indias, Libro IX, Titulo XXVII, Ley IX.*
[23]De Nava to Elguezabal, September 18, 1799.

within sixty leagues of New Orleans. He also drew attention to the fact, that along the western bank of the Mississippi from Punta Cortada to Puesto de Arkansas, there was not a single Spanish garrison to prevent the entry of foreigners.[24]

The intrusion just discussed was by no means a rare case. For in spite of the opposition of the Spaniards, many bold spirits took advantage of the unguarded frontier to push into the forbidden territory to trade with the wily Indians, who, with equal avidity, received favors from both Spaniards and intruders. The latter were also eager to trade with the Spaniards themselves, and found at least some of them bold enough to lay hold in this way upon a few of the comforts and even the bare necessities of life denied them by the short-sighted commercial policy of Spain, which forbade trade between the two Spanish provinces of Louisiana and Texas and refused to open a port for the exportation of the products of Texas to the Spanish ports of Vera Cruz and Campeche.[25] The temptation to violate the law was obviously great. The people had no inducement to devote themselves to agriculture—in fact, never raising sufficient crops for their own use. Foreign traders offered their wares at tempting prices in return for wild stock—practically the only medium of exchange upon which the natives could lay hands—and it is not surprising that many of them fell in with the plans of the intruders.[26] Although,

---

[24]Casa Calvo to Moral, March 8, 1800, in Morál to Elguezabal, April 26, 1800, and Casa Calvo to [Elguezabal], March 10, 1800.

[25]Such a system had been proposed at the end of the seventeenth century and again revived in 1778 by De Croix and Bernardo de Gálvez. Charles III who had imbibed many liberal ideas from a long residence in Italy, had given favorable consideration to the proposal, but nothing had been done in the matter because of the benighted condition of the people, the lack of funds, continued war between France and England, and strained relations between Spain and the United States. Priestley, *José de Gálvez, Visitador-General of New Spain, 1765–1776*, pages 24–45.

[26]Previous to the beginning of the period under consideration, permission had sometimes been given to persons living in Louisiana to come to Texas to secure horses for the government so that there

upon assuming the office of governor of Texas Elguezabal had issued an order absolutely prohibiting all traffic across the Texas-Louisiana frontier,[27] he had been unable to achieve any degree of success in spite of the fact that he had insisted vigorously upon the execution of these instructions.[28] Sometimes over one thousand head of stock were slipped across the border in a single month;[29] and, in spite of all efforts, clandestine trade went merrily, no doubt connived at by certain local officials and greatly enjoyed by many of the settlers.

Territorial aggressions.—Not all of the intruders of the time were considered mere traders, however; for some were believed to have designs upon Spanish territory. In such cases the government was forced to make even greater exertions to repel attacks. As a filibuster, James Wilkinson's *protegé*, Philip Nolan, is, of course, the conspicuous example. In his case the Spaniards were thoroughly aroused because his scheme had such an element of the mysterious. For instance, it was charged that he wished to engage in contraband trade; that he had designs upon the rich mines of Mexico;[30] that he was in league with Wilkinson, who, for years, was to exert a powerful influence upon the Spanish immigration policy, and that he intended to occupy Spanish territory by means of support from the British government.

---

would be no incentive to contraband trade with the English and the Americans; but the privilege had been so far abused that the authorities in Texas had soon felt compelled to interfere.

[27]De Nava to the Governor of Texas, March 19, 1799.

[28]Elguezabal to Guadiana, September 1, 1801.

[29]An illustration of the aggressive trade methods of the intruders is furnished by the case of Carlos Boyle who had located at Nacogdoches in 1796. He had secured permission from the Spanish authorities to place a boat upon the Trinity with the avowed purpose of facilitating travel between Nacogdoches and Béxar. But it was not long before he was introducing contraband goods under cover of his concession. But as soon as this procedure became known, he was ordered out of the province and a close watch was placed upon the mouth of the Trinity to prevent the possible landing of boats at that point. Morál to Elguezabal, June 26, 1800.

[30]Winsor, Justin, *The Westward Movement*, 369, 395.

Although the Spaniards were never able to determine which of these motives was the true one, they did know that there were great possibilities of danger in the situation, since Nolan numbered among his followers Englishmen, Americans, and Spaniards who had gone with him to Louisiana after an earlier trip to Texas in quest of stock.[31] That these fears had their foundation in fact is certain. There were a number of Americans who formed independent plans for invasion; and others, like Clark and Blount, of Tennessee— some of them even high in the councils of the government— who were willing to listen to plans for an American or even a joint American and British attack upon Spanish territory. But as the Spanish authorities were on the alert, they were able to dispose of Nolan and his ridiculously small following in short order. However, others soon took up similar plans; and the defenders were forced to remain constantly on guard.

From all the evidence considered it is quite clear, then, that at the beginning of the nineteenth century, the Spaniards felt compelled to be on their guard against the Indians, whom they tried to conciliate; against Spanish vassals of Louisiana, whom they really distrusted but feared to antagonize; against the French, whom they did not feel justified in definitely classing as either friends or foes; against the English, whom they kept under constant surveillance; and against the Americans, whom they feared most of all. Throughout the period to be considered, the Spaniards never lost their distrust of foreigners, although the authorities finally permitted the entry of a number who had located in Louisiana and who had there been made Spanish vassals. They had yielded in the first case because they had hoped that in this way they could form a buffer against the English of Canada, weaken the United States by drawing away part of her citizens, and perhaps induce the newcomers to set up a separate government in the West.[32] The struggle

---

[31]Músquiz to Elguezabal, July 2, 1801.
[32]Phelps, Albert, *Louisiana*, 149–177.

The Opening of Texas to Foreign Settlement 55

was to be staged under somewhat different conditions beyond the Sabine.

Imperfect execution of exclusion policy.—In January 1799, José María Guadiana, Lieutenant Governor, who was stationed at Nacogdoches, wrote to Governor Muñoz, saying, that, in obedience to orders, he had refused the second request of a certain "Hriala Wiggins and Hare Crow,"[33] inhabitants of Rapides, Louisiana, to hunt bear, beaver, and deer near Nacogdoches. He had also ordered out of the province Juan McFarrel, an American who had a passport from the commandant of Natchitoches, and had decided to keep an eye on Samuel Davenport, another American, who had been going in and out of Nacogdoches for years, and who, at that time, was associated in business with Eduardo Morfil, of Natchitoches, and William Barr, of Nacogdoches. Both of the last named men, he said, bore good reputations and were engaged in furnishing supplies for Indian trade at Nacogdoches.[34] The presence of these men in Texas naturally raises the question as to the number of foreigners who, by fair means or foul, had managed to gain entry into Texas by 1801.

Foreigners in Texas in 1801.—No census of Texas for this year has been found; but a list of foreigners in the jurisdiction of Nacogdoches in January, 1804, furnishes the information desired. In this register the commandant records the name, nationality, and term of residence of each person.[35] It contains the names of sixty-eight foreigners, of whom fifty had lived in the jurisdiction more than three

---

[33]The Spanish spelling of proper names has been followed except in cases where the real names of foreigners have been determined from original signatures.

[34]Guadiana to Muñoz, January 3, 1799.

[35]It is, therefore, possible to determine roughly how many foreigners there were in the jurisdiction of Nacogdoches in 1801 and to ascertain practically how many there were in the whole of Texas, since, at that time, not many had passed further into the heart of the forbidden territory. However, Lorenzo Reveque and Pedro Longueville may possibly have lived at Béxar at that time. Salcedo to the Governor of Texas, April 14, 1809. *Cf.* List for December, 1799.

years. Of these fifty, thirteen were Americans, among
them being Santiago Dill and Samuel Davenport whose cases
may be taken as illustrations of the means employed for
gaining entry into Texas. Dill was a native of Pennsylvania. He had taken the oath of allegiance to the Spanish
government in 1794, during the administration of Miró,
Governor of Louisiana. He had immigrated into Texas in
1800. Davenport was also a native of Pennsylvania, a married man, thirty-seven years of age, and an Indian trader
by occupation. He claimed that he had left home when only
sixteen years of age and had gone almost directly to Louisiana, at that time under Spanish rule. According to his own
statement, he had gained the confidence of the Spaniards by
his good conduct, and had been allowed to become a partner
of William Barr, the accredited Indian agent. Barr was
the most prominent Irishman who had settled in Texas before 1801. He, too, had taken the oath of allegiance under
Miró. He had first come to Texas, so he said, for the purpose of securing stock to take to Pittsburg, where his parents
lived; but had been so pleased with the country that he had
settled at Nacogdoches with the consent of the commandant
at that point. He had been living in that *pueblo* since 1793,
having been appointed Indian agent by Commandant-
General Phelipe de Neve. Of the seven other Irishmen
listed, Santiago Conilt, who had entered Texas in 1786, may
be named as the pioneer. The English were represented in
a much smaller proportion than the Americans or Irish.
Nevertheless, they had entered Texas quite early, for
Crisostome Yucante, a native of Canada, had preceded
Conilt to Texas by a few years, having located in 1783. Of
the nine Frenchmen named as early settlers, Juan Sarnac, a
native of Rochelle, and Guillermo Bebe, a native of Louisiana, had lived at Nacogdoches since 1788. Among other
Frenchmen located at Nacogdoches and who had been born
in Louisiana, several claimed a residence of twenty years.[36]

---

[36]*Padron que manifiesta los Estrangeros*, January 1, 1804; *Expediente Sobre Extrangeros*, May 8, 1810; affidavit of Barr, June 16, 1809; and affidavit of Davenport, June 16, 1810. *Cf.* Appendix 2 and 3.

Thus the settlement of foreigners at Nacogdoches had begun as early as 1778 with the entry of two Frenchmen— one from France, the other from Louisiana. Within the next few years, several other persons of French extraction had joined the pioneers. In 1783, the English had begun to send representatives to the region, while three years later the Irish had appeared upon the scene. By 1789, the American movement toward Texas had commenced; and by 1801, the stream of immigration, gaining strength from all these sources, had attained respectable proportions. Some of these settlers had come from Louisiana, some from Canada, some from the Atlantic seaboard, and others from far-away Europe. Although the majority were listed as farmers and laborers, many were engaged in trade as a means of earning a livelihood. Naturally, the traders made up a shifting population; and, hence, discrepancies in various census reports are not to be wondered at.[57]

It is hard to reconcile the presence of this large number of foreigners with the exclusion policy of the Spanish government just outlined, unless it be remembered that many of those who had been permitted to enter Texas were considered worthy of confidence because, like Barr and Davenport, they had previously lived in Louisiana, and had there taken the oath of allegiance. However, Guadiana was accused of having freely permitted the entry of many foreigners contrary to the strict orders of the commandant-general.[38] Although, on January 3, 1799, he promised to obey orders in future, his conduct was not satisfactory to his superiors. So, when selecting his successor, they decided

---

[37]*Padrón de Nacogdoches*, December 31, 1798. Nacogdoches Archives—to be indicated henceforward as N. A. For instance, Roy [Rueg?] a German who was reported in 1828 to have resided in Texas for about thirty years does not appear on any of the lists of early settlers at Nacogdoches.

[38]De Nava to the Governor of Texas, March 20, 1798, and Elguezabal to the General Commanding the Eastern Provinces, November 30, 1800, in Translations of Historical Documents in the Archives of Bexar County, 1st Series, Part IV, Adventures and Private Expeditions into Texas, No. 1, Document 8, N. A.

to change the commandant at this place every five or six months to prevent him from forming any secret entangling alliances with the people of the United States.[39] To the new commandant they repeated former orders and, likewise, gave new instructions that communication across the border must be restricted to gathering information of the activities of the enemy.[40] But owing possibly to ill health De Nava was unable to enforce these instructions. However, in the summer of 1800, Nemesio Salcedo, the most exclusive of all exclusives, who was in office many years and who was to have a decisive influence on the colonization of Texas, was assigned to duty in the Interior Provinces for the especial purpose of guarding against a threatened English attack.[41] Naturally he made every effort to keep out all other intruders as well. The fact that two foreigners, Martin Doyle and a certain Aroberson, who had been staying at Nacogdoches, were ordered out of the province in June, 1803, probably indicates that, for at least a short time, he was able to secure obedience to his orders.[42] However, at this juncture the unexpected retrocession of Louisiana to France compelled him to modify his policy sufficiently to permit the transfer to Spanish soil of all vassals of Louisiana who were displeased with the change of sovereignty. The history of the transfer of a number of these persons to Texas will now be traced; for, in spite of the fact that the Spanish authorities constantly felt afraid of the Americans as a nation, they allowed their strong desire to settle Texas to outweigh their first sober judgment. Indeed, they evidently half persuaded themselves that such Americans as desired to settle in Spanish territory were hostile to the government of the United States and would thus be effective guardians against the advance of the great body of Americans. They

---

[39]De Nava to the Governor of Texas, May 14, 1799.

[40]Muñoz to Moral, June 22, 1799.

[41]Cédula, August 26, 1800. However, he did not assume office until the end of 1802. N. Salcedo to the Governor of Texas, November 4, 1802.

[42]Elguezabal to the Commandant-General, June 22, 1803, draft No. 80 in *Quaderno Borrador*, December 8, 1802–June 30, 1803.

failed to take into account the characteristic longing of every frontiersman for a home and better living conditions for his family and underestimated the lure of the wide field in Texas where he seemed to meet all the elements demanded for finding happiness and making a fortune.

CHAPTER I

Admission of Spanish Vassals from Louisiana, 1801-1803

Immigration from Louisiana.—Spain receded Louisiana to France in the treaty of San Ildefonso; but, as the transfer was kept a profound secret, no important results followed immediately in Texas. However, the news at last leaked out and Bernardo Martin Despallier, a Frenchman who was later to justify the premonitions of the Spaniards, soon asked permisison to settle in the Spanish dominions to escape his enemies in Louisiana. He declared that he had suffered financial reverses in Santo Domingo; that he had then returned to his native country, Louisiana, where he had been honored by military appointment under Governor Carondelet; that, during the war with France, he had conducted himself in accordance with his position and his duty to the Spanish king; that, as a result, he had gained many enemies; and that he now desired to end his days in peace in Texas, where he could be looked upon as a faithful Spaniard since he understood that Louisiana had been transferred to France.[1] Later in enumerating his services to Spain Despallier claimed that he had been appointed captain of the mounted militia by Carondelet in 1794; and that, thereafter, he had always been ready to sacrifice himself to serve his king;[2] that he had discovered plots against the crown during the recent war with France; that he had given warning of the "infamous project" of Nolan; and that, through the aid of his uncle, Valantin Layssard, he had done much to defeat the intruder.[3] Despallier was not admitted at this time, but like his kinsman, Layssard, he was nothing if not persistent, and his history will have to be considered later. His case was an unusual one;[4] for it was

---

[1]Petition, January 18, 1804, Appendix 4.
[2]Petition, January 7, 1809.
[3]Petition, October 17, 1801.
[4]The only other case noted in the Béxar Archives is that of Nicole Welch, a retired major of the American Army, who appeared with

not until the spring of 1803 that the inhabitants of Louisiana began to show signs of general discontent. In April of that year, the governor of Texas wrote to the commandant-general asking what he should do, since the settlers of Louisiana frequently came to him seeking admittance into Texas, declaring that they objected to the transfer of Louisiana to France. The commandant-general, who recognized the necessity for developing the territory under his control and who desired to furnish a refuge for the vassals of Louisiana, "abandoned a foreign country,"[5] was not long in deciding upon a course of action. In May he ruled that all petitions must be received but that each applicant must prove that he had been a Spanish vassal in Louisiana and must submit a passport or other documentary evidence of good character before he could be received as a settler. As a further precaution, each person was to be required to furnish a statement of the size of his family and the amount of goods he intended to introduce. Those who did not submit absolute proof of fidelity to the Spanish government were to be induced to settle in Nueva Viscaya or in Coahuila, where lands would be assigned them. To make assurance doubly sure, he required that all petitions should be presented to him for final decision.[6] These stipulations gave an intimation of the cautious nature of the commandant-general. This point is an important one; for, even from this time, may be traced the beginning of the differences between him and his bolder fellow-workers who were later placed in Texas. These differences eventually led to bitter feeling and finally brought colonization work in Texas temporarily to an abrupt close. But, for a time, the work went steadily forward. Salcedo's regulations soon received royal approval and, thereafter, events moved rapidly.

On September 24, 1803, the king issued a decree permitting all Spanish vassals in Louisiana who might migrate to

his family at Rapides in October, 1800, seeking a location within the Spanish dominions. Layssard to Elguezabal, October 3, 1800.

[5]N. Salcedo to Ceballos, June 7, 1803, *A. G. I. S.* Mex., *legajo* 18, No. 27, June 7, 1803.

[6]N. Salcedo to the Governor of Texas, May 23, 1803.

the Spanish dominions to bring in their personal effects free of duty.[7] On November, 1803, he approved the commandant-general's immigration regulations,[8] thus opening the door of the Interior Provinces to such Spanish vassals of Louisiana as could persuade the local authorities that they bore a good reputation and professed the Catholic faith.

Among the first to apply for admission into Texas was a certain Irishman, Guillermo Williams by name, who desired to settle at Nacogdoches. He brought with him recommendations from Captain José Vidal,[9] of Concordia, "the nearest post to the United States." As was to be expected, the commandant-general was not willing to have the applicant locate where temptation to contraband trade would be strongest; and he therefore instructed him to settle at Béxar, where his conduct could be watched.[10] In fact, all evidence goes to show that, at the outset, the commandant-general intended to place all immigrants in or near Spanish settlements so that the magistrates could keep a watchful eye on them.

In August, 1803, José de la Baume presented a petition asking to be received as a settler. He claimed that as soon as he learned that Louisiana was to be ceded to France, he was filled with the desire to follow the flag which his ancestors had defended with such signal valor and that he had come to Nacogdoches to locate. He had soon realized that this place offered but little opportunity for one of his profession, a physician and herb dealer, and but little work for the eight negroes he owned. He therefore asked to be allowed to move to Béxar or to Bahía.[11] This, of course,

---

[7]Decree, September 24, 1803, Copy in Aguirre to Elguezabal, March 2, 1805.

[8]N. Salcedo to the Governor of Texas, March 27, 1804.

[9]Ugarte to Elguezabal, April 3, 1803. For Vidal's plan for establishing settlements on the Mississippi as a barrier against the spread of the Americans, see documents in *A. G. I. S.*, *legajo* 10, No. 6, September 27, 1800–February 26, 1801.

[10]Ugarte to Elguezabal, June 3, 1803.

[11]Petition, August 4, 1803. See Appendix 5 and Burlage and Hollingsworth, *Abstract of Valid Land Claims Compiled from the Records of the General Land Office and Court of Claims of the State*, 635.

The Opening of Texas to Foreign Settlement 63

fell in with the plans of the commandant-general who gave him a permit to locate at Béxar, or, if he preferred, at some point in Nueva Viscaya, provided he could show the proofs of loyalty required by the order of May 23.[12] Juan Pedro Walker, a native of New Orleans, and Florenço Millan, a native of the kingdom of Castille, presented themselves at Nacogdoches with the plea that they did not wish to remain in Louisiana since it was soon to be turned over to the French, and then was to be sold to the Americans.[13] The commandant issued immediate orders for their reception, not even waiting to be sure that they intended bringing their families.[14]

Through the recommendation of Felix Trudeaux, of Natchitoches, the commandant of Nacogdoches was ordered to admit Juan de Bassily and family if these same conditions could be met.[15] Similar privileges were extended to a certain Francisco Chabus who had been a Spanish vassal for seventeen years. He, too, was permitted to settle at Béxar with his family and his slaves; but he was to be warned that all contraband trade with Louisiana was strictly forbidden.[16] However, he was to be urged to locate in Nueva Viscaya. This did not suit Chabus, for he had his heart set on securing lands at Nacogdoches and probably never accepted the offer, although he continued his efforts to secure a permit to visit the interior of Texas and protested against being compelled to sell his property on the frontier before immigrating.[17]

Among other petitions was that of Juan Valentin Duforest, a native of New Orleans, whose father had served in the veteran army of Louisiana for twenty-nine years and

---

[12][Elguezabal] to N. Salcedo, October 12, 1803, draft No. 141 in *Borrador*, June 6, 1803–December 21, 1803.
[13]Ugarte to Elguezabal, September 2, 1803.
[14]Ugarte to the Governor of Texas, October 10, 1803.
[15]N. Salcedo to the Governor of Texas, September 12, 1803.
[16]Petition, September 30, 1803; N. Salcedo to the Governor of Texas, November 21, 1803; [Elguezabal] to N. Salcedo, October 26, 1803, Draft No. 156, in *Borrador*, June 6, 1803–December 21, 1803.
[17]Chabus to Ugarte, April 4, 1804.

who had held various offices of trust under the Spanish government. Duforest declared his intention never to stray from Spanish rule and selected the Province of Coahuila as a place of residence.[18] This was a very unusual case, for the immigrants almost to a man desired to settle in Texas rather than farther toward the interior in accordance with the wish of the commandant-general. Whether they really wished to follow the flag, as they claimed, to engage in contraband trade, as their conduct indicated, or even to secure lands in the Spanish dominions, as certain authorities charged, cannot be determined. Certainly all applicants sturdily protested their affection for the Spanish flag, but few could later square their deeds with their words.

A very unusual case was that of Captain Vidal. In the latter part of 1803, he presented a petition asking to be allowed to settle at Nacogdoches. In support of his plea, he claimed that, upon learning of Nolan's plan for entering Texas, he had warned the Spanish authorities, explaining to them that he feared, if Nolan succeeded, the Americans would by degrees penetrate into those precious possessions which it was important to guard from the ambition of the United States.[19] In transmitting Vidal's petition, the commandant of Nacogdoches urged that lands be assigned him until official action could be taken on his case.[20] Although the governor was not satisfied with the documents presented, he suggested that the applicant be allowed to settle, because of the good reputation he bore, and that the petition of his companion, Santiago Ferrold, be favorably considered since it was reported that he, too, was a faithful vassal of the king.[21] Vidal was finally allowed to locate temporarily at Nacogdoches, but orders were issued that he was not to receive lands until his case could be thoroughly investigated. Ferrold, also, was to be admitted because he had

---

[18]Duforest to the Commandant-General, October 5, 1803.

[19][Vidal] to the Commanding Officer at Nacogdoches, October 6, 1803, in translation, 1st Series, Part IV, No. 1, Doc. 2, N. A.

[20]Ugarte to Elguezabal, October 21, 1803.

[21][Elguezabal] to N. Salcedo, November 1, 1803, Draft No. 158, in *Borrador*, June 6, 1803–December 21, 1803.

The Opening of Texas to Foreign Settlement   65

lived in Louisiana, but he was to be urged to settle in Coahuila.[22] No further reference to these cases has been found; but since, a few years later, Vidal was still living in New Orleans, it is probable that he was not permitted to locate permanently at Nacogdoches. He therefore probably did not choose to emigrate at all. In fact, there is nothing to show that any of the applicants just mentioned took advantage of the permisison granted for settlement, save José de la Baume, who finally located at Béxar. The small proportion of actual settlers in comparison with the large number of applicants will be noted throughout the whole period under consideration. That Nacogdoches was at this time the point of greatest interest, both to Spaniards and foreign traders, who often used immigration as a cloak to secure entrance into Texas, will be seen at once, but other regions were now to receive attention.

Proposed settlements between Béxar and Nacogdoches.—On November 2, 1803, just before the actual transfer of Louisiana to France, Juan Ugarte, who at this time was commandant of Nacogdoches, suggested the establishment of one or two settlements between Béxar and Nacogdoches as a means of furnishing the necessary supplies for the maintenance of Nacogdoches. This was made necessary, Ugarte said, by the orders forbidding all trade with Louisiana. Unfortunately, this proposal can not be found, but its main points can be gathered from an opinion rendered by the governor of Texas on January 18, 1804.

Disapproval of governor.—The governor acknowledged that it was a long distance from Béxar to Nacogdoches, and thence to the frontier of Texas, and that on the way there were *arroyos* and other fertile spots suitable for the location of settlements as has been stated by Ugarte. But he said that there were as good or better sites near Béxar where the lands could be irrigated. Even at the capital, all the lands had not been cultivated, because the population was small and the *people did not relish the work demanded by agriculture.* He then gave a backward glance

---
[22]N. Salcedo to the Governor of Texas, November 10, 1803.

at the history of colonization in Texas. The abandonment of the *presidios* of Orcoquisac on the Trinity, and of Adais on the extreme Texas-Louisiana frontier and the removal of the troops and settlers to Béxar, in 1773, had been caused, he said, by the fact that the people of Texas were not agriculturists and because the Indians of the North, the Comanches, and the Lipans, had kept up a constant warfare against Béxar. Even with this massing of population, he explained, the region between Béxar and Nacogdoches had not been explored and settled until some of the settlers of the abandoned *presidios* had established the post of Bucareli at Paso de Tomás on the Trinity in 1774. He next recited the story of the abandonment of Bucareli and of the informal establishment of the *pueblo* of Nacogdoches by these same settlers, and claimed that the move had been necessary because of Indian depredations, and floods which had destroyed goods, crops, and finally, even the settlement of Bucareli itself. Thereafter, he said, these settlers had maintained a precarious foothold at Nacogdoches without even the protection of troops until 1795, when a small garrison had been furnished them. From this melancholy recital of events, the governor naturally drew the conclusion that there were not enough people in Texas to develop even Béxar, Bahía, and Nacogdoches, and he, therefore, believed that it would be impossible to establish the settlements proposed by Ugarte, unless *settlers should be brought from other provinces and adequately protected from Indian depredations after being located.*[23] The governor's disapproval temporarily ended the plan; but it was revived later when the necessity for erecting a buffer against the Americans, who by this time had unexpectedly secured possession of Louisiana through Napoleon's decision to sell it rather than to have it fall into the hands of the English, was more keenly felt. It will therefore be again the subject of discussion.

---

[23]The Governor of Texas to the Commandant-General, January 18, 1804, Draft No. 184 in *Quaderno Borrador*, January 4, 1804–December 19, 1804. For a detailed account of the events mentioned see Bolton, *Texas in the Middle Eighteenth Century*.

The Opening of Texas to Foreign Settlement 67

Texas in 1803.—The condition of Texas at the end of the French *régime* in Louisiana is admirably set forth in a report made by the governor of Texas to the commandant-general in June, 1803. In this report the governor declared that Texas then had only three small settlements, namely, the capital, San Antonio de Béxar, the *presidio* of Bahía del Espíritu Santo, and the *pueblo* of Nacogdoches. He estimated the population of Béxar at twenty-five hundred, that of Bahía at six hundred and eighteen, and of Nacogdoches at seven hundred and seventy. To this number he added the settlers located at the various missions, making a total of four thousand civilized persons in Texas. He gave an interesting picture of the province and deplored the absence of any industry save a slight attempt to cultivate the soil. He described the consequent sufferings of the people and showed their dependence upon the meat of wild animals for actual subsistence. He even claimed that the people were saved from actual starvation by the use of wild horse meat and prophesied that Nacogdoches would have to be abandoned if contraband trade were cut off. It was clear, however, he said, that the smuggler would take advantage of these conditions; that Americans, Frenchmen, and Indians from the United States would be attracted by the fertile lands of Texas; and that the peculiar conditions created by the retrocession of Louisiana to the French and its subsequent sale to the United States would encourage the entry of foreigners into Texas.[24] The United States took possession of Louisiana in December, 1803;[25] and the Spaniards

---

[24] See Appendix 6. *Cf.* Report, January 30, 1805, and Elguezabal's discussion of Indian relations, December 8, 1802, in *Quaderno*, December 8, 1802–June 6, 1803.

[25] Napoleon's instructions to the prefect of Louisiana to receive the province from the Spaniards and then deliver it immediately to the commissioners to be appointed by the United States to receive it came to the motley residents of New Orleans, "white, black, yellow, red, Frenchmen, Spaniards, African, mulatto, Indian, and the tall lanky Westerner in coonskin cap and leather hunting shirt" like "a clap of thunder out of a clear sky." In *The Opening of the Mississippi*,

were thus brought face to face with the aggressive American. It must not be thought for a moment, however, that the French were eliminated from the contest by this sale; for Napoleon soon let it be known that he had formed even more ambitious schemes than those for the erection of a French dependency in the comparatively unimportant province of Louisiana.[26] The whole Spanish Dominions of

---

597–603, Frederick Austin Ogg gives a most graphic and touching picture of the transfer of authority from Spain to France, on November 30, and of the final lowering forever, on December 20, of the tricolors of France into the waiting hands of the guard of honor which had held a death watch over their national emblem. Then the Stars and Stripes were flung to the breeze amid the shouts of the Americans and the firing of salutes from the armed vessels on the river.

[26]In 1804, the Governor of Louisiana, W. C. C. Claiborne, wrote to Madison declaring that he had discovered with regret that there existed among the people of New Orleans "a strong partiality for the French government" and that there was cherished in some circles a sentiment that "at the close of the war between England and France, the great Bonaparte would again raise his standard in the country." Claiborne to Madison, January 10, 1804, *Official Letter Books of W. C. C. Claiborne, 1801–1806*, Rowland Dunbar (ed.), I, 330. During this same month he reported the presence at New Orleans of some twenty or thirty troublesome young adventurers from Bordeaux and Santo Domingo. He described them as "men of some information, desperate fortunes, and inflated with the idea of the invincibility of Bonaparte and the power of the French Nation." He charged that they were mortified at the possession of Louisiana by the United States and that they semed determined to "sour the inhabitants as much as possible with the American government." As to the means used by them, Claiborne stated that they relied upon "the dissemination of falsehood (which among the uninformed and credulous pass current)" and upon the fomentation of division among the Creoles of the country and the Americans in New Orleans. These men, he claimed, were able to exercise a very great influence since the language, manners, and customs of the people were French and because the mass of the pople were so densely ignorant, Claiborne to Madison, January 24, 1804, *ibid*, 345–346. Again, in February of the same year, he complained of a considerable immigration from the French West India Islands. He reported the arrival of a vessel with about one hundred French citizens on board, and the

America were soon to be his objective. The stage was merely set for the preliminary skirmishes which were to decide the ownership of Texas.

Since the difficulties Spain had to meet in defending her territory have been described and a picture of conditions in Texas at the beginning of the struggle has been given, it will now be possible to take up the main thread of the story and to show the steps by which Spain attempted to erect a buffer against the Americans; for since Louisiana had been lost to the defenders of "liberty" in fulfilment of the prophecy of the viceroy of Mexico made some years before,[27] nearly all faithful Spaniards recognized the necessity for carrying out his injunctions to fortify and guard Texas, now once more a barrier province for the purpose of preventing an invasion of American colonists and of wild Indians whom the enemy could easily gain over as allies. However, their desire to develop the country outweighed their inherent distrust, and they flattered themselves that they could form a buffer of these immigrants who came knocking insistently at the fast-closed door.

---

expected arrival of another vessel from Jamaica, with several hundred Frenchmen who had been refused asylum on that island. He declared that he did not consider these immigrants the best possible settlers for Louisiana but supposed that he would have to accept them if they sought a residence in his jurisdiction. He again called attention to the prevalence of the opinion that Lousiana would again revert to France upon the conclusion of the European war. He called especial attention to Laussat's remark that "the harvests of Louisiana were not yet secured to the United States," Claiborne to Madison, February 6, 1804, *ibid.*, 363–364. See also Claiborne to Madison, February 6, 1804, *ibid*, 388. Again in 1805, Claiborne declared that it had been rumored that certain discontented persons were contemplating a mission to France to call the attention of the Emperor to the province, Claiborne to Madison, June 6, 1805, *ibid*, III, 79.

[27]Branciforte to the Prince of the Peace, May 27, 1796, *A. G. I. S.* Mex., *legajo* 5, No. 64 of April 23, 1796.

CHAPTER II

DECISIONS FOR A BUFFER AGAINST THE UNITED STATES
1804–1805

Increased emigration from Louisiana.—Many of the inhabitants of Louisiana were displeased with the retrocession of that territory to France and a still larger number were angered by its sale to the United States. Consequently, while Ugarte's plans for the establishment of settlements were in abeyance, a movement of Spanish vassals, consisting of Spaniards, Irishmen, Englishmen, Frenchmen, and disguised Americans, continued into Texas. The immigrants now claimed that they desired both to follow the Spanish flag and to escape the "harsh rule of the United States."[1] To this stream a number of Indian immigrants were added; for, after the transfer of Louisiana to the United States, the Spanish authorities, desiring to erect the strongest possible buffer against aggression, quickly reversed their former policy in regard to these applicants.[2]

---

[1]Moses Austin ascribed this dissatisfaction to Wilkinson's arbitrary regulation in regard to the forms required for surveying and proving claims to lands to meet the demands of the law of Congress in regard to the matter. Austin, *Representation to Congress of Conditions in Louisiana, 1806*, (original), Austin Papers. Claiborne believed that the people were leaving Louisiana for Texas because of the ease with which lands could be secured from the Spanish authorities, and the prevalence of the opinion that the subjects of Spain were free from taxation. Claiborne to Madison, February 16, 1802, *Letter Books*, I, 47. He felt that it was due also in a large measure to the action of the French of Louisiana, who stirred up animosity against the American government, and the dissatisfaction of the people with the judicial system of the new government. Claiborne to Madison, January 24, 1804, *ibid.*, 346, and June 15, 1806, *ibid.*, III, 231. *Cf.* Gayarré, Charles, *History of Louisiana*, IV, Chap. I.

[2]So convinced were the Spaniards that the Americans intended making some hostile move that orders were issued calculated to prevent the approach of the Americans toward the Texas-Louisiana frontier and especially to forestall any attempt to run the boundary line. N. Salcedo to the Governor of Texas, May 6, 1804. Naturally,

The civilized immigrants, of course, could secure entrance under the commandant-general's order of May 23, already cited, if they were able to convince the authorities that they were Spanish vassals and desirable citizens; and certain regulations were soon drawn up for the purpose of more carefully culling the applicants.

Immigration regulations.—On March 27, 1804, the commandant-general instructed the governor of Texas to receive all petitions presented by settlers of Louisiana, to admit those entitled to reception under previous orders, and to designate the location assigned each applicant. He decreed that as before, immigrants might settle in Texas, Coahuila, or Nueva Viscaya, but ordered that no newcomers should be allowed to remain in or near Nacogdoches. He thought it wiser to leave this post with its existing scanty population, rather than to have it settled by Louisianians who, because of their connections and their knowledge of the country, could carry on contraband trade. For the same reason, he wished immigrants to remain at Nacogdoches no longer than was absolutely necessary for a provisional decision upon their petitions. The governor was required to report the names of the favored applicants in all cases, and to indicate the locations to be assigned to them, in order that the proper authorities might be notified. The commandant-general was in favor of settling the immigrants near Béxar, suggesting likewise that American deserters who had been given an asylum by the Spaniards in an effort to weaken the enemy should be brought to the capital and assisted in selecting locations. He desired that all immigrants having trades or professions should be urged to settle in Coahuila since they would be safer there.[3] A little later, the territory in which the immigrants might settle was enlarged, when the viceroy, who at first had refused to admit the Louisianians into the territory under his

---

therefore, the commandant of Nacogdoches was opposed to the entry of any Americans into Spanish territory. Ugarte to the Governor of Texas, June 3, 1804.

[3]N. Salcedo to the Governor of Texas, March 27, 1804.

direct control,[4] reversed his decision, upon learning of the king's decree of November 9, 1803, and declared that no inconvenience would result from their entry. However, he ordered that all business in Louisiana should be finished by them prior to immigration, because no journey back to that region would be permitted.[5]

Petitions.—Juan Curon, an Irishman and a settler of Ouachita who desired to locate at Nacogdoches, was one of the first to present a petition at this time.[6] The commandant of Nacogdoches forwarded the petition with the statement that the applicant was a good man and that he would furnish the people of Texas a good example of the proper cultivation of the soil so that they could avoid the poverty and suffering so continuously experienced.[7] Texas apparently continued to be deprived of this much-needed example; for no final decision of this case has been found.

During 1804, there were thirteen successful applicants for settlement in Texas or further toward the interior. Several of them expressed a preference for Nacogdoches. This, of cours, was not permitted and most of them evidently failed to take advantage of the permission to locate at other points.[8] In fact, Christian Hesser, who in spite of

---

[4]N. Salcedo to the Governor of Texas, May 22, 1804.

[5]Uranga to Elguezabal, February 11, 1804, and N. Salcedo to the Governor of Texas, April 24, 1804.

[6]See Appendix 7.

[7]Ugarte to Elguezabal, April 1, 1804. *Cf.* Recommendation of Tejeira [Commandant of Ouachita], February 3, 1804.

[8]Estevan Despallier and Valentin Layssard, who promised to immigrate with their families, were given permission to settle at Béxar, Bahía, or further toward the interior. N. Salcedo to the Governor of Texas, May 22, 1804.

Daniel Clark, an Irishman, a native of Opelousas, wished to enter the Interior Provinces, or even to go into the territory under the personal command of the viceroy to put up certain mining machinery. [Elguezabal] to the Commandant-General, July 18, 1804, draft No. 266 in *Quaderno Borrador*, January 4, 1804–December 19, 1804.

Bernardo Guisarnot, of Natchitoches, begged to be allowed to live at Nacogdoches, since he could not afford to remove to Béxar with his family. Ugarte to Elguezabal, July 4, 1804. He insisted on this point; but was finally informed that he would not be received at

The Opening of Texas to Foreign Settlement 73

prohibitory orders located at Nacogdoches, is the only applicant known to have settled at this time. Later, however, two applicants, Edmond Norris and Hugo Coyle, immigrated, the former locating at Nacogdoches and the latter settling on the Trinity river.

Certain Indian tribes of Louisiana at this time also began to show signs of discontent with the treatment they received

---

all unless he would locate in the interior. N. Salcedo to Cordero, July 14, 1804.

Nicolas Urbano Carlos Canel, a native of France and a Spanish vassal, declared that he would be satisfied with any suitable location that might be assigned him in the Interior Provinces, as he simply wished to escape American rule. Petition, July 4, 1804: Ugarte to Elguezabal, August 4, 1804. The compliment was at once effective, and he was given permission to locate at Béxar.

Francisco Olivares, a native of Valencia, a resident for some years of New Orleans, of Natchitoches, and of Nacogdoches, wished to move with his family to Béxar or to Bahía, because the American government did not suit him. He really wished to remain at Nacogdoches since his wife was a native of that place and since he also owned lands there. Petition, August 4, 1804.

Christian Hesser, a native of Germany and a resident for some years of Natchitoches, disliked American rule so much that he agreed to settle with his family at any point the governor might select. Petition and List of slaves, household goods, etc. introduced by him, August 5, 1804. He actually showed his allegiance to the Spaniards by becoming a resident of Texas.

Manuel Alvarez de Guitán, of Vera Cruz, who had lived some time at New Orleans, was content just to enter Spanish Dominions in order to escape American rule, but wished to remain in Nacogdoches. Petition, August 30, 1804. Of course, this last request was refused in view of the existing regulations; but he was nevertheless given permission to reside elsewhere.

Edmond Norris, an Irishman, like the majority of the applicants considered, asked to be allowed to locate at Nacogdoches. Ugarte to Elguezabal, October 4, 1804. It is known, however, that he did not become a settler until several years later.

Another applicant, a poor carpenter, Alexo. Guelete, wished to move from Nacogdoches to Béxar in order that he might secure employment.

Hugo Coyle, an Irishman, who had been employed as a surveyor in Louisiana, and Pablo Lafitte, a Frenchman of Bayou Pierre, which was within territory claimed by both Spain and the United States, at the hands of the Americans, and commenced begging protection from "their friends, the Spaniards." So insistent were they, that the authorities finally yielded, and it became necessary therefore to work out some system for their reception.

Indian situation.—A letter of May 22 from the commandant-general to the governor of Texas gives an idea of the Indian situation on the frontier just before the sale of Louisiana to the United States. In this communication, Salcedo suggested to Elguezabal that, since the whole of Louisiana now belonged to the United States, it would certainly be a good thing to take steps to hold the friendship of the Indians of that province, so that they would not be tempted to break off existing treaties with the Spaniards. To this end, he gave orders that such Indians as appeared at Béxar were to be told that the Americans, without any cause whatever, had drawn away certain of the Indians from their allegiance to the Spaniards, as had been shown by Nolan's expedition and the proposed incursion of his follower, Robert Ashley. They were also to be warned against the treachery of the Americans by the cruel treatment of the Alabamas, Choctaws, and Apalaches, who had been compelled to traverse the deserts of the United States to settle near their protectors, "the Spaniards."[9] Although he was anxious to hold the friendship of the Louisiana Indians, Salcedo was by no means anxious to grant them entry into Texas.

---

applied for admission. Ugarte to Elguezabal, November 4, 1804. However he did not take advantage of this permission for several years; and his case will receive attention later. There was delay in the case of Lafitte, owing to the fact that, by order of October 13, 1801, he had been expelled from the jurisdiction of Nacogdoches for aiding the accomplices of Nolan to escape. Elguezabal to N. Salcedo, November 21, 1804, draft No. 316 in *Quaderno Borrador*, January 4, 1804–December 19, 1804.

Still another applicant was Franco. Bosie, of Natchitoches, who was permitted to go to Béxar in order that a location might be assigned him. [Elguezabal] to N. Salcedo, September 19, 1804, draft No. 326 in *Quaderno Borrador*, January 4, 1804–December 19, 1804.

[9]N. Salcedo to the Governor of Texas, May 22, 1804.

Indian immigrants.—Early in 1804, Valentin Layssard asked permission to introduce three hundred Tinzas and Apalaches, who had been living near Opelousas, Avoyles, and Rapides.[10] Influenced perhaps by the governor's suggestion that Layssard was seeking some personal gain, Salcedo at first objected, claiming that sufficient proofs of the good conduct of the Indians in question had not been furnished and that the addition of new tribes would greatly increase the troubles of the government in keeping peace between these immigrant Indians and the more numerous friendly tribes in Texas and along its borders. At the same time, Salcedo rejected Layssard's request that he be made commissioner for the friendly Indians of Texas, saying that the office was already filled by William Barr.[11] The Apalaches themselves claimed that they desired to immigrate to Texas because they preferred the rule of Spain to that of the United States; and as the greater portion of them were Catholics, they asked that arrangements be made for religious instruction. Their reception was favored by the commandant of Nacogdoches, who thought that they would furnish a good example to the surrounding tribes; and there were others to plead their cause,[12] for Juan Manuel de Salcedo while serving as governor of Louisiana had already written to his brother, Nemesio, urging him to admit them because they were faithful Catholics, good citizens, loved the Spaniards, and hated the Americans.[13] Soon afterwards, the governor of Texas reported that upon investigation, he had learned many favorable things concerning the Tinzas or Apalaches, and agreed to their admission because they were quiet, devoted to agriculture and hunting, were Catholics, had many customs similar to the Spaniards, disliked the Americans, were related to many

---

[10][Elguezabal] to N. Salcedo, February 29, 1804, draft No. 201, in *Quaderno Borrador*, January 4, 1804–December 19, 1804. Luis Tinza was chief of the Apalaches. Ugarte to Elguezabal, August 1, 1804, and N. Salcedo to the Governor of Texas, May 21, 1804.

[11]N. Salcedo to the Governor of Texas, March 13 and 26, 1804.

[12]Ugarte to Elguezabal, April 3, 1804.

[13]J. M. de Salcedo to N. Salcedo, November 11, 1803.

tribes of Louisiana and would be able to influence these to become the friends of the Spaniards.[14] These arguments were effective; and the commandant-general assigned them lands toward the coast between the Sabine and the Trinity where native tribes of the North would not be likely to disturb them. He forbade them to extend their settlement beyond the two rivers named, placed them under the jurisdiction of the authorities of Nacogdoches, and charged them to be self-supporting and to keep the Spaniards informed of the movements of other tribes.[15]

Although this was not a general order, other Louisiana tribes soon used the decision as a precedent and secured admission, among them being the Koasates, the Choctaws, and the Alabamas, who were said to be closely related to the Tinzas. But in spite of the fact that the Spaniards had hoped the immigrant Indians would strengthen the barrier in process of erection, their hopes were vain, because the immigrant Indians were more open to foreign influence than the native tribes. Besides, it must be said that their location, although a favorable one so far as avoiding trouble with the native Indians was concerned, was from the standpoint of the government an unfavorable one, if contraband trade were the true reason for their coming. The fact that there was a good harbor at the mouth of the Trinity and that a lucrative contraband trade had been carried on for years between the Louisianians and the Indians of this region made it an ideal spot for the commercially inclined.[16] To add to the difficulties of the government, the coast country about the mouth of the Trinity also became more and more popular among civilized immigrants, who came seeking relief from the "harsh rule of the United States," and plans for a general colonization movement to this point were soon proposed.

---

[14][Elguezabal] to N. Salcedo, April 11, 1804, drafts Nos. 216 and 228, in *Quaderno Borrador*, January 4, 1804–December 19, 1804.
[15]N. Salcedo to the Governor of Texas, May 8, 1804.
[16]Bolton, *Texas in the Middle Eighteenth Century*, 407–412.

Marín de Porras plan.—Among the first to urge the formation of a buffer against the United States by the establishment of settlements in Texas was the bishop of Nuevo León, who visited Texas in 1804–1805. As a result of his observations he made the following plea:

> In general, the country, whose riches are chiefly agricultural and whose climate is much like that of Old Castile, merits attention, particularly, so far as the question of settlement is concerned, because the adjoining Americans are bestirring themselves and are determined to escape from the narrow confines of their forests into the open plains. My visit to my parishioners at Natchitoches has given me an opportunity to plumb the ideas and intentions of these Republicans.

To meet these dangers, he offered to bear the expenses of such men as might wish to abandon the scattered ranches of Nuevo León to take upon themselves wives, and to aid in forming compact settlements in Texas where they could receive religious instruction.[17] However nothing came of the suggestion.

Brady's' and Despallier's petition.—Another plan for the establishment of a settlement in Texas during this early colonization period is referred to in a petition presented by Father Brady, of Louisiana. He explained that he was acting as priest at Baton Rouge and wished to continue as religious guide to certain families who desired to immigrate to Texas because of the sale of that province to the United States. He was not without special qualifications for this position. In 1795, he had gone to Louisiana, under royal orders to serve the missions of Louisiana where the tenets of the Catholic church were to be explained to the foreign vassals who had lately settled there. First, he served as assistant priest at Natchez, where most of his hearers were English and Irish. Later, he was placed at Nuestra Señora del Carmen, on the Colorado, where he had an opportunity to speak Spanish and French. Due to his knowledge of

---

[17]The Bishop of Nuevo León to Caballero, March 7, 1804, *A. G. I. S.* Guad., 104–2–19, March 7, 1804.

these languages and to his thorough theological training, he had been able to perform his duties with zeal and success.[18] He could, therefore, with perfect truth, claim that he understood the languages of the settlers of Baton Rouge, where all three languages were spoken; and that, consequently, he would be able to encourage them to be industrious.[19]

But Brady also had much larger plans in mind. On April 10, 1804, he and an associate, our former acquaintance, Bernardo Martin Despallier, who declared that Casa Calvo, Boundary Commisisoner of Louisiana, was the originator of the plan proposed, asked to be allowed to introduce into Texas a number of families from Rapides and Baton Rouge settlements which, in the main, were inhabited by *Frenchmen*. The reason assigned was the retrocession of Louisiana to France and its final sale to the United States. The projectors explained that numerous noble, influential, and prosperous families, as well as some of lowlier state, desired to settle in the Interior Provinces so that they might continue to enjoy the pleasant rule of Spain. The proponents could not definitely state the number desiring to come, but thought that more than one thousand families—about two hundred of whom were Spaniards—would migrate as soon as they could dispose of their property, provided they should be permitted to come by land and by sea. The advantages to be derived from this immigration were then set forth under twenty-five heads.

In the name of the proposed immigrants, the petitioners stated their reasons somewhat as follows: Their devotion to the Catholic religion, which had led them to settle in Louisiana, where their children had been born and educated, made irksome a further residence in a land where religious faith and observance were a matter of indifference. They appreciated the pleasant Spanish rule, and therefore were desirous of following the flag and defending it, if need be, with their blood. The king of Spain had already been put

---

[18]Statement of the Bishop of Louisiana, October 31, 1801.
[19]Petition, April 10, 1804.

to great expense in providing for the settlement in Louisiana of these same families, some of whom had been brought over from the Canaries[20] and others from Acadia,[21] Canada, Germany,[22] and Spain."[23] The petitioners were now ready to repay previous favors by personal service, and begged not to be abandoned to a foreign power. The solemn pledge of the government to protect them should be carried out, and the petitioners should be allowed to proceed at once to the nearest Spanish settlement. The possibility of war with the United States should be kept in mind and a situation in which the petitioners, if left in a foreign territory, might be compelled to take up arms against Spain, should not be created. The transfer of Louisiana to the United States had come about through the fortunes of war and not through any desire on the part of the petitioners; and their loyalty should be recognized. Their immigration would be beneficial to the crown, since they would protect Texas against invasion from an adjacent country. It would weaken a powerful neighbor and increase the strength of Spain by developing the poor, unsettled region of Texas into a rich and populous province. They would devote themselves to agriculture, engaging particularly in the cultivation of tobacco, hemp, cotton, and other staples, and would thus enable the government to secure supplies for the navy without applying to foreigners. Their presence would prevent Indian hostilities and stop Indian expenses. The strong tide of immigration from Louisiana, due to its

---

[20]The use of the Canary Islands had been favored for the settlement of Florida, Louisiana, and Texas. Indeed, the first permanent settlement in Texas had been effected by Canary Islanders or *Isleños* as they were called. Austin, "The Municipal Government of San Fernando de Béxar, 1730–1800," in the Quarterly of the *Texas State Historical Association*, VIII, 277–352.

[21]Fortier, *History of Louisiana*, I, 152–158; and Duvallon, Berquin, *Vue de la Colonie Espagnole Du Mississippi où des Provinces de Louisiane et Florida Occidentale*, 51.

[22]*Ibid.*, 251–252.

[23]Fortier, *History of Louisiana*, II, 60; for character of the population as a whole, see Duvallon, *Vue de la Colonie Espagnole*, 248–252.

change in ownership, should be turned toward Texas. The settlement of these immigrants, contrary to the usual procedure, would occasion no expense to the royal treasury. The mail service would be improved. Supplies could be furnished troops on the frontier. Many men of varied accomplishments would put new life into industry. In case a port were opened, commerce would be increased and the coasts could be watched. The duties to be collected at the proposed port would maintain the government of the Interior Provinces. Contraband trade would be prevented. Communication with foreign countries would be cut off, since the new settlers would furnish supplies for the develment of Texas and for the Indians. The opening of this port, *without which the families could not immigrate,* would encourage the laziest to work. In case the opening of the port should be opposed by the *Consulado de Mexico,* arrangements should be made for the distribution of the products of the country through the said department, or through some company at Vera Cruz, Havana, or some other point.[24]

As an opening wedge this plan was original and far-reaching. The suggestion that a port be opened for trade between Texas and other points must have occasioned great surprise among the exponents of the exclusion policy then in vogue; and many must have been struck later with the similarity of this plan to Napoleon's schemes for free trade with the Spanish dominions of America. But the idea was to grow more and more familiar and at last to become one of the vital points in the colonization program.

Recommendation of the governor.—The governor considered this petition so important that he at once referred it to the commandant-general, at the same time pointing out a few of its unusual features. He reminded Salcedo

---

[24]Petition, April 20, 1804. See Appendix 8. For the organization and powers of the *consulado*, see Priestley, José de Gálvez, 70–74.

that the presence of many nationalities and many non-Catholic religions had been tolerated in Louisiana,[25] and asked to be informed whether Protestants were to be admitted into Texas and, if so, whether certain nations were to be excluded. He remarked that the government did not permit the cultivation of tobacco by private individuals, and suggested the Guadalupe river as a suitable place for the location of these families in case they should be received. The advantages possessed by this situation were water, plains, woods, and proximity to lakes and lagoons connected with the harbor of Matagorda, which would prevent the great expense occasioned by overland transportation. The letter of transmittal ended with the suggestion that should the families be allowed to come to Texas, arrangements would have to be made to prevent the introduction of contraband goods.[26] The governor did not mention the fact that the location of the settlement so near Béxar would make it easy for the authorities to keep a strict guard against all contraband traders, although this must have been in his mind. Despite its unusual features, the commandant-general at once granted the petition. And, desiring to guard against the entry of Protestants, to remove the settlers as far as possible from the temptation of contraband trade, and, at the same time, to furnish them with a desirable location, he drew up a set of regulations, containing twelve articles, as follows:

(1) *Not even negroes, mulattoes, or servants could be introduced unless they were Catholics.*

---

[25]Cox, I. J., *The West Florida Controversy*, 21–22; Roosevelt, Theodore, *The Winning of the West*, IV, 252–253; and Sparks, Jared, *American Biography*, XXIII, 169–170. As an especially interesting instance of this religious tolerance in Louisiana, the case of Baron de Bastrop may be cited. When making a contract for the introduction of families into Louisiana, he had exacted a promise of religious tolerance for non-Catholics. Petition, June 20, 1796, in *A. G. I. S. Sto. Dom.*, La. y Fla., 86–7–17; June 20, 1876–June 16, 1797.

[26]The Governor of Texas to the Commandant-General, April 25, 1804, draft No. 230, in *Quaderno Borrador*, January 4, 1804–December 19, 1804.

(2) *All settlements were to be on the Guadalupe river.*

(3) *Lands were to be distributed according to the size of the family and the amount of property any given applicant might possess.*[27]

(4) *All kinds of plants and seeds could be brought, save those like tobacco, that were raised under government monopoly.*

(5) *No commerce could be carried on through Matagorda or neighboring harbors, and no trips could be made into the Gulf without previous knowledge of the government.*

(6) *Immigrants could also settle at Béxar, Bahía, or any of the settlements of Coahuila, Nueva Viscaya, or in the territory under the direct control of the viceroy.*

(7) *No settlements could be made at Nacogdoches.*

(8) *Necessary aid would be given immigrants.*

(9) *No tax was to be placed on personal property, tools, etc.*

(10) *Contraband trade was to be guarded against.*

(11) *Immigrants must settle up all business matters before leaving Louisiana, as they would not be permitted to return.*

(12) *Brady's appointment as priest of the settlement must be decided by the Bishop of Monterrey.*[28]

The verdict of the bishop must have been unfavorable for Brady is not heard of farther in the colonization plan here indicated, although he had been very active in securing permission for the inauguration of the work.[29]

His personal character may have had something to do with this decision; for later Father Sedella, of New Orleans, warned the Texas authorities that it was quite possible that Brady—who called himself a Spaniard and who claimed to be bringing in only Spanish Catholics—was really preparing a plan that would force the government to redouble its vigilance in constructing barriers against infidelity. He declared that he had known the petitioner for many years

---

[27]*Cf. Recopilación, Lib. IV, Tit. V. Ley. IX.* It must be remembered that the lands of Texas were considered practically worthless because of the presence of so many hostile Indians. *Paracer*, November 12, 1800. The only record of the purchase of land found in the Béxar Archives is that of eighteen *sitios* for which only one hundred *pesos* were paid.

[28]N. Salcedo to the Governor of Texas, May 23, 1804. N. A. See Appendix 9.

[29]Ugarte to Elguezabal, September 4, 1804, and October 4, 1804.

and expressed the opinion that as the leader was, so would his followers be. He suggested that it would, therefore, be better to leave Texas with its mountains and other natural defenses than to cultivate and develop it as a dwelling place for Spains secret enemies, disguised as Spaniards.[30]

Although Brady ceased to be active Despallier continued to push the plans. When acknowledging receipts of the commandant-general's immigration regulations, the governor reported that he would have Despallier come to Béxar to settle all details for the establishment of families.[31] Salcedo thereupon again drew attention to the fact that, while he was not prohibiting the entry of settlers by sea, he expected every exertion to be made to prevent them from communicating with foreigners through any harbor whatever and to keep them from going out upon the Gulf without the previous permisison of the government.[32] Despallier was not satisfied with this ruling and soon attempted to secure more favorable terms.

Godoy-Grimarest plans.—While Despallier's plans were being perfected, a movement toward the settlement of Texas had been begun at the court of Spain. At the same time, orders were issued for dividing the Interior Provinces into two commandancies general as an additional means of offering a more effective front against the Americans. The project originated with Manuel Godoy, the Prince of the Peace, to whom, it was said, the Province of Texas had already been granted by Charles IV.[33] The execution was entrusted to Pedro Grimarest and Luis Baccigalupi. The division of the territory was considered imperative, because, on account of the sale of Louisiana to the United States, Texas was once more a frontier province. Supplies were to be collected in

---

[30]Sedella to the Governor of Texas, November 10, 1804.

[31]N. Salcedo to Elguezabal, July 17, 1804.

[32]Elguezabal to the Commandant-General, June 20, 1804, draft No. 204, in *Quaderno Borrador*, January 4, 1804–December 19, 1804.

[33]"British Correspondence Concerning Texas," *Southwestern Historical Quarterly*, XIX, 293; Smith, Ashbel, *Reminiscences of the Texas Republic*, 27. For Godoy's interest in Florida, see Cox, *The West Florida Controversy*, 241.

Coahuila, pending the arrival of the troops and colonists from Spain and Santo Domingo, and preparations for the distribution of lands were to be made. Settlements were to be established on the coast and provisions were to be made for examining the regions along the Rio Grande and the Colorado and the bays of Espíritu Santo and Galveston.[34] Additional *presidios* were to be founded and the frontier gradually pushed forward; while the colonists were to be governed by a mixed military and civil system, so that proper subordination might be preserved and the people still left free to develop the region.[35] From this outline, it will be seen that the ostensible object of the new undertaking was to form a buffer against the United States through the development of Texas; and not, primarily, to restrain the Indians as stated by Bancroft.

But owing to the European wars Grimarest was unable to carry out the division of the Interior Provinces and no evidence has been found to show that he introduced any settlers into Texas; although an American on the Louisiana border reported to the United States government that a large number of colonists had come into Texas at this time.[36] The project was not forgotten; and as soon as the fortunes of war would permit it was revived. Although plans for the establishment of European colonists in Texas at this time were thwarted, there was nothing to deter enterprising Texans from considering other colonization plans.

Barr's petition.—During 1804, William Barr became interested in the formation of a settlement at the abandoned *presidio* of Orcoquisac and wrote to the commandant-general in regard to the matter. He explained to Salcedo that, if

---

[34]Caballero to the Viceroy, May 18, 1804.

[35]*Real Órden de 30 de Mayo de 1804, dividiendo las Provincias en dos Comandancias*, Appendix 10. Instructions for Grimarest, July 12, 1804, in *A. G. I. S.* Guad., 103–6–17, July 8–13, 1804, also July 18, 1804; *ibid.*, 103–6–17, July 8, 1804–November 26, 1804.

[36]Bancroft, H. H., *North Mexican States and Texas*, II, 11. This, of course, may have been only a ruse of Napoleon to gain control of Texas through his tool, Godoy. Four years later he used almost exactly the same tactics for massing his troops in Spain.

his trade with the Indians of the North was to be successful, it would be necessary to prevent unlicensed traders from visiting them. He asked that the sale of intoxicating liquors to his wards be prevented, and that he be allowed to sell in Florida the horses obtained from the Indians of Texas. He promised to bring immediately to the proposed settlement forty of his own negroes, and to introduce two hundred Catholic families from Louisiana within the space of two years. In the meantime, he wished to continue the practice of securing articles for Indian trade in New Orleans, and to bring these goods in his own vessels to Orcoquisac in case the settlement was approved.

Despite the commercial dangers involved, Salcedo at once decided that there was no reason why Orcoquisac should not be resettled. He therefore authorized Barr to introduce the negroes in question and instructed him to make reports of all Catholic vassals in Louisiana who wished to locate at that point.[37] Barr's plans came to naught; but many similar plans were advanced immediately by other would-be colonizers.

Casa Calvo-Minor's plans.—For example, John Minor, a native of Pennsylvania and a citizen of Natchez, who wished to follow the religion of his ancestors and to live under the Spanish flag, asked to be admitted into the Interior Provinces about this time. He stated that he had lived under the Spanish flag for sixteen years, five of which had been spent in the service of the king in a company of Louisianians organized by Governor Gayosa. He asked that the condition requiring papers to be submitted by immigrants be suspended in his case because he had come to Texas prior to the issuance of such orders on a mission for Casa Calvo to examine the country along the coast of Texas

---

[37]N. Salcedo to Barr, August 29, 1804. For the efforts of Father Delgadillo to have a mission placed at Orcoquisac, see Elguezabal to the Commandant-General, August 15, 1804, draft No. 276, *Quaderno Borrador*, January 4, 1804–December 19, 1804. For adverse decision of proposal in the grounds that the government of the Interior Provinces was to be changed, see N. Salcedo to Elguezabal, September 11, 1804.

from the Trinity to the Sabine for the purpose of marking the boundary between Spanish and American territory, and had neglected to bring the documents in question.[38] He said that he had been instructed by his brother, Estevan Minor, and by Casa Calvo to examine the lands along the lower Trinity and between that river and the Sabine so that if a suitable location were found and this region remained in the possession of Spain, a large number of Louisiana families might be placed at this point.[39] The ruse of presenting himself as a settler may have been due to a suspicion on his part that the plan for examining the coast preparatory to running the boundary line would not be approved by the authorities of Texas. Indeed, a few days later an unfavorable reply on the proposition was received. He had been detained at Nacogdoches until Salcedo's decision upon his petition could be received.[40] On March 4, 1805, the governor recommended the rejection of the applicant, saying that Ugarte, who had urged favorable action, had made a mistake in regard to his character. He was therefore ordered out of the province.[41]

Minor was closely connected with Aaron Burr, who, it was charged, planned to bribe the western states to separate from the Union by offering them the plunder of the Spanish countries further to the west. The suspicions of the Spaniards were quite natural. Minor was merely Casa Calvo's agent and though the plan failed at this time it was by no means abandoned, as will be seen when his patron's activities are later considered. Casa Calvo may possibly

---

[38]Petition, October 16, 1804.

[39]Ugarte to Elguezabal, October 1, 1804, and accompanying documents. *Cf.* with Barr's plans. Spains' claim to this territory had been disputed by France See Kerlérec to the Viceroy, April 18, 1787, *A. G. I. S.* Sto. Dom., 87–7–11, July 26, 1756–July 22, 1757, pp. 29–30. Estevan Minor was a brother-in-law of Philip Nolan, *Louisiana Historical Quarterly*, IX, 100.

[40]N. Salcedo to the Governor of Texas, October 22, 1804, and Elguezabal to N. Salcedo, November 21, 1804, *Quaderno Borrador*, January 4, 1804–December 19, 1804.

[41]Valle to Elguezabal, April 5, 1805.

have been indebted to the French traveler, C. C. Robin, for the idea of locating Louisiana families on the Texas-Louisiana frontier; for Robin had explained to him that the region between Louisiana and Mexico was very valuable and that, if nothing were done to prevent it, the Americans would occupy it. He urged that the Spaniards forestall their rivals, predicting that immigrants would come in from both Europe and America as they had done to the Ouachita settlement in Louisiana. At the same time, he called attention to the advantages to be gained by the introduction of *French immigrants,* believing that they would prove more than a match for the American backwoodsmen who were anxious to secure lands in that region. His enthusiasm for French immigration is peculiarly interesting in view of Napoleon's subsequent ambitions in regard to the seizure of the Spanish dominions of America.[42]

In the light of this information, the fact that Despallier was a Frenchman, and that he, too, was carrying out Casa Calvo's plans, assumes additional interest. Despallier's further activities will, therefore, deserve careful consideration.

Despallier's new plans.—In furtherance of his colonization plans, Despallier explained that the majority of his settlers were well-to-do and that their removal to Texas would involve considerable expense. The preparation of the soil for cultivation and the construction of houses would occasion delay and consequent loss. As a partial compensation, he asked that he be allowed to place immigrants upon the Trinity rather than upon the Guadalupe, since the former situation offered superior facilities for the exportation of the products of the contemplated settlement and, likewise, a more healthful climate. He argued that lack of communication with Vera Cruz, Havana, and other ports would prevent the development of the proposed colony,

---

[42]*Memoire par C. C. Robin, Auteur du Voyage a la Louisiane et les Colonies, and Conduite que doit tenir la France Relativament au continent de L'Amerique Septentrionale par C. C. Robin,* in Paris Archives. *Affaires Etrangeres, Etats Unis,* Vol. 61, pp. 337–341. Transc. U. of T. Cf. Cox, *Early Exploration of Louisiana,* 62–64.

and added that the restrictions upon the exportation of stock to Louisiana, by depriving the immigrants of the means of overland transportation, made the opening of the Port of San Bernardo absolutely necessary. This, he thought, would benefit the whole country. He promised that his colonists would observe the laws in every detail and would defend the country against its enemies.[43] He laid especial stress upon the point that the poor alone could come by land and that, too, at a great disadvantage, while the rich, with their stock, slaves, furniture, tools, etc., would come only by sea.[44] When this second petition reached Salcedo, he refused to make any concessions, but referred it to the king, and suggested that Grimarest, the new commandant-general of the Eastern Interior Provinces, who was to be entrusted with the task of developing Texas and of aiding Spain's vassals, might take favorable action.[45] As has already been seen, however, Grimarest never assumed command of the territory assigned him, and the matter had to wait the decision of the king. Finally, on September 9, 1805, the king granted the desired permission for locating on the Trinity but stipulated that no immigrants were to be received whose lack of fidelity to the government could be questioned.[46] And thus Salcedo's determination to allow no settlements at a distance from Spanish magistrates was finally defeated. Despallier also won his contention for a port in Texas; for the king ordered Bahía de San Bernardo opened, in view of the fact that the great distance to Vera Cruz, the nearest recognized port, made it impossible for the settlers of Texas to secure necessities and to export products under existing conditions.[47]

Casa Calvo-Clouet plan.—In the meantime, Casa Calvo's plans for settlement at Orcoquisac were being pushed by

---

[43]Despallier to the Viceroy, December 5, 1804, in *A. G. I. S.* Mex., *legajo* 18, No. 28, December 5, 1804–January 8, 1805.

[44]Elguezabal to N. Salcedo, December 5, 1804, *ibid.*

[45]N. Salcedo to the Governor of Texas, January 1, 1805.

[46][Cordero] to the Commandant-General, May 20, 1806.

[47]Proclamation of N. Salcedo, February 11, 1806.

The Opening of Texas to Foreign Settlement 89

other agents. On June 12, the commandant of Nacogdoches reported the arrival at Atascocito, near Orcoquisac, of Juan Garnier and Pedro Arsenaux, residents of Attakapas, who had come to select a suitable spot for the location of *three hundred Louisiana families* who had promised Casa Calvo to settle in that region.[48] In his instructions to the governor, Salcedo stipulated that none of the persons were to be admitted until he had furnished proof that he would comply with the conditions previously imposed. At the same time, he informed the governor that, since Barr's petition of the previous year for the settlement of Louisiana families at Orcoquisac had been granted, Garnier and Arsenaux must go directly to Béxar to explain their plans, the character of their families, etc. In case the agents, upon examination, appeared to be loyal—and Salcedo seemed to doubt that they were—they were to be received. Such families as could not come by land to the Guadalupe river might be permitted to come by sea. Other suitable places for location were to be suggested by the governor, in case all seemed well; and the agents were to be informed in order that some suitable person might be appointed to distribute lands to them.[49]

On October 18, 1805, the governor gave permission to Lieutenant Brogné de Clouet, acting head of the three hundred families from Attakapas, for whom Garnier and Arsenaux had negotiated, to select a suitable location for his settlement anywhere between the Trinity and Béxar, or in the region about Béxar itself, under the conditions already imposed.[50]

---

[48]Valle to Elguezabal, June 12, 1804. But little has been obtained in regard to Arsenaux. It is known that Garnier was a Spanish vassals and a Catholic. He had been baptized in Sainte Ange, France, and had been carried to Attakapas when only four years of age. In spite of this long residence in Spanish territory, he understood the French language only. Affidavit, October 10, 1805.

[49]N. Salcedo to the Governor of Texas, July 9, 1805.

[50][Cordero] to the Commandant-General, October 18, 1805, and draft of permit of same date.

As a result of these concessions, steps were at once taken to transfer families from Louisiana to Texas. In November, 1805, the commandant of Atascocito reported that he had been informed by two Indians from Attakapas that certain Spanish and French families had sailed from Louisiana for the abandoned *presidio* of Orcoquisac; whereupon orders were given for the reception of these families and of the Tinzas Indians, who also desired ot settle in the vicinity[51] But the proposed colony never materialized. It was soon rumored at New Orleans that Casa Calvo was expending considerable sums of money among the Indians and that he was prepared to pay Spanish troops who were to come to the frontier. This, taken in connection with the facts that the Creoles of Louisiana were discontented, that troops did arrive, and that the lands in question were believed to be within Louisiana, led the United States government to ask Casa Calvo to retire from that province.[52] Furthermore, Casa Calvo became dissatisfied with the location and finally departed for Spain and his name is heard no more in connection with the history of colonization in Texas, his place being taken by Clouet who, as a reward for introducing Louisiana immigrants, demanded permission to import and export goods through the port of Vera Cruz.[53] But, before considering further attempts to carry forward these plans, it will be necessary to record certain events which were to have an influence upon subsequent colonization activity in Texas.

Detachment on coast.—It will be remembered that, at the beginning of the period under discussion, Nacogdoches was the objective point of the majority of immigrants, but that during 1804 contraband trade in horses became such a menace that Ugarte had suggested that the Spaniards living between Nacogdoches and the frontier and who protected

---

[51]N. Salcedo to Cordero, November 2, 1805; see also Cordero to Commandant of Bahía, November 25, 1805.

[52]See Cox, *Early Explorations in Louisiana*, 69–71.

[53]Clouet to the Viceroy, February 14, 1807, in *A. G. I. S.* Mex., 90–1–18, January 12, 1807 October 27, 1807.

those engaged in this trade be settled just west of Nacogdoches and that a detachment of twelve or fifteen men be placed at Orcoquisac, or at Atascocito, for the purpose of cutting off the trade along the coast. This he deemed necessary because parties sent out from Nacogdoches to intercept traders were rendered useless by fatigue by the time they reached this region.[54] The detachment was really stationed at Atascocito because the stream furnished water for the horses and was nearer than Orcoquisac to the road leading to Attakapas and Opelousas, along which the contraband traders frequently travelled.[55] In spite of all precautions, however, contraband trade had continued, and, through a mistake on the part of Salcedo, objectionable immigrants soon secured entry.

A loop-hole.—In the summer of 1804 Salcedo issued an order that soon gave rise to conditions which facilitated the entry of objectionable foreigners, even though he at once tried to correct his mistake. He ruled that, owing to conditions in Louisiana which made it oft-times impossible for the would-be immigrant to secure documents proving his identity, character, etc., mere statements of belief might be accepted instead.[56] Now, as has been pointed out, the authorities at Nacogdoches were not very careful about the exclusion of objectionable foreigners, anyway;[57] and this order gave them the opportunity of admitting many who could not have passed the test, if strictly applied.

Additional precautions against Americans.—Of course, Salcedo had never intended that the Americans, who were now actually asking that a large portion of Texas be erected into a neutral territory,[58] should be granted any of the privileges that the government was prepared to extend to its own vassals living in Louisiana. Indeed, he had issued

---

[54]Ugarte to Elguezábal, November 4, 1804.
[55]N. Salcedo to the Governor of Texas, July 1, 1805. For poor accommodation for troops, see Valle to Elguezabal, April 6, 1805.
[56]Ugarte to Elguezabal, October 4, 1804.
[57]Ugarte to Elguezabal, August 1, 1804.
[58]Bancroft, *North Mexican States and Texas*, II, 10.

orders forbidding either their entry into or their traveling through Texas, although American deserters and run-away slaves were still being received.⁵⁹ Others shared in this dislike and frequent protests were made against the settlement of Americans in disputed territory along the boundary,⁶⁰ and against the entry of various exploring expeditions sent out by the United States to ascertain the exact extent of the new territory acquired by the Louisiana purchase. Vigorous measures were taken also to prevent the execution of the plans of these explorers. Still another event which had an important bearing upon the history of the times needs to be mentioned—the appointment of a development advocate to assume the management of Texas affairs.

The governor, a colonization advocate.—In July, 1805, the health of Governor Elguezabal had so failed that the commandant-general consented to appoint governor *ad interim* in order that the critical situation in Texas—due to the military activities of the Americans along the frontiers and the consequent threatening movements of the Indians might be adequately dealt with.⁶¹ The appointment fell upon Antonio Cordero, governor of Coahuila, who was to be charged with the additional duty of guarding, with special vigilance, the isolated post at Nacogdoches,⁶² and the abandoned *presidio* of Orcoquisac,⁶³ where the Americans might be expected to make an attack.⁶⁴

---

⁵⁹N. Salcedo to the Governor of Texas, May 21, 1804, Ugarte to Elguezabal, June 3, 1804, and Ugarte to Elguezabal, July 4, 1804.

⁶⁰Casa Calvo to Elguezabal, June 19, 1804.

⁶¹Yturrigaray to N. Salcedo, August 3, 1805, in *Carpeta Numero* 2, June 12, 1804–December 28, 1807.

⁶²Cordero to Elguezabal, August 10, 1805.

⁶³N. Salcedo to Cordero, August 20, 1805.

⁶⁴Yturrigaray to N. Salcedo, August 10, 1805, in *Carpeta Numero* 2, June 12, 1804–December 28, 1807. The Spaniards, likewise, feared an attack from England, and there was considerable evidence to support this view. Valle to Elguezabal, June 4 and 11, 1804. In May, 1805, Claiborne reported to his government the existence of a rumor that an English armed vessel would soon enter Lake Pontchartrain for the purpose of coöperating with the Mexican insurgents, Claiborne to Freeman, May 13, 1805, *Letter Books*, II, 54. Later in discussing

The new governor was no novice in military and administrative affairs. According to Thrall, he had been brought from Spain by Gálvez in 1772, to aid in reforming the administration of Spanish America.[65] Cordero himself said of his services on the frontier that he had been in the Interior Provinces since the creation of the office of commandant-general, entering in the capacity of *alférez de dragones* with Cabellero de Croix; that in 1777 and 1778, he had taken no small part in organizing such troops as were added to the presidial companies, who had done much toward preventing Indian hostilities; that he had served also under De Neve, Rengel, Ugarte, and de Nava in their military activities on the frontier;[66] and that in 1800, he had founded in Coahuila the *villa* of Cuatro Cienegas and the *villa* of San Andreas[67] de Nava. He assumed his new office in Texas in September, 1805,[68] and owing to the continued illness of Elguezabal, remained for several years and undertook to carry out a few of the liberal ideas he had gained from his long experience on the frontier.

Observation corps on the Trinity.—One of the first precautionary steps taken by him was that of sending an observation corps to the Trinity river in September, 1805, with instructions to locate on either bank of the river at the most suitable place that could be found. The corps really took up a position at, or near, the intersection of the *Camino Real* and the Bahía Road;[69] and, as they became the nucleus of a civil settlement, it is necessary to consider the reason for selecting this particular region as a place of operations. According to Cordero, the principal object of the corps was

---

the strength of the insurgents under Miranda he expressed surprise that England had not already given effective aid, Claiborne to Jefferson, June 22, 1806, *ibid.*, 342.

[65]Thrall, Homer S., *History of Texas*, 528.
[66]Cordero to Bonavía, July 21, 1809.
[67]Portillo, Esteban L., *Apuntes Para la Historia Antigua de Coahuila y Texas*, 466–476.
[68]Elguezabal to Amador, September 9, 1805.
[69]See map between pp. 59–60. *Cf.* Austin's map of 1822, Archives U. of T.

to aid the commandant of Nacogdoches to preserve the friendship of the Indians along the Trinity and the Brazos. The Indians were to be informed that they were to be protected in case any other nation dared to disturb them in the occupation of a country which had been under Spanish protection from time immemorial.[70] Not content with this step, Cordero lost no time in making other plans for developing the province and thereby defeating the Americans in their attempts to secure territory.

Two additional settlements suggested.—On September 24, 1805, he protested against the adverse decision of his predecessor in regard to settlements along the road from Béxar to Nacogdoches and pointed out certain reasons why this verdict should be reversed and at least two settlements established, one on the Trinity and one on the Brazos. At the same time, he saw no reason for opposing the formation of settlements on the Guadalupe, or the San Marcos,[71] or even in the vicinity of Béxar. He insisted that the security of the province would be almost assured by the settlements on the Trinity and Brazos since the necessary transportation of troops, ammunitions, and foodstuffs would be made possible, and prompt communication would be provided for. He reported that he had already arranged for four citizens to go to the Trinity with stock and provisions to provide the detachment with milk, meat, and other necessities, with the understanding that they were later to be the founders of a new settlement at this place, provided his plans met with the approval of the superior government. He reported, also, that he would take steps to plant a settlement on the Brazos if permitted to do so, and said that security would thus be assured, commerce in furs be increased, and the

---

[70]*Instruccion a que ha de averiguarse el capitan Don Pedro Nolasco Carrasco, en el mando del cuerpo de tropa de observacion que va a entrar en las margines del Rio de la Trinidad.* September 17, 1805.
[71]Cordero may have had in mind Godoy's and Grimarest's plans for locating families on the San Marcos. Kennedy, William, *History of Texas,* I, 309. This plan was still being considered as late as 1808. Smith, *Reminiscence of the Texas Republic,* 27.

Indians given a new motive for behaving themselves. Salcedo's permission for the formation of a buffer of native Texans was at once granted; and, on October 18, Cordero issued a proclamation[72] calling for volunteers from Béxar to become founders of the two new *villas,* Santísima Trinidad de Salcedo upon the Trinity and San Telésforo on the Brazos, promising them lands and the usual exemptions and privileges. But the interest among the natives was not so strong as that among Louisianians; and before considering the results of Cordero's efforts it will be necessary to study the plans of other vassals from beyond the frontier.

Bastrop's plan.—At the end of 1805, there appeared in Texas a man who was to have a great influence upon the subsequent history of the region—no less a person than Baron de Bastrop, who, in spite of his strongly-protested anti-American sentiments, later actually opened the way for the movement which was to end in the acquisition of Texas by the United States. It will be remembered that Bastrop had secured from Governor Carondelet, of Louisiana, the promise of a grant of land at Ouachita as a reward for the establishment of a settlement which should serve as a barrier against the Americans, that he actually introduced a small number of colonists, but that a new governor had forbidden him to continue his efforts because it was feared that he was introducing Americans—the very people the colony was designed to exclude. Bastrop had later succeeded in securing a contract for furnishing supplies to the Indians on the Ouachita. But misfortune still pursued him. The sale of Louisiana to the United States prevented his reaping the expected profits; for the Americans themselves at once began to establish trading houses throughout the newly acquired territory.[73]

Naturally, Casa Calvo, too, was displeased at this turn of events, and conceived the idea of establishing rival trading

---

[72]Cordero to the Commandant-General, September 24, 1805, N. A. And Salcedo to the Governor of Texas, October 8, 1805.

[73]*Undated petition of Bastrop,* A. G. I. S. Sto. Dom., La. y Fla., 86–7–12, July 7, 1799, and Cox, *The West Florida Controversy,* 144.

houses in the Interior Provinces for the purpose of defeating the American plans. He, therefore, despatched Baron de Bastrop to Texas to consult with the authorities in regard to this plan. Bastrop was not an entire stranger to the officials of Texas. In 1801, the commandant of Ouachita had tried to secure stock from Texas for Bastrop's colony.[74] Upon arriving in Texas, Bastrop presented Casa Calvo's letter of recommendation, in which he was introduced as a faithful vassal of the king and a resident of Ouachita, who desired to immigrate to Texas with his property, and who, therefore, desired a location suited to his needs. He was accompanied by three slaves and a *French* servant and claimed to have an important communication for the government in regard to the Alabamas and the Koasatis.[75] On September 23, 1805, he presented a request to be allowed to bring into the Interior Provinces a part of the immigrants he had placed on the Ouachita with the consent of Baron de Carondelet, together with the Choctaw Indians whom he had settled there under the orders of Casa Calvo and Juan Manuel de Salcedo. Although in Louisiana he had been careful to secure a pledge that his colonists would be allowed the same freedom of conscience as that granted at Baton Rouge, Natchez, and other points in Louisiana, he now assured the commandant-general that he would introduce only desirable Catholic immigrants, all mechanics or industrious laborers, who would be a benefit to the country. He expected much aid from the Indians also since they were skillful hunters and brave warriors, and could protect the frontiers against the Americans, the Osages, and other Indians in case a war broke out. He promised that neither he, his civilized immigrants, nor the Indians from the Ouachita would ever abuse the favor—if they were received.[76] Finally, he wished to be allowed to secure in

---

[74]Tejeiro to Elguezabal, May 23, 1801.
[75]Valle to Elguezabal, August 13, 1805.
[76]Petition of Bastrop, September 23, 1805, Trans. U. of T.

Texas the necessary animals for the transportation of the proposed settlers. The plan was considered entirely satisfactory by Cordero who argued that the establishment of the Indians in question would effectually restrain others of the same tribe remaining in Louisiana from taking up arms against the Indians of Texas, and that it would be easy to compel the immigrant Indians to make peace with the Texas tribes with whom they had been at war.[77] The commandant-general expressed his willingness to give every possible encouragement and assistance to Bastrop.[78] He took the precaution to prevent this permit for the transfer of settlers from coming to the knowledge of the Americans for fear that some of them might in this way gain entry. Bastrop's settlers, like those to be brought in by Clouet, were to be located anywhere between the Trinity and Béxar. With his petition for settlement, Bastrop also presented a paper setting forth the object of his visit and discussing the American menace. In this he covered the ground from the beginning of Carondelet's rule in Louisiana to the time of writing, and emphasized the "daring land-hunger of the infamous class of Americans" who were forcibly and arbitrarily shaping the policies of the American government. He described their forts, their Indian allies, their efforts to draw away from their allegiance other tribes who had always been friendly to the Spaniards, their establishments on the Missouri and at other points always thought to be Spanish territory.[79] So important did Cordero consider this information, that he sent it to Salcedo by special messenger, and suggested that the detachment on the Trinity be increased and that Nacogdoches, Orcoquisac, and Matagorda be thoroughly guarded to prevent any invasion until aid could be sent from Spain.[80]

---

[77]Cordero to the Commandant-General, September 25, 1805, with petition of Bastrop, September 23, 1805.
[78]N. Salcedo to Cordero, October 10, 1805, in *A. G. I. S.* Guad., 104–2–10, May 25, 1805–March 11, 1819.
[79]N. Salcedo to the Commandant-General, October 18, 1805, N. A.
[80]Cordero to the Commandant-General, September 25, 1805.

This warning, of course, but strengthened Salcedo's suspicions of his next-door neighbors, although he did remark that Bastrop's statement had no other support than that given by the writer's own reputation. Bastrop's protestations probably gained a favorable hearing on the petition for admission, but his cherished plans for Indian trade were not allowed.

However, none of his plans were ever carried out, for when he returned to Louisiana to prepare the minds of the Indians for emigration, he was forced to suspend action because of the presence of American troops upon the border. Besides, he himself had to confess that the Indians were so well treated by the Americans that they did not desire to emigrate at all.[81] He was therefore left free to concentrate all his attention upon his commercial plans, which evidently lay quite close to his heart and as his activities in this field extended far beyond the phase now under discussion his name will appear frequently hereafter. In the meantime, the governor's colonization plans were being carried forward.

Three additional settlements authorized.—In response to a proposal by Cordero, submitted on November 15, 1805, Salcedo agreed to the location of three other new settlements in Texas, one on the Colorado, one on the San Marcos, and one on the Guadalupe. These new centers were not to be started, however, until those on the Brazos and Trinity had been given the necessary number of settlers. Immigrants from Louisiana were to be located at Béxar and at Bahía, or were to be distributed among the new settlements so that their conduct could be watched. However, in granting this permission, Salcedo drew attention to the fact that the greater the dispersion of the settlers the greater would be the difficulty of protecting them and that it was not wise to found a settlement with only a few inhabitants.[82] All these plans came to naught save those for San Marcos and

---

[81]Petition of Bastrop, January 30, 1810, in A. G. I. S. Guad., 104–2–20, January 30, 1810–February 13, 1810.

[82]N. Salcedo to Cordero, December 16, 1805.

since this *villa* was not founded until the end of 1807 discussion of the matter is for the present deferred.

Cordero's plans were bold. He believed that Nacogdoches would have to be abandoned unless its settlers could secure new life through additional immigrants and be induced to devote themselves to serious labor so as to provide themselves with the necessities of life through commerce with the settlements to be found between that point and the capital.[83] In addition, he wished to extend his operations to the westward.

Settlements to the west of Béxar.—Indeed, it was at this time that he planned the establishment of the *villa* of Nueva Jáen[84] in the Frio region.[85] A settlement was really begun there at this time but owing to the press of other matters and the difficulty of securing an adequate water supply the orders for its foundation were not fully carried out. Later the Texas authorities tried to revive the project[86] but nothing came of their plans. So no further mention of the *villa* need be made.

Summary, 1805.—At the end of 1805, therefore, permission had been secured for the founding of settlements on the Trinity, the Brazos, the Colorado, the San Marcos, and the Guadalupe, and even at Béxar and at Bahía, if desired; while one *villa* had actually been founded. Besides the immigrants who were planning to come in singly[87] or in

---

[83]Cordero to N. Salcedo, November 19, 1805.

[84]Jáen was a province in Spain.

[85]See map between pp. 101–102.

[86]León to Cordero, March 15, 1886, and Bonavía to Ugarte, May 29, 1809.

[87]To the names already mentioned may be added that of Henry Parr, an Irish Catholis, a weaver by trade, who wished to locate at Nacogdoches or at Béxar. Petition, September 9, 1805, and affidavit of Davenport and McNulty, September 6, 1809. Another case of interest was that of Juan Drybread who had resided in the district of Cape Girardeau in 1798 and who wished to settle in the Spanish dominions. As he had borne a good reputation and had taken the oath of allegiance at Baton Rouge, he was allowed to settle at that point. Affidavit of Larrimer, October 19, 1805, and of Grand Pré, May 16, 1806. He later immigrated to Texas. Dumas Belabre, a Frenchman

groups, there were several ambitious colonization plans under way, which may have had a common origin and which certainly seem to have had one point of similarity—the desire to secure a good location for commerce. It will be noticed, however, that all immigrants were expected to be Catholic vassals of good character. According to the provisions of the laws of the Indies, lands were to be distributed to immigrants in proportion to the size of their families, their ability to aid in the development of the country, etc. No Americans were to be received. On the contrary, so great was the feeling against them, especially because of their insistence on enlarging the boundaries of Louisiana as much as possible,[88] that orders were issued to cut off all communication with Louisiana and to permit no foreigners to enter Texas. Indeed, in August, 1805, Salcedo instructed Cordero to stop all intercourse with the United States, in case war broke out as a consequence of the failure of Monroe's negotiations to secure Texas.[89]

This order was to be enforced by imposing the death penalty for disobedience. The enemy was thus to be prevented from securing stock in Texas. As a further means of weakening the United States, all slaves escaping across the Sabine were to be declared free.[90] During the summer of 1805, on account of the presence of American troops on the Texas frontier, Spanish officers charged with the defense of Texas were on the *qui vive,* expecting a hostile

---

who had lived at Natchitoches for a short time, received a grant of two hundred *arpents* upon the Trinity. This he expected to cultivate by slave labor. He took possession, built a house, and started cultivating and improving the grant. However, he was compelled to return to Louisiana to bring in his slaves and the tools needed for further work, leaving a Spaniard as a caretaker during his absence. In January, 1807, he sold the grant to Juan Santiago Paillette, of Natchitoches, for the sum of two hundred dollars in cash. Petition, November 6, 1805, and appended documents. Ben. C. Franklin Papers, Archives U. of T. Whether or not the purchaser ever came into Texas is not known.

[88] An unsigned letter from Madrid, July 6, 1804.
[89] N. Salcedo to the Governor of Texas, October 2, 1805.
[90] N. Salcedo to Cordero, August 20, 1805.

movement at any time.[91] But the tide of immigration from Louisiana was setting strongly toward Texas and interest in the proposed *villa* on the Trinity was especially strong. This is shown by an extract from a letter, dated "Opelousas County, Territory of Luciany, August 18, 1805," and addressed to one of Nolans' companions, "Simon McKoy, in his Catholic Majesty's dominions near Mexico." The writer declared that since the sale of Louisiana the inhabitants of that territory were much dissatisfied with the American rule, that it was understood that the Spaniards were erecting a town on the Trinity river and were offering encouragement to immigrants, and that most of the inhabitants of Opelousas were selling their lands in hopes of securing other lands there.[92] It will now be necessary to trace the development of the various settlements provided for, and to describe the growing differences between the commandant-general and the Texas authorities over the question of immigration.

[91]N. Salcedo to the Governor of Texas, August 20, 1805, Yturrigaray to N. Salcedo, December 3, 1805, in *Carpeta Numero* 2, June 12, 1804–December 29, 1807, and Cordero to N. Salcedo, January 14, 1806.

[92]Bound with Valle to Elguezabal, September 19, 1805. *Cf.* Brown, John Henry, *History of Texas*, I, 42, and Claiborne to Madison, June 15, 1806, *Letter Books*, III, 331.

CHAPTER III

ESTABLISHMENT OF VILLAS AND DIFFERENCE OVER MANAGEMENT OF IMMIGRANTS, 1806–1807

1806

Founders from Béxar for Villa de Santísima Trinidad de Salcedo, 1806.—In response to the governor's call for founders for the new *villas*, there set out from Bexar, on December 20, 1805, a colony of settlers for the Trinity. There were probably five families, consisting of fourteen persons, as follows: Pedro Cruz, wife, two sons, and one daughter; José Manuel Casanova and wife; José Luis Durán, wife and two sons; Francisco Travieso and one son; and José Aldrete, who died at the mission of San Juan during the same year.[1] Upon reaching the Trinity, they found twenty-three Louisiana immigrants already upon the grounds.

Founders from Louisiana.—Bernardo Despallier and family had arrived in Texas as early as February, 1804, while Geronimo Herrn[ánde]z and family had immigrated at the beginning of 1805. To these settlers there had been soon added, Miguel Quinn, who came in October, 1805, Juan Magee and family, Enrique Seridan and family, Rebecca Seridan, the wife of Juan Lunn, who remained in Louisiana for a while longer, and Hugo Coyle, who came in December, 1805.[2]

Organization of villa.—From this time forward plans for the establishment of the new *villa* were carried out with vigor. Instructions for the organization of the settlement and for the admission of other approved settlers were issued to the commandant at that point, Pedro Nolasco Carasco, who had assisted Cordero in the establishment of the *villa* San Andres de Nava in Coahuila a few years before.[3] It

---

[1]N. Salcedo to Cordero, October 5, 1806, and list of settlers, October 6, 1809.
[2]*Padron General de Trinidad*, March 22, 1809. See Appendix 11.
[3]Portillo, *Apuntes*, 470–6.

was Cordero's intention to have Carasco repair to the Brazos as soon as his work was finished at Salcedo, in order that he might there establish the *villa* of San Telésforo with other settlers who had presented petitions for admission. However, interest can be centered upon the *villa* on the Trinity, since in the case of San Telésforo matters never progressed further than the selection of a name and the location of a detachment of troops at the intersection of the Brazos and the *Camino Real*. In the erection of Villa de Salcedo, Carasco was expected to follow the instructions for the settlement of *villas* in the Interior Provinces sent him on December 19.[4] These were really the rules which had been laid down for the establishment of the *villa* of San Pedro de Pitic, in Sonora, and other new *villas* planned for the Interior Provinces, approved August 22, 1783. Under these regulations, which were an amplification of the laws of the Indies to meet the special conditions on a frontier infested with hostile Indians,[5] lands were to be granted to persons establishing a civil settlement under the protection of a detachment of soldiers. Lands were to be distributed according to the size of the family brought in by a prospective settler, the amount of tools he possessed, and his ability to aid in development projects. Matters of local arrangement were to be left largely to the judgment of the governor of the province in which the *villa* was to be placed; but the settlers were to be required to occupy and improve their grants and to be ever ready with horses and arms to defend the country against all enemies.[6]

---

[4]Carrasco to Cordero, January 4, 1806.
[5]See item 4461 in Chapman, Charles E., *Catalogue of Materials in the Archivo General de Indias for the History of the Pacific Coast and the American Southwest.*
[6]N. Salcedo to Cordero, June 16, 1806, and N. Salcedo to Cordero, April 19, 1809. Land Office Records, Vol. 58, No. 203, Doc. No. 10 and Appendix 12. For the manner in which these villas were to be laid out see map plan of San Fernando de Béxar, between pp. 102-103.

The exact date of the establishment of Villa de Salcedo cannot be determined from the evidence at hand; but it must have been begun prior to or on January 23, 1806; for on this day Juan Ignacio de Arrambide, lieutenant of the presidial company of Béxar, and, likewise, commandant and *justicia* of Salcedo, issued title to a *solar* of land to José Luis Durán and his heirs and assignees. The said *solar* was to have a front thirty *varas* in width, and the grantee was to be required to fence his land and build a house thereon, to keep the premises clean, and to perform such other duties as were required of citizens.[7] The work of founding the new settlement was completed before February 20, 1806,[8] the cost of establishing the *villa* and building the priest's house amounting to 1,652 *pesos*.[9] *Solares* and *suertes* were later distributed to other settlers;[10] although definite titles could not be issued owing to the want of accurate surveys.[11]

Additional settlers.—This new *villa* possessed attractions for even the people of favored Nacogdoches. For instance, José María Mora soon asked to be allowed to move from Nacogdoches to Salcedo because of loss of stock from wild animals and because of the greater convenience he would enjoy in the new settlement. In return for the privilege, he promised to hold himself in readiness to defend the dominions of the king.[12] But for some reason the move was never actually made. The majority of the immigrants desiring to settle at this place were from Louisiana. Among those who came in were Pedro Lartigue, a surgeon of many years' experience.[13] Santiago Fierr and family, Juan Si, and Feredicte Esctozman and family. The number was further

---

[7]*Cf. Recopilación, Lib.*, IV, *Tit.*, XII. *Leges* III and XI. See N. Salcedo to the Governor of Texas, April 7, 1809.

[8]N. Salcedo to Cordero, March 25, 1806.

[9]N. Salcedo to Cordero, December 5, 1806.

[10]Sáenz to N. Salcedo, March 6, 1809.

[11]Prieto to M. de Salcedo, July 22, 1809.

[12]Petition, March 26, 1806.

[13]Certificate of Cordero, March 31, 1806, and Petition of Lartigue, August 8, 1806.

increased by the arrival of two Italians, Vicente Micheli and his son, who moved from Nacogdoches.[14] Although special stress was laid upon the settlement on the Trinity, the governor made plans for settling other portions of Texas, though he was handicapped by the conservatism of the commandant-general.

Disagreement over Location and Treatment of Immigrants

Deferred settlement at Nacogdoches.—In January, 1806, the governor wrote to the commandant-general, reporting that many of the Louisiana immigrants insisted upon remaining at Nacogdoches. Personally, he was thoroughly in favor of allowing them to do so, claiming that it was impossible to organize an effective defense of the frontier because the small number of people at that point could not supply the troops with the necessary provisions. He explained, too, that the great distance from Nacogdoches to other settlements in Texas made it impracticable, and, indeed at times, impossible to supply food for the troops from these interior points. He, therefore, urged the necessity of establishing settlements in that region and asked to be authorized to undertake the work.[15] The effect of the decision to cut off all communication with the United States was also feared by the commandant at Nacogdoches, who insisted that the citizens of Nacogdoches, the friendly Indian tribes, and, indeed, the whole province of Texas, would suffer from such an arrangement. He even claimed that the settlers of Nacogdoches would actually starve for lack of supplies, and that immigration from Louisiana would be

---

[14]Vicente Micheli had also lived in Coahuila and at Béxar. While in Coahuila he had failed for a large sum and had immediately thereafter asked for permission to establish a cotton gin at Béxar, promising to bring a carpenter from Opelousas to assist him in its construction. This permission had been immediately granted. Petition, April 17, 1801.

[15]Cordero to the Commandant-General, January 28, 1806.

retarded.[16] He, too, therefore, asked for a modification of the order.

In reply to Cordero's request, Salcedo promised to consider the proposed settlement as soon as those settlements already authorized had received the necessary quota of immigrants; but he asked that all petitions of those desiring to locate at Nacogdoches be forwarded to him for special consideration.[17] By these instructions he intended to indicate that formal settlement might be considered later, but that individual immigrants must still be watched with the accustomed vigilance. So when, on May 20, the petitions of Carlos Salie and Manuel Dorván, who wished to locate in the jurisdiction of Nacogdoches, were forwarded to him, he not only refused to allow them to remain there, but declared that they must show a clean record before being received at all. Salie must furnish proof that he was no longer in the employ of Casa Calvo; while Dorván must give satisfactory evidence in regard to his character.[18] Not discouraged by this delay, Cordero continued to favor plans for the settlement of other regions, but because of Salcedo's opposition he was again forced to delay operations.

Rejected settlements west of Béxar.—In May, 1806, José Antonio Ramírez, of Nuevo Santander, asked permission to place thirteen families on the Nueces. He desired an unsettled region, because the proposed immigrants wished to engage in stock raising. Of course, the project was viewed favorably by Cordero, who wished to facilitate communication between Texas and Nuevo Santander; and, to carry out this plan, he proposed the establishment of a *pueblo* for the applicants and the granting of lands for ranches, in accordance with the *cédula* of the king of February 14, 1805, providing for the distribution of *sitios* and *realengas*.[19] He

---

[16]Rodríguez to Cordero, December 5, 1805.
[17]N. Salcedo to Cordero, February 25, 1806.
[18]N. Salcedo to Cordero, June 16, 1806.
[19]Cordero to the Commandant-General, May 1, 1806. This *cédula* required all lands granted by the kings to be occupied and improved at once. N. Salcedo to the Governor of Texas, April 7, 1809.

Up to this time it had been the custom to sell large quantities of grazing lands for a mere song. This was objected to by many; and

could do no more, however, than to secure a promise from Salcedo that the matter would be considered as soon as other settlements already provided for could be established.[20]

Salcedo was not always obliging enough to promise future consideration, but on occasions peremptorily refused to permit settlement in certain regions peculiarly suited to contraband trade. The story of the attempt to establish a settlement at Orcoquisac furnishes an illustration of his attitude.

---

the *Consejo de Indias* called upon the governors of Nuevo Santander, Nuevo León, Coahuila, and Texas for information as to the best means of dealing with the trouble in that section of the country. In reply the governor of Nuevo Santander suggested that no person be given lands unless he were able to settle them. This was to be done because the vast stretches of unsettled, undeveloped lands held by the stock-raisers made it impossible to provide for an effective system of Indian defense. He suggested the following prices as equitable for the lands granted small proprietors: Twenty-five *pesos* per *sitio* for non-irrigable lands; fifty *pesos* for those which could be irrigated; and one hundred *pesos* for those supplied with running water. But the governor of Nuevo León believed that one price for all classes of lands—thirty *pesos* per *sitio*—should be fixed upon. This price was to be paid in installments of three *pesos* per year for ten years. The governor of Coahuila inclined toward the belief that ten, twenty and thirty *pesos*, respectively, should be asked for the three classes of lands indicated. Because of these various opinions a special *junta* was called to meet in San Luis Potosí to consider the matter. It recommended that not more than thirty *sitios* be sold to men of wealth and not more than eight or ten to poor persons. They, too, believed that the condition of settlement should be imposed, the time to vary from one to two years. They advised that preference be given those not already possessing land, the more industrious of this number being favored most of all. The *junta* suggested the following prices: Ten, thirty, and fifty or sixty *pesos*. The last named price was considered fair by the *fiscal* who reviewed the whole matter. However, he objected seriously to the proposal that the payments be made on the installment plan since the laws (*Ley XVI, Tit. XXVI, Lib. VIII*) fixed the mode of payment. He opposed any statement in regard to the requirement for settlement since the limit for occupation was named in *Ley. XI, Tit. XII, Lib. IV., Consejo*, November 23, 1804, in *A. G. I. S.* Mex., 88–1–4, November 23, 1804–December 15, 1804.

[20]N. Salcedo to Cordero, June 3, 1806.

Opposition to settlement at Orcoquisac.—Upon learning of the proposed opening of the port of Bahía de San Bernardo, a considerable number of *French* immigrants had come in from Louisiana with the avowed intention of settling at Orcoquisac. The fact that they came in such numbers aroused the suspicion of Cordero; and he had determined to investigate the real intentions of the applicants in order that no contraband trade should be carried on under cover of immigration, although he seems to have had no suspicion as to their loyalty to the Spanish government. He was perfectly willing to consider a settlement at this point and felt, also, that he had authority under existing regulations to issue lands to applicants. In transmitting certain petitions to the commandant-general, he suggested that it would be better to establish a formal settlement and to grant lands of Spanish measurement under existing regulations, than to issue them under the French system proposed by the petitioners. He, therefore, asked for instructions in the matter. The applicants in this particular case were Juan Bautista le Conte, Jose Darbain, Juan Bautista Anti, Remigio Lambre, and Agustin Langlois, who had asked for five hundred and eighty *arpents* of land to be distributed among them.[21] In ruling upon these applications, Salcedo reminded Cordero of the order that immigrants from Louisiana were not to be permitted to settle in any portion of the district of Nacogdoches, but were to be placed either in the new *villas* provided for, or to be induced to locate in more interior provinces. He reiterated his instructions that until the *villas* already provided for had been established no new settlements should be undertaken; reminded Cordero that the number of *sitios* which might be granted to any person were already fixed, varying according to the size of the family and the amount of property owned by the applicant; and ordered the settlement of the applicants near the places already selected, because he feared

---

[21]Cordero to the Cammandant-General, May 28, 1806.

that troubles would arise if numbers of *foreigners* were allowed to live at a distance from the Spanish magistrates.[22] This decision, which called into question not only the commercial but the political motives of the applicants, so offended the would-be immigrants that not one of them ever entered Texas. They were probably a part of the immigrants that Clouet had planned to bring in; for their petitions were drawn up in exactly the same form as a dozen or so others found in a folder marked *año de 1805 y 1806 Emigracion y Establecimiento en esta Prova. de Trescientas del Atacapa.*[23] Among others who seem to have belonged to Clouet's followers may be named the Texas Daniel Boone, who is said to have been a nephew of the noted Kentucky pioneer. He was a native of Carolina, although he had been a resident of Opelousas for twelve years prior to his immigration to Texas. He protested vigorously against being forced to remain under American rule and asked to be admitted with his family and goods.[24] Action in his case was favorable; and for years he served as gunsmith for the soldiers at Béxar.[25] According to family traditions, he was killed by the Indians about 1817.

Among others having similar desires to settle in Texas were James Milaclon and Matias Lee, both Americans who had been citizens of Opelousas for twenty years, and who preferred the rule of Spain to that of the United States.[26] No further mention is found of Lee, but Milaclon is probably identical with the Santiago McLaughlin who settled at Salcedo in October, 1806.

Maria Magdalena Venua, Sebastian Venua, or Benoist, as he signed himself, natives of Great Britain and residents of Opelousas for eighteen years, and Francisco Mercantel, a native of Opelousas, like those already mentioned, planned

---

[22]N. Salcedo to Cordero, June 16, 1806.
[23]N. Salcedo to Cordero, July 15, 1806.
[24]Petition, June 11, 1806. See Appendix 13.
[25]See bill, March 4, 1809, and N. Salcedo to the Governor of Texas, April 18, 1809.
[26]Petitions, June 9, 1806.

to bring their families and goods with them for the purpose of escaping American rule.[27] There may also be mentioned Jose Nicolas Landres and Louis Dannequien, in habitants of Lafourche de los Chetimachas, who wished to settle in Texas in pursuance of their determination to follow the Spanish flag.[28]

Daniel Colman Jones, an Irishman and a native of Halifax, desired to immigrate with his family and close relatives, and the families of two friends, John Ronells and Benjamin Thomas. These applicants were all Catholics who had lived several years in Louisiana before it was sold to the United States, and who expected to take advantage of the law permitting the entry of Louisianians into Texas. With Jones's petition, is found that of John Andreton, an Irishman, and a native of Brunswicke, Virginia, who hoped to bring his family, a son-in-law, and a friend, David King. These applicants, likewise, were all Catholics, and had all lived under the Spanish flag about eight years. Included in this same document, was the petition of Guillermo Gardner, an Irishman, who had lived in Opelousas more than seven years. He, like the others, desired to bring in his family, his stock, and his tools.[29] In the archives for this period, there is also found the petition of Juan Fear, an Irish Catholic, who had lived in Louisiana nineteen years. He planned to settle at Orcoquisac with his sons-in-law, Patricio Gurnet and Juan Nevil, Catholics and Spanish subjects, and with other relatives to the number of twenty-six persons.[30] The records show that part of these applicants were ordered received in case they were able to prove themselves worthy of trust,[31] but there is nothing to indicate that any of them ever became actual settlers, save María Magdalena Venua, who was afterwards expelled from the province for immorality,

---

[27]Petitions, June 11, 1806.
[28]Petitions, July 15, 1806.
[29]Undated but with certificate of good conduct for Juan Andreton, dated July 30, 1806.
[30]Petition, August 13, 1806.
[31][?] to Cordero, September 20, 1806.

The Opening of Texas to Foreign Settlement 111

Daniel Boone, who lived at Béxar, and Santiago McLaughlin, who settled at Salcedo. The explanation of the failure of the remainder to settle may possibly be found in the refusal of the commandant-general to allow settlement at Orcoquisac.

Check on immigration.—In refusing the request of some of Clouets' families to locate at Orcoquisac, Salcedo cited several previous orders in regard to settlement of Louisianians, and gave instructions to place them in the settlements already begun.[32] That this refusal to allow settlements at Orcoquisac had the effect of checking immigration in some cases is suggested. For instance, Father Domingo Joachin Solana declared that it was quite possible that a rich and educated Irishman of New Orleans, Juan Evalvez, who had signified his intention of taking up lands for the establishment of a settlement in Texas, might change his mind because none could be secured at Orcoquisac. Nevertheless, Solana forwarded Evalvez's petition in order that the case might receive consideration.[33] But the applicant was evidently disappointed, for he was heard of no more in Texas.

Other petitions.—In spite of these checks to immigration, petitions continued to come in. In October, 1806, Juan Francisco Warnett, Baron de Lambercy, requested lands on the Trinity. He desired a sufficient quantity for fifteen persons and six hundred head of stock.[34] At the same time Francisco Marceau Desgraviers asked the same favor.

---

[32]N. Salcedo to Cordero, July 15, 1806.

[33]Solana to Cordero and accompanying passports of same date, September 25, 1806. For petition of Solana, for payment of his expenses from New Orleans to Texas, see N. Salcedo to Cordero, December 13, 1806. He was appointed acting curate at Atascocito, and he at once proceeded to issue orders necessary for causing all persons within his jurisdiction to observe all the rites of the church. Solana to Herrera, February 29, 1807.

[34]Petition, October 22, 1806, and Ugarte to Cordero, November 4, 1806. Both these documents were found in a folder marked *Solicitudes á Emigracion no complidas.*

Whether their failure to immigrate was due to the fact that they could not secure lands at Orcoquisac cannot be determined.

Another prominent person who sought entry was Juan Eugenio Marchan, an experienced seaman, who claimed that upon learning of the opening of the port of San Bernardo he had come all the way from Florida to Texas to become a settler and to continue his occupation as a pilot. According to his story he attempted to bring a load of tools for the cultivation of the soil and provisions for his workmen in accordance with the permission granted by the opening of the port; but that on account of his inability to make a successful landing he was compelled to take his goods to Attakapas and return by land.[35] His request to be allowed to explore a portion of the coast country and to return to New Orleans for goods was naturally regarded by many as a very suspicious thing. Nevertheless, he was finally received as a settler, although he was forbidden to locate at the new port where as yet adequate investigations preparatory to its opening had not been made.[36] He was likewise refused permission to settle at Atascocito, Orcoquisac, or Nacogdoches;[37] and it was not long until he was expelled from the province because of his love for trade. Another petitioner was Guillermo Cork, a carpenter, who asked permission to go to Natchitoches in company with a certain Mr. Richards[38] and family to secure tools so that he might return and settle at Salcedo or at some other convenient place.[39] But, like the majority of the applicants considered, he was never heard of again.

---

[35] Viana to Cordero, November 24, 1806.

[36] N. Salcedo to Cordero, February 24, 1807. A great deal of interest was manifested in the coast region from the Sabine to the Trinity. N. Salcedo to Cordero, January 13, 1806. This interest was heightened by the rumor that an American was planning to examine the whole coast as far as the Rio Grande. Cordero to the Commandant-General, January 14, 1806; and Instructions to Moreno, January 25, 1806.

[37] N. Salcedo to Cordero, April 20, 1807.

[38] It is possible that he was referring to Mordicai Richards or to Estevan Richards, who were in Texas at this time.

[39] Petition, September 7, 1806.

The Opening of Texas to Foreign Settlement 113

During this year, Francisco Roquier and ten other citizens of Louisiana came to Texas, asking to be received as settlers. They wished to be allowed to take back with them enough horses to bring their families and goods. In ruling upon this case, Salcedo declared that they must meet the requirements of existing orders concerning the admission of Louisianians and the extraction of animals necessary for transportation;[40] but no evidence has been found to show that they actually settled. On the contrary, it is possible that this same Rouquier was later forbidden to settle in Texas because he had waited too long to become a settler and because his conduct had been suspicious.[41] Juan Filhiol, who had previously been commandant at Ouachita, was also granted permisison to locate in Texas,[42] but no further mention of his name has been found. Juan Carlos Casili, or John Cashily, as he signed himself, also presented a petition for settlement during 1806, and was given the desired permit by Cordero. However, before he arrived at his destination he was arrested as a contraband trader. His goods were seized and sold, and he was ordered to return to Louisiana. Nevertheless, several years later he returned to try his chances once more.[43] But whether or not he ever really became a *bona fide* settler cannot be determined. Edmond Janson and David Chote, who claimed to be Spanish subjects attached to that government, asked permission to settle in the Spanish Dominons, offering to locate at any point the commandant-general might think best.[44] As was to be expected, they were given permission to enter; but since their names do not appear on any of the lists of new settlers it is probable that they did not take advantage of the generosity of the government.

---

[40]N. Salcedo to Cordero, May 6, 1806.
[41]N. Salcedo to Cordero, July 13, 1807.
[42]Viana to Cordero, June 4, 1806, and Cordero to Viana, June 15 on margin of first document.
[43]Petition, May 12, 1806, and Petition addressed to *Junta de Govierno* [probably 1811].
[44]Certificate signed by Delachais, August 13, 1806. N. A.

A priest, Juan Maguire, wished to serve the king by selecting a good location at Matagorda and by drawing about him families from Louisiana whose reputations gave promise of loyalty to the government. He must not have been successful for no further mention of his colonists is found, although later he was at Béxar.[45] The last petition found in the Béxar Archives for the year 1806 is that of Amos Hubbard, an American, a Catholic, a millwright, and a resident of Louisiana for four years and of Nacogdoches for one year. He brought with him a certificate of good character, and asked for five leagues of land at Salcedo so that he might settle there with his family to work at his trade, and to cultivate the soil.[46] But he, like the majority of petitioners, seems never actually to have entered Texas.

Indian immigrants.—The old policy of permitting the entry of Louisiana Indians believed to be favorably inclined toward the Spanish government was continued. Cordero was firmly persuaded that not only the chief native tribes, such as the Tonkawas, Tawakonis, Comanches, Texas, Orkokisas, etc., but the immigrant tribes of the Coasatis, the Alabamas, and Choctaws, as well, were but waiting a favorable opportunity to take arms to aid the Spaniards against the Americans.[47] Permission was therefore given for the entry of the Pascagoulas and additional Choctaws. The latter were permitted to settle along the Sabine as that they would be near the Tinzas and permission was given for enlarging the territory already fixed for the settlement of immigrant Indians. At the same time, further precautions were taken to prevent communication with Louisiana.[48] At the end of 1806, Salcedo gave instructions for the admission of the Choctaws to be located so as to

---

[45]Ugarte to Cordero, August 25, 1806, and Affidavit, December 28.
[46]Petition undated with recommendation of Viana, December 21, 1806.
[47]Cordero to N. Salcedo, June 16, 1806.
[48]N. Salcedo to Cordero, August 16, 1806.

form, with other Indians of the province, a cordon along the frontier.[49]

Continued commercial restrictions.—During 1806 another attempt was made to secure a reversal of the order prohibiting trade with Louisiana. It was even suggested that the royal order providing for the opening of the port of Bahía de San Bernardo necessarily carried with it the privilege of free trade with the United States.[50] This, however, was promptly denied[51] and so determined was Salcedo to prevent contraband trade that he even issued orders for suspending actions looking toward the opening of the port in question.[52] Later, he even refused to allow the purchase in Natchitoches of the paper necessary for government correspondence and administered a sharp rebuke to the commandant of Nacogdoches for attempting to evade orders.[53] Although besieged with petitions for commercial concessions, he remained firm. Bastrop's petition to establish an Indian trading house at Béxar, on condition that he be permitted to export five hundred horses per year to Louisiana, was refused; while Barr's continued efforts to secure permission to trade with Louisianians were unavailing.

Contraband trade.—But in spite of orders to the contrary, goods were constantly brought from Louisiana to Texas and sold. On one occasion the commandant of Atascocito even defended this custom, claiming that it was absolutely necessary as supplies were needed for the sick at that place, where there was not a person left well enough to kill a beef or make a *tortilla*. He reported, however, that he had refused the traders permisison to exchange brandy with the Indians for peltries, and claimed also that he had charged them not to bring in any more goods to sell, but that he had

---

[49]N. Salcedo to Cordero, December 5, 1806. Later, permission for the entry of certain bands of Choctaws and Apalaches was refused. N. Salcedo to Cordero, August 11, 1807, and Cordero to Viana, August 18, 1807.

[50]Commandant of Bahía to Cordero, March 17, 1806.

[51]N. Salcedo to Cordero, April 21, 1806.

[52]N. Salcedo to Cordero, April 26, 1806.

[53]N. Salcedo to Cordero, July 15, 1806.

told them that they would be received as settlers should they return with their families.⁵⁴ This was doubtless a bid for their entrance, for once settled, all knew they could easily carry on the forbidden trade *sub rosa*.

Exclusion of Americans.—Salcedo's refusal to allow intercourse with Louisiana was a natural one at this time, especially in view of the report that a party of ten or fifteen hundred men were said to be gathering in "Quientoc" [Kentucky] to take possession of the unsettled regions of Texas and those portions inhabited by the Indian tribes.⁵⁵ Indeed, so grave was the situation considered, that Salcedo sent orders to Simón de Herrera, governor of Nuevo León, to assume immediate command of the frontier, *where reinforcements were being massed.*⁵⁶ At this time Herrera was also charged with the duty of making preliminary examination of Louisiana immigrants, as it was believed that his position would easily enable him to investigate the character of applicants;⁵⁷ but this arrangement was soon disapproved by Salcedo, and the old order of procedure was restored.⁵⁸ Salcedo's fears soon increased. In the summer of 1806, he received a warning through the intendant of Florida of the presence of a party in the United States who planned to raise a revolution in Mexico through the introduction of emissaries and seditious papers. Consequently, he issued instructions to his subordinates to examine with care all persons desiring to enter Texas and to permit no additional foreigners to cross the frontier unless supplied with proper passports and possessed of proofs of their fidelity to the king.⁵⁹

American deserters.—What to do with the American deserters was also a question at this time; and, following his usual conservative policy, Salcedo decided upon greater precautions. Those professing to be Catholics were to be

---
⁵⁴Herrera to Cordero, September 16, 1806.
⁵⁵N. Salcedo to Cordero, April 9, 1806.
⁵⁶N. Salcedo to Cordero, April 9, 1806.
⁵⁷Cordero to the Commandant-General, June 5, 1806.
⁵⁸N. Salcedo to Cordero, July 13, 1806.
⁵⁹N. Salcedo to Cordero, August 4, 1806, and December 10, 1806.

The Opening of Texas to Foreign Settlement 117

allowed to select locations in Coahuila or Nueva Viscaya, while those claiming to be Protestants were to be kept in Texas under the closest inspection.[60] The situation was somewhat relieved by Wilkinson's and Herrera's Neutral Ground Agreement[61] which temporarily settled the question

---

[60]N. Salcedo to Cordero, December 9, 1806.

[61]Copy of paragraph of letter written by a Spanish subject at Natchitoches to Samuel Davenport, November 8, 1806. The movement toward the delineation of a Neutral Ground between Spanish and American territory was begun in 1804 when representatives from the United States proposed to Spain that the country between the Sabine and the Colorado be made neutral. Later they modified their proposal, suggesting that the line be drawn between the Colorado and the Rio Grande. This suggestion alarmed the Spaniards who viewed the steady advance of the Americans to the westward with alarm. They at once threw a number of troops upon the frontier, some of them being even stationed beyond the Sabine. The Americans demanded their withdrawal and the Spaniards retreated to await instructions from their superior government. Wilkinson soon followed and the two armies were soon face to face, the Sabine between them. At this crisis, however, Wilkinson concluded that he must go to Natchez to make a great parade over his act in thwarting Burr's plan for an invasion of Spanish territory. He succeeded in patching up an understanding with Herrera, the commander of the Spanish forces who probably thought it necessary to come to terms with Wilkinson as a means of checking Burr's schemes. In so doing, both generals assumed unwarranted powers but, owing to the stress of the times, their work was allowed to stand. By this agreement the Neutral Ground was to lie between the Sabine and the Arroyo Hondo, the original western boundary of Louisiana under French occupation. Three reasons were suggested for Wilkinson's desire to enter into this agreement: 1st, that the United States was planning to declare war against Spain and desired to lessen watchfulness; 2nd, that he wished to be free to take part in the revolution which was being planned for the purpose of setting up an empire in the West, and, 3d, that he was interested in the formation of an army to coöperate with Miranda and Burr who would probably apply to England for assistance in revolutionizing the whole of the Spanish dominions in South America, Cortes to Herrera, November 14, 1806. Neither Spain nor the United States exercised any jurisdiction over the Neutral Ground and it became the refuge of all kinds of lawless and desperate characters. At various times the authorities of the two countries united in an attempt to exterminate them but to no avail. By the treaty of 1819, the limits of the entire section fell within Louisiana and disappeared forever. Garrison, George P., *Texas*, 128–131.

of boundary but because of continued rumors of invasion Salcedo did not relax his vigilance. Indeed, so suspicious was he that he visited Texas to make a personal investigation.[62]

Further immigration restrictions.—As a result, Salcedo decided upon a new step to prevent the entry of the enemies of Spain. Henceforth, all prospective immigrants were to be carefully examined as in the past. All those not possessing the requisite qualifications and those unwilling to settle at the points designated were to be refused admittance; while those already rejected and those who had located without the formality of presenting a petition were to be expelled from the province.[63] However, all cases in which settlers had left their families in Louisiana or possessed property there were to be referred to Cordero for final decision.[64] While professing a willingness to execute orders, Cordero was really able to defeat the plans of his superior.

Summary for 1806.—During 1806, despite trade restrictions, fear of American aggression, and the refusal of the commandant-general to allow any latitude in the location of settlements and the management of immigrants, considerable progress was made in the colonization of Texas. The *villa* of Salcedo was established by settlers from Béxar and a few Louisiana familes under the leadership of Despallier. Although Barr's unfulfilled contract had expired on August 23 and Bastrop had accomplished nothing, immigrants were still coming in singly and in groups and Despallier was continuing his efforts with comparative success. But discontent was beginning to manifest itself and during the next year immigration began to fall off.

1807

Discontent among the settlers.—Salcedo's restrictive orders were as displeasing to the immigrants as to Cordero.

---

[62]Letters of Salcedo to various authorities, dated, Béxar, December, 1806.
[63]N. Salcedo to Cordero, December 4, 1806. N. A.
[64]Cordero to Viana, January 20 and 28, 1807.

Upon being ordered out of Texas because he was a Protestant and because he had not gone through the necessary legal formalities, a certain Isaac Johnston gave a pathetic description of his attempts to follow the Spanish flag, and begged at least for time in which to prepare for his return to Louisiana.[65] Eleven families from Louisiana who had been located at Atascocito for more than a year talked of returning to Louisiana as soon as they learned that they could settle only in assigned places; while sixty of Clouet's families from Attakapas and Opelousas, who were already on their way to Texas, turned back upon learning of the requirements. In defense of his ruling, Salcedo pointed out that previous orders forbidding settlement at Atascocito had been clear and again demanded the execution of his orders and the removal to Villa Salcedo of the families already at Atascocito.[66] This did not put an end to Clouet's plans, although it seems probable that the Atascocito contingent represented practically the total results of his efforts. At the end of 1807, he was still trying to settle families, as is shown by a passport issued by him to the sailors Andres Veran and Antonio Molinar, who, in company with Joseph Olivero and Nicolas Bouquet, were expected to go to Atascocito to select a suitable place for location for such settlers as could be brought by land as soon as the king approved Clouet's plan.[67] But once more he failed. Salcedo not only refused to permit the examination of the region but ordered the arrest of the agents on the ground that their actions were suspicious.[68]

---

[65]Petition, February 22, 1807.
[66]N. Salcedo to Cordero, April 20, 1807. [Fragment.] See list of families, November 1, 1807, and *Padron*, Appendix, 11.
[67]Passport and Clouet to the Commandant of Atascocito, December 17, 1807. Doubtless these plans were favorably considered as a make-weight against Burr's activity, Folch to the Viceroy, March 20, 1807, *A. G. I. S.* Mex., 90–1–18, January 12, 1807–October 27, 1807. Clouet's promise that this immigration should occasion no expense to the royal treasury must also have been an attraction, Clouet to the King, September 17, 1807, *Ibid.*
[68]N. Salcedo to Cordero, March 8, 1808.

They were soon actually found to have a quantity of furs in their possession,[69] and therefore were finally ordered out of the province.[70] Since it is known that Clouet had accomplished nothing up to this time and that there was no prospect of any success in carrying forward his plans under the changed conditions,[71] no further mention of his work need be made. Even though settlers were not content with the regulations, many new applicants appeared during 1807 and several were able to secure entry.

Applicants.—Luis Parat, who had been living at Bayou de Los Ais for nine years, desired to move from this disputed territory to Salcedo, and asked to be granted all the privileges allowed other Louisiana immigrants.[72] The commandant of Nacogdoches recommended that his request be granted; but no further reference to the case has been found. At this time Edmundo Norris, who again applied for admission, was authorized to remain at Nacogdoches temporarily,[73] while Pedro Herrera, a native of Teneriffe, who had lived at Nacogdoches two years, was given permission to locate at Béxar. Whether he did so or not cannot be determined. Norris, however, succeeded in remaining at Nacogdoches permanently. A certain Arman and his son-in-law were ordered to locate at Salcedo,[74] and it is quite probable that they were identical with Zedo Charman and Elisha Nelson who located at that place in March, 1807. The privilege of settlement was granted to Germain Willet, a French Catholic from Canada, who had resided in and near Baton Rouge for two years. He asked permission to remain at Nacogdoches for some months until his sick wife could recover sufficiently to continue the journey to Béxar, where he expected to locate.[75] The governor granted the request but this kindness was repaid by treachery; for when

---

[69]N. Salcedo to Cordero, May 31, 1808.
[70]N. Salcedo to the Governor of Texas, August 5, 1808.
[71]N. Salcedo to Folch, September 27, 1806.
[72]Petition, January 3, 1807.
[73]N. Salcedo to the Commandant of Nacogdoches, May 14, 1807
[74]García to Viana, March 23, 1807.
[75]May 10, 1807.

the two months allowed had expired Willet escaped by stealth to Louisiana. Considerable red tape had to be unwound before Pedro Bray, a deserter from the United States army, who had lived for some years in Louisiana and Nacogdoches, was given permisison to settle at Salcedo instead of being expelled from the province according to orders.[76] He actually located at the place assigned to him. Gabriel Tacoma, a Louisianian, also desired to settle in Texas at this time,[77] but as his passport was not satisfactory he was detained at Nacogdoches and finally rejected.[78] Joshua Rees, of Pennsylvania, who had lived in Louisiana for eleven years and at Nacogdoches eight years, part of the time being in the employ of Barr and Davenport, was recommended as a desirable settler by the commandant of Nacogdoches, in spite of the fact that he had made trips back to Louisiana and had been accused of engaging in contraband trade;[79] and as was to be expected, Cordero issued a permit for his settlement at Salcedo, provided he were a Catholic;[80] and, strange to say, his name really appears upon the list of settlers of that place. In July, 1807, Hugo Coyle, who had been absent from Texas for a year and a half, was permitted to return to Salcedo;[81] while in September, 1807, Cordero gave to Guillermo de la Barre permission to locate in a settlement to be formed at the intersection of the Guadalupe river and the *Camino Real*.[82] There is no evidence to show, however, that he actually resided at this point. Later, lands were assigned to Bastrop, who hoped to make use of the splendid water power of the famous springs at that point. But, upon learning of the orders of

---

[75]Documents dated May 10–July 12, 1807.
[77]Affidavit of Blanc, May 11, 1807.
[78]Viana to Cordero, June 23, 1807.
[79]Petition and information, May 27–July, 1807.
[80]Cordero to Viana, July 19, 1807.
[81]Petition and connected documents, July 9, 1807. Coyle presented a passport reading "Arkansas, June 6, 1807, Please to let Mr. Hugo Coyle and Michael Lynch pass unmolested to Nacogdoches. J. B. Treat."
[82]Cordero to Labarre, September 15, 1807.

the commandant-general to postpone settlement at this place until the *villas* already provided should be completed,[83] he released all claim to the lands granted him. Anthony Glass, who on March 1, 1806, had been given permission to settle in Texas, declared that he had not been able to do so because the excitement occasioned by Burr's conspiracy had prevented the adjustment of his business. Therefore, in the fall of 1807, he asked to be allowed to come by water from Baton Rouge to Orcoquisac.[84] The fact that he brought neither his family nor his property aroused the suspicions of the commandant of Nacogdoches, who, at once, called the matter to the attention of the higher authorities.[85] The applicant was finally rejected because of his former filibustering activity and because of his connection with Dr. John Sibley, a veteran of the Revolutionary War who had located at Natchitoches in 1803, and who, as Indian agent from the United States, aroused the anger of the Spaniards.[86]

Miguel Solivello, who had received permission to settle in any of the new *villas* and to stay at Nacogdoches until arrangements for transportation could be made, remained at that point until the commandant protested. Thereupon, the governor ordered that he be compelled to depart at once.[87] Not all immigrants came directly from Louisiana. In June, 1807, Joseph de Goccazochea, at the Villa of Santa Anna de Camargo, issued a passport to Pedro Lartigue to go to Salcedo in accordance with the permit already issued him by

---

[83]N. Salcedo to M. de Salcedo, October 6, 1807, in *A. G. I. S.*, Mex., 104–2–10, June 23, 1806–March 14, 1819.

[84]Petition, October 21, 1807.

[85]Recommendation of Viana, October 22, 1807, with Petition.

[86]N. Salcedo to Viana, January 2, 1808. Sibley was instructed to hold frequent communication with the Indians of the region and to distribute merchandise among them. He was expected to conciliate all the tribes with whom he might come in contact and especially those who might be influential in case of a break between the United States and Spain. So successful was he in obtaining information that the United States soon made him permanent Indian agent and furnished him with goods for trading. Cox, *Exploration of the Louisiana Frontier 1803–1806*, pp. 164–166.

[87]Cordero to Viana, July 1, 1807.

Cordero. He was to be allowed to carry with him a large number of horses and mules, and was to be accompanied by Miguel de Larrua and eleven other adventurers.[88] Still another applicant was Guillermo Yanso, who was rejected because he was not a Spanish vassal.[89] Although a few of the applicants were rejected, many whose records were far from clear were received. Perhaps the most conspicuous case was that of José Miguel [McGill] Crow, who desired to locate at Bahía or at Béxar. Even while confessing that the applicant had been considered a suspicious person, Cordero gave orders for his admission, on the ground that his actions could be more carefully watched in Texas than beyond the borders.[90] And, quite as was to be expected, Crow did cause the Spaniards a good deal of trouble. It was only in rare cases that petitions for settlement were rejected. The only cases found are those of Juan Nes and Guillermo West, who were refused permission to locate at Salcedo because they were Americans. As a consequence, they were forced to leave the province.[91] Only one man, Amos Hubbard, is known to have been expelled.[92] These malcontents lingered along the frontier, lived among the Indians, and thus furnished a nucleus about which gathered fugitives from Louisiana and evil-doers from the Neutral Ground. It was also a rare thing for the petitioners to make good their promise to locate in Texas. In fact, of the large number of prospective immigrants named, only six are known to have settled—as follows: Edmundo Norris, Zedo Charman, Elisha Nelson, Pedro Bray, Joshua Rees, and José Miguel Crow.

Indian immigrants.—The policy of receiving Indian immigrants was still favored. Among those presenting petitions for land during 1807 were the Chickasaws, the Cherokees, the Guapasces, the Coasatis, and additional

---

[88]Passport of Goccacochea, June 15, 1807. See ante.
[89]N. Salcedo to Cordero, October 6, 1807.
[90]Cordero to Viana, July 1, 1807.
[91]Herrera to Cordero, February 2, 1807.
[92]Viana to Cordero, February 2, 1807.

Pascaguales, who resented the seizure of their lands by the United States.[93] They were admitted in spite of the fact that the Choctaws who had been previously taken on trial had committed hostilities against native tribes, and there had been talk of expelling them.[94]

Growth of Salcedo.—The *villa* of Salcedo was of necessity a favored spot for settlement during 1807. Among those not hitherto named as locating there were José Miguel de Sosa, of Acámbaro; Julian Lartigue, son of Pedro Lartigue; Juan Lunn, whose wife had immigrated in 1805; Juan Malrroni, an Italian; Silas Luci, an American; Bautista Canaliano, an Englishman, and Carlos Dupon, a Frenchman.[95] Santiago McNulty was also living at this new *villa* in May, 1807, although his name does not appear in the list of settlers due to his imprisonment for engaging in contraband trade.[96] This settlement however was no longer to enjoy the distinction of being the only new *villa* in Texas.

Establishment of Villa de San Marcos de Neve.—At the end of 1807, a new step in colonization was taken—that of bringing to Texas settlers from the interior of Mexico instead of from Béxar, as had been done upon one occasion, and from Louisiana as had been the general practice hitherto. In December, 1807, certain families from Refugio, below the Rio Grande, under the leadership of Felipe Roque de Portilla, who seems to have been financed by Cordero himself, were on the way to the San Marcos river.[97] According to previous promises, Cordero sent an escort to the Nueces to receive the party. He furnished money and supplies for the caravan, but declared that he would be unable to extend the same assistance to a second party which had planned to come, until the receipt of money from Saltillo.[98]

---

[93]Viana to Cordero, August 8, 1807, and N. Salcedo to Cordero, October 6, October 30, and December 1, 1807.
[94]Viana to Cordero, May 1, 1807, Cordero to the Commandant-General, May 14, 1807, and N. Salcedo to Cordero, June 15, 1807.
[95]Appendix 11.
[96]Petition May 7, 1807.
[97]See map, between pp. 101–102.
[98]Cordero to Portilla, December 16, 1807.

The Opening of Texas to Foreign Settlement 125

On January 6, 1808, the governor reported the establishment of the new *villa* of San Marcos de Neve at the junction of the *Camino Real* and the San Marcos river, and the appointment of Juan Ignacio Arrambide as *justicia*. At this time the population consisted of eighty-one persons, a large part of whom were from Refugio and the remainder from Béxar and Bahía. Seventy-nine *pesos* had been expended in establishing the settlement.[99] In approving these measures, Salcedo suggested that other settlements located in a direct line between Béxar and Nacogdoches would facilitate communication and transportation; and he therefore, for the time being, revoked previous orders for settlement at other points in Texas.[100] At the beginning of 1808, José Estevan García, a teacher, took up his residence at San Marcos, thus bringing the total number of settlers up to eighty-two; but he soon departed for Salcedo,[101] leaving the place with its original number of inhabitants. Portilla arranged for the transportation of six other families, four of whom had servants and two of whom had no capital save a large number of children; and Cordero promised to send troops to escort these families from the Nueces to San Marcos.[102] But they must never have reached their destination; for no additional names appear upon the list of settlers. Not much can be learned of the history of San Marcos, but the few details that are available indicate that its days were few and full of trouble. In the first place, the government had been compelled to aid certain of its poor families.[103] Then, on June 5, 1808, the settlement was visited by a flood. The water ran through the *plaza,* the people left their homes, and all confidence in the suitability of the location was lost.

---

[99]*Padron General,* July 12, 1809, Appendix 14.
[100]N. Salcedo to Cordero, May 2, 1808.
[101]Prieto to M. de Salcedo, December 4, 1809.
[102]Portilla to Cordero, August 29, 1808.
[103]*Noticia de lo subministrado a los Pobladores de San Marcos,* April 3, 1808.

Plans were made for moving the *villa*,[104] but they were never carried out. The Indians kept the settlers in constant alarm by frequent raids; and, in 1812, it was finally abandoned because of the attack of filibusters. In the meantime, however, interest in the colonization of Texas became of even more vital importance, in view of Napoleon's plans for world conquest.

---

[104]Granado to Cordero, June 7, 1808.

CHAPTER IV

AMBITIONS OF NAPOLEON AND PRECAUTIONS OF THE COMMANDANT-GENERAL, 1808

During 1808, the over-weening ambition of Napoleon Bonaparte brought a new element into the situation in Texas. Realizing the possibility of danger from this source as well as the probability of aggression from England[1] and

---

[1] In February, 1808, Vicente Folch wrote Claiborne that he had been warned that an expedition of 20,000 men was being fitted out in the ports of Great Britain for an attack upon the Spanish Dominions of America. Folch to Claiborne, February 11, 1808, in *Letter Books*, IV, 157–159. Long before this, Claiborne had feared that the English might be persuaded by Burr and his fellow conspirators to attack the Spanish Dominions and took precautions to see that the neutrality of the United States should not be violated. Learning of the agency of Richard Keene in an expedition proposed by Burr and his associates against the Spanish territory, he ordered Keene's arrest and added: "Mr. Keene is now supposed to be on his passage from Jamaica to New Orleans from which former place Mr. Burr expects, as is said, to receive the assistance of a British Fleet." Claiborne to Hall, January 2, 1807, *ibid.*, 78–79. For Keene's connection with Wilkinson and Burr, see Cox, *The West Florida Controversy*, 195, and Nile's *Weekly Register*, X, 1816, pp. 21–23.

In the Claiborne correspondence there are found other indications that the politics of Europe were to have effect in America. On December 29, 1807, he wrote Madison, reporting that General Moreau, who had been exiled by Napoleon, was expected at New Orleans within a few days but that, personally, he attached "no suspicion to the movements of that great but unfortunate man," and that he presumed that his visit to the territory had not caused the president "a moment's anxiety," or that he himself would have been "apprised thereof." *Ibid.*, 142. But uneasiness as to Moreau's movements soon became prevalent in the north—the government even sharing in this feeling. Claiborne, however, still had confidence in his protestations of favorable sentiment toward the United States and "his dislike of Bonaparte and the order of things in France." Nevertheless he reported a reserve between Governor Folch and the visitor and declared that the latter had been received at New Orleans with some coolness due to the suspicions expressed in the Atlantic States. Claiborne to Madison, February 1, 1808. *Ibid.*, 148–49. However, on February 17,

from the United States at this psychological moment, Salcedo took greater precautions than formerly to see that his orders were obeyed. Cordero did not realize at first the possible connection of the French menace with the immigration problem; and he went even farther than usual in his determination either to modify or to evade restrictive orders altogether. In this, he was aided by Herrera and by others who were soon placed upon the now vitally important frontier.

Aggressions of Napoleon.—By the cession of Bayonne, May 5, 1808, Napoleon gained complete ascendency over Charles IV and Ferdinand VII and secured from them title to the throne of Spain and the Indies under the pretext of desiring to settle family dissensions and to establish order in those revolution-cursed dominions.[2] He at once took steps to assert his claim to the whole territory thus ceded by making his brother Joseph king of Spain; by throwing additional troops into the Peninsula; and by sending emissaries

---

he declared that Moreau and Folch had contracted a great intimacy and that although their objects might be perfectly innocent, still he, himself, was *not without suspicions.* He further observed that Moreau seemed to have been well appraised of an approaching revolution in Spain, and that Folch, likewise, "had anticipated the event," and had expressed his determination to acknowledge no sovereign, save a member of the reigning family. Claiborne ended his letter thus: "My impression therefore now is, that the probable event of the dethronement of the King of Spain, has brought Moreau to this territory and that he (with Folch) contemplates assisting in establishing a separate Government in Mexico." Claiborne to Madison, February 17, 1808. *Ibid.,* 155–156. In the meantime, the Spanish authorities in the Interior Provinces seem to have had no suspicion of the possibility of interference by Moreau. In February, the commandant-general, having learned of Moreau's presence in New Orleans, wrote to Cordero saying that he did not believe Moreau would approach the Texas frontier but urging caution. Cordero to the Commandant of Nacogdoches, March 2, 1808.

[2]Martens, George Friederich von, *Nouveau Recueil de Traites,* 1808–1814, I, 60–62. For the events leading up to this cession, see Oman, Charles, *A History of the Peninsular War,* I, 1–20.

to America to announce the change in sovereignty,[3] charging them to stir up revolution which could contribute to the furtherance of his designs for assuming control. He likewise appointed a viceroy for Mexico, issued orders for sending troops and ammunition to certain points in America, and made preparations for seizing upon such provinces as might show signs of the very revolutions he had encouraged.[4] He hoped to aggravate class feeling to such a degree that the Creoles would be incited to attack the European-born Spaniards in retaliation for exclusion from a proper representation in the government. He instructed his emissaries to inform the Creoles that he planned to make the Spanish Americas free and to relieve them of certain exactions and restrictions imposed upon them by the deposed king. He declared that the only return he expected was the "friendship of the people and the commerce of the country." Naturally, a great many Spaniards feared that his plans were not quite disinterested as he had issued orders for the administration of poison to all authorities who might resist his rule. He offered both money and troops for the execution of his plans and expected to make special tools of the priests by inducing them first to spread discontent among the Creoles and then to urge the wisdom of securing an independent government through Napoleon's aid on the ground that he was "the agent of God sent to chastise the tyranny of kings." Presuming upon the neutrality of the United States—which he interpreted as friendship[5]—he

---

[3]Kennedy, *History of Texas*, I, 269, Cavo, Andres, *Tres Siglos de Mejico*, 248, Villanueva, Carlos A., *Napoleon y la Independencia de América*, 172, and Yoakum, *History of Texas*, I, 143–147.

[4]*Correspondence de Napoleon*, XVII, 246–248 and 350.

[5]As a token of his own feelings, he introduced his minister to inform the United States that he would offer no objection to the occupation of the Floridas. by that power if the government would aid him in the war war against England. *Correspondence de Napoleon*, XVI, 355. A few years later the Floridas and the territory lying between the Sabine and the Rio Grande were offered to the United States by Joseph Napoleon on condition that certain grants of land be reserved for the creation of a fund to maintain himself upon the throne of

sent a certain Desmoland, the chief of all his emissaries, to that country and instructed him to send out other agents to various points to spread the discord he himself so earnestly desired.[6] Under these circumstances, Texas was one of the most vital spots in the Spanish dominions of America. Consequently, it was not long until Salcedo's fears of foreign interference were justified. Indeed, as early as May, he learned that Octiviano D'Alvimar, an Italian[7] in the employ of Napoleon, was on his way to Mexico with other French officers and that the party would probably travel by way of Texas. It was reported that D'Alvimar was really a relative of Napoleon, that he had gone to Santo Domingo to aid in putting down rebellion there prior to invasion of Louisiana, that he had been commissioned to secure aid from Caracas, Carthegena, and Santa Fé, and that he had then returned to Havana ready to carry out further schemes.[8] A little later D'Alvimar admitted that he had been sent by Napoleon to take command of Mexico in place of "San Simon," whom he believed to have been appointed as viceroy by the emperor.[9] D'Alvimar did present himself at Nacogdoches asking to be allowed to go to Mexico City.[10] Naturally his request was denied and he was immediately arrested by the authorities in Texas who, as a unit, resented the open exercise of French interference. D'Alvimar was sent to Béxar as a prisoner of war. Very shortly afterward he was taken to the interior under guard and a little later

---

Spain, Russell to Madison, January 2, 1811, Reeves, *The Napoleonic Exiles in America*, 119–134.

[6]Bancroft, *History of Mexico*, IV, 1804–1824, pp. 70–81, Appendix 15, and Villaneuva, *Napoleon y la Independencia de América*, 171–179 and 229–247.

[7]N. Salcedo to Cordero, May 12, 1808. According to his own statement, D'Alvimar was born in Paris, Affidavit, August 5, 1808.

[8]Cavo, *Tres Siglos de Méjico*, 258–259, and *Charleston Courier*, March 18, 1808.

[9]Examination of Hernández, March 16, 1811. See supporting evidence in Ramos, Arispe, *Memorias*, Navarro, *Apuntes Historicos Interesantes de San Antonio de Bexar*, 6, and Turreau to Champigny, October 8, 1808, *Affaires Etrangerès*, VI, Transc., U. of T.

[10]D'Alvimar to Cordero, August 5, 1808.

The Opening of Texas to Foreign Settlement 131

was sent out of the country. This summary treatment gave him but little opportunity to sow the seeds of discord among the Spaniards of Texas. However, his journey may not have been in vain; for it is quite possible, as some suggest, that while being conducted to Mexico as a prisoner he was able to place in the mind of the priest Hidalgo thoughts which were later to bring on the revolution.[11] Indeed, the governor of Texas later called attention to the significant fact that the insurrection in Baton Rouge and in other settlements of the Floridas had occurred almost simultaneously with the revolution in Mexico, and that D'Alvimar had passed through each of these territories.[12] D'Alvimar's attempt ended in apparent failure. But reports continued to come thick and fast that Napoleon was following up his schemes with vigor; and further precautions were soon decided upon not only by Nemesio Salcedo, but even by the authorities in Spain, who now placed themselves once more under the protection of England.

Precautionary plans.—The supreme central *junta* of Spain, which had assumed control in the name of the imprisoned king of Spain, took up the matter of preventing the execution of Napoleon's plans in America. On November 12, in response to reports of the activities of French agents made by the viceroy of Mexico, the *junta* issued an order which provided for the arrest of all French agents venturing upon Spanish soil, and enjoined the strictest precautions to prevent any intrigues in Louisiana or other parts of the West so that the dignity of the Spanish crown might be upheld and all causes for misunderstanding with the

---

[11]It is rather significant that Hidalgo's rallying cry resembled the motto which, under Napoleon's instructions, was to be inscribed upon the banners of the revolutionists, and that his statement of the objects of the government he was planning to establish were in many points similar to the advantages promised by Napoleon. See Appendix 15. *Cf.*, p. 85 and 91–92 of Robertson, William Spence, *Rise of the Spanish American Republics.*

[12]*Historia, Operaciones de Guerra, 1810 y 1812*, August 8, 1809–March 31, 1812, Trans., U. of T.

United States avoided.[13] Necessarily, the *junta* was compelled to limit its activities in America to the issuance of proclamations, for at this time Spain was using every ounce of her strength in driving the invaders from the home territory.[14] The viceroy, too, had his hands full in attempting to counteract Napoleon's influence at his very door; and, in spite of the fact that he called for suggestions for the defense of Texas,[15] he was only able to send warnings and orders to that province. So in the final analysis the chief responsibility devolved upon the commandant-general; for, although the authorities of Texas, as has been said, were seemingly in perfect accord with him in detesting the French government, their anxiety to develop Texas made them strangely blind to the fact that the danger might present itself under various disguises. To guard against Napoleon's wiles, Salcedo ordered precautions taken to prevent the sending of seditious papers into Texas.[16] Yet defense against French intrigue did not prevent him from continuing a close watch upon the Americans who, he feared, would seize this opportunity to extend their frontiers.

Fear of Americans.—To forestall American agents, he made arrangements to send emissaries among certain Indian tribes.[17] He also determined to cut off more effectively all communication and trade with Louisiana, and to make additional efforts to prevent the entry of exploring parties from the United States.[18] He even forbade communication between Nacogdoches and the Spanish settlement of Bayou Pierre unless it became absolutely necessary to secure from it food or the services of a priest.[19] As a further precaution, he ordered twenty-seven slaves who had escaped from the

---

[13] Copy in N. Salcedo to Cordero, March 13, 1809.
[14] Declaration, June 6, 1808, in N. Salcedo to Velasco, August 24, 1808.
[15] N. Salcedo to Cordero, August 23, 1808.
[16] N. Salcedo to Cordero, December 3, 1808.
[17] Cordero to Soto, March 13, 1808.
[18] N. Salcedo to Cordero, January 12, 1808.
[19] N. Salcedo to Cordero, August 26, 1808.

United States transferred from Nacogdoches to Villa Salcedo, because he feared that should they be left at Nacogdoches the Indians would capture them and return them to their owners.[20] He declared to the viceroy that *the greatest question of the times was the holding of Texas—the buffer state—against the Americans.*[21]

Disagreement over defense.—In spite of the fact that the defense of other portions of Mexico was a grave problem, Cordero and Herrera, two of the strongest men of New Spain, were already in charge of affairs in Texas. In addition, Manuel María de Salcedo, a son of the former governor of Louisiana was now made governor of Texas.[22] He was instructed to see that no immigrants were received save those who were known to be faithful to the king and who had ceased to hold communication with any persons in Louisiana.[23] His lack of knowledge of local affairs was to be supplied by Cordero, who was instructed to remain in Texas for a time as the special representative of the commandant-general.[24] However, the new governor, like those already on the ground, believed that the best way to defend Texas was to develop it into a strong and self-supporting province through the introduction of settlers; and as the three had the courage of their convictions the commandant-general from the outset was seriously handicapped in carrying out his exclusion policy. Manuel Salcedo's liberal attitude is illustrated by his recommendation that immigrants be admitted whose fidelity might have been questioned by even the most disinterested observer. He said that they did not seem suspicious to him, since they had severed all relations with Louisiana and had made no attempt to return to that province; and as the majority of them had trades he thought they would make useful settlers.

---

[20] N. Salcedo to Cordero, May 31, 1808.
[21] N. Salcedo to the Viceroy, November 8, 1808.
[22] M. de Salcedo to the Governor of Baton Rouge, August 16, 1805, and M. de Salcedo to Cordero, September 12, 1808.
[23] M. de Salcedo to Cordero, December 11, 1808.
[24] N. Salcedo to Cordero, March 24, 1809.

He was unwilling to permit them to locate at Villa Salcedo but begged the commandant-general to allow them to settle at San Marcos, on the Guadalupe, or at Béxar.[25]

Evasion of orders.—During 1808, there were frequent infractions of the commandant-general's instructions. The correspondence between Nemesio Salcedo and Cordero concerning settlers at Orcoquisac furnishes an illustration of the tactics used by the local authorities to carry their point. Early in 1808, the commandant-general made a peremptory demand of Cordero to explain the statement of Father Solana that the settlers in the region about Orcoquisac were English and French whose language he could not understand.[26] In reply, Cordero evaded the point of the nationality of the settlers and stressed the statement that they were not *settled* at that point but merely *located there temporarily* because of lack of means of transportation.[27] There is abundant evidence that the commandant-general's orders were often disregarded. For instance, at the beginning of 1808, there landed at the port of Atascocito a very odd party of immigrants, consisting of five men, one woman, and a boy, all of whom showed evidences of French influence. The leader, Miguel de Larrua,[28] a Viscayan, claimed to be a Catholic, although he had no papers to support his assertion. According to his story, he had been educated in France, and had located at Nacogdoches in 1798 by permission of the commandant of that post. He possessed a passport issued by Cordero on February 6, 1807. He was accompanied by his son, who had been baptized at Nacogdoches, and by an Italian servant, Carlos Rumanoli. Rumanoli claimed that he too was a Catholic; and, like his master, he told a remarkable story to explain his inability to exhibit a certificate of baptism. Another man of the party was Juan Eugenio Michamps,[29] a native of Paris. He, like those

---

[25]M. de Salcedo to N. Salcedo, November 30, 1808.
[26]N. Salcedo to Cordero, February 13, 1808.
[27]Cordero to N. Salcedo, March 14, 1808.
[28]See *ante*.
[29]See *ante*.

already named, had passed through some thrilling experiences and, consequently, was unable to support his statement by documents. He had been led to immigrate to Texas, he said, by reading the king's proclamation which admitted all Louisiana vassals to Texas. He had brought with him his wife and two servants, Pedro Estevan and Pedro Flogny. His wife, Doña Rosa Francisca Vechan, a native of Nantes, was able to present a marriage certificate signed by a priest of New York. Pedro Estevan claimed to be a German and a Catholic but he, too, had lost his certificate of baptism. Pedro Flogny, a Frenchman, declared that he had lost his certificate of baptism during the insurrection of negroes in Santo Domingo. Despite the fact that in this Gallic party of seven only the woman and the boy could show any evidence of really being Catholics, they were all admitted with but little hesitation. In a note accompanying the report of the examination of the applicants, the governor wrote *"bueno"* opposite the name of Larrua; he expressed the opinion that Rumanoli, being young and a bachelor, might be useful at Béxar; he was willing to admit Michamps and his wife; and he felt that since Pedro Estevan had a trade he likewise should be admitted. He objected to admitting Pedro Flogny on the ground that he did not meet the requirements; but nevertheless the applicant was allowed to settle, mainly in order that the expense and inconvenience of the journey back to Louisiana might be avoided.[30] Besides, he hoped that Flogny would develop into a skilled farmer. All these suspicious immigrants were received by the local authorities as settlers, while Larrua was later actually granted permission to examine the coast country. In this way he was given every opportunity to gain information which would have been invaluable to Napoleon, if he had been able to push his plans for the seizure of Mexico, or to the United States, if a break had occurred between that country and Spain.

---

[30]*Expediente*, October 11, 1808, and order of Cordero, January 19, 1809.

In November another unusual case came up. The commandant of Atascocito reported the arrival from Louisiana of Carlos Tessier, who was on his way to Béxar with some personal property and certain effects belonging to the wife of the newly appointed governor. Tessier was allowed to continue his journey to Béxar because he had a passport to that point; but the crew of the boat in which he had made the voyage were kept under guard until further orders could be received.[31] Governor Salcedo really wished to employ Tessier as a secretary. When the commandant-general refused to allow this, he cast about for some expedient for keeping his *protégé* in Texas. He instructed him to present a formal petetion to be allowed to become a settler; and, until this petition could be acted upon, permitted him to remain at Villa Salcedo. The same privilege was to be extended to his two servants in case they were Spaniards and had lived in Louisiana during the Spanish *régime*. The boat crew was ordered back to New Orleans and the master was instructed to accompany them if he did not wish to become a permanent settler; at the same time orders were issued to guard against the introduction of contraband goods.[32] Tessier acted on the instructions of the governor, and in spite of the fact that the commandant-general refused this second request, he was able, through the protection of his patron, to remain in Texas for over six months.

Toward the end of December, there appeared, at Atascocito, Francisco de la Rosa, the leader of yet another party of immigrants. La Rosa was accompanied by two slaves and two servants. He had come up the Trinity river in a small boat from Culebra Island, where he had left the ship in which he had brought his belongings and his family, consisting of nineteen persons. He declared that he had come with the intention of settling at Béxar, and that he had brought with him all the necessary documents signed by José

---

[31]Cordero to M. de Salcedo, December 1, 1809.
[32]M. de Salcedo to Commandant of Atascocito, December 5, 1808.

The Opening of Texas to Foreign Settlement 137

Vidal, Vice-Consul at New Orleans.[33] The subsequent history of this case—which is a type of many others—is peculiarly interesting, because it clearly reveals La Rosa's secret motive for coming and the commandant-general's inability to impress the local authorities with his fear of contraband traders and foreign spies. Upon arriving at Atascocito, La Rosa described to the commandant the difficulties of bringing his vessel up the Trinity river and the dangers of leaving it at its actual location. He therefore begged to be allowed to continue his journey at once to the harbor of Matagorda. Fully convinced by these arguments, the commandant readily gave the desired permission; while Cordero instructed him to locate at Villa Salcedo or at San Marcos.[34] Naturally, the commandant-general objected to this free and easy mode of procedure, pointing out that La Rosa was evidently a contraband trader, that he must have evaded the United States authorities at New Orleans, since all ports in that country were closed by the embargo, or that he really must have come from some other port than the one named. Consequently he issued orders for the intruder's detention until his case should be decided by the king. But it was some time before the local authorities had any opportunity for carrying out these instructions; for La Rosa took his own good time in going from Culebra Island to his ostensible destination. Indeed, it was over two months before he was seen again in Texas. Finally, he reappeared at Atascocito with a story of a terrible storm which had blown him all the way to Campeche and of his final entry into Bahía de San Bernardo where he had been compelled to leave his vessel and to come to Atascocito in search of "food for his starving people." The commandant, seemingly oblivious of the fact that La Rosa could easily have been engaged in contraband trade during this long interval, at once permitted him to depart on another trip to seek the port of Matagorda. At

---

[33]*Diligencias.* December 28, 1808, and Cruellar to Cordero, December 28, 1808.
[34]Cordero to M. de Salcedo, January 19, 1809.

last, on April 8, he actually entered the harbor and presented the papers he had secured in New Orleans for the purpose of justifying himself in bringing goods expressly forbidden by law. These voluminous documents—which show him to have been a man of wealth, owning considerable property and a large number of slaves—were in legal form, but quite evidently had been prepared for the purpose of deceiving the Spanish officials; for Vidal, Spanish Consul at New Orleans, had granted him permission to bring three thousand *pesos*' worth of goods under the pretext that money could not be secured in New Orleans and that these supplies therefore were necessary for subsistence while awaiting permission for settlement.[35] In spite of all the suspicious circustances, the judge to whom the commandant-general submitted the case rendered a favorable opinion, ruling that La Rosa was eligible as a settler under the decree of September 24, 1803, since he was a Spanish vassal, showed a commendable intention of settling upon Spanish territory—although he had sufficient means to live anywhere he might desire—and had proved his good faith by bringing his family, whom had he concealed any hostile purpose in his heart, he would have left in a safe refuge. The judge called especial attention to the great advantages which would come to Spanish dominions if others of this class could be induced to immigrate, industry would awaken, commerce would flourish, and immense regions, now deserted, would become fruitful—all of which would be conducive to the spread of religion, the good of the country, the happiness of the people and the glory of the nation. Nevertheless, as a precautionary measure, the judge stipulated that La Rosa and his family should take the oath, that they had come with honest intentions, that they would be faithful vassals of the king, that they would submit to the local authorities, and that they would endeavor to live peaceably with their fellowmen. The commandant-general thereupon issued orders for their reception; but, still suspicious,

---

[35]Vidal to Zerbán, October 24, 1807, in *A. G. I. S.* Guad., 104–2–9, March 30, 1806–November 7, 1809.

stipulated that they should be located in Coahuila or Nueva Viscaya, and that they should promise to give information to the government of all persons whom they might suspect of disloyalty. He ordered that La Rosa's personal property be returned, the remainder of his possessions sold at auction, and the proceeds held until the final decision of the case. In the meantime La Rosa had appealed to the sympathies of the local authorities. He protested that he was not a condemned criminal, nor even a suspicious character— but a faithful Spanish vassal. He complained that he was actually exposed to death by starvation because of the detention of his goods, whereas he should have been rewarded for his acceptance of the invitation of the king to settle in his dominions. He felt particular resentment because he had gone through every legal formality necessary for the transportation of supplies for the purpose of avoiding this very calamity. The local authorities immediately took steps to release his property, claiming that he had rendered great assistance in making the observations necessary for opening the port of Matagorda and in securing the supplies essential to the development and defense of the country. As a result, the commandant-general was powerless to secure the execution of his precautionary measures and had to content himself with sending to Spain a protest against their arbitrary action. He said that everything indicated that La Rosa was a contraband trader, and that it was even possible that he had been sent as a spy by the United States to secure information in regard to the coast and navigable rivers of Texas.[36] While these suspicious characters, who were evidently contraband traders, and who might easily have been foreign spies, were using every exertion to gain entry into Texas, other immigrants were trying just as hard to escape from the province—possibly for the purpose of giving information to the enemy.

Suspicious action of settlers.—Discontent among the immigrants who had been transferred from Atascocito to Villa

---

[36]Documents in *A. G. I. S.* Guad., 104–2–9, November 21, 1798– September 5, 1809.

Salcedo continued; and some of them soon asked to be allowed to return to Louisiana. Part of them claimed that they desired to go for property left there at the time of immigration,[37] even though they knew that existing regulations forbade this step. Among those refused permission to return were Santiago Fear and Juan Debis. The latter declared that his stay in Texas had been exceedingly unpleasant, due to the continued illness of his wife and his inability to secure the necessities of life for his family.[38] The lack of permission did not deter some of the discontented ones from carrying out their plans for returning to Louisiana. A certain Salome Duxen procured a passport to Atascocito to secure property he claimed to have left there, and, forthwith, took *French leave* for Louisiana, accompanied by his wife and child and by his brother's family. To avoid a repetition of this occurrence, orders were given that, in the future, passports should not be issued save in rare cases and then that no person should be allowed to accompany the bearer.[39] It was also decided that should any be guilty of going to Louisiana without permisison and later return asking for forgiveness, they were to be rejected as settlers unless especially recommended for clemency by the commandant-general.[40] So when Miguel Ortís made a trip from Villa Salcedo to New Orleans without permission, he was arrested upon his return to Nacogdoches and ordered back to his home under guard.[41] However, this probably worked no hardship on him as he had already been to New Orleans and was merely on his way back home. If, as was frequently done, he had gone to New Orleans to give information to the enemies of Spain, he had already had all the opportunity he needed. It is certain that knowledge of

---

[37]N. Salcedo to Cordero, July 12, 1808.
[38]M. de Salcedo to Cordero, June 14, and July 12, 1808. Petition with M. de Salcedo to Cordero, January 19, 1809, and Cordero to M. de Salcedo, March 6, 1809.
[39]M. de Salcedo to the Commandant of Trinidad, December 5, 1808.
[40]Cordero to M. de Salcedo, December 23, 1808.
[41]Cordero to Commandant of Nacogdoches, April 18, 1808.

conditions in Texas was common in Louisiana. Indeed, Clouet wrote Cordero that all that went on in Texas was common knowledge in New Orleans and that doubtless this information had been given by those who had secured entry into Texas under pretense of being Spanish vassals.[42] Not all disloyal persons tried to return to Louisiana. Some, desiring to reap all the benefits conferred upon settlers, remained in Texas and carried on their private plans in a secret manner. For instance, Juan Dribread, in writing to his wife, expressed the desire to avoid a journey back to Cape Girardeau, Missouri, to bring his family out to Texas because he did not wish to lose the benefits of the probable rise in value of his lands.[43] Again, Juan Magee wrote exultingly to a brother at Coteilla, Louisiana, that he and another brother, José, held two pieces of land upon the Trinity which were well stocked with horses and cattle, and that "thanks to God" they were making something in the commercial line. He reported, too, that he had bought various other places which he expected soon to increase in value.[44]

Two *quadernos* in the Béxar Archives reveal the character of the commerce in which Magee was engaged. *Quaderno* number 1 is an account book, the first few items of which are as follows:

May 1st—Henry Poston [Genere Pon]................Mescal 1 peso
May 2nd—Wm. Burgess [Burxer]..................Taffia 4 "
May 3rd—Buges ....Mescal 4 "
May 4th—Patterson ....Mescal 4 "
May 4th—Patterson ....Mescal 4 "
       Patterson ....Taffia 4 "

These items are typical of the whole books of accounts, and strong drinks were almost the sole articles of merchandise in demand. Indeed, it was only on rare occasions that

---

[42]Clouet to Cordero, June 22, 1808.

[43]October 2, 1808. Letter No. 4 in bound volume of letters, October 2, 1808–April 18, 1810.

[44]October 2, 1808. *Ibid.*

Magee's customers did without their accustomed drinks to buy a small piece of calico, a few sticks of "pelloncey," or a pair of shoes. Even Magee's wife, a sister to the toper William Burxer named in the above account, purchased considerable amounts of liquor. But she was far outdone by a certain, as yet unidentified lady of the name of "Molly Ann."[45] Another *quaderno* contains a number of letters from Magee to his wife which show that he secured[46] considerable quantities of sugar and flour at Béxar, and a few dry goods at Natchitoches for his customers at Villa Salcedo.

Another settler, Miguel Quinn, in writing to a lawyer of St. Louis, stated that he had all his goods loaded on horses ready for a trip to St. Louis, but that he had been unable to depart because of the risk of discovery. He claimed that he had been three hundred leagues farther into the interior and that he had done some trading; but he declared that a trader could not always realize upon his goods because the market was too uncertain. He asked for information as to the price of horses at St. Louis, as he thought of carrying a drove to that place if the settlement of business matters with Mr. Hoistin [Austin?] at La Mina[?] demanded a trip to that region. He desired also to know if the Americans were really planning to press their claims to the Rio Grande and, if not, just where they did intend to stop so that he might buy lands in good locations in case it were known for certain that they would come into Texas.[47]

[45]*Quaderno* No. 1, Juan Megue, January 1, 1810.
[46]*Quaderno* No. 2, May 5, 1810.
[47]Quinn to Beulitt, October 1, 1808, Letter No. 37 in Letter-Book, October 1, 1808–October 2, 1810. This letter is peculiarly interesting since it shows a natural channel through which, at a very early date, the Austins could have gained information in regard to Texas. In writing to James Bryan, in 1816, Moses Austin said: "Judge Bullett has arrived from St. Louis." Austin to Bryan, January 22, 1816, A. P. Whether this judge was identical with the lawyer Beulitt, of St. Louis, cannot be proved, but the inference is strong. It is known that as early as 1813 Moses Austin's mind had turned to Texas as a possible field in which to recoup his losses in the mines of Missouri. He expressed the opinion that, after due consideration, he thought that

Defense of local authorities.—The authorities in Texas who were really responsible for the presence of these settlers were vigorous in their defense of their *protégés*. For instance, when the bishop of Nuevo León charged that the immigrants in Texas were not up to the standard in religious matters, the commandant-general naturally demanded an immediate explanation. Thereupon Cordero defended the accused against the charges of immorality, a propensity for contraband trade, and a lack of fidelity to the king; and maintained that the instructions concerning the admission of foreigners had been strictly adhered to, and that no rumors of disorder had reached his ears. He offered to submit evidence proving that he had received only those coming under the prescribed regulations. He repelled the insinuation that the new settlers were engaged in contraband trade and thus enabling foreigners to gain a knowledge of the province. He confessed that he always had been suspicious of Fedrico Zerbán,[48] one of the foreigners whom he had allowed to remain at Béxar, but defended this action upon the ground of necessity, claiming that Zerbán was the only physician available.[49] Cordero then gave a graphic description of the deprivations of the people and their limited trade with the Indians, and with the people of Béxar, Rio Grande, and Laredo in an effort to secure supplies and

"an adventure" to Texas would be both safe and advantageous. Austin to Bryan, January 4, 1813, *Ibid*. As early as 1819, Stephen Austin was at Natchitoches, where "his prospects were great" and where he was "in high spirits." Moses Austin to James E. B. Austin, August 12, 1819, *Ibid*. Indeed, the elder Austin may have considered removing to Texas as early as 1803; for in his petition of 1820 to the Spanish authorities at Béxar, he declared that many heads of families —he among the number—had often planned both in 1803 and subsequently, to immigrate to Texas but had been unable to do so because of their inability to dispose of their property and to introduce goods bought with the proceeds thereof and because of the opposition of the authorities of that province. Petition, December 26, 1820, *Ibid*.

[48]Zerbán had married Sara Moore, a slave owner. He had moved to New Orleans in 1790, and thence to Texas. Petition, February 10, 1802. See *ante*.

[49]For foundation for this suspicion see *ante*.

stock for the development of their settlements. He maintained that such cases of contraband trade as had been reported merely proved the vigilance of the authorities of the province. He explained, also, that the deserters and slaves at Villa Salcedo were there by special arrangement of the commandant-general, and that he was not at all responsible for their conduct.[50] The local authorities, having thus arbitrarily received objectionable applicants, stood firmly against all plans for expelling a single person.

Evasion of orders for expulsion.—But so flagrant were the offenses of certain individuals, who were not Catholics and who were guilty of represensible conduct, that the commandant-general ordered them out of the province, and warned them that they would be severely punished if they returned.[51] This was at once objected to by the immigrants affected. They claimed that they were practically a-foot because of the loss of great numbers of their stock, due to the extreme cold of the winter, and that they needed time to gather their few remaining animals which were scattered and to dispose of the small amount of "property accumulated by the sweat of their brows during their residence in Texas." Father Sosa made a plea for some of these condemned to exile, on the grounds that they had always wished to avail themselves of the teachings of the Church, but that they had not immediately reached the goal of their desires because they had to work for a living and could not perfectly understand the Spanish language. He reported, however, that they had at last become Catholics. It was also urged in behalf of one of these persons that he was particularly industrious, that he had proved his usefulness to the new settlement, and that he had shown his fidelity to the king through a peroid of twenty-five years.[52] The good father and the local authorities were unable to save all suspects, however; and Tomás Dallete, Juan Erondreque and wife

---

[50]Cordero to N. Salcedo, December 15, 1808.

[51]M. de Salcedo to the Commandant of Trinidad, February 4, and March 21, 1809.

[52]Sáenz to M. de Salcedo, February 22, 1809.

Serafina Esmiete, María Madelina Benua, and Remegio Bodro were finally expelled. Orders were soon issued for investigating the character of all other immigrants;[53] but the local authorities were able to prevent any additional expulsions.

On January 25, 1809, Governor Salcedo had offered to make a tour of inspection over the province and his proposal had at once been accepted by the commandant-general, who ordered him to prepare evidence in the case of objectionable immigrants at all settlements inspected, and to see that they were expelled from the province.[54] At the same time, he relieved Cordero of the duty of deciding upon the eligibility of applicants, keeping the matter entirely in his own hands.[55]

Summary for 1808.—During 1808 no great changes in the population of Texas had taken place owing to the conflicting views of the authorities. The commandant-general's suspicions were quite natural in view of conditions; but he was powerless to carry his point against the authorities of Texas. The plan of Cordero and his supporters to develop Texas by settlement and thus make it strong enough to resist threatened aggression was a wise one, but they were handicapped, not only by the restrictive orders of their immediate superior—which could easily be circumvented—but by the lack of funds and the want of faithful vassals essential to the plan and by the whole commercial system so persistently maintained by the supreme government. Since no special inducements for settlement were offered, no very desirable applicants appeared, and the authorities in Texas were compelled to let in many who were a drawback rather than an asset. It cannot be said that either of these policies, even though vigorously enforced, would have brought victory to the Spanish arms—for the continued advance of the Americans seems to have been inevitable;

---

[53]Sáenz to Cordero, March 2, 1809, and list of settlers, October 6, 1809, showing same number but different names.

[54]N. Salcedo to Cordero, February 13, 1809.

[55]N. Salcedo to Cordero, February 16, 1809.

but it can readily be maintained that nothing could be accomplished when both plans were frustrated. A small number of immigrants were received and the majority of them located at Villa Salcedo. The records for the year show the settlement at that place of José Manuel Lugo, a Guadalajaran, who with his wife had moved from Béxar; Francisco Lartigue, a son of Pedro Lartigue, whose entry has already been chronicled; José Juiroz, a native of Illinois, who immigrated with his wife and two children; Pedro Patterson, a carpenter; and Guillermo Burxer, who had moved from Nacogdoches.[56] By this time, however, the suspicions of the commandant-general had been so strongly aroused that he decided to put an end to all immigration from foreign countries.

---

[56]*Padron*, Appendix 11.

CHAPTER V

INSTRUCTIONS FOR CLOSING THE DOOR TO EMIGRATION FROM A FOREIGN COUNTRY, 1809

During 1809, owing to rumors of greater activity on the part of both the United States and Napoleon, the commandant-general carried his exclusion policy to its extreme; while the authorities in Texas, as was to be expected from their former attitude, not only failed to coöperate with him but even went so far as openly to defy certain of his plans. The activities of Mexico's enemies and the various steps in the contest between the commandant-general and the authorities of Texas will now be traced.

Fear of aggression by the United States and by Napoleon. Among the first warnings of the possibilities of renewed activity on the part of the United States in 1809, was that given by Valentín de Foronda, Spanish *Charge d'Affaires* at Philadelphia. On January 6, he wrote the commandant-general that a fleet was being collected at Norfolk for the purpose of transporting four thousand American soldiers to New Orleans. His suspicions were increased by the fact that he could secure from the United States government no satisfactory explanation as to the object of these warlike preparations although he surmised that the fleet was going to New Orleans to watch the movements of the English who had "signified their intention of visiting their friends, the Spaniards, at Baton Rouge." At the same time, he gave warning that rumors were afloat that troops were likewise to descend the Mississippi from Kentucky and Ohio and that Congress was planning to call out fifty thousand volunteers under Wilkinson, presumably, for use against the Spanish possessions.[1] Foronda was not alone in his suspicions; for Vicente Folch, commandant of West Florida, also gave information that the United States was making warlike

---

[1] Foronda to the Governor of the Interior Provinces, January 6, 1809.

preparations and expressed the opinion that Napoleon was encouraging this activity; while Marqués de Someruelos, Commandant of Cuba, declared that he thought it quite probable that Napoleon, who was planning to subjugate the entire world, was eager to support the plans of the United States. Someruelos, therefore, was insistent in his demands that the viceroy take immediate steps to guard Texas, Louisiana, Florida, and, indeed, the whole of New Spain. No help could be expected from the mother country owing to the fact that she was even then calling upon the colonies for aid in defeating the arch enemy in Europe.[2] Indeed, alarm was general, and both the United States and Napoleon were credited with various hostile intentions. José Vidal likewise joined in the chorus urging defense. He called attention to the temporary ascendency of the French party in the United States and wished precautionary measures taken.[3] In response to these appeals, the commandant-general and the viceroy began to outline plans for defense; but, owing to the lack of funds and the obstinacy of the local authorities, they actually accomplished little.[4]

Napoleon's usurpations in Europe and his continued employment of emissaries in the United States and Mexico certainly justified the suspicions of the Spaniards that he would undertake to secure a foothold in Texas, either by sending additional emissaries, by supporting the territorial claims of the United States,[5] or by combining these two means. The members of the supreme *junta* were much aroused, therefore, when they heard it rumored that Napoleon, having despaired of winning the Spanish vassals in America from their allegiance by ordinary methods, had

---

[2]Someruelos to Garibay, February 2, 6, and 12, 1809. *N.A.*
[3]Vidal to Garibay, February 13, 1809. *Ibid.*
[4]N. Salcedo to Bonavía, April 26, 1809, Garibay to the Commandant-General, March 17, 1809, and N. Salcedo to the Viceroy, March 25, 1809. For an idea of the limited resources at the disposal of the commandant-general, see *Carpeta* No. 2, June 12, 1804–March 14, 1809.
[5]N. Salcedo to Bonavía, June 22, 1809, and account of Spanish uprisings against French domination, May 10, 1809.

determined to send the deposed king and queen to America for the purpose of creating strife, under cover of which he intended to secure control. The *junta*, thereupon, issued orders to prevent the landing of the king and queen or their representatives at any Spanish American port.[6]

A new defender for Texas.—Indeed, so great was the uneasiness that the *junta* decided to send Bernardo Bonavía, the governor of Durango, to Texas to assist in executing the orders for the arrest of all French emissaries entering the Spanish dominions, so that all intrigues in the United States might be prevented.[7] Cordero was instructed to remain in Texas long enough to give the new second in command the benefit of his advice and then to return to Coahuila where he was badly needed.[8] Cordero, however, remained in Texas several months and continued his efforts to develop the province. As soon as his successor reached Texas, he, too, became an ardent adherent of the progressive party. As a result, the schism between the general and the local authorities continued.

Conservative plans of the commandant-general.—Among the most interesting papers relating to the colonization situation at this time is a letter from the commandant-general to Bonavía, ordering him to obtain from certain documents cited and from the three governors on the ground, all possible information as to the population of Texas, its boundaries and its Indian tribes, and to make suggestions for further defensive measures against the

---

[6]The Junta to Salcedo, March 1, 1809, in Salcedo to Bonavía, June 22, 1809. Appendix 16.

[7]N. Salcedo to the Governor of Texas, March 24, 1809. Orders for Bonavía's transfer to Texas had been issued two years previous but to no avail. Bonavía to Cornel, May 31, 1809. Bonavía had been named as governor of Texas in 1788 but apparently did not serve. For his connection with the plan of Charles III for the inauguration of reforms in the commercial system of Mexico, see Priestley, *José de Gálvez*, 32–37 and 312–390, and *A. G. I. S.*, Guad. 103–4–7, March 27, 1790–July 18, 1795.

[8]N. Salcedo to Cordero, March 20, 1809, and N. Salcedo to Bonavía, March 24, 1809.

threatened dangers. The commandant general's plan already included the defense of the frontier and the "almost impenetrable waste" in that region, and the strengthening of Villa Salcedo as a base from which to send out scouting parties and other troops necessary for the defense of the frontier. He also wished to place small detachments on the San Marcos and the Colorado rivers for the purpose of keeping open communication with the new *villa* and facilitating the transportation of supplies. He expected to fortify Béxar as a final rallying point in case of invasion, to strengthen Bahía, to stir the Indians of the coast, to prevent the landing of invaders, to place troops on the coast, and to select a port for landing supplies from Vera Cruz and other points so that the disadvantages of land transportation might be avoided. He did not wish, however, to fortify the port or to settle it until necessity might demand. That this scheme involved no new features and left out of account any additional settlement in Texas will be noted. In fact, he even contemplated abandoning Nacogdoches altogether. Among the reasons assigned for this were that the place could not be fortified adequately; that sickness was prevalent there both among the soldiers and the settlers; that the region thereabouts offered no means of subsistence; that some of the citizens were disloyal and ready to sell out to the highest bidder; and that the place would serve as an aid to the enemy in case of invasion. In view of the necessity for holding the friendship of the Indians in that region, he wished to take no action until one or two other points on the frontier could be selected as places of residence for Indian traders. In the meantime, existing orders prohibiting settlement at Atascocito were to be enforced.[9]

He also, at this time, evinced a growing hostility to foreign immigrants. In a letter written on April 2 he instructed the governor to enforce previous orders for the transfer of foreigners from Béxar to Villa Salcedo, and drew attention to the fact that the rich lands at the capital

---

[9]N. Salcedo to Bonavía, March 24, 1809.

had been reserved by the king for more meritorious, useful, and loyal settlers. The immigrants, he said, had been brought into Texas for the benefit of the country and not for their own profit, and they, therefore, should not expect to locate in settlements previously founded or upon lands already under cultivation.[10] This action had the effect of massing all foreigners on the Trinity river, in spite of his original intention to permit no aliens to locate at a distance from the Spanish settlements. Bastrop and Boone were probably the only persons already mentioned who were excepted from this sweeping order. In addition, Lorenzo Reveque, who was a very old man; Carlos Morasen, who served as an interpreter; José Rosi, who had opened a pottery factory, and Pedro Longueville, who had lived at Béxar for many years, were likewise permitted to remain.[11] There is no evidence to show how any of these foreigners reached Béxar, save in the case of Pedro Longueville who was a native of Bordeaux. He had come into Texas with Nolan, reaching the province in 1797. Later he visited Béxar in the capacity of a servant to Nolan. On account of not receiving any pay for his services he was compelled to remain at that point and to work for his living. After being cleared of the charge of complicity in Nolan's projects, he located permanently with the permission of the commandant-general.[12]

The commandant-general now began to regard the American deserter with suspicion, declaring it quite probable that the previous policy of the government in granting asylum to such persons was responsible for the appearance of a great number of criminals, who were to be feared because of their immorality. Such applicants were to be rejected in the future unless their good character could be

---

[10]N. Salcedo to the Governor of Texas, April 2, 1809.
[11]N. Salcedo to the Governor of Texas, April 18, 1809.
[12]Petition of Longueville with orders for gathering the necessary information, August 22, 1804, and the desired information, November 27, 1804.

established by reliable evidence.[13] Although the governor lost no time in transmitting these instructions to his subordinates,[14] it is quite evident that he was not in sympathy with the policy, believing, indeed, that a strict enforcement of the provisions of the law requiring all foreigners entering Texas to present properly authenticated passports would obviate all danger.

Progressive plans of authorities in Texas.—Bonavía reached Béxar on April 17; and, two days later, he called upon the other governors located at that point for their opinions upon the best means of developing and defending Texas. In response, each prepared a statement showing opposition to the conservative plans of the commandant-general.[15]

Cordero's plans.—Cordero, the original champion of colonization for Texas, believed that the protection of the whole Spanish dominions in America depended upon the security of Texas. He wished to organize a body of provincial cavalry and to maintain a sufficient mobile force on the frontier to inspire respect, even though actual invasion by the United States should not be attempted. Such troops would be sufficient to check any sudden hostilities which might be undertaken until reinforcements could be hurried to the rescue. He favored the fortification and settlement of the region about Nacogdoches, declaring that *population was the one thing needed to make the frontier respected.* He insisted that the lack of settlers in Texas and the abandonment of territory on the frontier had already led the Americans to assert a claim as far eastward as the Sabine and that withdrawal from Nacogdoches would inevitably encourage them to lay claim to the region between the Sabine and the Rio Grande. He believed that the Americans would have already penetrated into the region inhabited solely by Indian tribes if the settlement at Bayou Pierre had not been maintained. He, therefore, favored the location of additional

---

[13]N. Salcedo to Bonavía, May 12, 1809.
[14]M. de Salcedo to Bonavía, June 5, 1809.
[15]Report of *Junta de Guerra*, April 19–25, 1809.

settlers at Nacogdoches, on the rivers between the frontier and Béxar, and even on the coast. He suggested that the disease and suffering of the troops at Nacogdoches, so often referred to, could be avoided by a little foresight. He urged the opening of the port of Bahía de San Bernardo, which had been provided for three years before, expressing the belief that this measure would not only aid in the defense of Texas but would contribute to the development of all the Interior Provinces. He also favored the location of a general trading house at Béxar with sub-stations at Bayou Pierre and at Nacogdoches or Villa Salcedo so that the Americans could not so easily bribe the Indians to attack the Spaniards. His final recommendation was that the military commandant of Texas should be commander, likewise, of the Eastern Interior Provinces with the same powers as those formerly delegated to Pedro Grimarest.[16] While forming these views, Cordero had been taking steps to secure the much desired immigrants from the interior. This is shown by a letter from Father Puelles, of Zacatecas, who had lived at Nacogdoches for a long time and who was, therefore, familiar with the colonization plans for Texas. In March, 1809, he wrote saying that he had spread abroad the report of Cordero's accomplishments, his military ability, and his services to the government. He had heard general expressions of admiration and understood that many desired to enlist under Cordero's command. More than one hundred families, amounting to more than fifteen hundred persons, wished to secure transportation to Texas by enlisting for military service and then to settle there. Among the prospective colonists were several persons of unusual attainments. Puelles asserted that all classes, priests and parishioners, rich and poor, were desirous of serving with Cordero under the impression that Texas had been greatly benefited by his management of its affairs.[17]

Manuel de Salcedo's opinion.—Governor Salcedo's opinion of the best means for the defense of Texas was rendered

---

[16]Cordero to Bonavía, April 23, 1809.
[17]Puelles to Cordero, March 8, 1809.

on April 24. He believed that the situation was more critical than at any other time since the retrocession of Louisiana, because of the extensive claims to territory made by the Americans and their trade with the Indians. He insisted that it had not been possible to prevent encroachments because of the small number of settlers and soldiers in the province.[18] He praised the character of the settlers very highly, but explained that their enemies, the Americans, were resourceful, strong, agile, and brave, and, therefore, to be feared. He discussed, at length, the ease with which the foe could gain entry into the Spanish dominions, citing instances in which persons had penetrated into Texas from New Madrid, Natchez, and other points without being caught by the Spaniards. But he did not regard the situation as hopelessly bad and suggested plans for defense. He counted upon the loyalty of the Spaniards, their superior horses and horsemanship, their knowledge of the country, the friendship of the Indians and of the people of Lower Louisiana. He disapproved the abandonment of any territory, believing, like Cordero, that such a step would inevitably lead to new aggression on the part of the Americans. On the contrary, he desired to guard both the frontier and the coast, and believed a civil settlement necessary to support each garrison. In this connection, he ventured the assertion that even the detachment stationed at Atascocito needed a certain number of industrious settlers located in the vicinity in order that it might be kept supplied with meat, corn, and beans. He objected to the location of Villa Salcedo, preferring a spot nearer Béxar, if a situation suitable for the establishment of a large settlement could be found. Doubting the practicability of finding such a place, however, he favored strengthening the *villa*, at its existing location so that from that point Nacogdoches could be supplied, scouting parties could be sent out as needed, Indian tribes could be visited and held to their allegiance, and a

---

[18]He estimated the population at eight thousand persons, not counting the one thousand and sixty-nine soldiers. He must have included the Indians in his estimate.

rallying point could be prepared in case the troops at Nacogdoches should be defeated by an invading army. Even if an invasion were not to be feared, he felt the need for settling the province for the cultivation of its fertile lands. For this reason, he, like Cordero, favored the opening of a port on the coast.[19]

Herrera's opinion.—Herrera expressed his views on April 25. He, too, wished the force in Texas enlarged and the military commandant of Texas authorized to exercise the functions which had been delegated to Grimarest as commandant-general of the Eastern Interior Provinces. He, too, urged the opening of a port for the introduction of supplies for the army and the exportation of the products of the country. He strongly favored the development of Nacogdoches, because of its fertility and its strategic position, and suggested that certain changes be made to better sanitary conditions there. He not only denied the charge that the people of that region were lacking in fidelity to the crown, but declared that some of them had served the king with marked devotion. He wished to maintain the post at Nacogdoches and the settlement at Bayou Pierre, since abandonment would be a sign of weakness and consequently would serve as an incentive to further aggressions from the United States. He made no attempt to deal with the Indian situation, holding that Cordero's thirty-two years of service on the frontier fitted him to speak with greater authority; but he did wish a respectable force maintained in Texas to prevent the introduction of exploring and trading parties from the United States, even though actual war should not be declared by that country.[20]

Bonavía's opinion.—On April 26, Bonavía delivered his own opinion in regard to the need of defending Texas against further aggression. He discussed the gravity of

---

[19]M. de Salcedo to Bonavía, April 24, 1809.

[20]Herrera to Bonavía, April 25, 1809. For description of the Indians of Texas, see *Noticia de las Naciones en la Provincia de Texas que me dio, Don Samuel Davenport*, enclosed in M. de Salcedo to Bonavía, April 24, 1809.

the situation, dwelling particularly upon his own lack of men and means, upon the aggressive spirit of the Americans, and upon the consequent necessity for establishing a strong defense for Texas, *"the key to the Spanish dominions of America."* Then, after discussing some of the suggestions offered by the commandant-general in his letter of March 24, he paid tribute to the natural ability of those who had already been in charge but who, for lack of money and authority, had been unable to cope with the distressing situation. He acknowledged his own ignorance in regard to conditions and his own helplessness in case the necessary changes should not be made. He begged not to be made a scapegoat and urged that active preparations for defense be pushed while the Americans were still inactive. What seemed to surprise him most of all was that no knowledge of the wise measures for free commerce inaugurated under the liberal government of Charles III had reached the province and that its situation so near the sea and its possession of so many navigable rivers had not tempted any one to make an accurate examination of its harbors. He ended his tirade against the existing system by saying that he was dumbfounded that the province should be in so miserable a condition when it possessed every advantage calculated to make it the most prosperous region in Spanish America. Therefore, he did not hesitate to urge the absolute necessity of conferring extraordinary powers upon a commander to be named for the Eastern Interior Provinces, thus enabling him to deal directly with the Mexican minister to the United States, the president and congress of the United States, the governor of Havana, the viceroy of Mexico, the king of Spain, and, indeed, any other person whom the necessity of the case might demand. He maintained that the idea that the unsettled regions of Texas had served as a defense for the Spanish Dominions a mistaken one that had caused great trouble. He thought that those who supported this theory either did not understand the situation, or did not make any distinction between *uninhabited* and *uninhabitable* territory. The lands along the

frontier, on account of their fertility and of the neglect of
the Spaniards to occupy them—so long as the boundaries
were not definitely known—were alluring to foreign nations; and he believed that, if the possessors relaxed their
vigilance, the enemy would come in and occupy them. So
he decided that settlement by the Spaniards was the only
solution of the problem.[21] His final recommendation was to
place Texas in a state of defense and thus to hold what belonged to Spain until the limits could be marked.[22]

So convinced was he of the importance of this plan that
he wrote directly to the secretary of war in Spain as follows:

> I have the satisfaction of knowing that we who are in Texas
> are all in accord touching the plans for the defense of this
> province, although we are not in accord with the commandant-general, who is inclined to abandon certain points and to suspect
> the inhabitants [of these places] in spite of the fact that they
> have proved their fidelity. This is not the only point on which
> we are divided, for [I know] from things I have seen that he
> makes difficult and embarrassing the entry of vassals from beyond the border who desire to settle, and that he likewise [opposes] the formation of settlements when both objects should
> be pushed by all possible means, admitting all who desire to
> enter so long as there is no foundation for suspecting them;
> and, even though some should commit suspicious acts, the vigilance and vigor of the government should be directed toward
> [finding] a convenient remedy. According to my opinion, facilitating communication by sea and land and permitting free commerce would be the best means of increasing the population,
> for we must leave out of consideration the introduction at government expense of families, who would depopulate the place
> from whence they came, and, yet, would not permanently settle
> the points to which they were directed, bringing only unhappiness, at a great cost, as has been sufficiently shown by the past
> experience of our nation. *Wherever the people find prosperity,*
> *protection, and security, there they will go without being called.*
> Returning to the question of this province, I consider the plan
> you propose as sufficient, because the weak constitution of the
> United States does not make it dangerous as a conqueror but as

---

[21]Bonavía to the Commandant-General, April 26, 1809.
[22]N. Salcedo to Bonavía, June 25, 1909.

a greedy, aggressive knave who should be watched and held back beyoned the frontier.

It is an urgent and absolute necessity that the commandant of these Eastern Interior Provinces be independent. If not, you will lose time as [you have done] heretofore. I say this and repeat it because of its importance, in my opinion, and without any personal motives, for I am not trying to get anything. If I had been commandant-general of the Interior Provinces, I would have delegated the command of these [Eastern Provinces] by giving all possible authority to Colonel Antonio Cordero, who, to his expert knowledge of all questions, adds the accomplishments of the military profession and the happy faculty and ability of getting along with the Indians, as is proved by the tranquility enjoyed in his district of Coahuila, but not in this government with whose command he has been likewise charged.[23]

A study of these opinions shows that all those on the ground were unanimously in favor of encouraging colonization in Texas. But when acknowledging receipt of all these carefully prepared opinions, the commandant-general merely instructed Bonavía to make no changes whatsoever in the management of affairs until the viceroy had considered conditions carefully.[24] Therefore, the local authorities were driven to greater evasions to carry forward their cherished plans.

Additional recommendations of governor.—Not content with his previous presentation of the matter, Governor Salcedo, a few weeks later, prepared another paper upon the administration of affairs in Texas. In this, he insisted upon the advisability of at once fixing the boundary line between Spain and the United States and the absolute necessity for colonizing Texas. He favored the plan of securing immigrants from Louisiana, though urging the wisdom of excluding foreigners and suspicious characters and contraband traders. He reviewed the progress of the settlements provided for on the principal rivers of Texas and condemned the change of plans which had forced immigrants desiring to locate at Atascocito to move on to Villa Salcedo. He wished to place settlements on the Frio, the Nueces, or the

---

[23]Bonavía to Cornel, May 31, 1809.
[24]N. Salcedo to Bonavía, May 13, 1809.

Arroyo de San Miguel, as a means of facilitating communication with the provinces of Coahuila and Nueva Santander, and spoke of the attempt made to form a settlement on the Nueces in 1806 by immigrants from Nueva Santander. He even urged the location of settlements at Tortuga and at Palo Alto in the region occupied by the Tankawas and on the headwaters of the Colorado de los Tancahues. He claimed that these settlements would *aid in opening communication with New Mexico* and in stimulating the commerce with the Indian tribes. He believed that the cost of transporting colonists at the expense of the crown would be exceedingly high and that, perhaps, more favorable results would be secured by simply admitting those who might volunteer to come in, especially if they were allowed to carry on commerce through Bahía de San Bernardo. He made a strong plea for the admission of Louisianians, declaring that this step alone would carry out the wishes of the king to aid his former vassals of that region, and would, moreover, furnish a supply of good settlers for Texas. He believed the Louisianians would most surely come seeking the protection of the Spanish flag, if they were permitted to select locations suited to their needs. He thought that if they were permitted to do this, suspicious characters without definite destinations and obligations would no longer apply for admission, but that, on the contrary, all immigrants would bring their possessions and settle under the prescribed conditions, as their happiness would be assured by being located among people of their own kind. He urged the opening of the Port of Matagorda so that settlers could secure what they needed at reasonable prices and export the products of their toil. In conclusion, he enumerated the various natural attractions of Texas, its healthful climate, fertile lands, beautiful mountains and plains, convenient harbors—especially that of Bahía de San Bernardo—navigable streams, mineral wealth, and animal life, and predicted a splendid future for the province if colonization were continued.[25]

---

[25][M. de Salcedo] to [N. Salcedo], May 7, 1809.

Bonavía's supplementary suggestions.—As was to be expected, Bonavía ably seconded Governor Salcedo's efforts. In pursuance of his development plans he called another *junta*, this time, to consider the question of development since it was so intimately connected with the question of security for which he had been made especially responsible. At this meeting, held on June 19, he explained that the soldiers simply could not live in Texas unless there were sufficient settlers in the country to furnish them with adequate supplies. He maintained that agriculture, commerce, and the arts could not flourish without protection and that, if this were offered, settlers would come without the government being put to the trouble of seeking them or to the expense of paying for their transportation after they had been found. The first step he advised, then, was to protect those desiring to immigrate, after proper precautions had been taken to see that they would make desirable citizens. He also proposed to improve Béxar, to make communication easy between that place and other portions of the province[26] to permit the location of immigrants already in or yet to come in such unsettled portions of the country as they might prefer. Since settlements were the prime object it would be highly impolitic to frustrate the main purpose for so insignificant a detail as the selection of a location. The next and most important step he proposed was free communication by sea. If this were permitted, the regions near ports would be soon settled. He also desired certain changes calculated to carry out the real intent of the laws made in the regulations for the information of settlements. He, therefore, offered for approval the immigration regulations he had drawn up for the consideration of the commandant-general. The *junta* at once approved them and made several additional suggestions for furthering the ends discussed. One

---

[26]To secure this end, Bonavía desired to use the most direct road between Béxar and Monclova. This was the La Pita road opened by Cordero in 1805. He therefore gave instructions for carrying forward the work of establishing the *villa* of Nueva Jáen, begun in 1805, suggesting that the site be changed in case it be deemed desirable, Bonavía to Ugarte, May 29, 1809. See map, pp. 101–102.

of them was that certain families from the Rio Grande who had expressed a desire to immigrate at their own expense should be assigned lands at Mission San Francísco de Espada. As an inducement, the first fifty were to be granted their *suertes* absolutely free, while those coming later were to be charged a nominal sum. The *junta*, likewise, wished the government to appropriate money to assist all Louisiana immigrants in locating.[27] These regulations were exceedingly liberal, for, while all immigrants were to be required to prove themselves Spanish vassals of good character and adherents of the Catholic Church, practically all the prohibitions as to the introduction of goods were removed.[28] Bonavía transmitted his regulations to the commandant-general, claiming that his sole consideration was for the development of the province by attracting desirable citizens and preventing the entry of objectionable characters.[29] He hoped that immigration would be stimulated by gaining the confidence of the Spanish vassals of Louisiana and that unnecessary delay, expense, and inconvenience in the transportation of all good vassals of the king would be avoided.[30] But all these carefully worked out plans were doomed to failure, for the commandant-general's suspicions had only increased with the passage of time.

Order for prevention of immigration across the Texas-Louisiana line.—Within a week from the transmission of Bonavía's immigration regulations, the commandant-general had ordered all immigration into Texas from Louisiana stopped for fear that Napoleon might introduce emissaries in the guise of settlers.[31] Naturally, therefore, he rejected Bonavía's suggestion, declaring that the immigrants already

---
[27]Minutes of *Junta* in *A. G. I. S.* Guad., 104–2–25, June 19, 1809–June 28, 1809.
[28]See Appendix 17.
[29]Bonavía to Saabedra, June 28, 1809.
[30]Bonavía to the Commandant-General, June 14, 1809.
[31]N. Salcedo to Bonavía, June 22, 1809, see Appendix 17. For Cordero's defense against the charge of the lack of vigilance in guarding against the entry of French agents, see Cordero to N. Salcedo, March 12, 1809.

admitted had deceived the government as to their intentions and had failed to keep their promises to present proper documents. Moreover, conditions, said he, had so changed that it had become necessary to take this step even though the immigrants had proved themselves worthy of trust.[32] He was not alone in his belief, for the supreme *junta* became alarmed and issued orders to the captain-general of the Interior Provinces to place their respective frontiers in a respectable state of defense and to guard especially against any French intrigues in Louisiana, where a number of Napoleon's agents, certain American adventurers, and "a dangerous Spanish subject" were located. Plans were even considered for calling upon England for aid in forcing the United States to give an explanation of the proposed increase of troops.[33]

It is not to be thought for a moment that the authorities in Texas meekly acquiesced in the commandant-general's decision to close the door to immigrants from Louisiana. Each party had shown too much tenacity for this to be possible. But the question of immigration was not the only one upon which there was a difference of opinion. Before taking up the continued efforts of the local authorities to defeat the orders of their superior, it may be well to give an idea of the character of the immigrants actually entering Texas at this time and to discuss certain other differences on closely related questions.

Character of immigrants.—Although the authorities in Texas stood together in their defense of the immigrants who had been received, there is much to support the belief that the commandant-general was justified in thinking that many objectionable characters had really secured entry. One of his most frequent complaints was that of contraband trade. Among those falling under his suspicion several may be mentioned. Francisco Bermúdez, who had lived in New Orleans and who had later located at Monclova, asked to be

---

[32]N. Salcedo to Bonavía, July 10, 1809.

[33]N. Salcedo to Bonavía, June 27, 1809, and N. Salcedo to the Governor of Texas, November 7, 1809.

The Opening of Texas to Foreign Settlement 163

allowed to settle in Texas, but was refused because his conduct had been suspicious, and because he was believed still to be engaged in contraband trade.[34]

Francisco de la Rosa was apparently moved by a guilty conscience to explain some of the most glaring inconsistencies of his own acts by claiming that he had determined to immigrate to Texas as soon as he learned of the sale of Louisiana to the United States, but that he had been unable to settle up his business immediately. He, therefore, had not actually set sail for the port of Matagorda until December, 1808, and had been unable to reach his goal before April, 1809. He claimed that this delay, which had damaged his goods, was his sole reason for presenting the request that he be allowed to dispose of some of them. The local authorities seemed quite convinced of his innocence, and, instead of expelling him as a contraband trader, sent him to Vera Cruz to secure money and to make arrangements for the formal opening of the port of Matagorda. The commandant-general offered his customary protest, producing evidence to show that, whereas La Rosa claimed to have brought to Texas three thousand *pesos* in goods and to have carried only ballast on his trip to Vera Cruz, he had really carried more than nineteen thousand *pesos* worth of contraband goods; the greater part of these he had sold to the soldiers of Texas at a lower price than that prevailing at Saltillo and the remainder he had carried with him to Vera Cruz with the intention of disposing of them along the coast or on the Rio Grande where he had operated prior to his appearance as an immigrant.[35] His subsequent plans however came to naught as he lost his life in a storm encountered on the return voyage.

Miguel Larrua, who was probably La Rosa's brother-in-law, succeeded in arousing considerable excitement even in Texas by an authorized voyage along the coast from Louisiana to Matagorda. He had been engaged by the local

---

[34][Bonavía] to M. de Salcedo, May 31, 1809. See also N. Salcedo to the Governor of Texas, June 25, 1809.

[35]Documents in *A. G. I. S.* Guad., 104–2–9, March 30, 1806–November 7, 1809, and *Ibid.*, September 12, 1809–December 12, 1811.

authorities to make an examination of the proposed port of Matagorda.[36] But when they learned that he had introduced goods they ordered him to show all his plans and maps. He insisted, however, that he had nothing save a diary of the journey which he had already delivered to Cordero.[37] In spite of these suspicious circumstances, they finally received him as a settler on condition that he should locate with his family in Coahuila or Nueva Viscaya, and that they should all take oath that they had come with honest motives, that they would be faithful vassals of the king, observe the laws of the country, obey the constituted authorities, live in peace with their neighbors, and give information of any suspicious characters within their knowledge.[38] This permission was granted in spite of the fact that Larrua was not a model citizen.[39]

Every one seemed aware of contraband trade among the immigrants, save those directly responsible for its prevention. The Bishop of Nuevo León informed the governor that *all* those seeking entry into Texas *had no other object than contraband trade*,[40] while the commandant-general asserted that none had come save for contraband trade, to escape their creditors, or to better their fortunes.[41] The Texan authori-

---

[36]M. de Salcedo to Bonavía, July 4, 1809. For other attempts to examine this port during 1809, see N. Salcedo to Cordero, February 7, 1809, Cordero to M. de Salcedo, February 18, 1809, Herrera to Cordero, February 18, 1809, Cordero to Cuellar, March 5, 1809, Cordero to the Commandant-General, March 5, 1809, and Herrera to Cordero, March 23, 1809.

[37]Prieto to M. de Salcedo, September 6, 1809, and M. de Salcedo to Bonavía, September 22, 1809.

[38]Prieto to M. de Salcedo, October 6, 1809.

[39]When complaining of several troublesome persons who prevented the development of the new *villa*, the commandant of Villa Salcedo claimed that Larrua had not proved himself of value. He complained, too, that Juan McFalen was not content with being merely dissatisfied himself, but went about stirring up others, Prieto to M. de Salcedo, October 6, 1809.

[40]Bishop of Nuevo León to M. de Salcedo, April 10, 1809.

[41]N. Salcedo to Bonavía, August 16, 1809.

ties seemed willfully blind to the danger of permitting the entry of suspicious persons.[42]

Even Bernardo Despallier, who had been especially trusted and honored by the Spaniards, was guilty of the same crime[43] as well as refusing to aid in draining Villa Salcedo as a precaution against an epidemic of fever and of failing to perform other duties required of citizens.[44] His ingratitude appeared the more culpable because he pretended a great zeal in attracting certain tribes of Indians to the Spaniards and applied for some position which would give him an opportunity to defend the Spanish dominions against Napoleon.[45]

Among other flagrant violators of the trade laws were: Juan McFarland, Juan Magee, Miguel Quinn, Pedro Lestigue, and Juan Davis. Indeed, it was after investigating the case of Davis and other settlers of Villa Salcedo on trial for contraband trade, that the commandant-general instructed the governor to clear the new *villa* of ojectionable characters.[46] Up to this time no adequate punishment had been fixed for such offenders. Indeed, matters had rarely gone further than a harmless investigation, although in a few cases the penalty of expulsion had been named. It must not have been considered a very severe punishment since in many cases the immigrants were already anxious to return to Louisiana, while those who did not wish to abandon the province permanently could easily return after being expelled. Pedro Cruz was one of those anxious to leave.

---

[42]The case of José Hernández furnishes still another illustration of this attitude. He presented himself, with only a certificate of baptism into the Catholic Church, asking to be allowed to enter Texas to collect a debt owed him by Bastrop; and, although it was known that he had tried to buy a vessel at Pensacola, his presence was not resented. As was to be expected, however, as soon as the commandant-general learned of the case, orders were given for his expulsion. N. Salcedo to Bonavía, July 12, 1809.

[43]Petition of Despallier, January 7, 1809, and connected documents and evidence in case, December 4, 1809, and February 15, 1812.

[44]M. de Salcedo to the Commandant on the Trinity, May 19, 1809.

[45]Despallier to the Commandant-General, January 7, 1809.

[46]N. Salcedo to M. de Salcedo, February 2 and March 6, 1809.

He asked to be allowed to move from Villa Salcedo on account of the climate, claiming that he had lost five members of his family within three years.[47] Juan Davis, fearing, perhaps, that his misdeeds had been found out, begged to be allowed to return to Louisiana, because, due to the illness of his wife which prevented him from making a living, he had been unable to build his house or cultivate his land.[48]

As an example of those who made an unauthorized voyage across the frontier and received full pardon on their return, the case of Juan Sy is interesting. He secretly departed for Baton Rouge and, upon his return, threw himself upon the mercy of the local authorities, confessing that he had gone to sell some lands and that he had not applied for a passport for the simple reason that he knew it would be refused him.[49] It is quite possible that Sy as well as others who made good their escape across the border never to return, carried information to the enemy, for Baton Rouge and New Orleans—the goal of many lawbreakers—were even at this early date hotbeds of the revolutionists.

Perhaps the most striking case of the possibility of intrigue was that of Carlos Tessier, who, in 1809, was still trying to secure permission to settle in Texas. On May 4, the local authorities granted the desired permission on condition that he would be faithful to the king and defend the Spanish possessions even at the cost of his life.[50] The commandant-general, however, disapproved of this decision, and, after carefully examining the case, insisted that Tessier did not possess the qualifications required, that he was of French or other foreign extraction, that he had not presented evidence that he had been born in Spain, and that he had not made clear the nature of the offices held in Louisiana under the Spanish government. He pointed out, also, that the applicant contradicted himself when giving his motives

---

[47]Petition, August 25, 1809.
[48]Petition, undated, with M. de Salcedo to Cordero, January 19, 1809.
[49]Examination of Sy, October 15, 1809.
[50]Certificate signed by Sáenz, Sosa, Tessier, and others, May 4, 1809.

for making a trip from Louisiana to France, and that there was no evidence to show that he had actually gone to Spain, as he claimed. In fact, the commandant-general considered the whole case a suspicious one and felt that the action of the authorities had been highly discreditable. He, therefore, ruled that the petitioner should be expelled. He also issued orders that Eugénio Marchán be sent to Vera Cruz if he had returned to Texas in the face of previous orders for his expulsion.[51] Two Americans, Ira Nash and Calvin Adams, had been ordered to leave the province because they belonged to the class prohibited from entering under royal orders. But during the consideration of their cases they had been allowed to remain at Nacogdoches, from which vantage point they could easily have communicated with Spain's enemies, although orders had been issued for their arrest in case their actions seemed suspicious.[52]

It was quite easy to spread information in regard to the country as is shown by the case of a certain Santiago Claimorgan, who in 1809 traversed Texas without difficulty and returned to Islas Negras, in upper Louisiana, with maps and other materials.[53]

Differences over organization of presidial companies.—In accordance with his usual conservative policy, the commandant-general objected to Bonavía's proposal that the presidial companies of Coahuila and Texas be organized into regiments as had been the intention of Grimarest. In opposing this, he expressed the belief that under the existing system the presidial troops themselves would aid in the much desired development of the frontier establishments by settling in them after their terms of service had expired,

[51] N. Salcedo to Cordero, January 1, 1808, February 7, 1809, and N. Salcedo to Bonavía, August 16, 1809.
[52] M. de Salcedo to the Commandant of Nacogdoches, April 4, 1809.
[53] M. de Salcedo to Bonavía, September 30, 1809. The extent of Islas Negras has not yet been ascertained, but the town of Cape Girardeau, Missouri, lay within its boundary, while that of St. Louis did not. De Nava to Duque de Alcudia, November 3, 1795, in *A. G. I. S. Mex. legapo 18*, No. 5.

and by protecting them against the Indians who were still unmanageable.[54]

Governor's defense.—In answer, Manuel de Salcedo admitted that the establishment of presidial companies was the safest means of settling territory inhabited by savages, but denied that this was the best means for developing a desirable class of citizens. He felt that the presidial companies had already accomplished the object for which they had been organized and, therefore, believed that they should either be reorganized to fit them to cope with the well-drilled troops of the United States, or else that they should be placed in unsettled regions where it might be necessary to found new settlements. He insisted in this connection that the sale of Louisiana had entirely changed the aspect of affairs in Texas and that the most pressing question of the times was instant and effective defense and not the planting of settlements on the frontier. The *presidios* of Texas were such only in name, he said, since the civil authorities had superceded the military commandants, and as there were no real *presidios*, there was no longer any necessity for presidial troops.[55]

Cordero's opinion.—Drawing his conclusions from his experience on the frontier, Cordero also favored the idea of forming the presidial companies into regiments, pointing out that after a trial for thirty-two years the old system had proved to be inadequate. He explained that when the presidial troops had been first stationed along the frontier to form a buffer against the Indians, the families of the soldiers had been expected to become the sole inhabitants of the settlements established along the lines. He thought that it had probably been a wise measure to permit the soldiers to settle about the points they knew so well how to defend after their terms of service had expired. He maintained that all the benefits expected to spring from this system had already been experienced, since all *presidios* in Texas and Coahuila had become *lugares, pueblos,* or *villas,*

---

[54]N. Salcedo to Bonavía, June 27, 1809.
[55]M. de Salcedo to Bonavía, July 24, 1809.

and considered the time ripe for carrying out the royal order of May 30, 1804, providing for the reorganization of the *presidios* on the frontier and the creation of regiments instead.[56]

Herrera's views.—Herrera, too, supported the plan for forming the presidial companies into regiments, declaring that the settlements composed of such troops scarcely deserved the title of *presidios* partly because they contained such a large number of non-military settlers and partly because the civil authorities of the settlements had become entirely independent of the military commandants. He thought that the presidial companies had been organized to hold the Indians in check, and that since this result had not been accomplished, some changes were absolutely necessary if the attacks of the organized and disciplined American soldiers just across the border of Louisiana were to be repelled.[57]

Commandant-General's reply.—In spite of these arguments, the commandant-general insisted that the presence of the presidial companies would be a benefit to the province by affording the necessary protection to the settlers while engaged in agricultural pursuits and by offering a market for the products thus raised. Consequently, he opposed any reorganization of the troops so long as Texas was thinly settled and the means of communication with the interior provinces so inadequate.

Differences over disposition of deserters.—The disposition of deserters continued to be a question between the commandant-general and the Texan officials. Acting upon the advice of the *auditor de guerra*, the commandant-general soon decided that his order of May 12, for locating deserters at Béxar, was impracticable, and that it would be wiser to send them back at once to the United States.[58] This decision was opposed by the Texans. Governor Salcedo admitted that it was very hard to prevent the entry of French

---
[56]Cordero to Bonavía, July 21, 1809.
[57]Herrera to the Commandant-General, July 24, 1809.
[58]N. Salcedo to Bonavía, July 9, 1809.

emissaries disguised as deserters, but insisted that the commandant-general's plans also presented difficulties. He believed that an American soldier who desired to desert would burn all bridges behind him, and come to Texas with the firm resolution of remaining, because severe punishment would be meted out to him should he ever return to the United States. He thought that it would be cruel to refuse such men the asylum they expected to find under the protection of the Spanish flag, declaring that the deserters, being thus between two fires, would either be forced to swell the number of desperadoes living in the Neutral Ground, or to enter clandestinely and hide among the Indians. He favored receiving deserters under proper regulations, on the ground that the American army would be weakened by this action. As a means of guarding against all possible trouble, he proposed that all deserters should be carefully examined so that it should be known certainly that they were not impostors, and that they should then be sent on to Monclova, where they could be kept under strict surveillance and where by personal labor, they could repay the expense thus incurred. As a possible alternative, he suggested that the Spanish government might exchange all deserters. In this way he hoped to prevent an increase in the population of the Neutral Ground. He pointed out that even under existing conditions horse stealing was common, that the danger zone reached even to the Trinity, and that many foreigners were gaining great influence along the Sabine. He insisted that if the order closing the door against deserters were carried out, a clash of arms between the two governments would necessarily follow; for the American commanders, in seeking to recapture deserters, would[59] be sure to send an armed party in pursuit, contrary to agreement.

Bonavía's action.—In transmitting this communication, Bonavía declared himself of the same opinion except in regard to exchanging deserters. This suggestion he disapproved, believing that the refusal to admit them would

---

[59]M. de Salcedo to Bonavía, July 30, 1809.

not remedy the difficulties experienced and expressing himself as unwilling to answer for the consequences if the order were enforced.[60]

Insistence of the commandant-general.—The suggestions of the local authorities were not received with approval and were even made the occasion for charges of officiousness and of unfaithfulness to the Spanish crown.[61] But Bonavía seemed not a whit daunted by all these failures and continued sending suggestions for other development projects.

Differences over the opening of the port of Bahía de San Bernardo.—On July 30, Bonavía called a *junta* similar to those already held for the discussion of matters pertaining to the interrelated subjects of the defense, development, and settlement of Texas. The particular matter under consideration at this time was the plan for opening a port on the coast of Texas, a thing upon which he had insisted ever since his arrival. In his appeal to the *junta*, he declared that he had already sent Francisco de la Rosa to Vera Cruz to secure from the viceroy a person capable of making the necessary observations and markings for the proposed port, but reported that no favorable reply had been received. He still hoped that de la Rosa would be permitted to return with goods so that the trade already authorized by the king, but as yet refused by the commandant-general, might be inaugurated. He desired the opinions of his colleagues in Texas as to the proper restrictions to be placed upon the proposed trade. The *junta* unanimously approved the plan of opening the port under liberal conditions;[62] but as was to be expected, the commandant-general was deaf to all arguments, merely replying that there was no necessity for discussing the question as no vessel would be likely to arrive at that point except that of La Rosa which would probably

---

[60]Bonavía to the Commandant-General, July 31, 1809.

[61]N. Salcedo to Bonavía, August 13, 1809, and M. de Salcedo to Bonavía, September 15, 1809.

[62]Report of *Junta*, July 20, 1809.

have to be seized because it would be loaded with contraband goods.⁶³

The discussion in regard to the organization of the army, the disposition of deserters, and the opening of a port were heated, but the greatest energy of each contestant seems to have been reserved for a discussion of the immigration question.

Continued differences over immigration.—On August 21, the commandant-general wrote Bonavía that his order for closing the door to immigrants was absolute and that it must be taken to include both the Louisiana frontier and the Gulf coast, so that every means of communication with a foreign country might be removed. He charged that during the six years in which immigration into Texas had been permitted not a single individual whose presence was not harmful had come in. He even declared that not one had even approximated the requirements fixed by royal orders. In answer to Bonavía's objection of July 31 in regard to the difficulties in the way of immigration, he maintained that good Spaniards who might wish to immigrate to Texas in the future could do so by way of Vera Cruz, provided the approval of the viceroy could be secured and that Bonavía's estimate of the difficulties to be overcome was an erroneous one. In a spicy postcript he charged that there was evidence to prove that all Louisianians who had entered Texas were prejudicial to the development of the country, that they were all libertines, contraband traders, fugitives, and disturbers of the peace. Among the most objectionable, he cited Minor, Vidal, Despallier, Clouet, and Bastrop. He considered them underhanded rascals who pretended a love for the nation, which they really hated, and who demanded favors for selfish motives only, without a thought for the welfare of the country. He ended by charging Bonavía not to admit such people because they would soon prove to be "crows to pick out the Spaniards' eyes."⁶⁴

---

⁶³N. Salcedo to Bonavía, September 7, 1809.
⁶⁴N. Salcedo to Bonavía, August 21, 1809, Appendix 18.

Bonavía's rebuttal.—In reply to this spirited communication, Bonavía protested that he had no sinister motive in preparing the regulations governing the introduction of immigrants from Louisiana. No one, he said, distrusted people of French extraction more than he did, but he wished all possible consideration to be shown the Spaniards living there. He declared that they deserved attention both on account of their numbers and their character. He estimated that there were in Louisiana at least fifteen hundred men capable of bearing arms and about four hundred industrious Canary Island families who were anxious to leave the United States. He believed that not one of these would remain in Louisiana if encouraged to remove to Texas where there was such a crying need for this class of people. He ventured the opinion that these persons, unlike the residents of New Orleans and those who had been engaged in commerce, had not been "contaminated" by their association with foreigners.[65] On this same day, Bonavía wrote directly to Spain, setting forth his position in the matter. In this letter, he stated that the question of immigration from Louisiana was one of the most important problems confronting the men who were directing affairs in Texas. He explained that the development and defense of this unfortunate province was important as a means of maintaining the security of New Spain, and even of the whole Spanish dominions. Indeed, he considered this matter so important that he wished the supreme *junta* informed. He contrasted the policy of the United States in attracting settlers with that of Spain in discouraging immigration, pointing out that the United States sent agents to Europe to secure new people, while Spain discouraged the entry not only of those born in Louisiana under Spanish rule, but even of Spaniards who lived in that region. He mentioned a few of the difficulties placed in the way of those desiring to immigrate and then described some of the troubles experienced by those who were received. He claimed that the arbitrary assignment of places for their settlement in many cases

---

[65]Bonavía to the Commandant-General, September 20, 1809.

worked a great hardship and that sometimes the immigrants were even expelled without due legal process. This treatment, he insisted, made American supporters of those who, by the very nature of things, would otherwise have been adherents of Spain. He denied the charge of the commandant-general that the immigrants were libertines, contraband traders, and Protestants, claiming that there was no evidence to support these accusations. He acknowledged that precaution was necessary under the circumstances but pointed out the folly of losing adherents by such a shortsighted policy as that in force. Finally he asked that in the future all loyal Spaniards be received and that the immigrants already admitted be given justice.[66]

Persistence of the commandant-general.—All of the arguments of the Texan authorities were unavailing and the commandant-general remained a firm adherent of his exclusion policy, severely rebuking all attempt to evade his instructions. Indeed, upon learning of the presence in Béxar of an inhabitant of East Florida, under the pretext of collecting debts, but possibly for the purpose of carrying on a furtive negotiation with Bastrop, he complained that the whole thing had been in defiance of instructions and ordered the punishment of the guilty parties.[67] On the same day he called attention to the case of Daniel Hughes, an agent from the United States, who had visited Chihuahua, and, who, upon his return, had succeeded in carrying away with him a great number of horses.[68] He did not mention, as he might well have done, the fact that Hughes had had every possible opportunity to secure complete information as to the military strength of the Interior Provinces. The local authorities seem to have stood entirely alone in their feeling of security. As has already been shown, both the supreme *junta* and the viceroy had supported the commandant-general's policy. To add weight to these warnings, disquieting reports began to come in at the end of 1809 from

---

[66]Bonavía to Saabedra, September 20, 1809.
[67]N. Salcedo to Bonavía, October 6, 1809.
[68]N. Salcedo to Bonavía, October 6, 1809.

Onís, unrecognized minister to the United States. In October, he wrote the viceroy that it was well known that a number of inhabitants of Louisiana were entering the Spanish dominions under the claim that this right had been guaranteed them by the treaty of 1803, in case they were dissatisfied with the change in government. He drew his attention to the danger that both Napoleon and the United States might make use of this immigration to slip in their emissaries and agents.[69] In November, he wrote that there were at New Orleans a number of discontented Spaniards mixed with French and American insurrectionists who were planning to raise revolutions in both Spain and Mexico. Immediately thereafter Secretary of War Saabedra wrote the viceroy declaring that Francis Belmont had left France for Philadelphia under instructions from Napoleon with the intention of penetrating the Spanish dominions for the purpose of inciting a rebellion. A little later Saabedra wrote a letter giving information of the plans of certain citizens of Mexico for placing themselves under the protection of England in case the French succeeded in conquering the mother country. He thought the situation fraught with danger because of the presence in Louisiana of Wilkinson and of a great number of French families.[70] These conspirators, he said, were carrying on communication with Mexico City and with Vera Cruz by way of the Interior Provinces. He even gave the names of a number of prominent Spaniards who were acting as agents of these revolutionists and declared that he had warned the viceroy, the captain-general of Cuba, the governor of Pensacola, and the consul at New Orleans to take every possible step to exterminate them. He now charged the governor to render the above-named authorities all the assistance in his power.[71] He also gave warning that vessels were being equipped in the United States by Spain's enemies.[72]

---

[69] Onís to the Viceroy, October 21, 1809.
[70] Saabedra to the Viceroy, December 12, 1809.
[71] Onís to the Governor of Texas, November 24, 1809.
[72] M. de Salcedo to Bonavía, March 10, 1810.

The supreme government of Spain was so thoroughly convinced of the necessity for taking drastic measures to hold the people of America to their allegiance that orders were issued allowing the Spanish dominion a representative in the *junta*,[73] while almost at the beginning of the next year provision was made for allowing America to have representatives in the *cortes*. There were, however, two almost insuperable difficulties in the case of Texas. There were no natives capable of filling the position and no funds to pay the necessary expenses in case one could be found. Governor Salcedo was the choice of the people, but, because he was not a native, his election was declared illegal. This decision fell in with his own desires because he doubted his own ability and preferred to finish his work in Texas. After a long delay, a native son was elected but failed to serve.[74] Provision was later made for representation by any native of the province who might be in Spain; but this deferred representation gave an opportunity for the Creoles to become more and more discontented and disposed to listen to plans for insurrection.

Dangers from Indians.—Despite the efforts of the authorities to hold the friendship of the Indians, many attacks were made, not only on the new settlements of Salcedo and San Marcos, but upon Béxar itself. So frequent were the depredations of the Tankawas at San Marcos, that abandonment of that place was seriously considered and Bonavía was even warned that the whole policy of development would be thwarted unless the Indians could be controlled sufficiently to permit settlers to cultivate their lands.[75] Naturally, he concurred in this opinion and approved the proposed measures of defense.[76] At this juncture, a treaty was made with a part of the Indians[77] and no steps were taken either to punish the aggressors or to abandon the

---

[73]N. Salcedo to the Governor of Texas, May 12, 1809.
[74]*Expediente*, June 21, 1810.
[75]M. de Salcedo to Bonavía, July 3, 1809.
[76]Bonavía to the Governor of Texas, July 4, 1809.
[77]M. de Salcedo to Bonavía, July 15, 1809.

The Opening of Texas to Foreign Settlement   177

settlement. On November 15, 1809, Governor Salcedo even proposed to the commandant-general that Villa Salcedo be abandoned and that its faithful settlers be located at San Marcos. Whether this was thought necessary because of Indian depredations or because of its "anti-military" situation[78] cannot be determined since the letter in question cannot be found. Decision was deferred until the governor should make a personal observation during the inspection of the province which was being planned[79] and no steps were actually taken to abandon the place.

Immigrants.—In spite of all restrictions, a few Spanish immigrants continued to present themselves during 1809. La Rosa had brought with him to Texas the petition of Don Francisco Huguet, a Spanish vassal, who had been living at New Orleans.[80] The petitioner was warned by way of Vera Cruz not to attempt to enter Texas.[81] Luís Grande, of Nacogdoches. expressed a desire to locate at Villa Salcedo.[82] He was granted the desired permission and actually became a settler. There were forwarded from Nacogdoches the petitions of Francisco Martínez, José Hernández, Juan Bautista Laguardıa, and Francisco Matón.[83] José Hernández, however had already been ordered out of the province, and it is probable that neither Francisco Martínez, Laguardıa, nor Matón became settlers. It may be noted that Melchor Martínez was accepted as a settler and that another applicant, Manuel Bodoya, a Spaniard, was permitted to go to Béxar in connection with his location in Texas.[84] Toward the end of the year, the petitions of Guillermo Spahn, Juan Felipe Mims, and Juan Cortés were denied.[85] Juan Batista

---
[78]See *ante*, p. 154.
[79]N. Salcedo to the Governor of Texas, January 23, 1810.
[80]Bonavía to M. de Salcedo, June 12, 1809.
[81]N. Salcedo to Bonavía, June 12, 1809.
[82]Petition, July 4, 1809.
[83]M. de Salcedo to the Commander of Nacogdoches, April 20, 1809, and M. de Salcedo to Bonavía, May 10, 1809.
[84]Bonavía to M. de Salcedo, May 12, 1809.
[85]M. de Salcedo to the Commandant of Nacogdoches, August 4 and October 21, 1809.

Norrain, a Sardinian, was permitted to settle under existing regulations.[86] No evidence has been found to indicate that any of these applicants actually entered Texas. It is certain that a few additional immigrants came in prior to 1810, when the situation was radically changed, for, in addition to those already named, there appears upon the list of settlers at Villa Salcedo the names of Francisco Arduán and Miguel Hernández (noted as being at Attakapas in 1809), Mordecai Rechar (living at Béxar), James Merlan, José Giru, José Antonio Esquíbel, José Leal, and Francisco Lacomba. Among others listed, whose whereabouts were unknown, were: Francisco Oranday, Diego Samora, José Antonio Salinas, Juan Carlos, Francisco Sancerman, and Santiago Fil.[87] Between 1805 and 1809, there had died at Villa Salcedo, Francisco Gómez, Bernabe Treviño, Andres González, and Pedro Engle, who had for years served as Indian trader of the region. All the last named, save Engle, were probably Spaniards and consequently transfers from one portion of Texas to another rather than actual immigrants. Several of those noted in the first list may have been of the same character. Among the foreigners who had located in and about Nacogdoches, in spite of prohibitory orders, were the following: Louis Fonten, a native of France; Juan Cidre, born in Hanover; José Lucobichi, an Italian; Patricio Fitzgerald and Timoteo Barnett, from Ireland; John Leathem, from Noivel (?); Jonathan Hale Platt, a native of Massachusetts; Juan Loid, of Charleston; and Pedro Bolio, a native of St. Genevieve, Missouri.[88]

---

[86]N. Salcedo to Bonavía, July 10, 1809.

[87]*Lista de vecinos—desde 1805—hasta 1° de Octubre, 1809—lista de agregados*—October 6, 1809. Appendix 11.

[88]At Bayou Pierre were located the following: Juan Bilberg, from Germany; Juan Duponey and Carlos Bruillar, from France; Bautista Colet, a native of Louisiana; Pierre Bonet Lafitte, Luis Beltran, Sylvestre Poisset, Atanasio Poisset, Pedro Dolet, Remi Christi, all natives of Natchitoches; Miguel Benson, from Canada; Bisente Nolan, born in France; Juan Bolbado, born at Nantes; Santiago Guales, from the United States; Miguel Roben, from Natchez; Guillermo Estreche, a native of Nueva Mercia; and Dabit Gualteman, from

Proposed settlement on the Frio.—During 1809, José Antonio Ramírez, who had secured a promise in 1806 that his plans for settling on the Frio would be considered later, renewed his attempts, asking to be allowed to establish a new *pueblo* on that river. However, despite Cordero's approval, the commandant-general decided that existing conditions precluded the consideration of such a plan but promised that it might be taken up at a more opportune time.[89]

Cordero recalled to Coahuila.—In 1809, the progressive party lost one of its most efficient members when Cordero returned to Coahuila.[90] The others, realizing the futility of opposing the commandant-general openly, now changed their tactics and began to seek their ends by underhanded measures. Their plans were favored by the fact that no invasion of the enemy developed immediately. They were, therefore, enabled for a time to follow their plans although it brought no appreciable result on account of lack of funds, and the final entry of the enemy.

High-water mark of colonization.—Before considering the continued conflict, it may be well to pause for a moment to get an idea of just how much had been accomplished toward the development of Texas by 1809, since from this time forward affairs went from bad to worse until, taking advantage of internal troubles, the enemies of Spain finally succeeded in destroying the buffer that had been erected against them in Texas and forced the authorities to consider additional plans for development and defense. The best available description of Texas in 1809 is that given by Governor Salcedo when furnishing information for the deputy from Texas to the *cortes*. In this report the governor declared that from the time that Louisiana came into the hands of the Spaniards, to the coming of Cordero to meet the situation created by the sale of Louisiana, Texas had been under a purely presidial form of government and that the country had been

---

Germany. See affidavits, July 26, 1809, and August 2, 16, and 17, 1809.

[89]N. Salcedo to the Governor of Texas, April 17, 1809.

[90]N. Salcedo to Bonavía, June 6, 1809.

almost entirely neglected. Then affairs had taken a change for the better, owing to the coming of immigrants from Louisiana, the presence of additional soldiers needed to prevent aggression from the United States, and the activities of Cordero who took steps to afford adequate protection for the settlers and to regulate trade. He believed that conditions had so changed that the presidial system was now harmful to the province, since it left the governor with everything to do but with no means of carrying out a single plan for the good of the country. He estimated that there were one thousand and thirty-three soldiers in Texas and three thousand one hundred and twenty-two settlers, distributed as follows:

In the jurisdiction of Béxar	1700 persons
In the jurisdiction of Bahía	405 persons
In the jurisdiction of San Marcos	82 persons
In the jurisdiction of Trinity	91 persons
In the jurisdiction of Nacogdoches	655 persons
At Bayou Pierre and to the east of the Sabine	189 persons
Total	3122 persons
To this may be added the soldiers	1033 persons

He showed that in spite of the fact that the province was especially blessed by nature the inhabitants had led a very wretched existence owing to the fact that Vera Cruz, distant more than five hundred leagues, was the nearest legal port. He insisted that the sale of Louisiana to the United States had increased the dangers threatening the Spanish dominions, and that Spain must place sufficient troops in Texas to inspire respect, must settle and develop the province by opening a port, and must carry out the reforms planned by Grimarest. He insisted, too, that the popular idea that the United States was not to be feared was an erroneous one and gave reasons to support his contention. He pointed out that the question of controlling the Indians was one of great importance and that although all border Indians were then at peace, the government would have to offer them greater trade inducements than the United States was offering them, if even their ostensible friendship was to be retained. To meet this situation he proposed that trading houses be established and that *presidios* be founded among certain tribes. He explained that in all the six missions of Texas there were only three hundred and forty-three persons. In his judgment the whole mission system was cumbersome and led to but little good. In this connection he said:

> The Indians who are reduced to mission life are attracted not because the faith has entered through the ears—but through their mouths, because of gifts of something to eat and the charm of presents.

He thought that it would be easier to secure the desired results through trade and the establishments of settlements, since the priests alone could never teach them the Spanish language and the elements of religious doctrine. In regard to the introduction of immigrants from Louisiana, he thought that precautions should be taken to prevent the entry of disloyal and harmful persons, but that the government should not fail to protect those who were known to be faithful vassals. He favored an increase in the army of Texas and the establishment of the office of commandant-general of the Eastern Interior Provinces.[91] This description showing the meager results of six years' hard work must have seemed pitifully small to the authorities in Texas who had done all that men could do to fill the province with happy and prosperous settlers. To the commandant-general, suspicious of every person crossing the border from Louisiana, the number doubtless seemed all too large. The dangers of which he had often given warning were soon to materialize.

---

[91]Report, Salcedo, August 8, 1810, in *Historia Operaciones de Guerra años de 1810 y 1812*, August 8, 1809, March 31, 1813. Trans., U. of T.

CHAPTER VI

Opposition of Active Enemies, Headstrong Subordinates, and Rebellious Vassals, 1810

During 1810 the cares of the commandant-general increased, for by the end of the year he was compelled to deal with revolution at *his very door*. In the meantime he was not allowed to forget that there was danger from abroad. Indeed, so frequent were the warnings sent in from various sources that both Governor Salcedo and Bonavía began to feel alarmed, the former ordering the commandant at Nacogdoches to keep a watchful eye on the Americans to prevent the entry of exploring parties. Nevertheless, his instructions in regard to permitting the entry of immigrants were not specific, for he said: "Since the door is closed against the entry of all American deserters, I will only say that I depend upon your fidelity to carry out *my* instructions."[1] Almost immediately he wrote Bonavía complaining that his own cares and anxieties were daily increasing while his resources were continually diminishing.[2] Upon learning of the refusal of the United States to recognize de Onís as minister from Spain, Bonavía, too, became alarmed, fearing that the United States might be planning an attack upon Texas. He again urged, even more insistently, if possible, the necessity for providing for adequate defense.[3] He reported that many of the soldiers of Salcedo and Nacogdoches were a-foot without hopes of securing mounts. He declared that he still had faith in the ability of the viceroy to send help but at the same time he confessed that the Interior Provinces could furnish practically nothing. Still, he expressed the fear that recruits would have to be secured from Jamaica as the viceroy had not, as yet, sent any help. This,

---

[1] M. de Salcedo to the Commandant of Nacogdoches, February (?), 1810.
[2] M. de Salcedo to Bonavía, February 26, 1810.
[3] Bonavía to M. de Salcedo, January 24, 1810.

of course, led to a discussion of the necessity for opening the port of Matagorda so that troops could be transferred with greater efficiency. He ended by saying:

> We who are in authority cannot be idle. We must complain and beg again and again for the things which are absolutely necessary, since Texas is the most exposed point.[4]

Following his usual custom, the commandant-general issued precautionary instructions, forbidding the entry of any foreigner into Texas and expressing the belief that the viceroy would be unable to send help.[5] His fears were well founded, for the viceroy immediately wrote declaring that he would send no reinforcements until he knew exactly the strength of the army in Texas.[6] This was only a subterfuge, for Bonavía had given him this information repeatedly. The tension between Spain and the United States was somewhat relaxed by the offer of the latter to coöperate in the task of clearing the Neutral Ground of objectionable characters.[7] In reality the danger to Texas was increased by the move, for Lieutenant Augustus Magee, who was later to lead a filibustering party into Texas, was at this time sent to Nacogdoches to aid the Spanish troops in clearing the region.[8]

There was but little opportunity for enjoying this temporarily improved situation, for Napoleon continued to push his plans against the Spanish Dominions in Amesica with even greater vigor than before. At the end of 1810 Antonio Cornél wrote the commandant-general enclosing an intercepted letter written by Francis Belmont to Miguel José de la Azana, Minister of the Indies, informing him that an American in charge of a swift sailing vessel had offered to

---

[4]Bonavía to N. Salcedo, March 1, 1810.
[5]N. Salcedo to Bonavía, March 13, 1810.
[6]N. Salcedo to Bonavía, March 20, 1810.
[7]Bonavía to Eguía, October 17, 1810.
[8]Carr to Bonavía, July 7, 1810. The task was thoroughly done and all the houses in the region were destroyed, Guadiana to Bonavía, July 29, 1810.

carry passengers from France to the United States. In this communication Belmont requested Azana to furnish him money for the passage, on the ground that it would be productive of good to the new government. He likewise promised to give information of the whole continent of America and asked if it were possible for General Thureau [Turreau], of Washington City, to furnish him money for his expenses while in Philadelphia.[9] In April, Miguel Crow reported that a French vessel had arrived at the mouth of the Sabine to trade with the Indians and to secure support for some mysterious scheme. He declared that all the Indians —even to the women and children—had gone to meet the foreigners.[10] Onís continued to report every move of the enemy, sometimes giving the most detailed information as to the number and the names of various French agents landing at different points, together with an account of their plans for the distribution of literature.[11] For instance, he reported to the viceroy the arrival, at Baltimore, of *The Tilsit*, from Bayonne, under command of Dumelan [Desmoland(?)], having on board an emissary of Joseph Napoleon who was provided with secret commissions and seditious documents calculated to revolutionize the Spanish dominions of America. Other agents, so he said, had been landed at Norfolk having in their possession proclamations and letters which either were fictitious or had been secured from the Spanish king by force. These emissaries to the number of fifty had reëmbarked for other ports from which they exepected to send reports to four chief agents who were to establish themselves at various points. These leaders were thereupon to issue instructions for carrying forward these revolutionary plans. Onís enclosed a list of the emissaries in question, showing that some of the agents were to be placed in the Interior Provinces.[12] It is certain

---

[9]Cornel to N. Salcedo, January 2, 1810.
[10]Ruiz to Guadiana, April 4, 1810.
[11]N. Salcedo to Bonavía, April 16, 1810.
[12]*Cf.* the plan sketched in Appendix 15 and the list in Villaneuva, *Napoleón y la Independencia de América*, 238–241.

that Napoleon did continue his attempts to secure control in America. He endeavored to induce the Council of the Indies to issue orders calculated to bribe the people of Spanish America to acquiesce in his schemes; and, failing in this, he determined to issue proclamations in the king's name and planned to have them distributed by secret agents.[13] With characteristic despatch, he carried out these plans by issuing several orders, one of them granting free trade to the Spanish Dominions in America, even though in so doing he ran counter to the whole spirit of the commercial system then in vogue.[14] The regency, of course, immediately declared this order null and void.[15] The commandant-general being thoroughly convinced of the danger, thereupon instructed Bonavía not to permit the entry of a single foreigner from Louisiana and to make the most minute examination of the belongings of any inhabitant of Texas, who, upon any pretext whatever, might go from the frontier posts of the interior. Again, Onís wrote that Mr. Leger, a Frenchman who had lived on the German frontier and who spoke Spanish perfectly, had gone from Baltimore to Louisiana to organize a party in sympathy with the French cause among the Germans of that section. His intention was to locate at Ouachita, under the guise of a merchant, and to carry on his plans under the instruction of Desmoland.[16] About the same time, there arrived at New Orleans a Frenchman by the name of Lestigue who claimed to be on a mission for the *junta*.[17] Alarmed by these activities, the regency prohibited the debarkation of any foreigners in the ports of Spanish America unless carrying a passport from the proper authority which proved his identity and motives for coming. If, in spite of all possible

---

[13]Garay to the Viceroy, July 27, 1810.
[14]N. Salcedo to Bonavía, October 2, 1810. *Cf.* Art. 89 of the Constitution of Bayonne in Rios, *Código Español—de José Napoleon Bonapart*, 24.
[15]Decree July (?), 1810.
[16]Onís to the Viceroy, March 14, 1810.
[17]N. Salcedo to Bonavía, April 13, 1810, and Onís to the Viceroy, May 1, 1810.

precaution, an agent should slip through into the closely guarded territory, either by land or sea, he was to be immediately executed.[18] Naturally, the commandant-general approved this action and in addition ordered every precaution taken to prevent the entry of emissaries across the Texas frontier,[19] forbade all communication across the border so that the enemy could not secure horses for an invasion,[20] and provided for the arrest of any person entering the province from the United States, even though carrying a passport from Onís—since such documents might easily be forged.[21] These orders could not be carried into effect as Bonavía quite frankly informed the commandant-general, saying that he had not troops at his command to perform the ordinary duties required, much less to guard an extensive coast better known to the Louisianians than to the people of Texas themselves, who were without vessels and soldiers to patrol the long line of unsettled and defenseless frontier.[22]

The French agents were thoroughly familiar with conditions and naturally continued their efforts to revolutionize Texas while Onís continued to send warnings of their plans. He claimed that they were securing spurious passports, money, arms, and sympathizers in the United States for the purpose of revolutionizing Texas and the Floridas.[23] He also issued warnings against a band of Frenchmen in New Orleans who had received from one of Napoleon's agents arms and ammunition to use in an attack upon Texas or to raise a revolution therein, and charged that a certain Mr. Baudin, formerly a merchant at New Orleans, had asked Napoleon for money and ships to carry out his plan for revolutionizing Baton Rouge and Pensacola, preliminary to an

[18]Bordaxí to N. Salcedo, April 14, 1810.
[19]N. Salcedo to Bonavía, April 30, 1810.
[20]Proclamation, April 25, 1810.
[21]*Circular reservada*, May 6, 1810, in *Barradores de Oficios*, January 4, 1810–January 11, 1815.
[22][Bonavía] to the Commandant-General, August 8, 1810.
[23]N. Salcedo to Bonavía, June 25, 1810.

The Opening of Texas to Foreign Settlement 187

invasion of Texas. Onís, likewise, called attention to the activities of a certain "young Spaniard of evil conduct," the son of a merchant of Havana, who had come to America with a large number of Frenchmen, all on revolution bent. Indeed, so thoroughly was Onís aroused to the danger that he wrote to the viceroy demanding that troops be sent to Texas to guard against these emissaries who were more to be feared than the Americans who "were divided in their views, and so handicapped by commercial and financial troubles as to be incapable of launching a general attack."[24] Diego Morphi, Spanish consul at New Orleans, seconded Onís's efforts to give warning of the plans of the enemy for attacking Mobile and Pensacola with recruits secured by the promise of *one hundred acres of land* in the territory to be conquered.[25] These fears, shared by many in high authority, were not without foundation, for before the end of the year half of West Florida had actually been lost by Spain through revolution at Baton Rouge. Governor Salcedo believed that this revolution was no isolated event. He claimed that it sprang from the conspiracy of Burr and his followers and that it had grown under the revivifying influence of French emissaries. As proof of this, he called attention to Burr's visit to France.[26] As a matter of fact, examination of the records of the period shows that this charge of conspiracy had considerable foundation. For instance, the action of the representatives of West Florida, who presented a memorial to the United States government claiming that Spain's inability to govern the region forced them to erect an independent government conclusively shows the presence of foreign influence there.[27]

---

[24]N. Salcedo to Bonavía, June 25, 1810, and N. Salcedo to the Governor of Texas, December 24, 1810.

[25]Morphi to the Captain-General of Havana, November 18, 1810, in *A. G. I. S.* Mex., 89–1–19, November 11, 1810.

[26]For Burr's intentions, see Cox, *The West Florida Controversy*, 1798–1813, p. 311. For Napoleon's attitude toward Burr, see *Correspondence de Napoleón*, XX, 524.

[27]The declaration ran as follows:
"It is known to the world with how much fidelity the good people of this Territory have professed and maintained allegiance to their

Their declaration seems quite plausible and justifiable; but the representatives really had no intention of remaining free and independent. The president of the convention, at once, wrote to the secretary of state of the United States declaring that the weak and unprotected situation of the region would force its representatives to appeal to some foreign country for support, unless the United States, who was looked upon as a mother, would give direct and unequivocal assurances of protection. In support of this claim, he pointed out that the United States had already authorized

legitimate sovereign, while any hope remained of receiving from him protection for their property and their lives.

"Without making any unnecessary innovation in the established principles of the Government, we have voluntarily adopted certain regulations, in concert with our First Magistrate, for the express purpose of preserving this Territory, and showing our attachment to the Government which has heretofore protected us. This compact, which was entered into with good faith on our part will forever remain an honorable testimony of our upright intentions and inviolable fidelity to our King and parent country, while so much as a shadow of legitimate authority remained to be exercised over us. We sought only a speedy remedy for such evils as seemed to endanger our existence and prosperity, and we were encouraged by our Governor with solemn promise of assistance and coöperation. But those measures which were intended for our preservation he has endeavored to pervert into an engine of destruction, by encouraging, in the most perfidious manner, the violation of ordinances sanctioned and established by himself as the law of the land.

"Being thus left without any hope of protection from the mother country, betrayed by a Magistrate whose duty it was to have provided for the safety and tranquility of the people and Government committed to his charge, and exposed to all the evils of a state of anarchy, which we have so long endeavored to avert, it becomes our duty to provide for our own security, as a free and independent State, absolved from all allegiance to a Government which no longer protects us.

"We, therefore, the representatives aforesaid, appealing to the Supreme Ruler of the world for the rectitude of our intentions, do solemnly publish and declare the several districts composing this Territory of West Florida to be a *free and independent State;* and that they have a right to institute for themselves such form of Government as they may think conducive to their safety and happiness; to form treaties; to establish commerce; to provide for their common

The Opening of Texas to Foreign Settlement 189

its agents to engage France to intercede with Spain to relinquish any claim she might have to the territory in question, and that it had been spoken of in diplomatic correspondence as a part of the Louisiana cession. He claimed, too, that occupation had only been deferred because it was hoped that Spain would amicably consent to relinquish all claims. He asserted that the existing government of Spain was not recognized as legal and that any attempt to subjugate the revolting territory would be considered an invasion by a foreign country. He argued that since the emperor of France had advised the Spanish-Americans to declare their independence rather than to remain in subjection to the old Spanish government, he could not object to annexation to the United States. He finally asserted that, even though England was an ally of Spain, she would willingly consent to occupation by the United States to prevent the region from falling into the hands of the French exiles from the Island of Cuba and of other partisans of Napoleon.[28] The desired protection was forthcoming. On October 27, the president issued a proclamation ordering his agents to take possession of the territory in question as a part of the Louisiana Purchase,[29] while Congress, fearing

---

defense; and to do all acts which may of right be done by a sovereign and independent nation; at the same time declaring all acts within the said Territory of West Florida, after this date, by any tribunal or authorities not deriving their powers from the people, agreeably to the provisions established by this convention, to be null and void; and calling upon all foreign nations to respect this our declaration, acknowledging our independence, and giving us such aid as may be consistent with the laws and usages of nations.

"This declaration, made in convention, at the town of Baton Rouge, on the twenty-sixth day of September, in the year of our Lord, one thousand eight hundred and ten, we, the representatives, in the name aforesaid, and on behalf of our constituents, do hereby solemnly pledge ourselves to support with our lives and fortunes.

By order of the Convention.

JOHN RHEA, PRESIDENT,
ANDREW STEELE, SECRETARY.

[28]Rhea to the Secretary of State, October 10, 1810, *American State Papers, Foreign Relations*, III, 395–396.

[29]Smith to Claiborne, October 27, 1810, *Ibid.*, 397–398.

that England was planning to seize the region, soon, in secret session, passed the necessary legislation for a temporary occupation, subject to future negotiations and authorized the president to take possession of East Florida also in case the local authorities desired the protection of the United States or in case foreign governments should undertake to seize it.[30] Vicente Folch, Governor of West Florida, almost immediately expressed a willingness to deliver the territory to the United States for the purpose of avoiding further anarchy due to the alarm of the people, the influence of French agents in Louisiana, and the rapid spread of disorder. He stipulated, however, that the United States should assist him in preventing further attacks upon Mobile and Pensacola by Reuben Kemper,[31] who was shortly to appear in Texas in the role of a liberator. That the situation was a grave one for all the Spanish dominions in America admits of no doubt; and that the local authorities in Texas could not be depended upon to guard against the

---

[30] Act of January 15, 1811, in *A. G. I. S.*, *Legajo* 13, No. 9, January 15, 1811–April 4, 1818. For the action of the American authorities in Louisiana in forming public opinion in West Florida in favor of annexation to the United States, see Cox, *The West Florida Controversy, 1795–1813*, pp. 329–333.

[31] Folch to Smith, December 2, 1810, *American State Papers, Foreign Relations*, III, 398. As to Kemper's revolutionary activities, see Claiborne to Freeman, May 13, 1805, *Letter Books*, III, 54, and Cox, *The West Florida Controversy, 1798–1813*, pp. 152–168 and 457–486. The bitter animosity of Kemper and his equally famous brothers is characterized by one writer as follows: "There is no doubt that for some time the antagonisms between American and Spanish subjects were kept very much alive through the instrumentality of three celebrated giants of pioneer Mississippi, who were well known as the Kemper brothers. They were known to hate anything and everything belonging to Spain; they were implacable in hate; they had made many an aggressive excursion within the Spanish lines; had tried to capture Baton Rouge and fix on the crest of the hill an American standard. Through the influence of Governor Claiborne, however, the leaders were released by the Spanish authorities but the Kempers were secretly at work despite the promises repeatedly made by them. Favrot, Henry L., "Some of the Causes and Conditions that Brought About the West Florida Controversy in 1810," in *Publications of the Louisiana Historical Society*, 195, pp. 40–41.

entry of dangerous foreigners will now be further demonstrated.

Evasion of orders for expulsion.—As has already been shown, the commandant-general had long ago determined to rid Texas of all suspicious immigrants. He had first decided to carry out this purpose in connection with the inspection of the province proposed by Governor Salcedo early in January, 1809. But, as time had dragged on and no action had been taken, he had deemed it necessary to issue additional orders. Consequently, on August 7, 1809, he had instructed the governor to proceed at once on his tour of inspection, and to draw up a complete list of the foreigners in Texas so that all objectionable characters might be expelled in accordance with *Libro IX, Titulo XVII, Ley IX, of the Recopilación*.[32] Still no move had been made. On January 9, 1810, he returned to the attack. This time he wrote Bonavía, saying that he had examined the reports of foreigners living in the five settlements of Texas and had noted with regret that in all of them, especially in Villa Salcedo, there were a great number of foreigners who should never have been admitted. He considered them objectionable because of their nationality and their religion and because they had not been able to produce satisfactory papers. He enjoined instant obedience to previous orders for expulsion of foreigners and the other objectionable characters from Béxar, Villa Salcedo, and Nacogdoches. He criticised the previous laxity of the authorities and instructed the governor to start *at once* with as many troops as might be necessary and forbade him to return to Béxar until orders for expulsion had been carried out to the letter.[33]

Protest of governor.—Of course, the governor was not without arguments to explain his seeming shortcomings and to prevent the expulsion of such foreigners as had been admitted. In the first place, he pointed out that many of them had been received previous to the retrocession of Louisiana, and that there had been plenty of time for them

---

[32]N. Salcedo to M. de Salcedo, August 7, 1809.
[33]N. Salcedo to Bonavía, January 9, 1810.

to prove their good character. In the second place, he maintained that the delay in inspecting the province had been unavoidable. In the third place, he asserted that since nearly all foreigners in Texas had immigrated because of the sale of Louisiana, they were necessarily good Spaniards. He, thereupon, entered a vigorous protest against the whole policy of arbitrary expulsion, claiming that this step would increase in a neighboring province the number of evil-doers, who would harass Texas and carry on a lucrative contraband trade. He, therefore, asked to be allowed to clear the province of objectionable characters in his own way, and suggested that undesirables be sent further into the interior where they could be kept under closer supervision.[34]

Bonavía's position.—Naturally, Bonavía was ready to support the governor and to excuse himself for any wrongdoing. He, too, claimed that it had been necessary to suspend the execution of orders for the expulsion of foreigners and that its enforcement now would serve only to create excitement and lead those expelled to join the rabble in the Neutral Ground where they would be entirely beyond control. He insisted that Texas should be guarded, especially along the Texas-Louisiana frontier, but said that, owing to friendly relations between Spain and England, he had but little to fear from a naval attack by the French and Americans.[35]

Rejection of proposal.—The governor's request that he be allowed to dispose of foreigners as his judgment might dictate was instantly rejected by the commandant-general who severely reprimanded him for interpreting definite orders as conditional, and commanded him to carry out instructions without quibble.[36] But moved by the warnings

---

[34]M. de Salcedo to the Commandant-General, January 2, 1810, Draft No. 140 in *Borradores de Oficios*, January 21, 1810–October 20, 1810.

[35][Bonavía] to Commanding General, January 23, 1810, Doc. No. 1, in Translations of Historical Documents found in the Archives of Bexar County, 1810, *N. A.*

[36]N. Salcedo to M. de Salcedo, and N. Salcedo to Bonavía, February 6, 1810. The governor was expected to make a thorough examination

The Opening of Texas to Foreign Settlement

of Onís and by the protests of the Texan authorities, he finally yielded to the extent of admitting that he considered it unwise to expell all the foreigners at one time, because of rumors of the presence of a band of French and American revolutionists in New Orleans who would secure information and support from the immigrants in question. He finally ruled that those desiring to leave should be allowed to do so at once but that others were to be detained until arrangements could be made for their expulsion according to previous instructions.[37] Under no pretext, he decided, were they to be allowed to penetrate further into the interior. Nevertheless, practically nothing came of all these orders.

Inspection of Salcedo.—When he could think of no other excuse for delay, the governor finally set out from Béxar on March 11 and went directly to Villa Salcedo, arriving there on March 24. There, he at once proceeded to collect the required information in the case of twenty-three foreigners, arranging the evidence in two *cuadernos*. This was as far toward expulsion as he ever went. On March 30, he reported to the commandant-general that he had not informed those living on ranches in the vicinity that they must destroy all their property at these points and move within the two leagues assigned to the *villa*. Nor did he, according to his own testimony, take any steps in regard to illegal marriages among the immigrants, further than to have an informal conversation with the parish priest in regard to their religious conduct and their general reputation. He admitted, too, that he had not secured evidence in the case of Jacob Dorst, who was away at the time but who was well thought of by the commandant at Villa Salcedo. According to the governor, Dorst was a German who had lived for many

---

of the province from a military standpoint and to make suggestions for its defense. He was also to give, in a separate report, the names of all Indians, showing a disposition to receive Spanish citizens and missionaries among them. Bonavía to M. de Salcedo, March 1, 1810.

[37]N. Salcedo to the Governor of Texas, March 13, 1810.

years at Arcos, Louisiana, and who claimed to be a Catholic, as did his three sons, one of whom lived with him and two of whom were located at Nacogdoches. The governor also omitted from his list, Vincente Micheli, and Juan Lorenzo Boden, the latter a native of Natchitoches, who had married an Indian woman of that place. Having prepared the evidence mentioned, the governor took up the cudgels in defense of those of his *protégés,* listed in *cuaderno* No. 1, claiming that they were not prejudicial to the country. Rather, he insisted that the Spaniards had little to fear from the Americans of the laboring classes, especially if they, like the majority of the immigrants, had lived long under the Spanish flag. He spoke of their love of farming and of their contentment when located upon rich and well wooded lands where they could follow their natural bent. Observation had taught him, he said, that but few of this class ever left the Spanish dominions except under extraordinary circumstances. He argued, also, that there was no special objection to their professing the Protestant faith, since they were not very well grounded in their beliefs and could be easily won over to the Catholic church. He acknowledged that he feared the educated Americans, such as doctors, lawyers, and merchants and that he felt no confidence in the French, either educated or uneducated, Protestant or Catholic. He took occasion to speak of their restlessness and love of change and said that even the French Catholics concealed in their hearts an unplacable hatred for the Spaniards. In spite of the fact that at last he seemed to have come to a full realization of the danger, he was still bold enough to inform the commandant-general that he had decided to disregard the orders of March 13, and to carry out his own plans in regard to the management of foreigners. He transmitted the evidence he had collected, showing the good conduct and fidelity of the immigrants.[38]

Among the supporters of the governor was Father Maynes, parish priest of Villa Salcedo. In response to a request for an estimate of the character of the foreigners

---

[38]M. de Salcedo to N. Salcedo, March 30 and April 6, 1810.

there, he declared that they were quiet and law abiding, although some few were addicted to drink.[39] He thought that they were faithful vassals of the king and that those professing the Protestant faith had not attacked the Catholic religion or any of the rites of the church but that, on the contrary, they had attended services just as the Catholics had. He admitted that not all attended confession regularly, but claimed that this was due to the fact that they could not express themselves freely in the Spanish tongue.[40]

Bonavía again supported the governor in his efforts to prevent the expulsion of foreigners, even though he, too, had finally become convinced of the dangers from the French. The reported arrival at Baltimore of a French schooner carrying emissaries called from him a lengthy discussion of the intrigues of Wilkinson and of the great danger from the numerous French families located in Louisiana. He believed that the danger was increased by the inability and unwillingness of the United States to prevent trouble, and complained that the French had been allowed in that country to fit themselves out for expeditions against Spanish territory. Both he and the governor yet hoped to defeat the plans of Spain's enemies by making Texas strong enough to repel any invasion that might be attempted. To this end they continued to beg for troops as a preliminary step towards development. And, although these requests were not granted, they were actually able to carry their point touching the retention of the immigrants, for when the commandant-general received the two *cuadernos* in regard to the immigrants at Salcedo, he immediately returned them with instructions that they be referred to Bonavía for final decision.[41]

Victory for the Texas authorities.—This, of course, amounted to a virtual victory for the Texan authorities, and on May 30 Bonavía rendered the decision that such foreigners as had remained for any length of time in Texas

---

[39]See *ante*, p. 141.
[40]Maynes to M. de Salcedo, May 30, 1810.
[41]M. de Salcedo to the Governor of Texas, May 14, 1810.

should not be forced to return to Louisiana. He gave instructions that those who seemed objectionable should be removed into the interior, so that communication across the border could really be prevented.[42] On June 6 he made assurance doubly sure by writing the governor approving the measures taken in regard to the foreigners located at Villa Salcedo. He said that he had investigated the matter thoroughly and had already expressed his views to the commandant-general. He believed that there were but few persons whose immigration had not been in strict accordance with the regulations, and recommended that such immigrants as were willing to embrace the Catholic faith should be allowed to remain at Villa Salcedo. He then took up the few cases in which action seemed necessary, naming seven persons who should not have been admitted at all. Of these, Juan Magee, Miguel Quinn, and Juan McFarlan, all of Villa Salcedo, were connected with the charges of contraband trade made against Enrique Kuerke, originally from Kentucky but at that time an inhabitant of Nacogdoches. In their cases he decided that action should be suspended until the case could be tried.[43] Of the remaining five, three were to be permitted to remain, because it was believed that they would give no trouble. Of the two that were left, one was thought to be more deserving of instruction than expulsion; and, so finally, there was but one lone immigrant for whom there seemed no hope. Opposite the name of Guillermo Burgis [Burxer] he wrote "As a Protestant he should not have been admitted."[44] But there is no evidence to show that this one lone undesirable was ever really expelled. Although this was a complete anti-climax to the commandant-general's sweeping orders for expulsion, strange to say, he offered no protest against the decision.[45]

---

[42]Bonavía to the Commandant-General, May 30, 1810.
[43]See *Causa seguida a—Kuerke, Magui, McFarlan, y Brentón por contrabista, y haber hecho armas contra la tropa en defensa de la cavallada que llecvaron por la Luciana.* [January 1, 1810.]
[44][Bonavía] to M. de Salcedo, June 6, 1810.
[45]N. Salcedo to Bonavía, July 10, 1810.

The Opening of Texas to Foreign Settlement 197

In the meantime, having practically carried his point at Villa Salcedo, the governor went on to Nacogdoches, where he, at once, began to prepare evidence in regard to the foreigners in and near that settlement.

Inspection at Nacogdoches.—The *expediente* prepared at this time contains much interesting information. Each head of a family was required to give his name, age, birthplace, and religion and to state whether previous to his immigration he had been a Spanish vassal, whether he had taken the oath of allegiance and by whom he had been admitted. He had, also, to give information of all absences from the province and to explain the motives of any journey he might have made.[46] The names of only twenty-nine foreigners appear—some of them new settlers—although it will be remembered there had been fifty foreigners at that point in 1801.[47] The investigation revealed the presence of several who were not Catholics, some who had made numerous voyages to Louisiana, and a few who manifestly belonged to the proscribed American race. In fact, the settlers represented many nationalities. There was one Irishman from the old sod, one Italian from the Sunny South, and one German from Berlin. In addition there were Englishmen from both England and Canada and Americans from several points in the United States. Nothing daunted, the governor began to pursue his usual method. But when called upon for a report to support the governor's position, the priests gave no such optimistic recommendation as had Father Maynes, of Salcedo. On the contrary, Father Sosa, who admitted that he was not thoroughly familiar with the situation, described the suspicious communications that had passed between Napoleon's emissary, D'Alvimar, and Bernardo Dortolan[48] and complained of the failure of Santiago

---

[46]*Expediente sobre Exaranjeros—de Nacogdoches*, May 8, 1810.

[47]This may have been due to the fact that the settlers of Bayou Pierre were listed in the first report but not in the second. The fact that some of the immigrants had returned to Louisiana may likewise have affected the results.

[48]Bernardo Dortolan had come to Texas with the celebrated French trader, De Mézières, in 1779. Demézières to Cabello, October 26, 1779, in *A. G. I. S. legajo 70*, January 1, 1779–January 18, 1780.

Dill and Christian Hesser to observe their duties as Catholics. He also called attention to Hesser's love for the French and the Americans, and his lack of visible means of support.[49] Father Huerta de Jesús, who confessed that he, too, was handicapped by lack of knowledge, supported the testimony of Father Sosa in regard to Dortolan and Hesser, and added that Santiago Dill was not a Catholic and that he had no intention of becoming one.[50] Even the commandant of Nacogdoches, who had a good word for almost everybody, was forced to admit that many of the settlers were remiss in their religious life. In a letter written at this time, Father Sosa discussed plans for bettering conditions at Nacogdoches. He criticised the evil conduct of the soldiers and the dishonesty of the settlers but explained in extenuation that there was no opportunity for the settlers to dispose of their products to an advantage, and that this naturally tempted them to be lazy or to engage in a contraband trade. He proposed several plans for improvement, among them the establishment of a public school, the maintenance of the troops under a desirable financial system, and the development of some arrangement by which the settlers might dispose of their products to an advantage, so that they would be led to devote themselves to agricultural pursuits rather than to contraband trade. As a final recommendation, he proposed the establishment of missions among certain of the Indian tribes whom he believed to be anxious for religious instruction. He insisted, however, that the missions would have to be founded under a new system.[51] In transmitting the list of foreigners at Nacogdoches, the governor admitted that several individuals should never have been received at all, since they were neither Catholics nor Spanish vassals, but urged that the majority of them be allowed to remain. He did not suggest the expulsion of the Querque family and did not seem at all alarmed over the suspicious

---

[49]Sosa to M. de Salcedo, May 4, 1810.
[50]Huerta to M. de Salcedo, May 31, with Sosa to M. de Salcedo, May 4, 1810.
[51]Sosa to M. de Salcedo, May 26, 1810.

actions of Dortolan. As at Villa Salcedo, he made no effort to reach the outlying ranch houses.[52] Besides trying to prevent the expulsion of immigrants who desired to remain, he wished to keep in Texas the foreigners who really desired to return to Louisiana and the natives who wished to escape to that region. He wrote Bonavía in regard to this matter, suggesting that he try to prevent emigration from Texas to Louisiana because the *unfortunate people were ignorant of the blessings they were enjoying and of the dangers they would encounter by abandoning their country and their religion for trivial personal reasons.*[53] Bonavía answered at once that no legal steps could be taken in the matter but that the Spanish consul at New Orleans might be asked to try to persuade all fugitives to return.[54] As was to be expected, everything at Nacogdoches was finally arranged to the governor's satisfaction.

He did not inspect Bayou Pierre, although a number of foreigners were located there. He also failed to visit Atascocito on account of the rains;[55] and, since there were no foreigners at San Marcos or at Bahía, and only a few at Béxar,[56] this ended the examination of foreigners in Texas—one man only having been specifically declared objectionable and none having certainly been expelled.

Evasion of orders for non-intercourse.—The foreigners had been, indeed, highly favored. Discontent soon began to assert itself among them, while many of the Spaniards began to leave Texas for Louisiana without assigning any reason for their action. The governor naturally desired to prevent any large number of discontented vassals collecting on the frontier where the French and the Americans were said to be very active. Emboldened by the fact that he had

---

[52]*Informe*—May 19, 1809, and annexed opinions of commandant of Nacogdoches, May 19, 1810.
[53]M. de Salcedo to Bonavía, October 5, 1810.
[54]Bonavía to M. de Salcedo, October (?), 1810.
[55]M. de Salcedo to N. Salcedo, May 19 and May 22, 1810.
[56]The following foreigners are listed as residents of Béxar at this time: José La Baume, his son, Valerio; Pedro Girard, Pedro Longueville; and José La Grasse. List, December 31, 1810.

carried his point in preventing the expulsion of foreigners from Texas, he at once began trying to defeat the commandant-general's policy of non-intercourse by laying plans to secure the return of all exiles and fugitives.

Defiance of authorities in Texas.—While at Nacogdoches in the face of all dangers and in spite of orders he issued a proclamation in which he explained that arrangements had been made for the continued residence of foreigners in Texas, even though certain of them were not legally entitled to this privilege, and extending pardon to all citizens who fled to Louisiana through fear of punishment for contraband trade.[57]

Reprimand.—Upon learning of this, the commandant-general declared that the authorities in Texas had not only gone beyond their own powers but had even exceeded those conferred upon the commandant-general himself. He believed that nothing less than royal authority had been usurped; hence, he ordered that all persons presenting themselves in response to the proclamation should be arrested and tried for their crimes.[58] Influenced by civil disturbances, he almost immediately changed his mind, and the authorities in Texas scored another point.

Virtual victory for authorities in Texas.—On October 13, the commandant-general consented to let the proclamation stand and provided that those presenting themselves in response to it were merely to be examined so that the reason for their journey to Louisiana, the number of animals taken, and the places in which they had sought refuge might be ascertained.[59] A condition was thus created in which persons having a strong motive for securing entry into Texas—such, for instance, as exiled Spaniards, Frenchmen acting as envoys of Napoleon, or Americans desiring to aid in spreading "Liberty" throughout the world and to secure

---

[57]M. de Salcedo to Bonavía, September 3, 1810. For copy of proclamation, see Appendix 19.

[58]N. Salcedo to the Governor of Texas, October 2, 1810.

[59]N. Salcedo to the Governor of Texas, October 13, 1810, with the Governor of Texas to N. Salcedo, October 2, 1810.

The Opening of Texas to Foreign Settlement 201

possession of lands to which many believed the United States had a valid claim, could easily do so, while *bona fide* immigrants, who might possibly have brought the peace and prosperity dreamed of by the authorities in Texas, were debarred from entry save by the circuitous and expensive route through Vera Cruz. The situation was made worse by the fact that immigrants who had committed crimes were able to escape to Louisiana, leaving their helpless families a burden upon the already embarrassed government.[60]

But so sure were the local authorities of their ability to carry their every point, that although orders had been issued forbidding the consideration of any immigration petitions whatever, they openly favored the admission of a servant of Davenport's, Enrique Carr, who presented a statement from the commandant of Nueva Felicinia, proving him a Spanish vassal.[61] The final decision of this matter is not disclosed, although the commandant-general did not positively forbid the step, merely insisting that the applicant's documents be properly prepared by the consul at New Orleans before his case could be considered.[62] José Alvarado, a native of San Martín de Tesmeluca, near Mexico City, who, in 1806, had gone from Texas to Opelousas and there married, returned in 1810 with his wife and children and desired to settle in Texas.[63]

Nothing is known as to the decision in his case. It is probable that Pedro Antonio Sais, who wished to immigrate from the district of Nuevo Feliciana and to locate in Texas with his wife and children,[64] settled at Béxar, since the name Pedro Saez, a European, a married man, sixty years of age, appears upon a list of the inhabitants of the capital prepared in 1820.[65] During this year, the commandant-general permitted two other Louisianans to

---
[60]Bonavía to M. Salcedo, October 9, 1810.
[61]Bonavía to M. de Salcedo, September 4, 1810.
[62]N. Salcedo to Bonavía, October 1, 1810.
[63]Guadiana to the Governor of Texas, September 21, 1810.
[64]Guadiana to the Governor of Texas, November 2, 1810.
[65]List January 1, 1820.

settle on condition that they should come by way of Vera Cruz,[66] but it is not likely that they immigrated.

Establishment of Villa de Palafox.[67]—The local authorities now carried things with a high hand. In line with his former policy, Cordero determined upon the establishment of a *villa* upon the Rio Grande, about half way between the *presidio* of Rio Grande and Laredo. This *villa*, which was founded on April 27, 1810, was given the name of Palafox in honor of one of the Spanish patriots who had been most successful in opposing Napoleon's invading army. On this day, Cordero wrote to Juan José Dias giving him jurisdiction over the place and instructing him to distribute lands to settlers.[68] In September, the commandant-general approved the step, but reminded Cordero of the scarcity of money and the consequent necessity of erecting buildings at the expense of the settlers themselves.[69] Not much of the history of Palafox can be secured from the meager records at hand. It may be said, however, that it alone of all the *villas* founded in present-day Texas during the period under consideration survived the attacks of the invaders in 1813,[70] only to be abandoned from 1818 to 1826 because of Indian depredations. The Texan officers thus carried out several of their plans over the protest of the commandant-general, and for a time, they were as successful over the revolutionists who soon began an active campaign in Texas.

The Hidalgo revolution.—Although, for years, discontent had been smoldering among the Creoles of Mexico, and although tentative attempts toward an uprising had been made, it was not until September 16, 1810, at the town of Dolores, that general revolution was actually set in motion. Then, the priest, Hidalgo, who, it will be remembered, had been allowed to communicate with D'Alvimar when on his

---

[66]M. de Salcedo to Bonavía, September 11, 1810.

[67]See map, between pp. 201–202.

[68]Cordero to Dias, April 27, 1810, Document No. 8, Volume 58, Records of Land Office.

[69]Document No. 203, *Ibid.*

[70]Arredondo to the Governor of Texas, May 5, 1814.

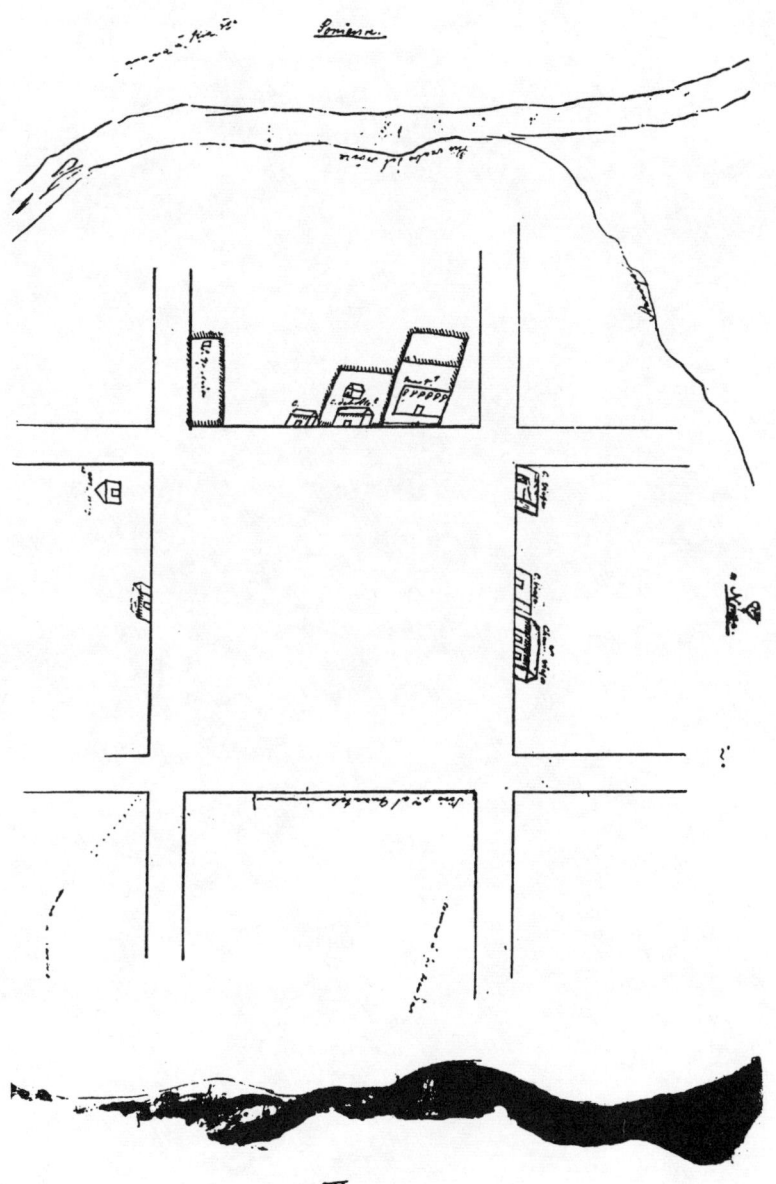

PALAFOX

way to Mexico, determined to put his cause to the test of arms. Consequently, the revolution so much desired by Napoleon was soon raging, and both the viceroy and the commandant-general,[71] made haste to do what they could to oppose it. The fact that there was but little money to be had and that the troops were ready to listen to the promises of the enemy, rendered their efforts at first weak and insignificant. Indeed, for a time, these authorities were so busy with the problems at home that they were unable to do more than to issue orders for preventing the spread of disaffection to Texas. An idea of the situation may be gained by examining a few of these orders. On October 2, the commandant-general charged the governor of Texas to take steps to avert invasions from the United States and to prevent the development of conspiracies in Texas. In reply, the governor explained that he had already taken all possible precautions, but that he had no resources on which to count.[72] The situation was not relieved by the action of the commandant-general in giving extraordinary powers to the governor to arrange with the consul at New Orleans for securing ammunition, arms, and other supplies;[73] and, to make matters worse, Bonavía was recalled to Durango to deal with the revolutionists at that point.[74] As a result, Governor Salcedo was left with no help save that of Herrera to oppose contraband traders, Indians, Americans, French, and Mexican revolutionists. Under these conditions, the governor did not lose heart, but, at once, devised vigorous defensive plans.

Ineffective preparations to prevent revolution in Texas.—
On October 26, he issued instructions to the commandant at Nacogdoches to keep a careful watch over the conduct of foreigners and suspicious vassals at that point and to call upon the commandant of Villa Salcedo for help in case it

---

[71]The commandant-general was thoroughly convinced that Napoleon was responsible for the revolution. Decree October 13, 1810.
[72]M. de Salcedo to N. Salcedo, October 2, 1810.
[73]N. Salcedo to the Governor of Texas, October 13, 1810.
[74]M. de Salcedo to N. Salcedo, October 27, 1810.

were needed. He warned him of the plans of the insurgents to assassinate all authorities who should remain faithful to the king and told him to guard against treachery even among his personal friends and to arrest anyone showing any signs of disloyalty or sedition.[75] As an additional precaution, he ordered Cristóbal Domínguez to Nacogdoches to assume command of the frontier posts, to guard against the entry of anyone from across the Louisiana border, and to prevent the carrying on of contraband trade.[76] All that could really be done, however, was to await the tide of events.

Nevertheless, on January 6, Governor Salcedo issued an appeal calculated to hold the people of Texas to their allegiance to the king. In this he said that the insurgents were attempting to make Mexico independent, that they were seeking to absolve themselves from their oath of allegiance by declaring that the king was really dead and that the Europeans were pretending that he was alive because they were trying to sell Mexico to Napoleon, but that in truth they were being led away by those favoring the French, or perhaps were being deceived by the emissaries of Napoleon. He vigorously repelled the charges of the insurgents that the European-born Spaniards were seeking to sell out to France and asserted that the insurgents themselves were merely appealing to the prejudice of the Creoles for the purpose of covering up their own treasonable designs of playing into the hands of Napoleon. He challenged his opponents to name a single European-born Spaniard who had been guilty of any suspicious or treasonable act since the beginning of Napoleon's attack on Spain. He cited the proclamation of the viceroy of April 18, 1809, as evidence that the higher authorities had taken every precaution to prevent the spread of Napoleon's influence. He even had the temerity to call attention to his own efforts to prevent the

---

[75]M. de Salcedo to the Commandant at Nacogdoches, October 26, 1810, in *Borradores de Oficios*, January 4, 1810–January 15, 1811.

[76]M. de Salcedo to the Commandant of Nacogdoches, November 21, 1810.

entry of either foreigners or Spaniards across the Louisiana frontier and, with more justice, discussed the measures he had taken for the peace and prosperity of the country. He enlarged upon the services of the European-born Spaniards and the excesses of the Creole insurgents and called upon the people of Texas to remain true to the beneficent king of Spain, and to their religion, and to present a solid front to the infidels, the cowards, and the traitors, who were being instigated to the attack by such a criminal as Hidalgo.[77]

Even in the face of these impending dangers, he gave indisputable evidence that trade with Louisiana was still one of his favorite hobbies. He wrote the governor of Nuevo León and Nuevo Santander that the commandant-general was considering the plan of granting the privilege of an annual fair to the people of Nacogdoches; he expressed pleasure at the prospect, since the people would be allowed to exchange mules, horses, and other products for articles they needed. He though this step was a wise one in view of the many plans of the enemies of the crown, for he felt that this evidence of the desire of the commandant-general to develop the Interior Provinces would help hold the people to their allegiance to the king and to prevent them from listening to the "sordid suggestions" of those who were seeking to carry out their private plans under the pretext of reforms.[78] By supporting this liberal commercial policy he placed himself in line with the progressive party of the *cortes* which had met on September 24, 1810. Immediately after securing their seats, the American deputies secured the passage of a decree placing the American provinces on the same footing as those of Spain by confirming the decree of October 15, 1810, which granted to them equal representation in the *cortes*, by extending to them the privilege of cultivating their native products and of developing manufactories and other industries, and by conceding to them an equal opportunity for official positions.[78] These belated

---

[77]M. de Salcedo to the Faithful Inhabitants of Texas, January 6, 1811.

[78]Decree February 9, 1811.

promises of sweeping reforms did not serve to placate the revolutionists, and it was but a short time until a member of the *cortes*—perhaps an agent of Napoleon—came to Texas for the ostensible purpose of aiding the insurgent cause, although he may have intended to betray that cause after having secured command.

In the meantime the governor was able to carry only a small part of the people of Texas with him. On January 18, a few of the leading citizens of Béxar, in mass meeting assembled, declared their allegiance to the king and their confidence in the local authorities. They also expressed the wish that the governor should make ready for the defense of Béxar and lead his loyal troops against the insurgents of Coahuila who were carrying everything before them.[79] The governor had hardly made his appeal before the wave of insurrection reached Béxar, and his followers began to drop away, for the inhabitants of Texas were not behind those of other regions in changing their political faith instantaneously as occasion might arise. Indeed, as Bancroft remarks:

> With wonderful facility the people could be royalists or revolutionists as the occasion demanded. In their principles they were greatly influenced by the weather. If Hidalgo rained his rabble upon them in the morning, the town—all that was left of them—were for the country. If Calleja's sun shone bright, it was for the king.[80]

The contest in Texas will therefore be of especial interest.

---

[79]*Junta Convocada*, January 18, 1811.
[80]Bancroft, *History of Mexico*, IV, 259.

CHAPTER VII

A Preliminary Testing of Nations and of Principles, 1811–1812

The Las Casas Revolution, 1811.—On January 23, 1811, Juan Bautista de las Casas, who had previously served in the army of Nuevo Santander, set in motion at Béxar a revolution against the European-born authorities in Texas. On this day, following the example of the governor, he issued appeal to the "Faithful Inhabitants of Texas," in which he criticized the local authorities for making plans to flee from Béxar and thus leave everything in confusion under the pretense of establishing their headquarters at Nacogdoches.[1] Under cover of this charge he seized upon both Herrera and the governor as well as upon the property and persons of the eleven other European Spaniards living in the province,[2] his avowed purpose being to maintain order, to defend the Catholic religion and to serve his country and his king. Deserted by their troops, Herrera and the governor could offer no resistance, and they were soon sent to Coahuila under guard. With the legal authorities out of the way, Las Casas succeeded in having himself elected as governor *ad interim*, but, within a few weeks, he was removed and a *junta governadora* composed of a president, a secretary, and eleven members was selected to direct the affairs of Texas.[3] Among the members of this *junta* were four men who had been supporters of the deposed authorities; further developments soon followed.

Counter revolution.—According to the invariable custom, this *junta* issued an address to the people, declaring their determination to obey the king, to defend the Catholic

---

[1] Proclamation, January 23, 1811.
[2] List of Prisoners, February 12, 1811. *N. A.* Navarro states that there were fourteen Spaniards seized at this time. Navarro, *Apuntes*, 8.
[3] [?] to Gómez, Vivero, and Cantú, February 8, 1811.

religion and the Spanish dominions, and to protect the people of Texas.[4] They sent commissioners to Monclova for the ostensible purpose of learning the true motives of the insurgents, but, in reality, with instructions to get in communication with the commandant-general or with Calleja, who was now in charge of the royalist troops.[5] These agents did not have to wait long to accomplish their purpose. Because of the treachery of Elizondo, a disgruntled revolutionary leader, they soon witnessed the capture of Hidalgo and his most trusted associates. As a result, the whole region was soon cleared of revolutionists.[6] The deposed Texas authorities were thereupon reinstated, Herrera returning in July, as governor, *ad interim*, and Manuel de Salcedo, who was soon sent to replace him, arriving in September. Salcedo did not assume office until the end of the year because of illness and his determination to force an adequate recognition of his previous services and to secure exoneration from charges of neglect in connection with the insurgent attack.[7] In the meantime, however, the way had been thoroughly prepared for his return. Juan José Zambrano, a member of the *junta*, managed to gain the support of all the people of Béxar and to turn the tide in favor of the European-born Spaniards, at first, by merely pretending to correct the faults of Las Casas's administration, and later, by charging that certain agents of the insurgents of Coahuila, who had passed through Texas on their way to the United States, were French emissaries who were planning to sell Texas to the United States.[8] The European-born Spaniards were thus, for a time, victorious.

---

[4]March 3, 1811, and Minutes of the *Junta*, March 6, 1811.

[5]Instructions, March 6, 1811, and the *Junta* to the Agents of Texas, April 18, 1811, Navarro believed that these instructions were made indefinite in order that the agents might play safe no matter which side might win. Navarro, *Apuntes*, 10.

[6]Muñoz and Galán to the *Junta*, April 3, 1811, and Menchaca to the *Junta*, May 7, 1811.

[7]M. de Salcedo to N. Salcedo, November 4, and December 16, 1811.

[8]N. Salcedo to the *Junta*, April 19, 1811, and Herrera to N. Salcedo, July 24, 1811. Navarro claimed that the people had learned definitely that Napoleon was sending a new agent to take charge of affairs. Navarro, *Apuntes*, 6.

The Opening of Texas to Foreign Settlement 209

The royalists of Texas were also encouraged to a continued resistance by the action of the regency in providing for the division of the Interior Provinces into two commandancies general.[9] This division was urged in the *cortes* by Miguel Ramos de Arispe, representative from Coahuila, who was one of the foremost American deputies.[10] He took it upon himself to plead the cause of Texas, since, at that time, no representative from that "unhappy province" had reached Spain. He prophesied that the government would realize the strategic importance of the Eastern Interior Provinces as soon as it learned *"how many foreigners had fixed their eyes longingly on the region."* He insisted that conditions were exactly the same as they had been in 1804, when the divisions of the Interior Provinces was first decided upon. He urged the necessity for the establishment of a representative system of government which would be capable of managing all departments and of assuring the development of the great resources of that region and thus bring wealth and happiness to thousands of persons. In this connection, he discussed the wisdom of carrying out plans similar to those adopted in 1804 for the establishment of settlers in Texas. He also claimed that while the existing commercial system had enriched a few, it had left the mass of the people in poverty and misery, thus proving to be the greatest curse of the Spanish dominion of America. The people of Texas were compelled, he said, to pay six prices for an article by the time it reached them. He urged that they be placed on an equal footing with the vassals of other regions, claiming that since Texas possessed most excellent harbors it was rank injustice to deny its people the enjoyment of the prosperity which would follow their use. He favored the opening of the Ports of Matagorda and Brazos de Santiago, on the Rio Grande, saying that this alone would attract settlers, who, through self-interest, would defend the province and bring to it the long desired peace

---
[9]Appendix, 20.
[10]Bancroft, *History of Mexico*, IV, 450.

and prosperity.¹¹ Although Ramos de Arispe was not able to carry all his points, his arguments were effective in securing the division of the Interior Provinces into the eastern and western divisions. But the fires of insurrection were not extinguished; they were merely smouldering, ready to be fanned into a flame by any chance breeze.¹² There was danger too that the conflagration would again spread to Texas from other points even though the fires at home were carefully guarded.

In July, 1811, the American deputies to the *cortes* despaired of getting any adequate representation and charged José Alvarez de Toledo, one of their number, with the duty of directing the insurgent campaign in the Interior Provinces.¹³ He was instructed to organize an army and to establish there an independent government similar to those established in other provinces of America. That the United States would be feared at this time of internal struggle was inevitable and that many foreigners would take advantage of this opportunity to carry forward their plans was to be expected. A review of the activities of the aggressors is, therefore, necessary.

Activities of the French.—Napoleon continued his attempt to foment trouble by sending additional emissaries to spread dissatisfaction in the Spanish domains. It was charged that at one time alone thirty French agents landed in the United States.¹⁴ Repeated warnings were sent to the authorities so that his plans might be frustrated.¹⁵ For instance, Onïs wrote the viceroy giving information of the presence in New York of a certain Greffe, a French of-

---

[11]*Memoria*, November 1, 1811, in *A. G. I. S.* Guad., 103–3–19.

[12]For the plans of Josef Menchaca to draw away the troops from their allegiance, see M. de Salcedo to N. Salcedo, February 20, 1812, and the *Junta* to Luna y Seguin, July 13, 1811.

[13]*A. G. I. S. Indif.*, 136–7–9, July 14, 1811–March 31, 1815. Certain insurgent leaders charged that Toledo had forged his credentials. *Memoria Politico-Instructiva Enviada de Philadelphia en Ayosto, 1821 á los Gefes Independentes del Anahuac*, 11.

[14]Sambrano to Herrera, August 10, 1811.

[15]N. Salcedo to the *Junta*, May 7, 1811, and N. Salcedo to the Governor *ad interim*, September 14 ,1811.

The Opening of Texas to Foreign Settlement 211

cer in Napoleon's Guard, who was making plans against the Spanish dominions in America.[16]

Among those arousing the greatest alarm was a certain Dr. Amblimont, who, it was said, had come from France to the United States to further Napoleon's purpose. The warnings issued against him stated that he intended to take advantage of the occupation of Florida by the confederated troops for the purpose of making his way from Philadelphia to New Orleans. From this place, he planned to send representatives into the Spanish dominions. He was said to be charged with the duty of ascertaining the best means of penetrating from New Orleans to the City of Mexico itself, of increasing the number of agents, and of sending them out with passports as citizens of the United States. Some of these agents were to point out to discontented persons the attractiveness of independence, while others were to approach men of wealth and standing and describe to them the horrors of revolution. In this way all classes were to be induced to appeal to the protection of the Emperor of France. In pursuance of these plans, the agents were to continue to excite the Creoles against the European-born Spaniards, and to arm them for the conflict.[17] Suspicion was not confined to the French.

Fear of the United States.—From the very beginning of 1811 the local authorities of Texas had complained to the United States of aggressions of certain Americans. In fact, as early as January 3, the *junta* wrote the commandant-general of the establishment of Americans in the Neutral Ground contrary to agreement.[18] No retaliatory movement was attempted because, as it was claimed, the Spanish authorities hoped that the United States would continue to coöperate with Spain in clearing the region of intruders.[19] Yet, so great was the prevailing distrust, that when the United States made promises of restraining her lawless

---
[16]The Viceroy to N. Salcedo, July 24, 1811.
[17]Venegas to N. Salcedo, October, 1811.
[18]N. Salcedo to the *Junta*, April 19, 1811.
[19]N. Salcedo to the Governor *ad interim*, September 3, 1811.

characters and actually took steps to do so, many royalists believed that this was but a preliminary step toward an invasion of Spanish territory. Naturally, the commandant-general, who attributed to the United States government the same motives that actuated a few of its most adventurous frontiersmen, was not slow to issue a warning that the United States would probably take advantage of the discontent within Mexico to carry forward its territorial ambitions, or even to spread the principles of freedom in the Spanish territory and thus gain possession of the disputed territory.[20] It was even feared that the United States might coöperate with Napoleon,[21] and severe criticism of the lack of energy on the part of the authorities in dealing with the French of Louisiana was indulged in.[22]

American "filibusters."—Although the United States government committed no hostile act, there were, at this time, quite a number of Americans eager to enter Texas. A striking example of the attitude of these adventurers is offered by the case of Dr. John Sibley and a confederate by the name of Smith.[23]

Writing from Natchitoches to Father Huerta, of Nacogdoches, in regard to the plans of the insurgents, Smith asserted that he had been born in a free country, and that, consequently, he believed in liberty and equal rights for all. He was ready, he said, to assist his companions, his neighbors, and his brothers, who had come to him asking for aid, in case they wished to defend their rights, their liberty, and their happiness, and to free themselves from the oppression of the king. He said:

> This is the time for you to embrace my offer. I will raise a thousand men and place them around your banners. I will aid you to defend the cause which you have so justly undertaken to support. The gods desire to protect you until victory

---

[20]N. Salcedo to the Governor of Texas, February 4, 1811.
[21]Letter dated New York, March 4, 1811.
[22]N. Salcedo to the *Junta*, July 9, 1811.
[23]Probably Juan F. Smith. See list of officers of insurgent army in *A. G. I. S. Indif.*, 36–7–9, July 14, 1811–March 23, 1815.

The Opening of Texas to Foreign Settlement 213

is gained. You should at once abandon your king, for he is unworthy to rule you because he has submerged his sovereignty beneath the tyranny of Napoleon and because he has spilled so much blood in the heart of his kingdom.

Smith tried to persuade Huerta that he could influence his parishioners to revolt by showing them that all men were born equal and that the tyranny of the king justified them in establishing a government for themselves. He asked to be informed if his offer was accepted, saying that considerable numbers of men were ready to march to the aid of the insurgents. In addition, he promised to enlist others who could easily be obtained in case they were needed.[24] Instead of adopting the suggestion, Father Huerta at once forwarded this letter to the *junta*, together with a paper setting forth the plans of Napoleon and declared himself ready to support the king.[25] His fellow priest, Father Sosa, was not so faithful; and, although the authorities immediately recalled him from the frontier, he managed to make his escape to the United States.[26] Smith collected only a small number of foreigners, but, in spite of the fact that but little resistance could have been offered, for some unknown reason, he made no attack. This alarm, however, had its effect upon the subsequent history of Texas, for one hundred and fifty soldiers were thrown forward from Béxar to Nacogdoches to guard the frontier. This left the capital under the protection of a mere handful of miserably equipped and unreliable soldiers, and finally led to the loss of the majority of the men who were transferred to Nacogdoches, since they were quite unable to remain true to the old *régime* when placed in this hot-bed of the revolutionists.[27] Contrary to his usual custom, the

---

[24]Smith to Huerta, April 19, 1811.
[25]Huerta to the *Junta*, May 20, 1811.
[26]N. Salcedo to the Governor of Texas, September 3, 1811. He soon repented of his defection, Sáenz to Herrera, August 19, 1811.
[27][?] to the Justice of the Peace of Natchitoches, June 26, 1811, [?] to N. Salcedo, June 26, 1811, and N. Salcedo to Domínguez, June 28, 1811.

commandant-general seems to have been but little impressed with the danger, explaining that he considered Smith merely a filibuster who had been incited to make an attack upon Texas by Napoleonic agents and who had been able to carry forward his plans because of lack of energy on the part of the United States government.[28] Nevertheless, he advised caution and reported that Cordero was sending two hundred men from Coahuila to aid in the defense of Texas. As usual, the governor had a very different opinion. He was so impressed with the danger that he instructed the commandant of the frontier to fall back to the Trinity if attacked by a superior force and to send information to Béxar so that proper defensive measures might be determined upon.[29] The authorities of Nacogdoches also considered the danger great; Sambrano, especially, protested against the insufficient defense of the frontier, declaring that this was the point of greatest importance, because over thirty emissaries of Napoleon had disembarked in Louisiana and because, even when uninfluenced by Napoleon, the Americans were greedy for the beautiful and fertile lands of Texas.[30] Domínguez, too, was very much afraid that an attack would be made. He went further and protested to the justice of the peace at Natchitoches against the expedition of over one hundred men against Bayou Pierre, under the leadership of Miguel Quinn and an American by the name of Taylor.[31] Domínguez was also much alarmed because Captain José Menchaca had fled from Nacogdoches to the United States accompanied by a number of insurgents. One of his chief charges against Menchaca was that he was influencing the Indian tribes to join the attacking party.[32]

---

[28]N. Salcedo to the *Junta*, July 7, 1811.
[29]Herrera to the Commandant-General, August 7, 1811, and N. Salcedo to the Governor *ad interim*, September 3, 1811.
[30]Sambrano to Herrera, August 10, 1811.
[31]Probably Joseph Taylor. See list of foreign officers in the insurgent army in *A. G. I. S. Indif.*, 136–7–9, July 14, 1811–March 31, 1815.
[32]Domínguez to Herrera, September 28, 1811, and enclosed documents.

The Opening of Texas to Foreign Settlement 215

Indian troubles.—His alarm, of course, was quite natural, and, indeed, from the very beginning of the Hidalgo revolt, the Comanches, the Tahuacanas, the Tankawas, and the Lipans had been giving trouble in Texas. Many reports of the activities of foreigners among the Indian tribes had been sent in[33] and appeal after appeal had been made to the commandant-general for protection.[34]

Of course no effective measures could be taken, owing to the lack of troops and supplies to carry on a vigorous warfare against the offenders, and so the old system of making presents was continued.[35] Besides, upon learning of the threatened attack of Smith and Sibley, the commandant-general charged Domínguez to preserve the most peaceful relations possible with the Indians, especially with "the Koasatis, the Alabamas, the Beloxis, the Choctaws, the Eylishes, the Nadakas, the Nacogdoches, and the Texas Indians," inciting them to hate the Americans for desiring to seize the lands held by these Indians under the authority of the Spanish king.[36] Upon the urgent request of the governor, Davenport, the Indian trader, was commissioned to secure in Louisiana the necessary presents for his wards.[37] So intent was the governor upon holding the Indians in check and preventing the entry of foreign traders that he proposed the establishment of a *presidio* on the Brazos among the Tahuacana Indians, to be garrisoned by troops of the company of Alamo de Parras, who were to be accompanied by their families. He also favored the plan of the archbishop of the college of Guadalupe for establishing a mission at this point. He prophesied that in time this would become a fine settlement, because the lands were

---

[33]N. Salcedo to the *Junta*, June 20, 1811.
[34]The *Junta* to N. Salcedo, May 8, 1811, and Herrera to N. Salcedo, August 29, 1811.
[35]N. Salcedo to the *Junta*, June 10, 1811.
[36]N. Salcedo to Domínguez, June 28, 1811, and M. de Salcedo to N. Salcedo, September 18, 1811.
[37]M. de Salcedo to N. Salcedo, September 11, 1811, and *Comision dada al Don Samuel Davenport, para la compra de efectos de regalos en la Louisiana*, December 21, 1811, and May 25, 1812.

fertile and well watered and the Indians anxious for missionaries and Spanish settlers.[38]

Discontent among soldiers.—This consideration for the treacherous Indians must have enraged the ragged soldiers of Texas, for, in spite of the efforts of the authorities to secure supplies from Louisiana, the soldiers were sternly forbidden by the commandant-general to exchange horses and mules for clothing from that place.[39] That they should be willing to revolt against such a system does not seem surprising. At the end of 1811, therefore, the royalists were not only surrounded by enemies, but had them even within their own midst.

Dangers everywhere.—In describing the strain under which he labored at this time, the governor complained that he and his supporters were menaced, on the east, by a troop of American bandits, eager for the slightest misunderstanding as an excuse to tread under foot the rights of the Spaniards; on the north, by the Indian nations, ready even without being influenced by the Americans to attack the weak and unarmed settlements; and, at the capital, by the followers of Las Casas, longing for an opportunity to fan into flames the smothered fires of insurrection. He showed that the danger from these sources was increased by the lack of supplies for the soldiers and the discontent among them due to the presence of revolutionary ideas. He was not entirely without hope of defending Texas against all foes. He relied upon the ability of the commandant-general, the support of the faithful vassals in Texas, his own determination to defend his country, and, above all, to Divine Providence, who would most surely bring final victory to the standard of the king.[40]

Partial conversion of the commandant-general.—By this time, however, the commandant-general, whose removal had already been decided upon, in spite of the fact that his

---

[38]M. de Salcedo to N. Salcedo, November 27, 1811.
[39]N. Salcedo to the *Junta*, June 25, 1811.
[40]M. de Salcedo to the Commandant-General, August 16, 1811, and N. Salcedo to M. de Salcedo, August 14, 1811.

every prophecy was coming true, was beginning to favor the plan of developing Texas. For example, desiring to show his interest in Texas and thus to gain adherents, he called upon the governor for a report of the conditions of the province in order that he might be able to carry out his wishes for improving the region.[41] Finally, upon the urgent appeal of the governor,[42] he even consented to the opening of the port of Matagorda in accordance with the decree of September 28, 1805.[43] For the purpose of preventing contraband trade, he considered the plan of establishing an annual fair at Nacogdoches where the settlers could exchange their surplus stock for manufactured articles.

Aggressive policy of the governor.—Thus, all too late, he was finally converted to the development policy which had been so warmly espoused by the governor, who, by this time, favored still more vigorous and aggressive measures. To this length, however, the commandant-general was neither willing nor able to go. Nevertheless, he asked for a report of the productions of Texas and for suggestions for increasing the output and for stimulating friendly relations between Spain and her American dominions through trade, a measure which was being greatly stressed by the *cortes*. But, despite his final partial conversion, he was handicapped by his conservative tendencies and by his lack of funds. Yet, in the midst of all these difficulties, the governor, realizing that he was face to face with a grave situation, wished to take certain preventative measures to weaken the enemy. He was resolved to do everything in his power to extinguish the fires of revolution. In March, he reported that the Comanches were evidently making plans to attack Béxar and other points, and proposed that several parties be sent into the enemy's country so that depredation might be

---

[41]M. de Salcedo to the Commandant-General, February 3, 1812, No. 39, in Series 31–44 of the same date.

[42]M. de Salcedo to N. Salcedo, draft No. 39 in *Libro*, February 5, 1812.

[43]M. de Salcedo to Morphí, February 15 and April 1, 1812.

prevented. In answer to this proposal, the commandant-general explained that a declaration of war against the Comanches had always been considered the greatest evil that could befall the province. He urged that the old system of conciliation be continued, since the government was confronted with such a great number of other important questions that nothing could be done. He merely instructed the governor to drive away to a reasonable distance any hostile parties who might attack the settlement and to reward in the customary way those who might come peaceably. He hoped by this plan to avoid a general Indian war. Instead of favoring any aggressive measures, he advised that the detachment on the Brazos be removed to the Trinity and that the troops on the Colorado be transferred to San Marcos, so that less opportunity for attack would be offered to the Indians.[44]

Continued foreign aggression and continued delay.—Although he was quick to issue orders, the commandant-general could not send the reinforcements so much needed.[45] An illustration of his futile policy is shown by his instructions of February 3, 1812, providing for more drastic treatment of the Americans caught in Texas without passports. These were issued with a view also of excluding Napoleon's emissaries,[46] and preventing communication across the Louisiana frontier.[47] But since the military force so much desired by the governor was lacking, these orders were not worth the paper upon which they were written. That the danger was increasing is quite clear. Some of the royalists even believed that a combined French and American attack was in contemplation.

For instance, Consul Morphí declared that the United States and the French minister at Washington were sending agents to Mexico to stir up the insurgents. He claimed that their plans had advanced so far that places of deposit

---
[44]N. Salcedo to the Governor of Texas, March 25, 1812.
[45]N. Salcedo to the Governor of Texas, August 6, 1812.
[46]N. Salcedo to the Governor of Texas, February 3 and 4, 1812.
[47]Garza to M. de Salcedo, March 6 and April 4, 1812.

for supplies for an invading army had been selected.[48] Onís continued his warnings. In January, 1812, he wrote to the viceroy in regard to the continued activity of revolutionary agents at Philadelphia, who hoped to make Texas part of the United States. He declared that he knew positively that Poinsett, an agent of the United States government, was residing within Spanish territory. He stated that the arrival of Bernardo Gutiérrez at Washington, his conference with officials, his contracts for munitions, his departure for Natchitoches, and his boast that the leader of the insurgent army had two American subordinate officers, Smith and Patterson, of Philadelphia, increased his alarm.[49] So convinced was he of the danger that he appealed to the supreme government, insisting that the United States was following up with tenacity its determination to enlarge its dominions at the cost of the Spaniards, and saying that a number of American recruits had gone to Texas to encourage rebellion there.

Plan of Morphí.—He advised that the plan for placing a military colony in that province should be carried into effect, at once, instead of after the conclusion of the war with France, as has been previously decided upon.[50] As Spanish troops were not available, owing to Napoleon's aggressions in Spain and to the activities of the revolutions in America, he proposed to the government that German and Polish soldiers, who had enlisted in Napoleon's army either through the use of deceit or force, should be detached from their allegiance and induced to settle in Texas, where they could devote themselves to agriculture and the useful arts, thus securing

---

[48]Morphí to the Commandant of Nacogdoches, April 26, 1812.

[49]The Viceroy to the Intendant of San Luis Potosí, April 3, 1812, with appended letter of Onís and N. Salcedo to the Viceroy, May 11, 1812, in *Libro*, May 12, 1812. For the policy of the government of the United States in sending agents to the revolting colonies of Spain, see Treat, *The Independence of the South American Republics*, 106–112.

[50]Onís to Duque de San Fernando, September 20, 1819, in *A. G. I. S. legajo*, No. 23, September 20, 1819–April 26, 1821.

their own happiness and the welfare of the province.[51] He wished to grant them *seven square leagues* of land upon the Gulf of Mexico near the Louisiana frontier, to exempt them from taxation, to allow them free trade with all nations, and to invest them with local authority. Only artisans and mechanics of good character were to be introduced. By this means, Onís hoped to weaken Napoleon and, at the same time, to place in Texas a body of troops which would some day inspire the respect of the United States.

The plan was not favorably regarded either by the local authorities or by the regency to whom it was referred for decision. The regency protested against placing a number of foreign soldiers in a region where everything was already in a ferment, and they did not wish to furnish money from a depleted treasury to enrich foreigners who had been contaminated by long years of association with the French and who would only await a favorable opportunity to ruin their gullible and poverty stricken benefactors by falling in with the plans of Spain's enemies, especially those of the United States where many Germans and Poles settled. They feared that as soon as the project became known Napoleon would send out, under the guise of settlers, his most trusted lieutenants who would claim to be Polish and German deserters. How easy it would be, they pointed out, for those men to deliver Texas into their master's hands as soon as a favorable opportunity presented itself. Recalling the case of Louisiana and West Florida, they even feared that Napoleon would immediately transfer the province to the United States to pacify that country while he invaded other Spanish territory in America. One member suggested that the project of securing settlers in the way proposed might be favorable as a war measure in so far as it tended to weaken Napoleon's army, but insisted that neither Germans nor Poles—who were all favorable to Napoleon's rule—should be located in Texas, since it was a buffer against the United States. He even believed that the whole plan was contrary

---

[51]Documents in *A. G. I. S.* Mex., *Legajo 4*, May 6, 1819.

to the laws of the country, which permitted the immigration of only such foreigners as were mechanics or craftsmen. He wished every precaution taken against surprise by the French as well as by the Americans who continued to push into Spanish territory and who had disregarded the treaty of 1795 by permitting the passage of Napoleonic emissaries through its territory, by allowing the army of French corsairs in its ports, by giving support to the insurgents, and by actually furnishing a leader from the insurgent army in Texas. He proposed as a substitute that German Catholics should be persuaded to desert Napoleon by inducing them to serve in the Spanish army at home by a promise of subsequent transportation to America where they would be continued in service. He desired that even greater precautions should be observed, stipulating that the deserters thus obtained should be sent out in small groups in regiments known to be faithful to the Spanish cause. He wished to make permission to settle contingent upon good behavior and suggested that *presidios* be founded and that lands be given these recruits in regions especially needing defense against the Indians. These precautions were favored by one other member who had made similar proposals to the *junta* as early as 1808. That body, however, finally decided to reject the whole scheme, insisting upon the enforcement of the law forbidding all intercourse with foreigners and repealing the order of September 24, 1803, which had permitted the immigration of Spanish vassals from Louisiana.[52]

Although John Robinson, a semi-official agent[53] of the United States, presented himself at this time, declaring that his government did not look with favor upon the movements of the revolutionists,[54] he was not believed. In fact, his proposal that trade be opened between the Interior Provinces

---

[52]*Expediente sobre remision a la Provincial Alemanes y Polacos para poblarla y otras fines*, A. G. I. S., 103–3–17, June 6, 1806–February 29, 1809.

[53]Cox, "Monroe and the Early Mexican Revolutionary Agents," in the *Annual Report of the American Historical Association*, 1911, V, 199–215.

[54]M. de Salcedo to the Commandant-General, October 27, 1813, and Bustamante to M. de Salcedo, November 14, 1812.

and Louisiana for the purpose of "tranquilizing the minds of the revolutionist, arousing their ambition, and increasing their prosperity" quite naturally angered Nemesio Salcedo and the commandant-general of the Western Interior Provinces to whom the proposals were presented, as they believed that such a thing was contrary to express sovereign decisions, to the best interest of the nation, and to the tranquility which the president of the United States seemed so ardently to desire.[55] The fact that Robinson soon openly espoused the revolutionary cause,[56] justified their suspicions. There were other circumstances which kept the Spaniards in alarm. Morphí gave warning of the departure from New York of a Creole of New Spain, Navarro by name, who had previously made a trip to Philadelphia to secure arms, ammunition and other supplies. In writing to José María Navarro, another official said:

> Informed of your determination to go to North America and of your desire to do something for King Joseph, using your influence, friendship, and relations in that place, and to share the fate of this Metropolis and remain united to it, I send you the adjoined papers which will serve you as credentials.[57]

Onís discussed, too, the suspicious activities of Tadeo Ortiz, of New Orleans, a close friend of the editor of *L'Amis de Lois* who was a rabid Bonapartist.[58] It was known at this time, too, that Gutiérrez had left New Orleans for the

---

[55]Conde to Apodaca, September 18, 1818, in *A. G. I. S.* Mex., *Leg.* 13, No. 41, April 8, 1817–November 30, 1818.

[56]Bancroft, *History of Mexico*, IV, 606, Note 40. On September 16 he issued at Philadelphia an inflammatory circular calling upon the Americans to join the Mexican revolutionists and requesting them to *rendezvous* at Nacogdoches on November 25, 1818. One of these circulars was addressed to Edward Hempstead and A. McNair, Parker, *Calendar of Papers in Washington Archives relating to the Territories of the United States*, Item 4667.

[57]Translated from letter in *coleccion de noticias y documentos para la Historia del estado de N. Leon por el ciudadano J. Aleuterary*. See Josef Navarro mentioned in Appendix 10.

[58]Morphí to the Commandant of Nacogdoches, April 26, 1812.

purpose of starting another revolution in the Spanish dominions. He had first applied to the United States for aid but he soon abandoned this idea because of the neutral policy of that government, and began to gather adherents in the southern states, where enthusiasm for the cause of the revolution was strong.[59] Upon learning of Gutiérrez's activity, Governor Salcedo again begged that sufficient additional troops be sent to Texas to meet all dangers, declaring that the province could no longer be held by the force already on the frontier. He also gave warning that the strained relations between England and the United States might lead the latter to support Gutiérrez's schemes as a makeweight against England's attempt to draw away the settlers of portions of the United States from their allegiance. When news of actual war between England and the United States reached Texas, the governor announced that this virtually amounted to a declaration of war against

---

[59]Filisola, Vicente, *Memorias de la Guerra de Texas*, 61. In regard to the attitude of the United States toward the revolutionists, Claiborne gave several interesting bits of information. He asserted that he had received no official instructions as to the treatment of Gutiérrez but that he had been advised by an *attaché* of the department of state that the government desired that the gentleman's return to Mexico be expedited. As a result, Claiborne instructed one of his subordinates to extend every possible civility to Gutiérrez and to advance him such funds as might be necessary to enable him to reach Natchitoches. Claiborne to Shaler, April 7, 1812, *Letter Books*, VI, 71–72. This must not be construed as indicating that Claiborne was strongly in sympathy with the revolutionists. Although wishing them well in the abstract and desiring them to be freed from European influence, he expressed the fear that they would not be good neighbors and voiced the wish that "it comported with the policy of the American government to take possession of the country as far as the Rio Grande." Claiborne to [?], June 21, 1813, *Ibid.*, 228–229. He expressed his disapprobation of the designs of various citizens of the United States to *rendezvous* at some point west of the Sabine and there take up arms to aid the revolutionists. He believed, however, that action should be delayed until the question of peace or war with England could be decided. Claiborne to Monroe, July 6, 1812, and Claiborne to Gates, September 10, 1813, *Ibid.*, 122–123 and 364–365.

England's ally, Spain.[60] In June he begged once more for troops to meet the threatened invasion of revolutionists from the Neutral Ground and again urged the establishment of the Eastern Interior Provinces as had been planned so many years before.[61] The commandant-general acknowledged that the situation was very grave, but said that detailed instructions were being prepared for placing Texas in the best possible state of defense. He pointed out that he was distracted by a thousand cares and charged the governor to do the best he could under the circumstances, since it was physically impossible to send aid, because of dangers in other provinces.[62] This, after all, was what the governor had to do, for in less than a month one of his many foes opened attack.

Indians force abandonment of San Marcos.—On July 27, a large number of Comanche Indians, together with some Tawakanes and Tawehash, attacked San Marcos, where was located the only detachment that it had been possible to maintain along the line from Béxar to Villa Salcedo. In spite of the efforts of the twelve or fifteen soldiers who were guarding the horses, the Indians succeeded in carrying off two hundred and five animals. No immediate aid could be sent from Béxar, as there was no time to call in from Bahía and the Frío the two hundred men deemed necessary for an expedition against the aggressors. The Indians had counted upon this delay, and made use of their usual tactics of laying the blame on other tribes. So it happened that a Comanche captain, perhaps fresh from the scene of action at San Marcos, immediately presented himself at Béxar with about two hundred persons. On the next day another Comanche arrived in great haste to recall the first party, declaring that a great number of Indians were coming against the Spaniards. By this subterfuge they were able to convince the governor that the Tawakanes were the aggressors and that these same Indians were also inciting six other nations

---

[60]M. de Salcedo to the Governor of Vera Cruz, August 6, 1812.
[61]M. de Salcedo to the Viceroy, June 25, 1812.
[62]N. Salcedo to the Governor of Texas, July 11, 1812.

to hostilities, instructing them to kill and steal everything in their pathway. The Comanches were included in this alliance, but the governor ascribed the uprising to the influence of foreigners, Spaniards, and negroes who lived among the various tribes. To meet the threatened attack, the detachment of San Marcos and the garrison of Bahía were called to Béxar, leaving Bahía to be defended by the citizens of the place. Nothing has been found to show what eventually became of the settlers of San Marcos, but they immediately abandoned the place,[63] leaving the residents of Villa Salcedo —where foreigners were in the majority—as the sole remnant of the colonization work of the period. After all exertions, only a small force of effective soldiers could be obtained. These the governor considered totally inadequate in view of the distance to Villa Salcedo, the necessity for keeping open communication, and the many difficulties to be encountered in the long journey; consequently he urged that additional men be secured and an active campaign made against the Indians. He was especially anxious to do this at once because he feared that the Americans would begin hostilities and effect a combination with the red men.[64]

American activities.—That there was danger from certain adventurous Americans is evident. On the same day that the Indian question was discussed, the governor reported that the United States had declared war against England, and, therefore, virtually against Spain. He claimed that he had reliable information that volunteers were being collected upon the Sabine for the invasion of the Spanish dominions to aid the insurgents of Texas. He prophesied that the United States would try to secure possession of Texas to the Rio Grande, and urged that measures be taken to defeat this purpose.[65] On August 6, a day of ill report, he gave

---

[63]They may have returned to their old homes in Refugio. A few years later the alcalde of this settlement bore the same name as the leader of the San Marcos band.

[64]M. de Salcedo to N. Salcedo, August 5, 1812.

[65][M. de Salcedo] to N. Salcedo, August 5, 1812, No. 192. Bound with 191 of same date.

information of the existence of a more subtle danger. He had learned that the commandant of Nacogdoches had furnished a passport to Pedro Lartigue and his son to return to Villa Salcedo, that they had set out with supplies, but that they had gone to Natchitoches instead.[66] He had, at last, realized that the foreigners in Nacogdoches and Villa Salcedo were secretly hostile to Spain; but he feared to order them to return to Louisiana, because he realized the danger of increasing the number of enemies on the border. As a precautionary measure he arranged for all faithful vassals to rally at Béxar in case of an attack from the United States.

Enmity of foreign element in Texas.—That the foreign element in Texas was really hostile to Spain is borne out by other evidence. Even Bernardo Despallier finally joined the insurgents, giving them the benefit of his knowledge of the country, acting as interpreter for the invaders, and furnishing them with supplies.[67] He was able to render them valuable assistance by enlisting the aid of many citizens of Rapides and Opelousas.[68] That all the funds for the supplies forwarded by him were his own seems doubtful. It seems possible even that at least a large part of the money to carry on this invasion may have been furnished by French or American sympathizers. At any rate, it was reported that arrangements had been made by Gutiérrez with the United States and the French minister at Washington to furnish all needed supplies, while the governor claimed that "a certain Spaniard of Mexico" had agreed with the French government to foment the insurrection.[69]

The fact that the United States had declared war against Great Britain naturally caused the Spaniards to guard more zealously their Texas frontier. In the summer of 1812, Trudeau wrote to the governor of Texas, saying that American volunteers were gathering in the Neutral Ground for

---

[65]M. de Salcedo to N. Salcedo, August 5, 1812, No. 193. Bound with 191–192.

[67]Procela to Montero, August 11, 1812.

[68]Masmela to M. de Salcedo, July 10, 1812, in translation of Documents found in the Archives of Bexar County, A.D. 1812. *N. A.*

[69]M. de Salcedo to Bustamante, May 10, 1812.

the purpose, he believed, of attacking Mexico,[70] while Governor Salcedo declared that as a natural consequence of this declaration of war, the United States had begun an attack on the Spanish dominions by taking Nacogdoches. He at once called for help, and gave warning that the whole kingdom would be lost unless his request was speedily granted. He stipulated that information of the attack should be kept from the insurgents, although he felt that the news should cause them, as Catholics and as patriots, to join the king's forces so that all foreigners might be expelled.[71]

Another American who deserted the royalist cause at this time was Samuel Davenport, the Indian trader. Forgetting the many favors he had received from the Spanish government, he went over openly to the insurgents and used all the resources at his command to forward supplies to them. It may be noted, too, that the son of James Wilkinson was among the invaders. Wilkinson's ostensible attitude toward the revolutionists may be ascertained from a letter written to the Secretary of War in 1812. He said:

> But while preparing for the defense of New Orleans, we should not be inattentive to the Mexican provinces; for it is a fact, derived from good authority, that Great Britain has appointed three commissioners to coöperate with the same number from the Spanish regency, expressly to effect a reconciliation, and restore the former relations between the provinces and the parent state. Whatever may be the effect of these negotiations, it is the obvious policy of Great Britain to acquire some direct or indirect control over the people of South America, and more particularly those of the Mexican provinces; and it appears to be our interest and our policy, to take measures to counteract these views, as it may be fairly inferred, that the Mexicans must become our enemies or our friends—enemies should the British intrigue prevail, and the ancient government be reëstablished—friends should the natives be enabled to assert and maintain their independence. . . .
> In this state of things, it might be presumptuous in a subordinate agent of the government to intrude his ideas on a subject of such complication and magnitude; yet it is too manifest

---

[70]Trudeau to M. de Salcedo, July 20, 1812.
[71]M. de Salcedo to Tovar, August 23, 1812.

to escape notice, that some concert should be effected with the native chiefs of the Internal Provinces, and that this government should be prepared to furnish them succors of small-arms, light artillery, ammunition, equipments, and field equipage, with experienced officers to instruct them, and select corps from the different branches of service, a *nucleus* for the revolutionists to rally around, and skeletons for them to form by. It would seem that no time should be lost in carrying this project into execution; and, preparatory thereto, a couple of light-armed vessels should explore the coast of the gulf west of the Mississippi to Grand river, and ascertain the entrance into El Espiritu Santo Bay, where La Salle landed. I have been informed, four or five fathoms of water may be carried into that bay, and that it is completely land-locked. The position is certainly the most convenient for maritime intercourse with those inhabitants of the province of Texas to be found east of Grand river.[72]

The Spaniards, too, realized the importance of Bahía del Espíritu Santo and one of them, at least, planned to forestall any attempt on the part of foreigners to locate there. This is clearly shown by the following quotation from the memorial presented to the regency by the secretary of the overseas dominions. He said:

The opening of Bahía de San Bernardo to the northward of Vera Cruz will give great impetus to navigation and commerce. Settlements should be established there before our neighbors occupy it. Such portions of its immense territories as are best suited to agriculture should likewise be utilized. It is better to supply Havana, Puerto Rico, Cartegena, and other points with flour, fruits, and other necessities from this point than from Vera Cruz. This will prevent the Americans from becoming rich at our expense as they are doing.[73]

But, due to an actual invasion of Texas, these plans could not be executed.

Seizure of Nacogdoches.—Gutiérrez with his queer assortment of Mexican revolutionists, Indian allies, French

---

[72]Foote, *Texas and the Texans*, I, 133–4. *Cf.* Yoakum, *History of Texas*, I, 144.

[73]*Memoria Presentada á la Regencia del Reyno por Don Giriaco Gonzales Caravajal, Secretario Interino—de la Governacion de Ultramar*, September 30, 1812, pp. 24–25.

followers, and American sympathizers, each intent upon the accomplishment of a different object, reached Nacogdoches on August 11, bringing *promises of support from nearly all the civilized nations of the world and actual assistance, both by land and sea, of men, arms, and whatever else might be needed in the fight against the Gauchipines, so that the Creoles might be independent and have the inestimable privilege of making their own laws, selecting the men who were to govern them, and of enjoying free commerce.*[74]

He called upon the inhabitants of the province to rally to his standard, explaining that he had secured the aid of a respectable body of American volunteers who had left their homes and families to aid him in his fight for liberty. He counted a great deal upon the valor of these men, the descendants of the heroes of 1776, who were anxious to draw their swords in defense of the cause of humanity and against European tyrants. As a reward for their assistance, he pledged them *free commerce in stock, the gift of lands for cultivation,* and *a share in the spoils of war.*[75]

His promises of foreign assistance had some semblance of truth so far as the United States was concerned, for President Madison had sent to Congress a message dealing with the revolt of the Spanish-American provinces, which had resulted in action favorable to the cause of independence. The committee to which the message had been referred, declared that, since a number of Spanish colonies of America had represented to the United States that they had been compelled to declare themselves free, Congress looked upon the move with friendly interest, felt great solicitude for the welfare of these neighbors, and, as soon as the said countries had attained the condition of nations, would establish amicable commercial relations with them. To ascertain the true condition in the rebellious provinces, Monroe even sent out confidential agents.

In the meantime, Gutiérrez and his followers encountered no resistance from the soldiers at Nacogdoches. Indeed, the

---

[72]Notice to the Inhabitants of Texas, September 1, 1812.
[75]Appendix 21.

troops deserted to the enemy almost to a man. In obedience to previous instructions, the commandant then withdrew to Villa Salcedo, reaching that point with a mere handful of men.[76] Upon receiving news of this catastrophe, the governor sent special messengers to the viceroy with appeals for help. He likewise called upon the commandant-general, the governors of Coahuila, Nuevo León, and Nuevo Santander, and upon Joaquin Arredondo who had been very active in hunting down Hidalgo's followers. He appealed also to the people of Béxar to do their part in defending to the last their holy religion against the attacks of these foreigners, Protestants, and heretics who sought to draw them away from their allegiance to their king and to their God.[77] He had good reason to call upon them, for the enemy was rapidly sweeping on. As had been prophesied, Villa de Salcedo really served as a rallying point for the enemy instead of as a defense for the Spaniards; and the citizens of that place, at once, became a part of the invading forces.[78] As a result, this *villa*, which was the last remnant of the buffer recently erected in that region, was soon abandoned by the royalists.[79] When called upon for an explanation of his retreat, the commandant claimed that he had been afraid that his troops would follow the example set by the company at Nacogdoches and desert to the enemy.[80] The road to Bahía and Béxar now lay open to the invaders. But, from this time forward, progress was somewhat slower.

Fall of Bahía and Béxar.—It was not until March 13, 1813, that the insurgents succeeded in capturing Bahía. In the meantime, they had secured additional recruits to the number of eight hundred Americans, one hundred and

---

[76]Diary, August 16, 1812.

[77]Proclamation, August 18, 1812.

[78]Morphí to Onis, November 27, 1812, and *Historia de Guerra de Independencia, Notas Diplomaticas, Tomo III, 1810.* Transc. U. of T.

[79]N. Salcedo to Montero, August 21, 1812, and M. de Salcedo to Garza, September 19, 1812.

[80]Garza to M. de Salcedo, September 20, 1812, with M. de Salcedo to Garza, September 19, 1812.

The Opening of Texas to Foreign Settlement 231

eighty Mexicans—under the leadership of the "traitor" Menchaca—and three hundred and twenty-four Indians, and, despite the fact that a number of royalist reinforcements had arrived from the interior of Mexico, they were able to seize Béxar where the majority of citizens and soldiers were anxiously waiting to join them. As a climax to their work, they treacherously put to death Herrera, who had been unable to obey orders recalling him to the Interior and Governor Salcedo who had voluntarily remained to sacrifice himself for his country.[81]. After this success, Guitérrez issued a proclamation filled with exultation and threats of vengeance. Among other things he said:

> Friends of the Mexican cause: The Independence of Texas, a desideratum long looked for and greatly wished by all nations except Great Britain and Spain in Europe, is at length accomplished! Thus far my brave countrymen become the warm and immutable advocates of independence, peace, and free commerce . . . they have evinced to all nations, that their revolution is just in its origin, useful in its progress, and honorable in its termination.
> The brave Americans have united themselves with the immortal Mexicans as brothers, as freemen, and as men defending the same just cause which liberates the slave, ameliorates the overbearing wants of the poor. Their souls are united in council and their arms are mingled in the field.
> I may therefore invite freemen from all nations to share in the conquests I have gained, and enjoy unmolested the rights and privileges of Mexican citizens. The trade and commerce of New Spain will no longer be confined to one or two powers but the whole Universe will enjoy a portion of her unknown riches. Vera Cruz will cease to be the one port by which the provinces will be supplied with foreign trade. The industrious patriot will hail with ecstacy and joy, the slow moving vessel that gently glides upon the waters of Matagorda, which comes to supply Texas. . . . The northern and eastern frontiers of Texas receive, by land, the trade of the Ohio, Missouri, and a greater part of the State of Louisiana. All the bays and harbors of the Gulf of Mexico and California will be opened in a short time to the trade of all commercial powers. The wealth of Potosi will be divided among those who merit the enjoyment of her stores.

---

[81]M. de Salcedo to the Commandant-General, October 27, 1812.

> Freemen of all nations! The fertile plains of Texas will no more be stained with the precious blood of patriots—here peace and comfort will smile, must smile, on renovated Mexicans until the end of time.

He paid his respects to his enemies in the following terms:

> The unaltered friends of Ferdinand VII now at the disposition of France, alone say that the advocates of our institutions are the oppressors of the people and the plunderers of their trade. But they shall more than ever feel the power and vengeance of an injured people. The people of Texas are now united and have convinced the enemies of republican government that their energy dies not in a day, but may be called out to defend their infant state against oppression. Hence, let her royal heroes fear and tremble.[82]

Gutiérrez's claim of undivided support from the Americans was unwarranted, and the spirit of vengeance here breathed soon lost his sympathizers. Indeed, the murder of Herrera and Salcedo had really marked the turning point of the war. His prophecy that the sway of the insurgents would be unchallenged was also false, for the royalists were soon able to drive all intruders beyond the border and to lay further plans for development.

---

[82]Proclamation of July 4, 1813, Niles' *Weekly Register*, V, 87–88.

CHAPTER VIII

THE TEMPORARY TRIUMPH OF PROGRESSIVE ROYALISTS, 1813

The European-born Spaniards, possessing a common purpose and superior officers, were soon able to rally somewhat from the consternation into which the first attack of the invaders had thrown them and to gather strength for the counter attack. In this they were aided by the inherent weakness of the enemy.

Weakness of enemy.—From the very nature of things, the insurgent army was a heterogeneous band, without common ideals, stable financial backing, definite plans, or able leaders. To make matters worse, the army had lost strength through the natural and growing distrust among its various component parts,[1] the death of Magee, one of its most active leaders, and the abandonment of a large number of other Americans who had been disgusted by the revolting cruelty shown in the murder of Commandant Herrera and Governor Salcedo. Not only had many Americans deserted the cause, but, because of the intensity of the struggle in Spain, Napoleon had failed to follow up his first movement with any degree of vigor. Although the French commander, Humbert, left Philadelphia in company with a number of Spaniards and certain French officers for the purpose of directing the campaign under Ex-Deputy José Alvarez Toledo —who was to replace the bloodthirsty Gutiérrez—he did not reach Texas in time to save that reckless leader from defeat. Before leaving Philadelphia Toledo and one of Humbert's subordinates had posed as opponents of Napoleon and confided to Onís their plan for betraying the insurgents into the hands of the royalists.[2] That treachery, the subtlest and greatest of all dangers, existed in the insurgent army,

---

[1] For description of the jealousies which prevented any effective campaign see account of the battle of the Medina by a participant, *A. G. I. S. Indif.*, 36–7–9, July 14, 1811–March 23, 1818, pp. 4–13.

[2] Onís to the Commandant-General, August 20, 1813. Appendix 22.

is shown by Toledo's subsequent return to Spain to receive numerous favors from Ferdinand VII, whom Napoleon soon released from prison on condition that he would expel the English from the Peninsula.

Strength of the royalists.—Another condition which aided the royalists in the contest was the final division of the Interior Provinces into two districts and the appointment of two aggressive leaders in the place of the ultra conservative, Nemesio Salcedo.[3]

The position of the commandant-general of the Eastern Interior Provinces was first offered to the able and determined Calleja. But he had declined the post, receiving instead, early in 1813, the appointment of viceroy.[4] His skill, energy, courage, and experience gave promise of a speedy termination of the revolution, for he was acknowledged by all to be the foremost soldier in Mexico. Immediately thereafter, Calleja appointed his personal friend, Simón de Herrera as commandant of the Eastern division,[5] in recognition of his services for Texas. But, owing to Herrera's untimely death at the hands of the insurgents, Joaquín de Arredondo, who was equally as energetic as his superior and who had already distinguished himself in the contest in the Interior, was placed in charge of the Eastern Provinces, while the determined Bonavía was made commandant-general of the Western Provinces.[6] Besides all this, discontent among the Creoles was no doubt somewhat dissipated for a time by the issuance of the liberal Spanish constitution of 1812. By its provisions they were declared citizens and given equal representation in the *cortes.* In addition to these privileges, they were allowed twelve of the forty representatives in the council which was to act as an advisory body to the king or his representative. They were likewise instructed to elect new *ayuntamientos*

---

[3]N. Salcedo to Venégas, November 22, 1812.
[4]Calleja to the Governor of Texas, March 4, 1813.
[5]Calleja to N. Salcedo, March 24, 1813.
[6]*Parecer del Fiscal,* May 11, 1814.

The Opening of Texas to Foreign Settlement 235

and to form provincial assemblies whose duty it was to encourage agriculture, commerce, and other important industries.[7]

Victory of royalists.—Thus favored, Arredondo was not only able to gain a decisive victory over the insurgents at the battle of Medina on August 18, 1813, but to capture and put to death many of the invaders in their frantic flight toward the Louisiana frontier. He thereupon confiscated the property of all persons believed to have supported the insurgents, ordered the destruction of all settlements owing their origin to the illegal location of foreigners, seized all insurgent sympathizers not lucky enough to escape, and issued orders for the arrest of any Napoleonic agent who might be found in Texas[8] and for the the execution of all traders, either Spanish or foreign, located at Nacogdoches,[9] leaving the place almost without an inhabitant. Not content with this, he sought to punish those who had escaped across the border. He granted amnesty to all citizens and foreigners who, through misunderstanding, had taken part in the revolution but who, as a sign of their repentance and their desire to live once more under the protection of the Spanish flag, would present themselves to the proper authorities. But he singled out Davenport and Despallier for special execration on the ground that they had treacherously sought to destroy the government which had received them as vassals. He offered five hundred *pesos* and permission to settle to any foreign Catholic who would murder the proscribed leaders and half that amount to any Protestant who could claim the reward. Five hundred *pesos* and lands in fee simple were promised for their capture

---

[7]*Constitucion Politica de la Monárquia Española*, March 18, 1812, in *Colección de los Decretos y Ordenes Que Han Expedido las Cortes Generales y Extraordinarias desde Septiembre 24, 1811, hasta Mayo 24, 1812*, II, 98–157.

[8]Arredondo to Domínguez, October 6, 1813.

[9]Arredondo to Morphi, October 25, 1815, *A. G. I. S. Indif.*, September 16, 1813, January 24, 1813, and Arredondo to the Governor of Texas, October 8, 1818, in *A. G. I. S. Mex.*, 13–5–22, October 31, 1818.

alive.[10] As a precaution against future danger, Arredondo instructed Domínguez, whom he appointed as governor *ad interim*, to carry out the royal order of May 24, forbidding the entry of any emissary from the United States and providing for the seizure of any person in Texas without a passport from a competent officer.[11] Those even suspected of being detrimental to the country were to be imprisoned.[12] It is probable that few foreigners were punished under this order, for the very good and sufficient reason that nearly all of them had taken flight long before. In fact, of all the foreigners known to have immigrated during the period under consideration only Daniel Boone and Vicente Micheli seem to have remained.[13] By the end of 1813, therefore, the royalists were in complete control of Texas. But before they had accomplished this result, Texas had been brought to such desperate straits that heroic measures were necessary if the province was to be held against foreign enemies and developed as its wonderful resources and strategic position demanded.

Condition of Texas, 1813.—Some conception of conditions in Texas at the end of the struggle for possession may be gained from a letter written by Domínguez to Arredondo in which he reported that no definite idea of the number of people in Texas at this time could be gained since so many of its inhabitants were wandering as fugitives in a foreign land. A little later Arredondo was actually compelled to suspend the work of administering the oath of allegiance to the constitution of 1812, because the settlements were without inhabitants and because suitable persons were not available as officials under the said constitution.[14]

---

[10]Arredondo to Domínguez, October 10, 1813. Appendix 25.

[11]Arredondo to Domínguez, December 4, 1813.

[12]Arredondo to Domínguez, October 6, 1813.

[13]Petition, September 12, 1814. When the insurgents entered Béxar, Boone continued to repair the firearms of the defenders until compelled to conceal himself to escape death. Arredondo to Calleja, December 20, 1813.

[14]Arredondo to Armiñán, March 18, 1814. Claiborne estimated that the defeat of the revolutionists had thrown upon the frontier at least

The Opening of Texas to Foreign Settlement 237

Although the royalists were in complete possession of Texas, they did not feel that their vigilance could be relaxed for a moment. Therefore, before leaving the frontier, Arredondo made arrangements for a defensive program in spite of the fact that the Indians were pretending a desire for peace, the United States had issued a proclamation prescribing punishment for such of its citizens as should aid in any attack upon Spanish territory,[15] and the French cause was waning due to the expulsion of Napoleon from Spain. Arredondo still felt that all enemies should be watched, claiming that contraband traders, who had begun to ply their trade almost before the smoke of battle had cleared away, the insurgents, whose leaders had escaped to the United States to plan new aggressions, and American filibusters, who were still anxious to accomplish their purpose, demanded constant attention. But his main reliance was placed upon the development of the threatened province into which the foreigners could now legally enter only by securing naturalization papers from the regency.[16]

Development plans of Arredondo.—That Arredondo favored the development of Texas can be easily established. On September 13, 1813, he issued an address to the people of Texas, declaring that the God of Armies had sent unexpected resources just at the moment when the usurper seemed ready to seize upon the possessions of the beloved king. He expressed the hope that after the awful example furnished by the inevitable defeat of those daring to raise a hand against the king, no one would be again deceived into aiding an insurrection. He then went on to inform his hearers that contraband trade carried on by certain faithless Spaniards with the hated foreigners through Natchitoches had contributed in no small degree to the misfortunes of the province, and implored them to cast from their memories forever this abominable crime, and never to

---

twelve hundred persons, most of whom were destitute. Claiborne to Macarty, October 16, 1813, *Letter Books*, VII, 272–273.
[15]Morphi to the Governor of Vera Cruz, April 20, 1814.
[16]Arredondo to the Governor of Texas, April 2, 1814.

buy from the enemy "goods dyed with the blood of their victims." He pictured the folly of so doing when the government was planning shortly to open the port of Matagorda in order that their happiness might be secured if they would only devote themselves to agriculture and the arts.[17] His promise of a law legalizing the use of Bahía was no idle boast, for action to that end had already been taken by the supreme government. By an order of September 6, both Bahía and Tampico were granted the privilege of exporting native products with exemption from the payment of duty for five years.[18] A little later, Arredondo admitted that the execution of the project for development demanded greater powers and resources than he had at his command. Nevertheless, he ordered a beginning made by the establishment of a fort at San Marcos in order that ranches might be opened between Béxar and that point so that agriculture might be developed and contraband trade destroyed.[19]

Coöperation of governor.—That Arredondo's subordinate, the governor, was a progressive goes without saying. Although confessing that he could give no data from personal knowledge, he nevertheless favored the opening of the port of Matagorda, claiming that this step alone would provide for the adequate defense of the province.[20] The viceroy, too, was also in sympathy with the proposed policy.

Attitude of the viceroy.—This was shown by the fact that he suggested that the plans advocated by Grimarest be revived and that two thousand men be sent to Béxar immediately.[21] His interest was still further proved by the fact that he sent Manuel Aranga as a special agent to Texas,

---

[17]Appendix 24.

[18]Report of Council of Indies on Arredondo's Recommendations for Development of the Interior Provinces. February 28, 1817, *A. G. I. S.* Guad., 103–3–23.

[19]Arredondo to the Governor of Texas, August 9, 1814.

[20]The Governor of Texas to Arredondo, December 1, 1814.

[21]Calleja to the Minister of War, January 24, 1814, *A. G. I. S. Indif.* 136–7–9, September 16, 1813–January 29, 1814.

charging him to make a thorough examination of conditions so that adequate measures for development might be taken.[22] In their progressive plans, Arredondo and the viceroy were supported by still higher authorities.

View of the cortes.—The *cortes*, too, was in sympathy with a development policy. As a general example of their attitude toward this question, the law of January 4, 1813, which again opened the way for the execution of the long deferred plans for settling Texas, may be cited. This law provided for the reduction of public lands to private ownership by the distribution of *suertes* to defenders of the country and to such citizens as possessed no lands. The preamble of the law declared it to be the belief of the *cortes* that the granting of public lands to private individuals was one of the measures which the good of the people and the development of agriculture and other industries most imperiously demanded. The law in question, therefore, provided that one-half of the public lands should be reserved as security for the payment of the national debt, while the remainder, with the exception of the necessary commons for settlements, should be granted in fee simple to the defenders of the country and to such citizens as might desire it.[23] Later in the same year, the *cortes* issued a decree providing that mission lands be distributed in accordance with the provisions of the law just cited.[24]. Not only was it now possible to secure laws under which development could be easily accomplished, but the authorities were able to consider special development plans.

Attitude of the regency.—As an example of the interest of the regency is furnished by the following order issued in February, 1813:

---

[22]Filisola: *Memorias* I, 81–82. Unfortunately, his report which doubtless would have outlined the policy to be followed, has not been found, although careful search for it has been made in the Archives of Mexico and Seville.

[23]*Colección de los Decretos y Órdenes desde 24 de Mayo de 1812, Hasta 24 de Febrero de 1813, Tomo III*, 189–193. See Appendix 23.

[24]Moza, *Código de Colonizacion y Terrenas Baldias de la Républica Mexicana*, 152–3.

Among the different objects which this government has had in view for a long time, when planning for and increasing the population of Texas by the greatest possible exertions, was that of preserving its ancient limits in that region and of placing an impenetrable or almost impassable barrier against the United States. This is second only to that of arranging for its prosperity and development. The enemy have continually tried to cross this barrier, and at times they have succeeded in doing so, establishing themselves at points which offer the least resistance to contraband traders and the best advantages for the successful outcome of their combinations which have been formed for evil purposes. Unfortunately, there has occurred and intervened a thousand things and adverse circumstances which brought to naught the arrangements and preparations for the accomplishment of the plan which has been considered. But it is a matter of great importance, as much for the benefit which those worthy and faithful inhabitants would enjoy by its being carried out— since it would render available to them all possible means for bettering their situation—as for the assurance of their political existence which might be endangered or even destroyed in the future by that neighboring power which believes it has a right to occupy that territory. Therefore, we, the regency of the kingdom, have taken into consideration this undertaking, which certainly requires careful examination from all angles, especially from a political view, as has been pointed out; and lacking data and information which might contribute to the certain success of the operation so that it may be carried out in the shortest length of time with the least expense and risk—since the opinions presented to the regency had been very diverse and contradictory— the matter is placed entirely in your hands in order that you may take the measures you may consider opportune in consultation with the commandant-general of the Interior Provinces, after hearing first the Bishop of Nuevo León, who, because he has travelled in Texas,[25] will possibly afford assistance from personal knowledge, and other persons whom you may consider in a position to give information concerning the matter and to clear up the question. You must regard as the prime object to be accomplished the increase of population, the development of commerce,

---

[25]The Bishop of León had been among the first to advocate the placing of settlements in Texas as a means of preventing aggression from the United States, see *ante* p. 77, and had later aroused the fears of the government by reporting the presence of a great number of forigners along the Texas-Louisiana frontier. See León to Elguezabal, February 4, 1805, and Salcedo to the Governor of Texas, July 29, 1805.

the creation of riches, and the opening of the most direct and expeditious communication with other provinces, be it either by land or by sea. For this reason, establishments and settlements shall be made on the coasts for the purpose of avoiding useless expenditure and in order that persons settling shall suffer the least inconvenience and not be exposed to the diseases which Europeans regularly suffer from in that climate.[26]

Not only was information requested but orders were issued calling for the execution of these plans and steps were soon taken to secure the much needed settlers.

Colonization contract.—On November 29, 1913, the *cortes* approved the Texas colonization plans of Colonel Ricardo Reynal Keene, an American who, since 1810, had been trying to secure military rank, commercial concessions, and colonization grants in Cuba, Florida, and other unsettled portions of Spanish America. His latest plan was to introduce a company of volunteers from Louisiana and to settle Irish Catholic families from Spain and its adjacent islands, and Spanish vassals from Louisiana. The decree of the *cortes* provided that aid should be furnished him upon condition that the provincial legislature and the military commandant thereof should aid him in selecting the most suitable locations which were to be distributed under existing laws. This same committee was to fix the amount of premium lands to be granted to Keene in payment for the trouble and expense of forming the colony. The most noteworthy condition affixed to the grant was that two-thirds of his settlers should be Spaniards—the others might belong to any foreign nation save the French, who held the king a prisoner, and from any province whatever save Louisiana where the French were in large numbers. All colonists, however, were to be Catholics.[27] Offering as it did, a combi-

---

[26] Minister of Foreign Relations to the Viceroy. Copy in Arredondo to the Governor, September 29, 1814. When considering these plans, the fiscal at Mexico City suggested that the money usually expended for Indian presents be used to secure the desired settlers, *Parecer de Fiscal*, May 14, 1813. Appendix 26.

[27] *A. G. I. S.* Guad., 105-1-9, April 27, 1820-June 17, 1820, and Appendix 27.

nation of nearly all the plans previously considered, this project was a fitting climax to all suggestions offered between 1801 and 1813. In it can be noted a similarity to Grimarest's plans for bringing soldiers and their families from Spain and Despallier's plan for introducing Spanish vassals from Louisiana. Although Keene did not ask to be allowed to make use of friendly Indians as had often been done, he added a new idea by requesting permission to introduce the Irish who were weak politically but who were known to be faithful to the Catholic religion. The exact conditions under which he was to operate were probably never fixed; and from the data at hand, it is not possible to determine the exact location of the lands he expected to receive as a reward for his work, although it is known that some of them, at least, lay in the region about Matagorda Bay. According to Kennedy, he was promised twenty-one thousand leagues of the very richest lands in Texas.[28]

To Keene, then, was offered the opportunity of becoming the first real *empresario* for Texas, since to none of his predecessors—so far as the available records show—had lands been promised as a reward for introducing immigrants. He was not able to earn this title, however, owing to an absolute and almost instantaneous change in the situation of affairs in the Peninsula.

At this time, Napoleon was harassed at every point. He was steadily losing ground before the victorious Wellington and was deeply displeased with Joseph for complaining of his reverses in the Peninsula and the prospect of the total loss of the rebellious American provinces. Reasoning perhaps, that a pliant tool on the throne of Spain was more useful than a helpless prisoner in France, he suddenly made

---

[28]Kennedy, *History of Texas*, II, 3. *Cf.* Memorial of Keene to the King, 1814, in which he outlines his ideas on colonization; adding the suggestion that Germans, who were suffering from Napoleon's oppression might also be glad to take refuge in Texas. *Memoria Sobre El. Asunto De Fomentar La Poblacion y Cultivo En Los Terrenos Baldiós En Las Provincia Internas.* Photostat U. of T. Original loaned by Mr. Thomas J. Streeter, of New York.

up his mind to release the cringing Ferdinand. He thereupon agreed, in the treaty of Valency, December, 1813, to liberate his captive upon condition that the English should be driven out of Spain.[29] The *cortes,* as was to be expected, indignantly rejected this condition. Not to be daunted, however, Ferdinand started for home. The *cortes* next refused him entry until he could prove that no Frenchmen accompanied him, for they greatly feared a trap. To this Ferdinand readily agreed. The Liberals were quick to follow up this advantage and forced him to take oath to observe the Constitution of 1812. But not to be cheated of his throne Ferdinand willingly assented, taking the oath only a few days before Napoleon acknowledged his defeat at the hands of the Allies. Ferdinand was, however, able to recover from this seemingly fatal stroke of fortune. By widening the breach between the Liberals and the Conservatives, he was even able to restore the old *régime* of 1808. How he accomplished this result and forced the Liberals to begin once more their long and bitter struggle for the reëstablishment of the constitutional system will now be traced.

---

[29]*British and Foreign State Papers, 1812–1814,* I, Pt. 2, pp. 1225–1230.

CHAPTER IX

FINAL PREPARATIONS FOR A SUCCESSFUL COLONY, 1814–1821

Growth of Liberalism in Spite of the Temporary Restoration of Absolutism, 1814–1819

Reactionary policy of Ferdinand VII.—In spite of his solemn promise to follow along the constitutional pathway, Ferdinand at once began to deprive the people both in the Peninsula and in America of the privileges granted them by the *cortes*. On May 4, he issued a decree dissolving that body and instructing the American delegates to remain at home or to return to that country, if by chance they had started for the Peninsula. In addition, he forbade the election of deputies to a new *cortes* until the revolutionary movements should subside sufficiently to permit plans to be worked out for calling that body.[1] He prohibited the election of political chiefs as provided for by the *cortes* and decreed that the provinces should be governed by captains-general and commandants-general, as of old.[2] He also rejected the constitution of 1812 and dissolved all American provincial assemblies authorized thereby.[3] In July following, he issued a decree in which he declared that the flood of evils which was overwhelming many of the American provinces and threatening the overthrow of the general government had demanded his attention from the very moment he had been restored to the throne by the intervention of Divine Providence. After mature deliberations as to the best means of restoring happiness and tranquility to his beloved vassals, he had decided, so he said, upon the restoration of the Council of the Indies, which had proved its loyalty to the rulers and its usefulness to the people of America almost

---

[1] Secretario de la Ultramar to Arredondo, May 24, 1814.
[2] Decree, May 4, 1814.
[3] Secretario de la Ultramar to Arredondo, May 24, 1814. Appendix 28.

from the discovery of that continent. He therefore restored
the council with the powers exercised by it in May, 1808.⁴
By this series of decrees, he had placed his vassals in exactly
the same distressing position they had held in 1808,
although, to soften the blow, he had held out to them vague
and indefinite promises of future reforms and had declared
that he intended to use only the kindest measures in drawing his rebellious children of America back to their
allegiance. In the Peninsula, many bitterly resented his
treacherous actions, feeling with Xavier Mina, who was
later to aid the insurgents of Texas, that

> Notwithstanding the sacrifices which the Spaniards had made
> for him, Ferdinand was oppressing Spain more cruelly than the
> French had when they invaded it; that the men who had most
> labored for the restoration of the liberty of the ungrateful wretch
> were loaded with chains in dungeons, or were flying from his
> cruelty; that serving such a king one served the tyrant of the na-
> tion, and, that by aiding his agents in the New World one degraded
> himself to the rank of executioner of the people, the innocent
> victims of a greater cruelty than that which the Spanish people
> suffered on account of the same principles at the most glorious
> epoch of their history.⁵

It was some years, however, before the progressives could
turn the king from his obstinate course, in which he was
greatly aided by the strictly neutral policy adopted by the
government of the United States,⁶ where the people, as a
rule, really sympathized with the struggling colonists. In
spite of this temporary check the revolution really gained
new impetus; for the justice of resisting the tyranny of
such a changeable and irresponsible ruler soon came to be
quite generally recognized.

⁴Decree, July 2, 1814.
⁵Proclamation of Mina, May 18, 1817, Niles' *Weekly Register*, XII, 1817, p. 335.
⁶Neutrality Proclamation, September 15, 1815, *American State Papers, Foreign Relations*, IV, 1. This was published in the *Gazeta de Mexico*. See also Proclamation of the King of England, November 27, 1817, Niles' *Weekly Register*, XIII, 1817–1818, p. 376.

As for the colonists in America, the fleeting glimpse they had received of a possible future of freedom and prosperity but added to their discontent since they placed but little faith in the king's promises of reforms or the viceroy's cunningly worded tender of pardon to all insurgents.

Viceregal pardons.—In celebration of the king's restoration to the throne, the new viceroy, Felix Calleja, offered opportunity to the insurgents to again reënter the folds of the faithful by extending the time granted under the amnesties of 1811 and 1812, upon condition that they surrender their arms and horses and give bond to be faithful to the king. Even the leaders were to be pardoned if they would leave the country. In the face of such seemingly hopeless odds, many revolutionists accepted the offer; while the viceroy saw to it that the people were kept constantly informed of the number of those deserting the insurgent ranks. Nevertheless many remained true to the cause and kept up a rather successful guerilla warfare. To add to the despair of the people of Texas, Arredondo, who had held before them an enticing prospect of development when trying to lure them back to the royalist fold, also began to show reactionary tendencies.

Arredondo's restrictive commercial policy.—He made it quite evident that, in spite of the fact that he had promised the opening of a port on the gulf and a fair at Nacogdoches, he did not favor trade with the United States. Indeed, he gave strict orders for preventing any but spies or mail carriers approaching the Texas-Louisiana boundary line and drew attention to the fact that commerce did not yield the profits expected by its devotees.[7] In line with this policy, he refused the petition of Apolinar de Masmela and Juan de Beramendi to bring goods into Texas from Natchitoches and even repealed previous orders for rounding up wild stock, because the people were thereby deluded into a neglect of agriculture.[8] Arredondo's insistence on farming seemed to be founded upon sound economic principles; but

---

[7] Arredondo to the Governor of Texas, June (?), 1814.
[8] Arredondo to the Governor of Texas, October 18, 1814.

it was impossible to carry out his orders because the people of Texas could not subsist upon the crops then produced. The unfortunate state of the province at that time is vividly described by the governor.

Deplorable condition of Texas.—In writing to Arredondo, he said:

> The misery to which this province is now unfortunately reduced —and this state of affairs is well known to you from many sources and an analysis of its cause would be almost officious— forces me to delineate most hurriedly the calamitous situation which is injuriously affecting the unfortunate inhabitants of this province. They are hopelessly lost in their misery. They have been weakened by their past misfortunes. They are complaining most piteously over the lack of sustenance for themselves and their families. They are lamenting over the crisis and weeping bitterly over their fate—especially when they remember the terrible misery which lies before them. Their fields will yield but little more than they are compelled to have for their daily sustenance. Under these critical circumstances, the regiment under my charge is forced to live entirely on meat, with no possibility of supplying itself with even a *tortilla*. So their misery has reached its highest possible point. I, therefore, hope that you will be convinced that the small amount of supplies received from Alferez Aresmendi will suffice only for bare subsistence for the time already indicated to you in detail; and I trust that you will alleviate their extreme suffering at once. Otherwise, we will be forced to use the remedy of violence, a redress absolutely necessary under the circumstances for the preservation of so valuable a troop and one which is cruelly neglected. This is the fate we have suffered for some months, and consequently, to relieve yourself entirely of the responsibility of dire consequences, you will take such steps as you deem necessary in this crisis.[9]

The complaint was also made that Arredondo did not furnish enough military protection against the Indians to enable the people to raise sufficient food, even though they had been fitted for the work and could have secured pay for the supplies they might have furnished the troops.

Indian depredations.—Many instances of the inability of the government to restrain the Indians can be given. Even

---

[9]The Governor of Texas to Arredondo, May 22, 1814.

while Arredondo was still in Texas and had at his command the troops with which he had expelled the invading foreigners and the insurgents, the Indians committed numerous depredations at Béxar and easily escaped punishment therefor.[10] In April, 1815, the *ayuntamiento* of that city called to the attention of the governor the many horrible murders that had been committed in the vicinity by their inveterate foes, and asked that a guard of soldiers be furnished to assist the farmers in protecting themselves while at work in their fields, which otherwise would have to be abandoned. A continued neglect of agriculture, they claimed, would entail still greater miseries and calamities.[11] The small force stationed in Texas was also unable to inspire the respect of insurgent leaders and foreign aggressors; for as soon as Arredondo withdrew from the province they again united in laying plans for another attack.

Activities of insurgents and foreign sympathizers.—On March 29, 1815, a correspondent from Natchitoches warned Morphí, the Spanish consul at New Orleans, that Toledo had left the first named place for Natchez, promising on his return to bring with him one thousand men and to have a much larger number join him later. The correspondent gave information, too, that Robinson had gone to the Sabine for the purpose of organizing the revolutionists of that region and of selecting military and civil leaders by the time Toledo should arrive; that in the face of Claiborne's proclamation imposing a fine and imprisonment on American citizens aiding the revolutionists Smith had also gone to the Sabine with other Americans and some Spaniards; and that Gutiérrez was supposed to have gone to New Orleans to hold a consultation with General Humbert. In transmitting this news, Morphí declared that Gutiérrez and Humbert were planning to coöperate with the pirates of Barrataria in an attack on Salcedo, Matagorda, the mouth of the Brazos, or even on Tampico, the point from which money

---

[10]The Governor of Texas to the Commandant-General, March 22, 1814.

[11]Petition, April 28, 1815.

coming from the interior was shipped to Vera Cruz; for they knew that if they could but secure funds their cause might be won.[12] However, Arredondo did not consider the danger very great and even gave orders for discontinuing the system of maintaining spies at Natchitoches so that all communication between Texas and Louisiana might be cut off.[13] Although no attack was made at this time, the remnant of the insurgents who had been driven across into Louisiana continued their efforts to launch another attack; and rumors of impending danger continued to come in.

The captain of a vessel from New Orleans declared that Humbert, who had secured a number of men from Ireland for service in the Spanish Dominions, was preparing to lead an expedition of fifteen hundred men—three hundred of them Spaniards—in an attack on Bahía; that still another revolutionist, Anaya by name, had sent out corsairs to attack the coast; that Wilkinson was encouraging the plans for independence and that the Americans were secretly giving assistance to the cause.[14] The threatened attack was postponed for some years and the people of Texas settled back into their customary routine, broken only by the return of a few exiles, the entry of a few immigrants, and the laying of additional futile plans for development.

Returning exiles.—In May, 1815, Christian Hesser secured permission to go to Bayou Pierre for his family so that he might again settle in Texas. He did not return for two years, and in the *interim* served as a second lieutenant of militia in Louisiana.[15] Although he had been guilty of contraband trading and of serving in the American militia, the authorities permitted him to again locate in Texas.[16]

A little later, José de la Baume sent his son back from Louisiana to Béxar to enlist the services of Baron de Bastrop

---
[12]Morphí to the Governor of Vera Cruz, April 20, 1814, and paragraph from Morales to his brother, May 14, 1815.
[13]Arredondo to the Governor of Texas, October 18, 1814.
[14]Statement of Váldez, April 19, 1814.
[15]The Governor of Texas to Arredondo, September 26, 1815.
[16]List of contraband goods in possession of Eser and companions, October 1, 1916.

in securing a pardon for the elder Baume's complicity in the revolution. Upon receiving the petition, Arredondo demanded of the governor an explanation of Bastrop's action in receiving communications from Louisiana when this was strictly forbidden. But the desired pardon was finally issued. At this time a few new immigrants,[17] the forerunners of larger bands to come, began to apply for admission.

New immigrants.—One of the immigrants, José Diles, was an American. Upon his arrival at Bahía when he asked to be allowed to settle, he gave information of the hostile plans of Juan McFarlan and his associates.[18] Another applicant was an European, lately from Havana, who desired to live in the Eastern Interior Provinces. A very interesting case was that of Bartolomé Lafón, who, while asking to be allowed to locate on the Neches, frankly admitted that he was interested in commercial schemes which he believed might prove advantageous to Texas. He even had the temerity to advertize his wares.[19] The only other immigrant entering Texas at this time, so far as the available records show, was Sylvanus Castleman, of Tennessee. However, he did not present a formal petition until some years later and his case can be passed over for the time being. In the meantime, new colonization plans were being laid by those who still hoped to develop the region and to make it safe against Indian depredations and foreign aggressions even though it seemed that there was slight hope of establishing a liberal colonization system so long as the king continued to exercise absolute power.

Zambrano's plan.—On August 28, 1815, realizing the absolute necessity for again taking some steps to alleviate the condition of the people of Texas, Arredondo had called upon Manuel Zambrano for a description of the unsettled triangular strip of territory extending from Béxar to the Rio Grande between Laredo and the *presidio* of Rio Grande and asked for suggestions as to the points on the frontier

---

[17]Arredondo to the Governor of Texas, November 15, 1816.
[18]Castañeda to Pardo, May 7, 1817.
[19]Lafón to Castañeda, June 1, 1817.

The Opening of Texas to Foreign Settlement 251

best suited for the establishment of large settlements and for the location of troops calculated to protect the commerce and agriculture of the Eastern Interior Provinces from Indian depredations. Zambrano felt the necessity for some forward step because, up to this time, Texas had not prospered although she had cost the king thousands of dollars. He even felt that it would be better to abandon the country altogether than to continue to hold it under the old system. Nevertheless, he was unwilling thus to encourage the ambition of the United States, and immediately suggested a plan by which he believed the country could be developed.

He described the country in detail, saying that it was extremely fertile and blessed with a delightful climate. He ventured the opinion that, if proper protection were provided, the choice region immediately around Béxar would sustain a population of two or three thousand without the necessity of importing grain. Production at this point could be stimulated by distributing the mission lands to men capable of cultivating them and able to use the irrigating system already installed. He maintained that the true frontier line lay on the segment of a circle drawn through Bahía, Béxar, Bandera Pass, and Aguaverde, and claimed that it was necessary to place garrisons only at the three passes which the Indians used in making their inroads into the region; *i.e.* Bandera Pass, Cañon de San Sabá, and the defile near Béxar. His plans provided for a line of *presidios* on two sides of the territory under consideration and that would make available for additional colonies a section of country capable of supporting a population of more than eight thousand people. Among the places pointed out as especially suited for new establishments was one on the headwaters of the Medina and one on the Guadalupe, where the soil was unsurpassed, the hunting good, the pasturage abundant, the climate salubrious, and irrigation practicable. He stated that the half-way point between Béxar and Aguaverde fell upon the Rio Frio, where another new settlement might possibly be located, if placed eight or ten leagues above the La Pita Road, where the water was good. But since this location was inferior to those on the Medina and on the Guadalupe, he favored the plan of passing beyond the river and selecting a spot half way between Bandera Pass and Aguaverde in the canyon of San Sabá. He felt that with this protection assured, Mexican citizens would be willing to go out as settlers and that even some of the inhabitants of Béxar, Bahía, and Palafox would be tempted to try their fortunes in this favored region. He urged that detachments be placed at once at the points indicated, and that quarters be built for them. He hoped that in addition to the families of the soldiers and a number of vagrants who might be secured in the Interior Provinces to help in the construction work, that families of means could be induced to move to the new settlement, where they would find a good market for their produce and be well protected against Indian attack.

He also suggested a method of financing poor families who might wish to join them. He called attention to the great damage done by the Spaniards by the Comanches, the Tancahuas, and the Lipans—especially since the revolution—and expressed the belief that depredations could be prevented by placing the Tancahuas in a mission, by declaring war against the Comanches in Santa Fé, and by driving the Lipans beyond the frontier line indicated by him or by waging an exterminating warfare against them.

His final recommendation was that the port of Matagorda be opened, as had been promised long before. In regard to this question, he said:

> These difficulties [Indian depredations] are slight as compared to the greater one which exists in Texas and even in the rest of the Interior Provinces. The work of the inhabitants of the region does not yield enough for the support of their families, since they have to pay two prices for the necessities of life, and, sometimes, even an advance of three hundred per cent. The merchants cannot lower their prices because of the great risk of transportation over the long intervening distances. It is necessary, therefore, for you to make every possible exertion to secure a port on the coast of Bahía de San Bernardo so that the people can be sure of supplies. Then you can even lower somewhat the

salary paid to the troops, since they can supply themselves at a smaller cost than hitherto. Besides, countless other advantages will flow from this action, such for instance as the exportation of the fruits which the province produces, and the increase of the population which is imperiously demanded.[20]

The plan might have been feasible if the desired protection could have been furnished. However, past experience gave little encouragement for the hope that this could be done. All the settlements placed in the region prior to this time, save Béxar and Palafox, had been abandoned because of Indian depredations and lack of facilities. Even these two places had made but little progress. Hence there remained but little hope that other settlements, if formed by Mexicans as planned by Zambrano, would be able to maintain their existence. Although no favorable action seems to have been taken upon the plan, Arredondo soon took other steps to urge the need of settlers for the region.

Arredondo's plan.—He stressed the necessity for developing the Eastern Interior Provinces, where commercial conditions were deplorable owing to the lack of a circulating medium, to the activity of pirates along the coast, and to the lack of sufficient ports on the Gulf. He claimed that under existing conditions the people were not self-supporting and that the revenues of the government never amounted to more than fifty thousand *pesos* per year. To remedy these conditions he suggested the opening of a port at the mouth of the Rio Grande, so that the addition to the original price of commissions and of exorbitant freight charges from Vera Cruz to distant points in the interior would not make prices prohibitive. He wished commerce permitted between this new port and Havana, Campeche, and other points on the coast, and stipulated that only such duties as were absolutely necessary for the maintenance of the custom house should be charged. He also requested that Bahía still be considered as a minor port, and that tobacco culture and manufacturing be encouraged. He recommended the granting of lands in small quantities for the

---

[20]Zambrano to the Commandant-General, September 4, 1815. N. A.

purpose of attracting settlers who were also to be provided with farming implements.

Approval of plan.—When passing upon this plan, the *contador general* maintained that the demand for a new port was unreasonable, since Tampico and Bahía had been made ports by order of September 6, 1813, and had been exempted for five years from the payment of all export duties. He promised, however, an additional fiveyears' extension of this privilege, approved the plan of granting land to the people of the Interior Provinces and expressed the opinion that this could be done at once by securing an order from the king who now had the sole power to grant lands. He stipulated that as far as possible lands of different qualities should be granted, and that the settlers should be required to cultivate their grants within the space of three years. He refused to furnish farming implements, but offered to make arrangements for furnishing them at cost and on advantageous terms.[21] But, as usual, no actual results were accomplished. Although not averse to granting land in Florida[22] to his court favorites since he expected to dispose of that province to the United States, it goes without saying that the king would never yield these commercial privileges as long as he was able to occupy the throne.

The King's offer of lands.—To ensure the continuance of existing conditions, he therefore instructed his representative in Mexico to make another attempt to draw away additional adherents from the insurgent cause. On January 30, 1817, Juan Ruiz de Apodaca, who had been lately named as viceroy, issued a proclamation calling attention to the fact that the recent success of the royalist troops forecast a complete victory within a short time. He explained that the king was desirous of winning back the allegiance of his

---

[21]*Papeleta* 18, February 28, 1817, *A. G. I. S.*, Guad., 103–3–23.

[22]See records of grants to Baron de Espes, Duke of Alagon, Captain of the King's Body Guards, Conde de Puñonrostro, one of the King's Chamberlains, and Don Pedro de Vargas, Treasurer of the Household, *Public Statutes at Large of the United States of America from 1789 to March 3, 1845*, 268–273. *Cf.* Fuller, *The Purchase of Florida, 1776–1819*, p. 309.

deluded vassals without further bloodshed, and offered to pardon every insurgent, without exception, who would appear before certain designated officials and take the oath of allegiance. The only condition he imposed was that the applicant must surrender his arms and ammunition, retaining his horses and mules to be used in cultivating his lands and in hauling his produce to market. As an additional inducement, he promised lands to all those who wished to settle down and enjoy the pleasures of home. But all the advantages were not on the side of the royalists and the cause of the insurgents—the triumph of which was to finally pave the way for a successful colony—received added impetus at this time and that, too, from an entirely new source the Peninsula and South America.

The Mina and Aury expeditions.—The conditions in the Peninsula are thus described by a contemporary:

> The most distinguished members of the *cortes*, including Ramos Arispe, the most celebrated generals, like the O'Donojus, in fact, all the thinking men of the Peninsula, being unwilling to bend their necks again to the tyrant, fled to nearby countries to escape the wrath of the king.

Xavier Mina, a nephew of the celebrated leader, Espoz y Mina, escaped to England where he secured a vessel, some money, and a number of men who were anxious to aid the insurgents of Mexico. Touching at Baltimore, he secured additional recruits and much needed financial assistance through Dennis Smith, a prominent merchant of that place. However, he learned of the severe losses of the insurgents in the interior of Mexico and decided to sail to the coast of Texas to coöperate with Luis Aury, a Frenchman who had suffered defeat while aiding the insurgents of South America, and who had come to Texas to coöperate with Gutiérrez.[23]

In the meantime, Aury had seized Galveston; and with the aid of Herrera, insurgent representative to the United

---

[23]Hernández y Dávalos, *Colección de Documentos para la Guerra de Independencia de Mexico*, VI, 916–923.

States, he had organized a government and had declared the place a port. This being done, Herrera had sailed for Boquilla de Piedras, on the eastern coast of Mexico, from which point he hoped to get in communication with General Victoria and the insurgent congress so that future operations might be mapped out. But unfortunately Herrera's vessel was lost at sea, Boquilla de Piedras fell into the hands of the royalists and communication with the insurgent leaders was thus cut off. Nevertheless Mina still wished to make the attempt. He persuaded Aury to land him on the coast near Tampico, but from this time evil fortune pursued him. He succeeded in penetrating for a considerable distance into the interior but was finally captured and shot. Aury sailed back along the Texas coast and landed at Matagorda, where he expected to find a good harbor. Due to unfavorable winds, he was, however, obliged to abandon the place. Despairing of accomplishing anything for Texas, he finally sailed away to aid insurgents at other points.[24] Once more the authorities were free to consider plans for preventing future invasions.

Williams' plan.—In 1817, Lacarriére Latour, under the *alias* of John Williams, was sent from Louisiana to Havana to urge the need of protecting Texas against American adventurers by means of colonies. After declaring that the majority of the American people were in favor of the insurgent movement against Mexico and that they had been made conscious of their ability to assist other oppressed nations by their late victory over England, he explained that the principal danger zone for Mexico lay in Louisiana, which was too far distant from the seat of government to permit the use of effective repressive measures even in case the governor should desire to act. He claimed that owing to this fact, the effect of Pike's alluring representation of the riches of Texas, and to the presence of English influence, the people of Louisiana, and even the government agents located there were extending aid and protection to the insurgents. He next described the wave of emigration which

---

[24]Niles' *Weekly Register*, XII, 1817–1818, pp. 330–334, and 396.

was flowing toward the south and west *in search of fertile lands,* uninterrupted by any impediment save one fort at St. Louis and one at Natchitoches. He then pointed out that these farmers who were accustomed to defending themselves against the Indians and the wild beasts of the region were a much more powerful instrument of aggression than the common soldier located at a remote post where drunkenness and other vices were prevalent, and that the point of greatest danger from these immigrants—both whites and Indians—lay along the Red River, where the climate was most delightful, the products the most varied, and the lands the most fertile, and at the same time the most reasonable in price. He said that these Americans had fixed their eyes upon the adjacent territory as had the Israelites upon the Promised Land and that they were willing to undertake any proposed expedition into it, since they had all to gain and nothing to lose. As a means of delaying the inevitable conflict and providing for at least the temporary exclusion of these intruders, he suggested the establishment of military posts in a Neutral Territory along the frontier to serve as a means of holding back the Americans, controlling the Indians, and of extending and regulating commerce. As a further buffer, he suggested the attraction to Texas of all the Creole inhabitants of Louisiana, the greater part of whom were located at Ouachita, New Madrid, and on the Arcas, the Blanco, and the San Francisco rivers. All of them, said he, followed agriculture in the summer and hunting in the winter, and would be glad to immigrate to Spanish territory, if given assistance in money, since they had been deprived of their land titles by the American government and had been robbed of the enjoyment of the Catholic religion because they were so scattered and because they had not the money to provide for religious instruction. As they did not like the Americans, he said, and did not mind living on the frontier, they would prove valiant defenders of the country. There were also, he claimed, many Indians who hated the Americans and who would gladly aid in the erection of a buffer against their further advance toward the Rio Grande.[25] The commandant-general of the Western Interior Provinces supported all of Williams' plans and urged that the proposed buffer be erected at once. But nothing came of his recommendations. At this time Governor Antonio Martínez took up the problem of developing and protecting Texas and his ideas will therefore be of interest.

Martínez' policy.—Martínez, who had assumed office on March 27, 1817,[26] was strongly in favor of an energetic development policy. In writing to one of his subordinates, he declared that he considered it one of his first duties to develop agriculture in the province and that, because of lack of laborers, it would not be possible to fill up the ranks of the soldiers with the settlers of Béxar as had been proposed by Arredondo.[27] Unfortunately, however, Martínez soon found that all his hopes were thwarted by the ill-feeling thus aroused. In addition, he received a reprimand from Arredondo for appealing directly to the viceroy for aid; and thereafter could get but few of his plans approved. Arredondo refused his request to be permitted to disband the useless militia in order that they might be able to devote themselves to agriculture.[28] Additional agriculturists were available, but, unfortunately, not of the nationality favored by Arredondo.

Proposed settlers from Kentucky and Tennessee.—In July, 1817, Fatio wrote Martínez from New Orleans, saying that he had learned upon good authority that there was in the vicinity an Irish American who claimed to be the advance

---

[25]Williams to Ramírez, in *A. G. I. S. Mex. legajo* 13, No. 41, pp. 3–31. But little information in regard to the writer has been found. *Bolton's Guide*, 65, has the following statement concerning him. "Report by A. L. L. of a plan in the United States to cause a negro insurrection, of the doings of Gutiérrez and of Victoria, and of pirates on the Gulf, undated, evidently by Lacarrieré Latour, *alias* John Williams, French engineer." *Cf.* Pérez *Guide to Cuban Archives*, 63, and *Notas Diplomaticas*, II, 80–95.

[26]Martínez to Apodaca, March 31, 1817.

[27]Martínez to Pérez, July 5, 1817.

[28]Arredondo to the Governor of Texas, August 20, 1817.

guard of two thousand five hundred Kentuckians and Tennesseeans, who planned to locate in Texas, and that these adventurers had already secured the promise of coöperation from the Indians.[29] Quite naturally the threat was resented by both Arredondo and Martínez; and steps were immediately taken to guard against the expected invasion as well as against the possible danger of a hostile expedition said to be preparing in London under the leadership of Lord Cochrane and a certain Robertson, as a result of the activities of insurgent agents.[30] The proposed American settlers did not appear in Texas and the threatened attack by the English leaders was diverted to South America.

The king became alarmed lest sympathy for the insurgent cause in America might lead even the European governments to render them aid and determined to forestall this result.

The king's plan for subduing the rebels.—The policy which was now beginning to take form in his mind can be gathered from the following quotation in the *Gazeta de Madrid,* October 7, 1817:

> The time has come for the courts of London, Vienna, and St. Petersburg to work together for their true interests, recognizing that there will not be any security for royal governments if they permit other independent governments in America. Each new government therein will be a new temptation and a very obvious cause for the belief that kings are less necessary by furnishing another example of a self governing people. The proposed action is not of particular advantage to Spain but of general interest, embracing the whole of Europe, whose ancient leadership and influence over the other portion of the globe would quickly disappear, if independence should succeed in placing its sovereign banners in regions so particularly privileged because of their natural advantages.[31]

While steps were being taken to convince the powers of the truth of the statement, other claimants for Texas lands appeared.

---
[29]Fatio to the Governor of Texas, July 12, 1817.
[30]Pérez to Martínez, May 10, 1817, and Secretary of State to Secretary of War, November 15, 1817.
[31]*Memoria Politico—Instructiva,* 8.

Lallemand's plan.—During the fall and winter of 1817, plans were formed at Philadelphia for the establishment of an asylum in Texas for a number of exiled Napoleonic sympathizers who had taken refuge in America. In March, 1818, a band of immigrants under the leadership of Charles Lallemand[32] reached Galveston and selected a location upon the Trinity about twelve leagues from the Gulf Coast, to which they had been directed by a gentleman from Boston.[33] This place, which was expected to become a new "mother country," was to be called Le Champ d'Asile. The settlers asserted that they had a perfect right to establish themselves at this point because it was not occupied by any other civilized nation and was only periodically traversed by the Indians. Yet they must have had some faint idea that their claim would be disputed; for they issued a proclamation stating that they were able to defend their title against any arrogant enemy that might appear. To make good this assurance, they organized themselves upon a purely military basis. Here they proudly hoped to become skilled agriculturists and to produce such quantities of valuable commodities as would attract the merchants of all nations to bring them European goods in exchange.[34]

Naturally, the Spaniards did not look upon these would-be agriculturists and merchants with favor, believing, indeed, that they were French royalists under a cunning disguise. In fact, long before they left Philadelphia, Onís issued warning against them, and protested to the authorities of the United States against permitting them to form their plans. In writing to the Spanish consul at New Orleans he said:

> As soon as you receive this letter you will inform the viceroy of New Spain and the commandants of all the military posts of the frontier that there is not a moment to be lost but that the

---

[32] For an account of Lallemand's career, see Niles' *Weekly Register*, XII, 1817, p. 208.

[33] Cienfuegos to the Viceroy, March 6, 1818.

[34] Hartman and Millard, *Le Texas ou Notice Historique sur le Champ d'Asile*, 44–48. *Cf.* Reeves, *The Napoleonic Exiles in America*.

territory must be placed in a state of defense against a general attack under the leadership of certain French generals which has for its object the proclaiming of Joseph Bonaparte as king of Mexico. This is not simple conjecture, but is a most positive proof of the conspiracy which is to be carried out as a prearranged insurrection of the Western States, but with a secret object known only to its leaders, of making Joseph a claimant to the throne of Spain and the Indies.

Fatio lost no time in transmitting this warning to the viceroy, the commandant-general of the Eastern Interior Provinces, and the governor of Texas.[35] As a result, the viceroy gave orders that immediately upon arriving in Spanish territory the intruders should be forced to leave, since under the laws and instructions of the king[36] no foreigners could be admitted. The introdurs succeeded in locating before the local authorities could make a protest. But as soon as their presence became known[37] the matter was reported to the viceroy who, in September, issued definite orders for their immediate expulsion.[38] In obedience thereto an expedition was sent out against them. Hearing that the Spaniards were approaching, the intruders abandoned Le Champ d'Asile without attempting resistance and retired to Galveston. Here they experienced great suffering because of a hurricane and the lack of food. At last, despairing of making a home for themselves on Texas soil, they managed to secure a few vessels for transportation. Some of them set sail for New Orleans, while others went overland to the same place, where they were supplied with the necessities of life by kind-hearted Frenchmen.

---

[35]Fatio to Arredondo, October 8, 1817.
[36]Apodaca to the Governor of Texas, April 7, 1818.
[37]Evidence, May 22, 1818. Suspicion was stirred to fever heat by the testimony of two Spaniards who had joined the colony in Philadelphia, but who abandoned it soon after reaching Texas. They reported that these French intruders, to the number of seventy-five, were supplied with arms, ammunition, and men, were erecting a fort, were constantly receiving recruits, and had sent a commissioner to different European ports and to different states of the union to gather additional men.
[38]Apodaca to Arredondo, September 22, 1818.

Thus the Spaniards had again cleared Texas of all intruders save such Americans as were illegally settled upon the extreme frontier. These the governor had already determined to put to the sword. However, he delayed action until he could seek advice from his superior. In reply, he was warned that such action would be extremely dangerous as sympathy was running high in the United States for the insurgent cause, and that the United States government there might be forced by public opinion to retaliate for the execution of its citizens.[39]

Sympathy for the insurgent cause.—The strength of this sympathy can be gauged from the following extract from Niles's *Weekly Register:*

> It appears manifest to us that the contest between Spain and her revolted colonies in America, is about to arrive at a very important crisis. Although as yet no foreign power has openly interfered in the dispute, it has been viewed with deep interest by Great Britain and in the United States; both of which, without acknowledging the independence of any of the colonies, have rather treated them all as free and sovereign states. Neither of these powers has received ambassadors from the colonies; but in both countries it is notorious that persons are resident and *acting* as such, to a certain extent; nor had either sent ministers to any of the colonies; yet it is known that individuals with a sort of diplomatic character have been, or are about to be, sent out by both. This state of things will not last much longer; it is true that the emperor of *Russia* has agreed to interfere between Spain and her revolted colonies. It is pretty confidently asserted that Alexander, on the 7th of May last, signed a treaty with Spain by which he engages to furnish the latter with five ships of the line, four freighters, and 16,000 men, to assist in "restoring tranquility"—for which he is to be paid by the cession of Minorca, and the two *Californias*. It is added that the squadron and transports are all in readiness in the Black Sea, but that the Ottoman Porte has refused them a passage through the Bosphorus, in spite of the pressing importunities of the Russian Ambassador at Constantinople. If this news is true, *England* must be at the bottom

---

[39]Martínez to the Inspector-General, May 23, 1818. Castañeda, who had been instructed to carry out the plan, protested most vigorously because of the lack of supplies. Castañeda to Martínez, September 11, 1818. Arredondo had favored the plan. Arredondo to the Governor of Texas, October 8, 1818.

of the opposition of the Turks; for they would hardly dare to refuse them a passage unless they calculated upon the support of some of the great European powers; and there are none but England that will dare to offer it.

In giving credit to this intelligence, we have the prospect of a war between *England* and *Russia,* and the complete emancipation of Spanish America, as its natural consequence. In which case the United States will assuredly come in as a party; for the result is more interesting to them than to any other country, Spain and her colonies in America excepted.

England will not quarrel with *Russia* because she loves freedom; but she is exceedingly jealous of her commerce; and will not willingly lose so valuable a branch of it as might be transferred from herself to Russia by such a procedure—and the *right* combined to the *expedient,* will induce the United States to assist the *Mexicans,* at least, in throwing off the yoke of Spain, with whom our relations have been in a very unpleasant situation.

A case is now before us that seems likely to urge to action. Certain persons claiming citizenship with us have been captured under the patriot flag, and are dungeoned at Havana, in the most cruel and unfeeling manner. Some of their companions have been demanded as British subjects and were given up. These men claim the protection of their country, and, if they have offended, demand a trial under its laws. What ought to be done in this case, is a question that may well interest the best heads of the nation.

It seems understood that some very important matters in regard to Spain and her colonies will occupy the attention of the next congress. In our own right and in that of oppressed humanity, we might lawfully declare war against Spain, and no doubt should have declared it long since, if we had not been apprehensive of embroiling ourselves with the *kings* of other countries, united to defend one another against the people. But we trust that this unholy alliance may soon be broken up; not because we wish war, but that every *nation* may freely regulate its own affairs—and, as sovereigns, declare war and make peace, as to them shall seem just. And this event is certain,—that if England would only balance the European powers, the United States could easily throw in such a weight of strength and influence as to immediately destroy every vestige of Spanish supremacy on the American continent. The world, in truth, is interested in the opening of so vast and rich a country to commerce; and if ought of a liberal and enlightened policy prevailed, would command it. . . .[40]

---

[40]Niles' *Weekly Register,* XIII, 1817–1818, pp. 97–99.

The possibility of the transfer of Spanish territory bordering upon the United States to European powers who might aid Spain in subduing the insurgents aroused government at Washington to action. The best mode of proceeding in this crisis was a question of paramount interest. As usual in a Republic where all could give expression to their views, there were widely divergent opinions. In March, 1818, Henry Clay made an impassioned plea to congress in behalf of the revolting colonies. He argued that Spain's action in delaying the payment of indemnities for past injuries justifies the United States in demanding immediate reparation and in recognizing every established government in Spanish America. He considered this a much wiser mode of procedure than the plan offered by some of seizing upon the Floridas, which, as he said, "the United States must eventually have." He believed, however, that Spain would pay rather than risk a war. He argued that even though Spain had not injured the United States, the colonies should be recognized as a matter of simple justice, since every nation had the right to be free and many of them had well established governments. He called attention to the fact that the United States had a most vital interest in the Spanish Americas from the standpoint of politics, commerce, and navigation. He also maintained that

> Once independent, whatever might be the form of government established in its several parts, these governments would be animated by an American feeling, and guided by an American policy.

He was unable, however, to carry his point, as the government was extremely anxious to secure the Floridas by treaty and did not wish to jeopardize this object by a hasty recognition. But the discussions incident to the treaty served to fix attention upon Texas. On this point, Niles' *Weekly Register* published an interesting article. The writer who had had an opportunity of examining Dr. John H. Robertson's *Map of Mexico* and *Louisiana,* drew attention to the astonishing difference in the claims to territory between the United States and Spain, declaring that the eastern boundary of the claims of the Spanish government, if established, would not leave a territory averaging one hundred miles in width west of the Mississippi River. He protested against abandonment of claims to the Rio Grande because:

> The territory proposed to be relinguished by the president contains about 697,216,000 acres of land, which embraces more than one-half of all the great rivers which water the plains between the Mississippi river and the Rocky Mountains; together with all the territory lying between the 40th and 48th parallel of north latitude, and the said mountains; and the Pacific ocean; and which at the average price of public lands, would produce a revenue of $2,784,868. This territory is greater than that of the United States previous to the acquisition of Louisiana.
> The total difference of the claims between the United States and Spain, to the same territory, amount to $1,024,928,000.

He described the coast country as follows:

> From the Sabine to the Guadaloupe river, a distance of at least 700 miles, by the meanderings of the coast, we find the land low, and the navigation dangerous for large vessels, with the exception of two points—Matagorda, at the mouth of the Guadaloupe, and Galveston, at the entrance of the Trinity river; yet all the other rivers which fall into the Gulf within that division, are navigable for small crafts, to a considerable distance.
> The land generally continues low and marshy, for ten or fifteen miles into the interior, and covered with live oaks, of an excellent quality for ship building, and at some distance up almost all those streams, there is good pine timber for masts and spars; a portion of this low land, which is above the level of the salt water, produces excellent rice, indigo, cotton, and sugar-cane, all of which may be cultivated to a very great advantage to a distance of three hundred miles north of the coast. There is another advantage which no other portion of North America possesses, which is that sugar-cane and wheat are produced on the same farm, with the greatest perfection—our informant observes that he has seen in the same field or lot wheat and the sugar-cane growing—the former equal to any he has seen in Virginia or Pennsylvania, and the latter infinitely superior in size and in the quantity of saccharine matter, to that of the first quality of which

he has seen in Louisiana, together with all the other vegetable productions which are common to those countries, in which the wheat and apple-tree grow to perfection and produce abundantly —there are also many valuable spices, medicinal plants, and a great abundance of cochineal. How far, therefore, it would be of national importance to possess that country, and amidst the numerous considerations which ought to be taken into view, the propriety of augmenting the quantity of lands proper for the culture of the sugar-cane, the cotton, the rice, and the indigo, and of securing to our government all the ship timber in the gulf of Mexico, is certainly worthy of national consideration.

The country lying between the river Guadaloupe and the Rio del Norte will never admit of a population except such as are attached to a pastoral life; hence, the Guadaloupe would serve for a good national boundary, in this section of the country, inasmuch as it passes through the western extremity of a rich country, which would admit of a very extensive population on the eastern side, and with the exception of the soil on its western bank, a very limited one for at least one hundred and fifty miles on that side. Such a national limit would facilitate an intercourse between the citizens, and the execution of the laws of both governments in time of peace, and would give a great superiority to our government in times of war, if at any future period an appeal to arms should be necessary.[41]

Naturally, the king desired to retain these treasures for himself, and realizing that the suppression of the rebellion was one of the surest means of doing so, he pushed his plans for securing aid from the Holy Alliance.

The king's appeal to the European rulers.—Having been convinced that the powers were ready to come to his assistance, he sent to all allies and friendly powers a circular, dated June 17, 1818, in which he stated the proposed pacification was to be effected, as follows:

> Ever since the fatal events, which produced, as a necessary consequence of them, the extension of the revolutionary germ to Spanish America, and excited in those Regions the destructive designs of separating his Subjects from their lawful Sovereign, the Government of His Catholic Majesty has laid down as unalterable principles for its conduct.

---

[41]Niles' *Weekly Register*, XV, 1818–1819, pp. 6–7.

1st. That of trying all means possible to human prudence for reuniting the misguided Men, employing those of moderation, and having recourse to those of severity with a most sparing hand; and,

2nd. That of seeking, in diplomatic relations, some line of policy for facilitating that re-union.

The emancipation of America, and its submission to its lawful Government, present sufficiently important considerations of policy for Europe to occupy herself in a question, which may generate a new order of things and communications, with respect to industry and commerce, as well as to policy, and which may perhaps be felt, in one of the alternatives, in a manner not indifferent to European prosperity; at the same time that it presents, also, in the other, a flattering and vast view, most analogous to the late arrangements which have so happily united all the true interests of the European powers.

The efforts of these powers have fortunately destroyed a similar ruinous system to that which originated and facilitated the American Rebellion but it still remains for them to suppress the system in Spanish America, the scene of its most serious and lamentable effects.

His Catholic Majesty, always keeping in view the two above-mentioned principles, desirous of avoiding the bloodshed, horrors, desolation and ruin, consequent upon a war of this nature, and of more closely connecting, by all possible means, his relations with the Sovereigns of Europe, his Friends, and Allies, was awaiting a suitable opportunity to submit to their consideration the important matter, and the result of the Communications which have passed at different times, and have been lately renewed and carried on in the most friendly manner, with his Royal Highness, the Prince Regent of Great Britain.

The insurrection of Pernambuco excited a sincere regret in His Catholic Majesty; and when he directed the attention of the Sovereigns, his Allies, to that event, it was necessary to point out to them the general interest which this vital question presented to all Europe.

It was with the greatest satisfaction that His Majesty received replies from his high Allies, which opened the way for commencing an important Negotiation, in order that, by the interference of the Powers in the unfortunate events in America, and their employing their powerful and enlightened Mediation, a reconciliation with the Revolted Colonies might be obtained, by such effectual means as would put an end at once to the evils and to the immorality and political mischief of this state of things.

The first steps were followed by frank, amicable, and confidential Communications, between the Powers and Spain, calculated to lead to this important Negotiation; and, as a well-founded hope may be drawn from them, that the Negotiation may now be undertaken in a manner likely to produce the happy results which from the object and the warmest wishes of His Majesty, he is of opinion that the opportune moment is arrived for declaring to the friendly and Allied Powers, in an official and solemn manner, the general and solid Bases upon which he has determined in his high policy to proceed in this great work, doing on his part, all that can be desired from his conciliating and humane disposition.

For this reason, therefore, and in order not further to retard, as far as lies in his power, the great advantages and results which may be expected from this Negotiation, His Catholic Majesty has commanded to be addressed, at the same time to each of the Powers, this Note, the object of which, after recalling to their consideration all that has been hitherto communicated to them by the Spanish Cabinet, is likewise to present and renew to his August Allies the following Bases:

1st. A General Amnesty to the Insurgents, at the time of their submission ("reduccion").

2nd. An equal consideration, in favour of qualified Americans, with respect to Employment and Honours, in common with European Spaniards.

3rd. The arrangement of the Mercantile Relations of the Provinces with respect to Foreign Powers, upon principles liberal and suitable to the new aspect and political position of those Countries and of Europe.

4th. The manifestation of an unequivocal disposition, on the part of His Catholic Majesty, to adopt, in the course of the Negotiations, whatever Measures,—as well in favour of his Ultramarine Provinces, as with respect to the manner of undertaking this interesting Enterprise,—as may be suggested to him by his High Allies, which shall be compatible with the real object in view, his high dignity, and the preservation of his Rights.

Upon these principles, His Majesty is of opinion that the Negotiation may be immediately set on foot, in such a manner that, the Powers guaranteeing to His Catholic Majesty the attainment of his wished-for object, by means of a friendly interchange and arrangement of measures, proposals, and efforts, it may bring to a happy conclusion the most sublime Transactions witnessed for Ages, and the most fruitful in results of general utility and universal importance.[42]

This was followed by a proclamation imposing severe punishment upon any foreigner caught aiding the insurgent

---

[42]*British and Foreign State Papers*, 1817–1818, Vol. V, 1217–1219.

cause.⁴³ At this juncture, however, Onís finally signed the treaty granting the Floridas to the United States in return for the acknowledgment of Spain's claim to Texas. But, loath to lose any of his territory, the king delayed ratification. As a result a number of Americans already angered by the "surrender of Texas" were aroused to the point of invading the province.

Long's expedition.—As was to be expected, the invaders were supported by Gutiérrez and other insurgents, their activities being no secret to the Spanish authorities. In June, 1819, the Spanish vice-consul, in writing to Fatio from San Luis de los Ylineses, declared that plans were afoot in that section of the country to occupy the Eastern Interior Provinces, and that certain men, under the leadership of Benjamin O'Fallen, were considering an attack on New Mexico. He believed that the danger was greatly increased by the presence of certain bands at Galveston, Trinity, Sabine, Natchez, and Natchitoches, who were planning to begin hostilities in September.⁴⁴ In regard to the plans of these persons, Trudeau declared that people collecting beyond the Sabine had passed through Natchitoches and Adais on their way from Opelousas and Attacapas to Adais and Llanos Doacum [Tehuacan?] and Pecan Point. He claimed that vessels had sailed from New Orleans with food for the people on the Trinity. He named Robertson, Aden [Adair], and Wambert [Humbert] as leaders and believed that there were two other leaders whose names he did not know. He gave warning that the main body of the expedition was at Natchez and that they lacked nothing in the way of supplies and equipment. He reported that, as soon as the conquest was complete, each soldier would be given a *league of land* as a recompense. He did not believe that the United States government was involved in the attack and expressed the opinion that the aggressors were merely a band of thieves

---

⁴³Decree, January 14 ,1819, in *British and Foreign State Papers*, VII, 1818–1819, pp. 1134–1135.
⁴⁴Ortega to Fatio, June 6 and 10, 1819.

who would commit a thousand crimes.⁴⁵ As to the motives of those joining in the expedition, the *Louisiana Gazette* said:

> By the treaty of Florida our government abandons the Province of Texas, a region most advantageously situated and which yields all the products of Western America. But now the cries of "Liberty" are passing from mouth to mouth. They are taken up by our countrymen along the frontier; for they are filled with the hope of contributing to the emancipation of a nation and desire to plant the Standard of Liberty. It is certain that there are not more than one hundred royalist troops in San Antonio. Considering the talent and knowledge of the leaders of the Army of the Republic we do not hesitate to announce that before three months have passed, news of the conquest of that rich country will be received.⁴⁶

In discussing these plans a Natchez paper declared that it was the intention of the invaders to drive out the few royalists troops in Texas, to organize a government like that of the United States, and to attract a number of immigrants by granting them lands.

The fears of the Spaniards were well founded. Long and his followers, who claimed to be outraged by the action of the United States in abandoning all claim to Texas, soon reached Nacogdoches and organized their government. Their Declaration of Independence read as follows:

> They have resolved, under the blessing of God, to be FREE. By this magnanimous resolution to which their lives and fortunes are pledged, they secure to themselves an elective and representative government, equal laws and the administration of justice, the rights of conscience and religious liberty, the freedom of the press, the advantages of liberal education, and unrestricted commercial intercourse with all the world.⁴⁷

The supreme council passed an act giving private soldiers who would serve during the war six thousand four hundred

---
⁴⁵Trudeau to Fatio, June 19, 1819.
⁴⁶*The Louisiana Gazette*, July 7, 1819, No. 2672.
⁴⁷Declaration, June 23, 1819, Niles' *Weekly Register*, 1820, XVIII, 31.

acres of land "of good quality to be laid off in tracts of six hundred and forty acres." Provision was also made for the sale of lands on the Attoyac and a commissioner was dispatched to Pecan Point to invite the settlers of that section to become residents of Texas and to promise bounty lands to soldiers and head-rights to settlers.[48]

The objects to be attained seemed exceedingly ambitious for so small a number. The Spaniards, who were already on guard, were more thoroughly aroused by the threatened seizure and immediately sent out an expedition against the invaders. In ordering their destruction, Arredondo provided for the payment of the force to be sent against them,[49] and before the year was over all intruders had been driven temporarily beyond the frontier and the province was once more a wilderness save for the settlements of Béxar and Bahía. In the meantime the Spaniards were busy with additional plans.

Martínez' plan, 1819.—In June, 1819, Governor Martínez entered his plea for settlers, explaining to the viceroy that his continued efforts toward the development of Texas had been absolutely fruitless because of the lack of resources. He reported that there was left in the province only two thousand settlers and four missions—one at Bahía and three at Béxar. He now wished to bring immigrants from beyond the border of the province and to locate them at Mission Concepción—the best preserved of the missions at Béxar—and asked especially for some twenty-five or thirty Tlascaltecan families from Saltillo. He was led to make this choice by the fact that the Tlascaltecans were industrious and loyal and had proved their worth through long years. To carry out his plan, however, he realized that he must have money for transportation expenses and for maintaining the families for some time after their settlement. The viceroy at once

---

[48]*The Texas Republican*, August 14, 1819, quoted by the *St. Louis Enquirer*, September 29, 1819, Winkler, E. W.. "The First Newspaper in Texas," *The Southwestern Historical Quarterly*, VI, 163–164, Appendix 30.

[49]Venadito to Arredondo, August 25, 1819.

referred the request to the intendant of San Luis Potosí, Texas being under that jurisdiction. Acevedo gave a very gloomy picture of the condition of Texas, expressed the opinion that settlers were certainly badly needed, but believed that especial inducements would have to be offered to the Tlascaltecans before they would consent to abandon home and friends for a residence in a far-away province infested with hostile Indians. Among the inducements considered absolutely necessary, he named lands, tools, work oxen, seed, maintenance for one year, and some especial reward or honor for settlement.[50] For a little over a century, the Spaniards in America had been interested in the solution of the problem of the development of Texas by means of settlers. That Martínez' plan presented no improvements upon that which in 1730 had contemplated the location of Tlascaltecans and Canary Islanders at San Fernando de Béxar, the first civilian settlement in Texas, is evident. Consequently, as no true solution had been found, the problems continued to attract attention.

Padilla's plan.—In 1819, Juan Antonio Padilla, of Mier, prepared a report of the Indian tribes of Texas for the commandant-general, and—seemingly as an afterthought—declared that the *mission lands* at Béxar, which had been practically abandoned by the Indians, were capable of supporting a settlement of Spaniards. He suggested that the desired immigrants might be secured if the lands, water, and ruined mission buildings should be distributed to such families as might voluntarily present themselves. He claimed that from the settlement of these missions, there would follow the advantage of increasing the population of the deserted province. The troops would have better means of securing a supply of the things they need, and the settlers would secure advancement. They would mutually aid each other in their work for the preservation of the missions, and for defense against the barbarians.[51]

---

[50]*Misiones, 1818–1821, Tomo* 3, Transc. U. of T.
[51]Hatcher, M.A., "Texas in 1820," in *The Southwestern Historical Quarterly*, XXIII, 60.

Although nothing has been found to show that any action was taken as a result of this suggestion, it must have served to keep the interest of the commandant-general fixed upon the question.

The king's land policy.—On Christmas day, 1819, moved perhaps by a desire to wipe out the last trace of the seemingly expiring rebellion in New Spain, the king issued a decree which proves that he recognized the necessity for granting lands to his vassals. Having hastily traced the development of a system of laws suitable to the Indies, he gave instructions calculated to prevent arbitrary rule by his representatives there until a new code which had been under consideration for a long time could be published. He declared that laziness was the foundation stone upon which all other vices were built and called for suggestions as to the best mode of distributing the royal lands so that all might have employment.[52] The result of this call will be traced in the legislation of the *cortes*. In the meantime, however, plans for special grants continued to be presented. A project for the formation of a buffer of Swiss and German settlers to prevent the repetition of filibustering expeditions was next considered.

Proposed Swiss and German colony.—Onís realized that his government would reap but little advantage from his success in the treaty of 1819 if colonists were not placed along the frontier and on the coast. Just as he was leaving the United States, he was asked by certain Swiss merchants who had already negotiated with the governments of Brazil and of the United States for the establishment of colonies of their countrymen in these countries, whether Spain had decided upon the establishment of settlements in Texas, in case the boundary question could be satisfactorily settled. Onís knew that for over a century his government had been seeking to accomplish this important object, and that the *junta* had planned to establish a military colony there the moment the war with France should cease. Therefore he

---

[52]*Notas Diplomáticas*, I, 550–558. Transc. U. of T.

at once began to describe to them the fertile soil and the splendid climate of Texas. He also promised that the king would look upon them with favor. So successful was he that the merchants appointed him as their agent to present their petition to the king. Onís was wise enough to avoid any request for money, but asked, instead, for *twenty leagues of land* on the Trinity or any other place they might select. Sixteen leagues were to be distributed among the colonists according to their ability to cultivate the soil, one was to be reserved for public buildings, and three were to be sold to provide a fund for the transportation of the settlers. In addition, he asked that settlers be supplied with the arms necessary to defend the country against all enemies. He reported that *three hundred colonists* were already promised and that within three years they expected to have *ten thousand Swiss militia who would be abundantly able to defend Texas against every enemy.* A similar proposition was made to him by certain Canadian families who desired to move to a warmer climate and more fertile plains. He wished to defer presentation of these requests until after the king had taken final action on the treaty; but upon the urgent request of the merchants and the ministers from Prussia and the Low Countries he consented to forward them at once. The king favored the plan but withheld decision until after he could make up his mind whether or not to sign the treaty negotiated in 1819.[53] By this time, however, the applicants had decided to settle in Spain and a splendid opportunity for securing settlers was lost. However plans for securing German immigrants were still strongly advocated.

Hecke's plan.—J. Val. Hecke, in his *Reise durch die Vereinig-staaten von Nord-Amerika in den Yahren 1818 und 1819,* devoted an entire chapter to a survey of the recent revolution in Texas and a proposal for the introduction of immigrants from Germany. He showed in detail how his plan would work. He claimed that a tract for colonization

---

[53]Onís to Duque de San Fernando, September 20, 1820, *A. G. I. S.* Mex., 23, September 20, 1820–April 26, 1821.

purposes could be most advantageously located in Texas and that its acquisition by purchase from Spain, who did not value it for use or for political reasons, could be arranged easily. In spite of Spain's lack of interest, he said, Texas was really exceedingly valuable from both an agricultural and a political standpoint. He estimated that it was larger than Germany and could be made a most valuable country if the German government would encourage the immigration of Germans and would undertake to care for them for a season after their arrival in order that they might not be destitute—as was often the case in the United States. He suggested that the government might grant them free lands or support them for five or ten years after their arrival in Texas. He estimated that, by this time, the immigrant would have been able to clear at least fifty acres of rich soil. This would yield vegetables and grain for food and also wheat that could be sold at $1.50 per bushel. This would bring in an income of over a thousand dollars per year.

In addition it was quite possible, said he, that the mountains contained rich ores, since they belonged to the same range as the mountains which contained the mines of Potosí. He believed that these mines could be worked by incorrigible criminals, and by petty thieves and lawbreakers who could be transported for the purpose. This would serve to empty the prisons in Germany and would give the criminals a new chance at life. He especially stressed the commercial advantages that might accrue to the home government, pointing out that all trade with the Indians would be in the hands of the Germans, that Galveston Bay would provide a good harbor, and that from that point the trader would be able to reach Rio del Norte, Mexico, the Mississippi, Missouri, Ohio, Sabine, and the Red River. He believed that through this channel the immigrants would be able to secure tropical vegetables and could cultivate cotton, indigo, and sugar. The sum needed for the project would not be great and could be secured, he suggested, through the organization of a company similar to the East India Company, the government being required only to send out troops for the protection of the settlers. He prophesied that within ten years Prussian commerce would have an unusual development and that the proposed colony migh easily have one million inhabitants. To prove that the Indian trade was undoubtedly lucrative, he stated that the Americans, the English, the Russians were all after it, the latter confining its activities to the Pacific coast region. He recommended that at least ten thousand ex-soldiers be sent out as immigrants and that six hundred acres of land be given each of them as a reward. In connection with this proposal he discussed the impetus it would naturally give to the growth of the navy and pointed out that England had reached her position of world power through its command of the seas.[54]

American interest in Texas.—It was but natural that Spain should exert herself to encourage immigration as a makeweight against the commercial plans of her enemies. Many Americans still had their attention focused on Texas. In writing in May, 1820, to Monroe, Jefferson said:

> Your favor of the 3d is received, and always with welcome. These texts of truth relieve me from the floating falsehoods of the public papers. I confess to you I am not sorry for the non-ratification of the Spanish treaty. Our assent to it has proved our desire to be on friendly terms with Spain; their dissent, the imbecility and malignity of their government towards us has placed them in the wrong in the eyes of the world, and that is well; but to us the Province of Techas will be the richest state of our Union, without any exception. Its southern part will make more sugar than we can consume, and the Red River on the north, is the most luxurious country on earth. Florida, moreover, is ours. Every nation in Europe considers it such a right. We need not care for its occupation in times of peace, and, in war, the first cannon makes it ours without offense to anybody. The friendly advisements, too, of Russia and France, as well as the change of government in Spain, now ensured, require a further and respectful forbearance. While their request will rebut the plea of proscriptive possession, it will give us a right to their approbation when taken in the maturity of circumstances. I really think, too, that neither the state of our finances, the condition of our country, nor the public opinion

urges us to precipitation into war. The treaty has had the valuable effect of strengthening our title to the Techas, because the cession of the Floridas in exchange for Techas, imports an acknowledgment of our right to it. This province, moreover, the Floridas and possibly Cuba, will join us on the acknowledgment of their independence, a measure to which their new government will probably accede voluntarily. But why should I be saying all this to you, whose mind has had possession for years?[55]

Henry Clay used even more expressive language in his speech before Congress, as the following extract will show:

> The question was by what race shall Texas be peopled? In our hands it will be peopled by freemen, and the sons of freeman, carrying with them our language, our laws, and our liberties; establishing on the prairies of Texas, temples dedicated to the simple and devout worship of God, incident to our religion, and temples dedicated to that freedom which we adore next to Him. In the hands of others it may become the habitation of despotism and of slaves, subject to the vile dominion of the inquisition and of superstition. He knew there were honest and enlightened men, who feared that our confederacy was already too large, and that there was danger of disruption, arising out of the want of reciprocal coherence between its several parts. He hoped and believed that the principles of representation, and the formation of states, would preserve us a united people. But if Texas, after being peopled by us, and grappling with us, should, at some distant day, break off, she will carry along with her a noble crew, consisting of our children's children. The difference between those who might be disinclined to its annexation to our confederacy, and him, was, that their system began where his might, possibly, in some distant day terminate; and theirs began with a foreign race, aliens to everything that we hold dear, and his ended with a race partaking of all our qualities.
>
> The last resolution which the second resolution affirms is that it is inexpedient to renew the treaty. . . . Let us proclaim the acknowledged truth, that the treaty is prejudicial to the interests of this country. . . . Let us put aside the treaty; tell her to grant us our rights, to the utmost extent.[56]

---

[55]Bergh, Albert Elery (editor), *The Writings of Thomas Jefferson*, XV, 251–252.

[56]Mallory, Daniel, *The Life and Speeches of the Hon. Henry Clay*, Vol. I, 457–460.

At this juncture there transpired in Spain certain events that were favorable to the development of liberal colonization plans. These events will be briefly traced.

Reëstablishments of Liberal Institutions and Preparation for Successful Colony, 1820–1821

Re-adoption of the Constitution of 1812.—In March, 1820, a revolution broke out in Cádiz among the troops awaiting orders to embark for America to oppose "the insurgents and rebels" in that region. Their leader at once proclaimed the Constitution of 1812 which had been so summarily revoked in 1814. Thereupon, Espoz y Mina, who had consistently defended the liberal cause, placed himself at the head of the patriots in the northern part of the country, while the rest of the Peninsula arose in arms to force its re-adoption.[57] As a result, the king declared his willingness to return to the constitutional path. He again took oath to support the constitution; and, as a pledge of his affection for his rebellious vassals, set at liberty all who were imprisoned or detained at any point in the kingdom for political opinions.[58] This, of course, involved the reëstablishment of the *cortes* which had always been most liberal in its policies. Just how to proceed in view of this new turn of events was the question that faced the king and the *junta*.

Plans for calling the cortes.—The difficulties to be overcome in inducing the Americas to send delegates to the new *cortes* were thus described:

> The method of giving legitimate representation in the cortes to our brothers across the sea remains to be decided. We are united to them by the sacred bond of religion and of a common law. We are accustomed at all times to share with them our fortunes and our misfortunes; we are of the same blood; and, together, we form the great Spanish nation. Neither the great distance across the sea, nor the vicissitudes of time, nor the domestic dissensions which now threaten the destruction of our

---

[57]Niles' *Weekly Register*, XVIII, 1820, p. 137.
[58]Decree of March 8, 1820. Appendix 29.

country, nor even injury—if, indeed, this could be remembered between brothers—are sufficient to destroy the tender ties of nature and of fortune which bind us together. So, despite the sad events of the last six years, which we have deeply regretted without being able to raise our voices in protest, Spanish territory includes the same provinces mentioned in article 10 of the constitution.

In issuing the call for a new *cortes,* the *junta* said:

> We hope that their representatives will attend, and it would be neither legal, just, nor decorous for us to deprive them temporarily of the vote they are entitled to cast in all important matters touching the good of the country—especially now when the time has come for pardoning mistakes and forgetting offenses. We should all unite once more under beneficent government. The time has arrived when the voice of liberty crosses the enormous space of the high seas which divides the two worlds. It resounds on its waves, and likewise on the shores of the new world, and returns to our borders crying, peace, concord, and liberty.

To meet this situation, the *junta* provided for the selection of thirty substitutes to act until the delegates from overseas could arrive. Much pleased with their labors, the *junta* exclaimed:

> Citizens, you now have the *cortes,* that impregnable bulwark of civil liberty, that guarantee of the constitution, and of your glory. You now have the *cortes,* you are now free, and the terrible evil genius of tyranny has fled affrighted from your shores to a less dangerous region, dragging his bloody chains behind him.[59]

The king imcediately issued a decree reëstablishing all the decrees previously issued b ythe *cortes* for the development of the American dominions.[60]

Reëstablishment of land laws.—This made it possible once more for the *ayuntamientos* and the provincial assemblies, who were charged with the duty of developing agriculture and commerce, to distribute lands under the law of January

---

[59]Address of the *Junta,* March 24, 1820.
[60]Decree, April 15, 1820.

4, 1813. Not content with this, however, the new *cortes* made a most notable advance toward the goal of a successful colonization system. On November 8, 1820, it determined to take all possible measures for hastening the distribution of lands under the old law of January 4, 1813. It therefore issued a decree calling for a report from each settlement of all vacant lands in its jurisdiction, with a statement of the titles under which the lands were already held, their quantity, their approximate value, and suggestions for the best means of distributing them to those who had served the country as soldiers and to such citizens as possessed no land but desired to become home owners. Provisions was made for examination of those reports and recommendations so that a workable plan for the desired distribution might be formed.[61] But the *cortes* took even more radical steps, among the most important being an amnesty pardoning all insurgents who would accept the constitution and take the oath of allegiance to the king.[62] On September 28, 1820, it even reversed the age-long custom of excluding foreigners from the Spanish dominions by issuing a decree offering inviolable asylum for the persons and property of all foreigners upon condition that they respect the political constitution and the laws of the monarchy. It was specifically stipulated that such foreigners as embraced this offer would be safe from all prosecution for political opinions.[63] Naturally some time passed before this good news

[61]*Decretos de las Cortes*, VII, 345–346. Appendix 31.
[62]Decree, September 27, 1820, *Ibid.*, VI, 243–244.
[63]Decree, September 27, 1820, *Ibid.*, VI, 52. Appendix 32. The king had already established a precedent for this policy. Moved by a desire to increase the white population in the Island of Cuba, he had issued, in October, 1817, a decree abrogating all laws providing for the exclusion of foreigners from that island. The proposed immigrants, however, were to agree to the following conditions: to profess the Roman Catholic religion, to take the oath of allegiance to the king of Spain, and to prove that they were industrious and honorable, and possessed some talent or training that would enable them to be self supporting. If these conditions could be met, lands were to be granted to the newcomer. He was to be exempt from the payment of tithes for fifteen years—a favor not bestowed upon the natives of

reached Texas and the authorities still sought a solution of the colonization problem along the accustomed lines. Another step of importance to Texas taken by the *cortes* was that of urging the king to sign the Onís Treaty, which gave promise of preventing further advance of the Americans to the west. A hasty survey of the European situation at the time aids in an understanding of the matter.

European diplomacy.—The Russian-Spanish understandin is thus described by a writer who has made a close study of the diplomacy of the Onis Treaty:

> Heretofore [prior to 1817] Spain had hoped for an alliance with England as the most likely to sustain and increase her power. A strict alliance between Great Britain and Portugal, and the views of the former power on the subject of the revolted Spanish colonies furnished the proper instruments for Mr. Tatishoff, the Russian minister at Madrid, a man bitterly hostile to England and every thing English, by which he gained the entire confidence of the Spanish king and succeeded in withdrawing Spain from her connection with England. Rumors were abroad of a Russian plot which were given some credence because of purporting with the well known, inordinate ambition of the czar, and yet so extravagant and absurd as, on their face, to be incredible. Russia wished to secure a footing in the Mediterranean and would endeavor to wheedle Spain out of Majorca or Minorca. Russia might secure Texas in America. . . . For these cessions, Russia was expected to use her influence with the revolted colonies but Spain was expected to eagerly accept the chance of success offered as "the king imagined that if he had the great Emperor Alexander for his friend he had nothing to fear."[64]

Another writer declares that Spain needed money to enable her to reconquer the colonies and that one of her foremost financiers, Marqués de Yrujo, conceived the idea of recouping her loss of the mines of Mexico and Peru by selling lands. Great Britain would buy, he said, the Island of

---

the island, and citizenship was to be granted after a residence of five years. Extract from *Journal du Commerce*, December 5, in *The Louisiana Courier*, February 13, 1818, Library of the Louisiana State Museum, New Orleans.

[64]Fuller, Hubert Bruce, *The Purchase of Florida*, 273–4.

Cuba; France, Santo Domingo; Denmark, Puerto Rico; Sweden, Margarita; Holland, the Province of Guiana; Russia, the Californias; and the United States, Florida.[65] Another writer believes that Russia was also to promise to aid Spain in crushing out the rebellion in America by furnishing vessels for the transportation of troops. He declares that this offer was really a farce, because Tatishoff, who was really a member of Ferdinand's *camarilla*, sold to the king at an exorbitant price a number of vessels that were utterly unfitted for use.[66] In the meantime, the problem of defending and developing Texas pressed for solution.

Defense of Texas.—Fruitless attempts were still being made by the local authorities to guard against the Americans and to afford the proposed settlers protection against the Indians. In February Arredondo wrote to Martínez saying that he had been unable to maintain a detachment at Nacogdoches, that he had informed the viceroy of the situation, and that, as a result, he had been instructed to make a report as to the best means of safeguarding the frontier so that effective steps might be taken to this end. Arredondo therefore asked Martínez to assist in the preparation of the report.[67] Naturally, the governor favored all these plans. He was especially interested in protecting the coast region, as he feared that the insurgents might make an attack at that point. He therefore refused permission for the abandonment of Mission Refugio because it would serve as a base from which the whole region might be watched and the Indians held in check.[68] In spite of his desire to defend this section, he was unable to furnish the necessary troops from Béxar because the companies at that point were badly depleted.[69] But the strained relations existing between Arredondo and Martínez would have prevented any effective coöperation, even though money and

---

[65]*Memoria Politico-Instructiva*, 141–2.
[66]Hume, Martin, *Modern Spain*, 200.
[67]Arredondo to the Governor of Texas, February 2, 1820.
[68]Martínez to the Commandant of Bahía, March 22, 1820.

troops had been available.[70] Nothing daunted by the great number of plans that had previously failed, the *ayuntamiento* of Béxar now openly joined the ranks of the colonization enthusiasts.

Plan of the ayuntamiento, 1820.—On November 15, 1820, the *ayuntamiento* of Béxar made an appeal for help to the provincial assembly recently established under the new constitution. They suggested that a vigorous campaign be waged against the Comanches and the Lipans and that immediately thereafter a line of *presidios* be placed between Aguaverde and Nacogdoches, those in Texas to be located on the San Sabá, the San Xavier, the Brazos, the Tortuga, the Trinity, and at Nacogdoches. In addition they advised that the coast be protected by the establishment of one *presidio* at Atascosito and another *half way between the Brazos and the Colorado*. Behind this line of defense they wished to form a cordon of settlements by granting to all the inhabitants of the province *sitios* and *labores* on the San Antonio, the Medina, the Guadalupe, the San Marcos, the Colorado, the San Sabá rivers, and at any other place that might be suitable. Like Padilla, they favored the distribution of the *lands of the missions* at San Antonio, save those of Concepción, which they wished reserved as municipal lands. In conclusion they said:

> Since the inhabitants of the province have within their midst so excellent a port as is the port of Matagorda, where at first and second hand the goods needed could be received with the greatest ease, and that too, perhaps, in exchange for the products of their own soil without the necessity of expending any money whatever, we can find no reason or justice to convince us that we should be deprived of a benefit which nature has so liberally bestowed upon us. For this reason, we repeat the request for the opening of the said port in order to destroy, at its own roots, the odious contraband trade across the frontier of which some of the citizens of this place are accused. We have not yet seen progress made in this manner. Yet, if some practice it, it is not from ambition to accumulate riches, but because of the miseries they suffer and the ease with which they can relieve their sufferings

[70]Camuñas to Martínez, June 16, 1820.

by the sale of horses, in which there is at least fifty per cent profit in current money or in very useful goods. In this way, they supply their necessities. And, if this is the only relief these inhabitants receive, there is no reason for depriving them of it by seizing upon the contraband goods they accumulate.[71]

To hope for any practical and immediate result seemed little short of visionary, in spite of the fact that all thinking persons were convinced of the necessity for developing the province if it were to be held against the Americans and if it were to enjoy the blessings of liberty which were becoming so well known to the people of Mexico. It was the unexpected that happened.

Moses Austin's plan.—At this time there arrived at Béxar, Moses Austin, who had been a Spanish vassal in Louisiana prior to its delivery to France and later to the United States. Through the influence of Baron de Bastrop, he was enabled, after exhibiting proof of his former Spanish citizenship, to present a petition to the governor, drawn up in such a form as to meet the approval of all higher authorities to whom it was submitted. In this position he stated that he had been forced to remain in Louisiana up to this time because of his property and his family, but that upon hearing of the establishment of the *new political constitution*, which did not prevent the removal of emigrant families, he had resolved to come to Texas for the purpose of securing permission to settle at a point which seemed best suited to the cultivation of cotton, wheat, corn, sugar cane, and other products. He also represented *three hundred* other Louisiana families who were likewise desirous of taking advantage of the king's former promise of receiving Spanish vassals as might voluntarily desire to immigrate into Texas.[72] He claimed that at the time of the

---

[71]Hatcher, "Texas in 1820," in *The Southwestern Historical Quarterly*, XXVIII, 67–68.

[72]This right was confirmed by Art. 5 of the treaty of February 22, 1819, *Treaties, Conventions, International Acts, Protocols, and Agreements between the United States of America and Other Powers, 1776–1809*, II, 1653.

transfer of Louisiana he, with many other families, had planned to move but had been unable to do so because of the opposition of the local authorities of Texas. The heads of the families now wishing to enter were nearly all men of means and all were industrious. They promised to bring sworn testimonials of their good character and to bind themselves to defend their adopted country whenever necessary against Indians, "filibusters," and other enemies that might attempt aggressions. They also promised to obey all existing laws.[73] Favorable recommendation, legislative action, and final approval were immediately forthcoming. Soon thereafter it became generally known that the *cortes* had opened the Spanish Dominions not only to Louisiana, but to all foreigners[74] and the success of Austin's plan seemed more certain, for with the rich but undeveloped lands of Texas[75] before them and the press of a disastrous panic behind them, the immigrants composed of many nations, needed no urging westward.

The success of this plan was forecast by the character of Stephen F. Austin who, due to the untimely death of the pioneer father, assumed the responsibility for peopling Texas with settlers from the United States. In writing to his cousin, Mary Austin Holly, he said:

> When I explored this country in 1821, it was a wild, howling, interminable solitude from Sabine to Bexar. The civilized population had not extended beyond the margins of the Sabine in that quarter; and was confined, on the west to the towns or villages of Bexar and La Bahia, where were isolated military posts. I

---

[73]Petition, December 26, 1820, A. P. Appendix 33. *Cf.* Wilkinson's plan for introducing Spanish vassals from Florida and Louisiana, *The Hispanic American Historical Review*, I, 175–180.

[74]Appendix 32. For the liberal colonization law of June 27, 1821, encouraging Spaniards and foreigners to settle in Spanish America, see *British and Foreign State Papers*, 1820–1821, VIII, 1303–1309. Due to the establishment of the independence of Mexico this law had no effect save to encourage the liberals of that country in their favorable attitude toward foreign immigration.

[75]For the condition of Texas at the beginning of the Anglo-American movement, see map, between pp. 283–284, and Appendix 34.

found the country so much more valuable than I expected that the idea of contributing to fill it with a civilized and industrious population filled my soul with enthusiasm. I can with truth and a clear conscience say that none of the sordid and selfish motives which influence the mass of adventurers had any weight in determining me to attack the wilderness. I commenced on the solid basis of sound and philanthropic intentions and of undeviating integrity.[76]

The Spanish dream of two centuries was to become a reality, although the complete success of the revolution, which broke out anew in Mexico in 1821, was needed to give additional warmth to the welcome extended to foreigners[77] and especially to the Americans, some of whom had aided in the final establishment of the long-desired independence.[78]

Conclusions

From the mass of material considered in this study, several facts stand out with clearness.

(1) Through the retrocession of Louisiana to France and its subsequent sale to the United States, Spain was forced to permit the entry into Texas of certain foreigners to whom she had previously granted citizenship in return for settlement in Louisiana at a time when she hoped to erect along the Mississippi an impassable barrier against further foreign aggression. Among those thus admitted

---

[76]July 19, 1831, A. P.

[77]For the liberal colonization law of the Empire and of the Republic of Mexico, issued on January 4, 1823, and August 18, 1824, see Austin, S. F., *Translation of the Laws, Orders, and Contracts of Colonization*, 30–33 and 40–41.

[78]Indeed, the "filibuster" General James Long, who had entered Texas in October, 1821, after Texas had accepted the Plan of Iguala, laid claim to especial favors because of his services in the cause. He tendered the continued services of his band of men, declaring:

If you think us worthy to serve the Mexican army and navy you will please order us on duty, or should we be deemed unworthy to fight for the country of our adoption, another disposition may be made of us; for my own part I prefer death before such disgrace; and if it awaits me, I have to request that it may come soon. Long to Iturbide, December 26, 1821, *Relaciones Exteriores, Año de 1821*, Transc. U. of T.

were Englishmen, Irishmen, Frenchmen, and Americans, practically all of whom, while protesting their love for the Spanish flag and claiming that they were good Catholics and upright citizens, really had personal, commercial, or territorial schemes to forward and who easily opened the way for the entry of many who were neither entitled to the name of vassals, nor worthy to be designated as faithful Catholics or desirable citizens. As a result of her conciliatory policy, Spain was also constrained to admit into these jealously guarded precincts certain Indian tribes, who were naturally hostile to the Spaniards and who had been stirred to a greater dislike by the foreigners with whom they had been previously associated.

(2) With these immigrants and with natives from Mexico and Spain, the more progressive spirits among the officials of Texas planned to erect a buffer against the entry of all foreigners and, especially, against the further advance of the Americans. At the same time they desired to develop the "poor, neglected province," into the prosperous region forecast by its splendid natural advantages. To accomplish this purpose, they desired to open a port upon the Gulf and to attract other colonists to settle within its borders. It was their intention to place these immigrants in settlements located upon the principal rivers and upon the extreme Texas-Louisiana frontier.

(3) In spite of Spain's restrictive commercial policy, Antonio Cordero, who in 1805 was made governor *ad interim* of Texas, actually succeeded in establishing the *villa* of Santísima Trinidad de Salcedo, upon the Trinity River. At the outset, it contained only thirty-seven settlers, but within three years its population had increased almost threefold. This rapid growth was in marked contrast to that of the older settlements of Texas which had been founded by natives alone. This creditable performance was soon followed by the establishment of the *villa* of San Marcos de Neve upon the San Marcos River by native colonists from Béxar and Bahía and from the Rio Grande. In the beginning, it contained less than one hundred inhabitants; and,

like all other settlements formed by natives, it never grew at all. The founding of these two *villas*, whose very existence has been unknown to many close students of Texas history, was accomplished in the face of great difficulties, for the commandant-general, afraid that objectionable immigrants—and especially Americans—were being admitted, revoked the order for opening a port on the Gulf and forced all immigrants to settle in assigned places, steadfastly refusing to permit them to locate at Nacogdoches or upon the coast as many of them desired to do. In spite of this difference of opinion the local authorities continued to lay plans for additional settlements, and even succeeded in beginning the foundation of Villa de Nueva Jáen on the Frio River, and in establishing on the Rio Grande the *villa* of Palafox, which even yet exists. At the same time they continued to urge the abandonment of the outgrown presidial system of government; the division of the Interior Province into two commandancies; the admission of Spanish vassals from Louisiana; greater latitude in the location of settlers; and the opening of a port through which the people could export their products and secure the necessities of life at a reasonable rate. One of their number even advocated free trade, claiming that "wherever people find prosperity, protection, and security, there will they go without being called."

(4) But in 1808 Napoleon began to lay plans to secure control of the Spanish Dominions of America. The naturally cautious commandant-general soon learned that this self-styled "Scourge of Tyrants" had actually sent emissaries to Texas to stir up revolution, and that he was perhaps planning to send his prisoners, the king and queen of Spain, to America the more easily to create greater divisions in order that he might step in and gain control. To circumvent these plans, the commandant-general ordered that all immigration from Louisiana should be stopped. This was opposed by Cordero and his colleagues on this vitally important frontier. In spite of warnings that Napoleon was planning to rule the world and that the United States was supporting him in the attempt, they believed

The Opening of Texas to Foreign Settlement 289

that Texas could still be saved by the introduction of a large number of immigrants who would defend it against all enemies.

(5) While the local authorities were laying these plans and, in spite of opposition, were carrying them into effect, Napoleon continued his efforts to bribe the Spaniards of America to acquiesce in his schemes for aggrandizement by offering them the free trade which they had long been denied. He also notified the authorities of the United States that he would not oppose the occupation of the Floridas if they would help him defeat the English. To add to the fears of the commandant-general, the United States actually took possession of West Florida to prevent its falling into the hands of the French or the English. To meet these dangers, the commandant-general ordered all communications across the frontier stopped and instructed the governor of Texas to expel from the province all foreigners who were not loyal supporters of the Spanish cause.

(6) These instructions, however, had no practical results since the local authorities not only succeeded in sustaining the reputation of most of the immigrants, but actually protected those whom they themselves were forced to confess should never have been admitted. Besides this, in utter defiance of the commandant-general's orders, they invited back to Texas all exiles who had been forced to leave the province to escape punishment for contraband trade. Thus was created a situation which made possible the entry of exiled Spaniards, designing Frenchmen, and adventurous Americans, while a large number of Spaniards who were living in Louisiana, and who might possibly have been induced to come to the aid of their country, did not receive sufficient encouragement to overcome their natural distastes for emigration.

(7) At this juncture, true to the prophecies of the commandant-general, the enemies of Spain invaded Texas. Among their numbers were some of the Indians who had received so many favors from the Spaniards, a number of Frenchmen, who were acting as agents of Napoleon, a few

Americans, who were anxious to see Mexico free but who probably failed to penetrate Napoleon's true designs, and certain Creoles, who were beginning to feel their nationality and who were willing to receive assistance from any source which promised aid for the establishment of independence. These men actually succeeded in invading Texas, in assassinating the two representatives of the liberal policy left in Texas, and in destroying every trace of the buffer which had been erected at the cost of so much effort. The commandant-general may have considered this assassination a just retribution for defiance of his orders; but it is more likely that he deeply regretted the event, since he was beginning to realize the possibility of defending Texas by placing therein a buffer line of colonies as proposed by these victims. The commandant-general even consented now to permit the opening of a port and promised to consider the establishment of an annual fair at Nacogdoches so that the people could secure supplies without being forced to engage in contraband trade. The heartless murder of the opponents of the liberal policy proved to be the turning point of the war, for the best spirits among the invaders soon abandoned the savage native leaders. Consequently, the competent Arredondo, who had been placed in command of the newly erected Eastern Interior Provinces, was able to defeat the invaders at the battle of Medina, in August, 1813, and to clear Texas of all foreigners who showed the least sympathy for the insurgent cause.

(8) By this time all Spanish authorities, from the *cortes* down to the newly appointed governor *ad interim* of Texas, were a unit in believing that the development of Texas was an imperious necessity if further aggression was to be prevented and the unhappy country restored to its original condition and then developed as its resources demanded. In fact, all authorities now desired that the port of Bahía should be opened and that colonists should be induced to locate in Texas. As a result, laws for the distribution of lands to soldiers and other desirable settlers were passed by the *cortes*. A contract was even made with an American

The Opening of Texas to Foreign Settlement 291

who had become a Spanish vassal to introduce into Texas immigrants from Louisiana and from Spain.

(9) At this juncture, however, Napoleon released Ferdinand VII from captivity and recognized him as king of Spain and the Indies, upon condition that the English should be expelled from Spain. Ferdinand at once repealed all the liberal colonization laws which had been passed by the *cortes* and forced a return to the status of 1808. Conditions in Texas were distressing. But, although actually deprived of the hopes of a *free port*, of a free *government*, and, except on the caprice of the king, of *free lands*, the people did not despair and continued to beg for settlers so that the country might be protected against Indian depredations, piratical exactions, and foreign aggressions. The old idea of using Spanish citizens as colonists still prevailed. These, of course, could not be secured. The use of Germans and Swiss in the erection of the desired buffer was favorably considered; but before definite action could be taken the applicants had decided to settle in the Spanish Peninsula. American and French adventurers were anxious to secure lands in Texas but as they entertained ideas hostile to the existing government and they were rigorously excluded. The idea of securing Spanish vassals from Louisiana was now revived. In support of this policy it was urged that the Creoles of Northern Louisiana had demonstrated their ability to deal with the Indians and that because they hated the Americans for depriving them of their lands would prove their mettle by holding back the tide of American immigration into Texas. But before any action could be taken two important events transpired—the treaty of 1819 definitely abandoned Texas to the Spaniards and the king of Spain consented to reëstablish the liberal colonization laws of the *cortes* providing for provincial assemblies and granting power to the *ayuntamientos* to distribute lands. While the king called for suggestions for the best means of developing Texas, the *cortes* even granted inviolable asylum in all Spanish territory to forcigners, thus absolutely reversing the age-long policy of exclusions in vogue at the beginning

of the nineteenth century. The authorities were thus able to avail themselves of the offer of Moses Austin, a former Spanish vassal who had long desired to emigrate to Texas, and who now promised to introduce reputable Catholic vasvals from Louisiana. This promise, executed by Stephen F. Austin, the first *empresario* of Texas, in obedience to the dying request of his father, gave to Texas a *free port* through which to export the supplies produced on the *free lands* granted to the settlers, and, a little later, through the final triumph of the liberals in the Revolution of 1821, the *free government* for which the people had been longing. That these settlers would wish to become a part of the great Republic of the North was a foregone conclusion. The way was thus prepared for the extension of the frontiers of the United States to the Rio Grande.

APPENDIX

1. Exclusion of Foreigners from the Spanish Dominions of America, 1784.
2. Number of Foreigners on the Texas Frontier, 1801.
3. Attractions of the Province and Mode of Entry *via* Louisiana, 1795–1801.
4. A Frenchman Seeks Refuge in Texas, 1803.
5. Conditions in Texas at the Beginning of General Immigration, 1803.
6. Another Frenchman Follows the French Flag, 1803.
7. An Irishman Prefers Spanish to American Rule, 1804.
8. A Frenchman and an Irishman Plan a Colony for Texas, 1804.
9. The Commandant-General Admits Reputable Spanish Vassals from Louisiana, 1804.
10. The Prince of the Peace Decides upon a Buffer against the United States, 1804.
11. Description of the Villa System of Colonization.
12. An American Frontiersman Desires Lands in Texas, 1806.
13. Natives and Emigrants from Louisiana Establish Villa Salcedo, 1806.
14. Native Texans and Emigrants from Interior of Mexico Found Villa San Marcos, 1807.
15. Napoleon Seizes the Spanish Throne and Incites Rebellion in the Colonies, 1808.
16. The Commandant-General Closes the Door to Foreign Immigrants, 1808.
17. The Local Authorities Favor Colonization as a Means of Defense, 1809.
18. The Commandant-General Defends his Exclusion Policy, 1809.
19. The Local Authorities Persist in their Plans, 1810.
20. The Regency Provides for a Buffer Colony in Texas, 1811.
21. Insurgent Leaders Promise Lands to American "Filibusters."
22. Insurgents, Frenchmen and Americans, Continue Aggressions, 1813.
23. The *Cortes* Grants Lands to Faithful Citizens and Soldiers, 1813.
24. A New Commandant-General Promises Commercial Concessions, 1813.
25. He Expels Foreign Invaders and Pardons Mexican Insurgents, 1813.
26. The Regency Determines to Colonize Texas, 1813.
27. The *Cortes* Encourages an American to Introduce Foreigners into Texas, 1813.
28. Released by Napoleon, the King of Spain Abrogates the Constitution of 1812–1814.

29. The King Re-accepts the Constitution of 1812, 1820.
30. An American "Filibuster" Promises Lands to the President of the Texas Republic, 1820.
31. The *Cortes* Insists upon the Distribution of Public Lands, 1820.
32. The King and the *Cortes* Offer Foreigners an Asylum in Spanish Territory, 1820.
33. Moses Austin Asks Permission to Introduce Louisianians into Texas, 1820.
34. The Condition of Texas at the Beginning of the Anglo-American Colonization Period, 1820.

THE APPENDIX[1]

DOCUMENT NO. 1

EXCLUSION OF FOREIGNERS FROM THE SPANISH DOMINIONS OF AMERICA

The Commandant-General to the Governor of Texas, May 14, 1874.[2]

By the laws of title twenty-seven, book nine, of the *Recopilación de Indias*, the introduction and settlement of foreigners in the Spanish Dominions of America is expressly forbidden, especially in the coast settlements. It has been repeatedly ordered that those who have

---

[1] The thirty-four documents contained in the Appendix furnish an outline of the determined struggle of the royalists of Spain and Mexico to hold Texas against insurgent and foreign aggression from 1801 when, through the retrocession of Louisiana, it became a buffer province, until 1821, when detailed plans had been worked out for its colonization—especially as a barrier against any further expansion of the United States to the southwest. In this struggle, the defenders encountered two almost insuperable difficulties. In the first place, they were unable to induce any great number of the natives of Mexico to face the dangers of Indian depredations and the loneliness of the exposed frontier where they were forced, by dint of hard labor, to wring a bare subsistence from the soil. Besides, after 1808, when Napoleon had disclosed his determination to seize upon all the Spanish Dominions of America, the authorities were never, for any length of time, free to turn their attention from military defense against the insurgents whom this arch conspirator stirred into action. In spite of this preoccupation, however, they continued to lay careful plans to strengthen the province against invasion by the use of any colonists they could secure—so long as they were thought not to be open partisans of France, during the time of Napoleon's ascendancy, or of the United States, while she persisted in her determination to secure Texas either through purchase or the use of bluff. It is interesting to note that, in her eager desire to colonize the much coveted province, the authorities, in the end, completely reversed the attitude they had at first assumed towards foreigners and that, after the signing of the Onís Treaty of 1819, they were even willing to admit from Louisiana such persons as had lived in that region during the Spanish occupation and were willing to come into Texas to aid the almost despairing authorities in subduing the Indians so that the country could be developed as desired. It is also interesting to note that the lands of Texas were offered alike by royalists, insurgents, and foreign invaders in an effort to secure defenders for each cause. Of these documents, twenty-two are from originals in the Béxar Archives, two from the Nacogdoches Archives, and one from the *Austin Papers*, and seven from copies of documents in other collections; as follows: one, from the Bancroft Library; one, from *Archivo General de Indias*, Seville; one, from Villanueva, *Napoleon y la Independencia de América;* and four, from *Colección de Los Decretos y Ordenes de las Cortes*. Two are translations by unknown authors; one, from Niles' *Weekly Register* and the other from *The British and Foreign State Papers*. One only was originally in English, a letter from James Long to Major Ripley. The source of each document will be indicated in a footnote, save in the case of those from the Béxar Archives, where the usual system will be followed. The remainder were translated by the writer.

[2] This order shows the hostile attitude maintained for years by the Spaniards against all foreigners and the especial care they took to prevent the entry into Texas of the proscribed individuals. This policy was in full force at the beginning of the period under discussion.

introduced themselves without the proper license shall be searched for and apprehended and that, after the punishment fixed by the laws shall have been imposed, they shall be sent by the first opportunity on registered vessels to the Kingdom of Spain to the *Casa de Contratación*.

Because of the failure to observe these reiterated, just, and equitable orders, there has resulted a toleration which, if it continue any longer, may produce very grave and prejudicial consequences to our kingdom; and, since it is advisable to avoid these by every possible means, I command you to make use of whatever measures you may think proper and timely to arrange that there be made immediately the most punctual and exact examination of all the foreigners who may reside in any settlement, *hacienda*, or ranch within the province under your charge and that there be prepared lists or reports of those found, expressing clearly and distinctly their christian and surnames, their nationalities, the places of their birth, their conditions, their present residences, the size of the family of each and the number of their children, their real estate and such other property as they may possess, the professions, occupations, or employments in which they are engaged, and the time that has elapsed between their arrival in this kingdom and the preparation of the said lists. These reports you will have prepared with the greatest brevity and accuracy; and as soon as they are finished you will send me the originals in order that, in view of them, I may dictate such further measures as I may think necessary. In the meantime, you will be very careful and transmit the strictest orders to the justices in the province so that all foreigners found there who have no well-known or fixed and lawful residence—whether they be travelers or traders, or have entered under any other pretext whatever—may be arrested and put under guard. The records of the usual verbal examination made in such cases and all the papers found upon them shall be sent me for my decision. . . .

Arispe, May 14, 1784.
PHELIPE DE NEVE.

Don Domingo Cabello.

NO. 2

NUMBER OF FOREIGNERS ON THE TEXAS FRONTIER, 1801, CENSUS OF NACOGDOCHES[1]

PUEBLO OF NACOGDOCHES

LIST OF THE FOREIGNERS IN THE PUEBLO AND IN ITS ENTIRE JURISDICTON, WITH A STATEMENT OF NAMES, NATIONALITIES, CONDITIONS, AGES, TIME OF RESIDENCE, AND OCCUPATIONS

	No.
Don Samuel Davenport—American, native of Pennsylvania, married, thirty-seven years of age, residence of eight years, partner of general purveyor for the friendly Indians of Texas, farmer	1
Juan Macfallen—American, native of Virginia, married, thirty-six years of age, residence of six years, agriculturist, has with him his father-in-law, Julies Sanders, also an American, native of Carolina, widower, fifty-four years of age, agriculturist with residence of two years	2
Santiago Dill—American, native of Pennsylvania, married, thirty-one years of age, residence of four years, farmer and trader	1
Reimundo Querque—American, native of Virginia, married, forty-five years of age, residence of four years, farmer	1
Enrrique Querque—American, native of Virginia, bachelor, thirty-one years of age, residence of three years, farmer	1
[Antonio?] Pared—American, native of North Carolina, bachelor, thirty-six years of age, three years residence, carpenter	1

---

[1]This report shows that, in spite of the laws and orders providing for the exclusion of foreigners, many managed to secure entry into Texas. According to the report of one official certain foreigners had secured permission from the commandant at Natchitoches to settle upon the lands left unoccupied by the removal of the *presidio* of Adaes and its missions. Some of them became ranchmen, some farmers and some Indian traders, each being assigned an Indian *pueblo* on condition that he make a yearly gift to the church. Report, May 14, 1792.

For transient settlers, other than those named in the list for 1801, see Cabello to Neve, March 1, 1784, Report of Nacogdoches, May 14, 1792, and December 31, 1793, and lists of inhabitants of Texas, May 31, 1792, and of San Fernando de Béxar, December 31, 1793. In 1793 there had also arrived at Béxar a German physician, Agustin Guillermo de Spangenburg, Muñoz to Nava, December 31, 1793, and February 11, 1794, in *Quaderno*, January 4, 1794. He removed to Coahuila a little later, Muñoz to Nava, May 7, 1794, *Ibid*. Another transient who created a great deal of excitement was Juan Calvert, an Englishman, born in Philadelphia, and a Presbyterian, who presented himself at Béxar, desiring to become a Catholic. He wished to secure employment as a silversmith or a gunsmith, Muñoz to the Commandant-General, June 9, 1874, *Ibid*. However, he, too, went further to the interior and later wished to leave the Spanish Dominions for Islas Negras, Letter No. 294, 315, 338, and 347 in *Quaderno*, February 26, 1793. So far as can be ascertained, he never returned to Texas.

Guillermo Suel—American, native of Pennsylvania, bachelor, forty-one years of age, residence of fifteen years, farmer.............. 1
Guillermo Jonston—American, native of Virginia, bachelor, forty-six years of age, residence of two years, farmer.............. 1
Santiago Eliot—American, native of Pennsylvania, bachelor, twenty-three years of age, residence of four years, agriculturist.... 1
[?] Guemble—American, native of North Carolina, bachelor, thirty-six years of age, residence of eleven years, carpenter.... 1
Juan Bouquer—American, native of Virginia, married, sixty-one years of age, residence of thirteen years, carpenter.............. 1
Juan Debis—[American, native of Virginia], bachelor, thirty-one years of age, residence of six years, agriculturist.............. 1
Josue Ris—American, native of Pennsylvania, bachelor, forty-one years of age, residence of six years, agriculturist.............. 1
Miguel Cro—American, native of South Carolina, married, thirty-five years of age, residence of seven year, farmer.............. 1
José Hinson—American, native of Virginia, bachelor, forty-four years of age, residence of two years, farmer.............. 1
Rafael Sims—Englishman, native of New England, married, thirty-seven years of age, residence of twelve years, farmer...... 1
Juan [Biens?]—Englishman, bachelor, thirty-one years of age, residence of one year and eight months, farmer.............. 1
Don Guillermo Barr—Irishman, native of the capital of Munster, bachelor, forty-one years of age, residence of nine years, chief of traders for friendly Indian nations of Texas and gunsmith 1
Santiago Conilt—Irishman, born in Louisiana, bachelor, twenty-three years of age; has two younger brothers, bachelors, eighteen and sixteen years of age, residence of eighteen years, farmer.............. 3
Santiago Maconilt—Irishman, native of the capital of Munster, bachelor, forty-four years of age, eight years residence, farmer 1
Juan Oconor—Irishman, native of the capital of Connaught, bachelor, thirty-six years of age, residence of six years, farmer.... 1
Juan Bron—Irishman, bachelor, forty-six years of age, residence of three years, farmer.............. 1
Juan Oconor—Irishman, native of the capital of Connaught, bachelor, thirty-nine years of age, residence of three years, tailor 1
Juan Fontan—Frenchman, native of Bollona, married, forty-two years of age, residence of six years, baker.............. 1
Juan Rosales—Frenchman, native of Bordeaux, married, thirty-three years of age, residence of seven years, carpenter and farmer 1

Don Bernardo Dortolan—Frenchman, captain of mounted militia of Natchitoches, residence of eight years, widower, farmer.... 1
Don Juan José de la Baume—Frenchman, native of Longuedoc, widower, fifty-six years of age, residence of two years, farmer _____ 1
Santiago Christen—Frenchman, native of Piedmont, married, fifty-seven years of age, residence of six years, farmer _____ 1
Luis Reliquet—Frenchman, native of the Archbishopric of Nantes, married, forty-three years of age, residence of eight years, merchant _____ 1
[Guillermo] Pallar—Frenchman, native of Samolo, bachelor, thirty-six years of age, residence of one year, farmer _____ 1
Juan Laforçada—Frenchman, native of Bordeaux, thirty-four years of age, bachelor, residence of two years, farmer _____ 1
José Barbie—Frenchman, native of Sabollar [Savie?], bachelor, forty-one years of age, residence of three years, farmer and hatter _____ 1
Salvador—Frenchman, married, forty-two years of age, residence of eight years, farmer _____ 1
Pedro Bosquec—Frenchman, native of Bordeaux, married, forty-nine years of age, residence of nine years, trader for Tankawa Indians _____ 1
Don José Capuran—Frenchman, native of Ballone, married, forty-seven years of age, residence of nine years, merchant _____ 1
Juan Sarnac—Frenchman, native of La Rochelle, widower, sixty-one years of age, residence of twenty-six years, merchant..... 1
Nicolas Pon—Frenchman, native of New Orleans, bachelor, forty-nine years of age, residence of eight years, agriculturist _____ 1
Estevan Goguet—Native of Arkansas Post, Louisiana, married, thirty-five years of age, residence of twenty-five years, farmer _____ 1
Santiago Lepin—Native of Louisiana, married, forty-five years of age, residence of seven years, farmer _____ 1
Guillermo Bebe—Native of Louisiana, married, thirty-one years of age, residence of seven years, hatter _____ 1
Pedro Engle—Native of the capital of Louisiana, widower, fifty-three years of age, residence of twenty-six years, trader for Tankawa Indians _____ 1
Don Pedro Doleo—Native of Natchitoches, Louisiana, married, fifty-seven years of age, residence of twenty-three years, farmer _____ 1
Andres Balentin—Native of Natchitoches, married, thirty-seven years of age, residence of eleven years, farmer _____ 1
Franco. Pridomo—Native of Natchitoches, married, sixty-nine years of age, residence of nine years, farmer _____ 1

Anto. Dibua—Native of Natchitoches, married, thirty-four years
of age, residence of eleven years, farmer.. 1
Sebastian Pridomo—Native of Natchitoches, widower, forty-two
years of age, residence of three years, farmer............................ 1
Franco. Morvan—Native of Natchitoches, married, sixty-two years
of age, residence of twelve years, farmer...................................... 1
Pedro Laviña—Native of Natchitoches, bachelor, thirty-five years
of age, residence of eight years, farmer... 1
Juan Ignacio Pifermo—Native of Natchitoches, bachelor, thirty-
five years of age, residence of twelve years, farmer............. 1
Franco. Bart—Native of Punta Cortada, bachelor, thirty-eight
years of age, residence of six years, trader for Nacogdoches
and Anadarko Indians.. 1
José Tecier—Native of Canada, bachelor, forty-five, residence of
eight years, farmer.. 1
Guillermo Guelet—Native of Canada, married, forty-four, residence
of four years, merchant... 1
Crisostome Yucante—Native of Canada, married, sixty-five, resi-
dence of twenty-one years, farmer... 1
José Morel—Native of Canada, bachelor, thirty-seven, residence of
three years, farmer 1
Pedro [Tecier?]—Native of Louisiana, bachelor, fifty-three, resi-
dence of three years, farmer... 1

57

DESERTERS

Juan Bin (Scotchman) 1
Juan Nicolas (American) 1
Miguel Bruno (Irishman) 1
Guillermo Numans (Irishman) 1
Santiago Brirns (American) 1
David Korkens (American) 1
Roberto Tarp (American) 1
Franco. Born (Irishman) of County of Denegal.................................. 1
Franco. Macoy (Irishman) 1
Juan Debis (American) 1

[Total] 67

Nacogdoches, January 1, 1804.

JOSE JOAQUÍN UGARTE.[2]

---

[2]*Cf. Padron de Familias*, December 31, 1799.

NO. 3

ATTRACTIONS OF THE PROVINCE AND MODE OF ENTRY VIA LOUISIANA, 1795–1801

AFFIDAVIT OF A FOREIGN VASSAL[1]

Commandant,

Don Pedro Samuel Davenport, general trader for the Indian nations of the Province of Texas, and citizen of the Pueblo of Nacogdoches, with due respect, make known to you that, in compliance with the proclamation of the viceroy of New Spain, published in this *pueblo* by order of the commandant-general of the Interior provinces, I do state:

That I am the legitimate son of Don Guillermo Davenport[2] and Doña Ana Davidson, now deceased, natives and former residents of the town of Carlisle, Cumberland County, Pennsylvania;[3] in the United States of America.

That, having lost my parents by death when still very young, I set out from my native country when sixteen years of age and, almost without delay, went to the Province of Louisiana, entering it twenty-four years ago. There, in different locations, I engaged in commerce, being employed by well known firms of that branch of business and engaging in said business on my own account.

That, fifteen years ago, I came to this *pueblo*, where, without any difficulty, I settled; since, during that period I mention, Louisiana, where I was already known was, like this *pueblo*, under Spanish rule. Shortly after settling in said *pueblo*, because of my conduct and the honesty I have always shown, I earned the confidence of the Spanish government and was made a partner of Don Guillermo Barr, the

---

[1] This affidavit shows that commerce was the chief attraction which drew foreigners to Texas. It also illustrates the ease with which they secured entry through Louisiana just prior to the beginning of the period under consideration.

[2] "God save us Spaniards!" had been the prophetic exclamation of an inhabitant of Natchez, in 1787, upon the arrival of the commissioners sent out from Georgia to mark the boundaries of that state. One of the number was Don Guillermo Davenport, who brought with him his wife, two children and certain other persons. That he had come to stay was evident; and alarm over the possible loss of Natchez to Georgia or to the United States became general among the Spaniards. Profit to Miró, June 25, 1785, and Miró to Galvez, July 1, 1785, in *A. G. I. S.* Mex., 86–6–17, June 14, 1785–July 1, 1785.

[3] In a list of families of Nacogdoches, December 31, 1799, Davenport is listed as a native of Philadelphia. Quite a number of others had come from that city, among them being one Englishman and two Americans, Mr. Querque and Guillermo Fils. It will also be remembered that Moses Austin was a merchant of that city prior to his removal to Virginia and thence to Louisiana, from which place he finally, in 1820, visited Texas to arrange for the immigration of his family and a number of colonists.

general trader for the Indian nations of the province. This employment I have discharged for ten years to the satisfaction of the said government.

That, seven years ago, I married María Louisa Gañon, a native of Natchitoches, Louisiana. . . .

That my age is forty-five years, my religion, the Roman Catholic. Of this I have given proofs to the public here that can be supported by witnesses and certificates. Likewise, I have proofs that I have always tried to show my personal affections for the Spanish government not only in this *pueblo* but also in Louisiana.

That I have papers to prove my identity; but this is because, although I started from my native town with them, while I was traveling through the Indian country of the United States in company with other persons, the Indians attacked us, killed three of the company and the rest of us were able to escape only with our lives, all papers being lost, mine among them. Therefore, not having taken the precaution to secure others—since I have been and am known to the inhabitants of Louisiana and this *pueblo* and province—I present to you this statement (which I sign under oath— in fulfillment of the provisions of the said proclamation. . . . June 16, 1809.

S. DAVENPORT.

NO. 4

ANOTHER FRENCHMAN FOLLOWS THE SPANISH FLAG, PETITION OF LA BAUME.[1] AUGUST 4, 1803

Commandant-General,
My dear Sir,

Desiring to follow the Spanish flag, under which my ancestors were reared and which they defended with such signal valor, as soon as I learned of the retrocession of Louisiana to the French Republic, I moved with the proper permits, to this post of Nacogdoches last year in the time of Commandant-General, Pedro de Nava; and, recognizing the fact that this place is inadequate for the exercise of my profession as a doctor and a druggist and, at the same time, poor in opportunity for making use of the work of my eight negroes, I humbly beg that you will be kind enough to give me leave to move, with my family, goods, and equipment to Béxar or Bahía, . . .

JOSÉ DE LA BAUME.[2]

Nacogdoches, August 4, 1803.

---

[1]This is the first petition found showing the usual explanation given by the inhabitants of Louisiana for desiring to settle in Texas; i.e., a love for the Spanish flag and a dislike for remaining in Louisiana after its retrocession and subsequent sale to foreign powers.

[2]*Cf.* Juan José de la Baume listed in Appendix 2.

NO. 5

CONDITION OF TEXAS AT THE BEGINNING OF THE GENERAL IMMIGRATION MOVEMENT, 1803

Informaion in regard to the Province of Texas, its extent, population, and the occupation of its inhabitants, with a statement of the branches of agriculture in which they are engaged, given by Lieutenant-Colonel Don Juan Bautista Elguezabal, Governor of the Province of Texas, ot the commandant-general.[1]

The Province of Texas, whose exact extent to this day is unknown contains only three small settlements, to wit: San Antonio de Béxar, Bahía del Espíritu Santo, and the *pueblo* of Nacogdoches. The first named is the capital, the second is a *presidio*, situated to the southeast of the capital, at a distance of fifteen leagues from the coast, and the third is a *pueblo* on the frontier of Louisiana.

Villa de San Fernando, or by its other name, Presidio de San Antonio de Béxar, contains two thousand five hundred persons, including the company [of soldiers stationed there]. Its location upon the fertile bank of a river gives it peculiar potentialities which have not been developed because of the general poverty of the citizens. They confine their labor to planting corn, though not in great quantities; for experience has shown that when a quantity is planted, if abundant crops are raised, the [yield] is useless, because of the lack of a market—to the planting of beans, chili pepper and some sugarcane. From all these [products] it is customary for [the people] to provide themselves with rations for a year except in the case of the last mentioned product which benefits only two or three persons who make a small quantity of sugar. The rest [of the cane] they sell or eat. A loom or a manufactury has never been known nor are there any cotton fields. Wool is very scarce; for those who have any send it to Saltillo in order to manage to sell it. Besides, there are not over one thousand head of sheep in the whole province. It has been found that no profit will result from [raising sheep]. There are no flour mills. Other branches of agriculture are entirely unknown. The same is true of all kinds of arts. There is a notable scarcity of cattle. For this reason, a lack of meat is almost continuously experienced; and so it is that, if the semi-annual slaughter of buffaloes which takes place in the months of May and October did not in a measure relieve the misery, the majority of the families would no

---

[1]This report is included in the Appendix since it shows the condition of Texas at the beginning of the colonization era of 1801-1821. It seems surprising that the would-be immigrants could have felt the affection they expressed for the Spanish government which had been unable to develop the potentially rich province during an occupation of almost a century.

doubt starve. The catching of wild horses—and there is a great abundance in the province—is the second thing which attracts the attention of the settlers.

On the opposite bank of the same river is the mission of San Antonio de Valero, secularized some years ago. Its actual population, counting the company of San Carlos de Parras, amounts to three hundred and sixty-two persons. Its inhabitants plant corn, beans and pepper. Don Antonio Baca alone—and he is a settler of Béxar, who owns land and water there—raises sugar-cane. The crops are scant for the reasons already explained [in connection with] Villa de San Fernando.

Following the course of this river, there are found, about a league distant from each other, four missions, for the most part in ruins although in olden times they were exceedingly rich. Their population amounts to three hundred persons. Among the few Indians are settled a number of Spaniards and people of caste. They are occupied—as are all others—in planting corn, beans, and pepper, in catching stock, and in killing game at the accustomed times.

The *presidio* of Bahía is situated at a distance of forty leagues down the river from Béxar. It contains, counting troops and settlers, six hundred and eighteen persons. It lacks water for irrigation. This is the reason that, although the citizens plant annually in season, they rarely raise crops. The company secures its supply of grain from Béxar. An irrigation ditch could be constructed and all the evils that have been experienced could be remedied, but this demands funds—which the people absolutely have not.

In the jurisdiction of this *presidio* are three missions called Nuestra Senora del Rosario, Espíritu Santo and Nuestra Señora del Refugio. All these together contain two hundred and fifty persons of the Araname, Karankawa, Coco, Cujane and Mayeye nations. The first two missions are in a deplorable state, having absolutely nothing with which to support their respective Indians. The ministers who have served them have acquired cattle from the stipend which his majesty dispenses to them as a reward for their industry. The other mission is in a better condition as regards stock. From the product of these, they provide food for the Indians and pay for their servants. In all three, the planting of corn has been confined to one season which rarely yields; as they have no water.

The *pueblo* of Nuestra Señora de Nacogdoches contains six hundred and sixty settlers. It is situated about one hundred and fifty leagues to the northeast upon the frontier of Louisiana, from whence all the settlers obtain such articles as are necessary for the maintenance of life. Because of its proximity to Louisiana and because of the insuperable difficulties presented by the extensive, unsettled region [intervening between Nacogdoches and this place] which is full of rivers and liable to terrible floods, the settlers are deprived of the hope of securing anything for their subsistence from these regions. If it should be attempted to deprive them of the benefit [of trade with Louisiana] the families would be reduced to starvation or would be forced to move their dwelling places. Its settlers are engaged in hunting bear, deer, and buffalo, and in planting, at great expenditure of labor, what is absolutely necessary for their food. They also capture stock for their personal use on their ranches.

From this description, it is shown that in the entire province there are four thousand people of all ages and sexes—the three companies which at present garrison it being included in this number. It is shown, too, that its lands are fertile beyond all others of America, that there is absolutely no commerce nor industry, that the lack of these branches of trade, together with the exceedingly small population which is so much scattered, as has been shown—and to this must be added the great number of Indians which occupy it—are the principal causes for the general poverty which the settlers suffer.

June 20, 1803.[2]

NO. 6

A Frenchman Seeks Refuge in Texas,

Petition of Despallier[1]
(January 18, 1804)

His Excellency, the Governor,

Pardon me if I take the liberty of writing you again when I have just written; but circumstances and my unhappy situation force me to do so. In the first petition which I have already forwarded to you—the commandant having told me that time was pressing—I was not able to give you an idea of my situation. Having lost all my goods in Santo Domingo, I thought there was nothing to do but to return to my native country—the Province of Louisiana—where, at the time, Baron de Carondelet (May God preserve his life) was in command. Here I found all the assistance I could expect from a superior officer and from a kind hearted man like him. He was good enough to give me the appointment as captain of the mounted militia in the Legion of Mississippi; and, during the war we had with France, I conducted myself as my position and my fidelity demanded,[2] as did

---

[2]Draft in [Blotter], December 8, 1802–June 30, 1803 [after draft No. 90].

[1]Despallier's case illustrated the Frenchman's general attitude of pretended friendship for the Spaniards.

[2]This pretended devotion to the Spanish government was insincere; for, a little later, when the enemies of Spain invaded Texas, the petitioner, who had been received as a Spanish vassal, turned against his benefactors. That he was seeking his own commercial advancement may be inferred from his conduct. That he was a tool of Napoleon may also be true.

the commander of Rapide, my uncle, Valentine Layssard. This gained for us a great number of enemies as was the case with all officers who were faithful to the prince and who earnestly desired to perform their duty. The realization that I have a great number of enemies everywhere has impelled me to try to reach you in order to learn whether, under your protection, I could be considered a good Spanish citizen; and, when I have talked with you and have made known to you my family, I think you will give me the title. Doubtless, you have persons at San Antonio who are acquainted in New Orleans and who must know my family—the Facindes, the Florios, the Régios, the deceased Mr. de Tréveque, who was major of the regiment of New Orleans, and the deceased Mr. Layssard, perpetual commandant of the post of Rapide, who was called La Four. In a word, all my relatives are among those who have been devoted to Spain. This I can say without fear and I am able to give you proofs of all I have had the honor to submit to your Excellency, if you will permit me to settle in your government. I will bind myself to go to New Orleans to provide myself with a [removal] permit from that government and with the certificates of my conduct. My reason is that I am told that the French have secured Louisiana; and you may believe that, if this is true, our enemies will show themselves, because we have placed so many obstacles in the way of their wicked plans. This is why I desire to retire to a government where I hope to spend the rest of my days....

      Your humble and obedient servant,
        B[ernard]o M[art]in Despallier.

NO. 7

An Irishman Prefers Spanish to American Rule, Petition of Curon [April 1, 1804.[1]]

Commandant-General,

I, Juan Curon, Apostolic Roman Catholic, native of the Province of Munster, Ireland, married, having a family, resident of the Province of Louisiana for ten years, and recently removed to the *pueblo* of Nacogdoches, in this province, which is under your command, appear before you in due form, and say that the government of the United States does not suit me while that of the crown of Spain does. I, therefore, respectfully ask that you be kind enough to grant me permission to locate with my family in the said *pueblo* of Nacogdoches in this said province under your command. I have always been a faithful subject of our sovereign (may God bless him). I, therefore

---

[1]This petition illustrates the displeasure of certain settlers of Louisiana at the sale of that province to the United States which resulted in an increased number of applications for admission into Texas.

send two documents in order that you may be informed of my honorable conduct and truthfulness.

NO. 8

A Frenchman and an Irishman Plan a Colony for Texas, Petition of Brady and Despallier, 1804[1]

Commandant-General,

Friar Juan Brady, barefooted Carmelite, formerly parish priest at Rapide and, at present, parish priest at Baton Rouge, and Don Bernardo Despallier, captain of militia of the said post in Louisiana, in the name of the citizens of the above mentioned settlement, by whom we have been commissioned to come to this post of Nacogdoches to speak in their behalf, say to you, with due respect, that we are moved solely by the hope of serving both Majesties to explain to you our situation and desires in the following terms:

In view of the fact that the said province has been retroceded to the French Republic and they have sold it to the United States of America, numerous noble, influential, and rich families, as well as some poor ones, desire to move to the provinces under your command in order that they may live under the Spanish flag and enjoy the same kind treatment that they, as well as their predecessors, have previously enjoyed.

The number of families who desire to immigrate can not be given exactly; but it is certain that the universal love and loyalty felt for the Spanish government is so great that we are satisfied and believe there will be more than a thousand families, more than two hundred of them of the Spanish nation, who will come as soon as they can sell their lands and collect the value of their property in case you will permit transportation either by sea or land, according to which is the least expensive and difficult to them.

1. The reasons which may move your kind heart to accede to our petition are first and foremost religious reasons. For love of religion, we came to settle in Louisiana, where our children have been born and educated and where we had hoped to live and die; but your kind heart can not permit us to remain in a land where religion is a matter of choice and where its observance is looked upon with indifference.

2. Also, since we have experienced the great kindness and friendship of the Spanish government, we desire still to be under its dominion and protection so much that we will shed our blood for it and for its defense, leaving our descendants to the care of its pious king; and we desire that our wishes may be laid at his feet, trusting that he will not scorn his faithful vassals.

---

[1]This is the first definite plan for the establishment of a colony in Texas to serve as a buffer against the Americans who had just secured possession of Louisiana.

3. The third reason is that the king, our sovereign (may God bless him) has expended large sums from the royal treasury for the benefit of these same vassals, bringing some of them from the Canary Islands, others from Acadia, others from Canada, others from Germany, and others from France and from Spain; and, now, that they can repay this favor with personal service and property—a service for which they gladly offer themselves—it is not possible that he will abandon them to a foreign power.

4. We beg that you will consider this point and make known to the sacred Majesty of our sovereign that, because of his royal promise, we abandoned our native countries with the intention of populating the colonies under his command; and, now since we believe [this colony] is to be turned over to foreigners, we hope that he will keep his promise by permitting us to move to the nearest posts of the Province of Texas which posts are under your command.

5. That with the passage of time it may happen that his Catholic Majesty may have some disagreement or wars with the said Americans as a foreign and aggressive power; and we do not desire to bear arms against a king so good and kind, who has loaded us with benefits we are unable to return; nor do we wish to use a knife against our brothers, the Spaniards, whose absence we regret and whose withdrawal has been exceedingly painful to us.

6. The deciding motive which should impel you to yield to our petition is that the sale of Louisiana has been the result of war and the effect of jealousies among the nations and is not due to our faults and demerits. Besides, in no manner does it meet our desires; as we have always been loyal, faithful and submissive to our sovereign.

7. The seventh reason which should move you as a faithful and permanent vassal of our king, is that the greatest number of advantages will come to the crown through our admission; for a large numbers of vassals like this established along the frontier can make the limits respected by an invading enemy from an adjoining government, who will, it is quite natural to expect, attack, if unsettled, a frontier which should be guarded with a larger number of troops and loyal settlers who will defend it as the key to the Kingdom of Mexico.

8. If this large number of persons leave Louisiana for your provinces, it will greatly weaken the strong neighboring American government and will greatly increase the royal interest of our sovereign; since it is probable that the kind reception given them and permission for the coming not only of these thousand families but of many more —and these the most influential of the said province—will make this poor unsettled Province [of Texas] rich, populous, and fruitful.

9. From the industry of these influential and industrious vassals the government can secure supplies for the royal manufactories, since they are all industrious persons, who by application and labor, can

give great value to the country because of their large numbers, their slaves, their servants, and their goods. And these are advantages needed for successful settlements.

10. These citizens are coming to develop those branches of agriculture which will bring benefit to the king and to the public. For instance, tobacco, cotton, cane, and other things necessary for the royal navy can be secured by our government without the necessity of making application to foreign countries. They, likewise, can supply with their products and manufactories, sails, woods, and other articles as well as meats and all kinds of beverages.

11. This large number of people being settled, the invasions of the Indians who constantly harrass this neighboring province—because they see the region so unsettled—will end. At the same time, the expenses of the royal treasury will cease, as much because the Indians will be restrained as because of the large number of troops kept on the frontier can be reduced.

12. Since they will have their families and goods and possessions in the country [these people] will necessarily defend it at all times and fight with all possible vigor and determination because there will be involved not only the sovereign's interest, but also their own.

13. You may rest assured that we speak as faithful vassals of our king when we say that this is the critical time and moment for settling these places; and that it should not be allowed to pass; for almost all the citizens of Louisiana are greatly excited and displeased by the new government and the events just transpired.

14. His Majesty has always spent a good deal of money in settling this province; but to people it under these conditions will cost nothing since all these vassals who desire to immigrate, if given permission by you, will pay for their transportation and location from their own funds.

15. This unsettled country being peopled, the grave inconveniences and calamities which have been experienced during the time I have been here will cease; and I have just learned that the mail has been lost in the torrent of a river through lack of settlers and canoes to carry it over. Likewise, in spite of the wise measures taken by the chief who governs [these regions], I have seen this place subjected to great calamities, of even serious and pressing hunger and want of provisions through lack of people to cultivate these splendid lands and of a market for their products.

16. That, having settlers well supplied with provisions, it will be possible to furnish any number of troops that the king may need on the frontier in a sudden and unexpected emergency; and it will not happen, as I have just seen it happen here, that troops who have been on an expedition will have to beg for food and not be able to secure adequate supplies for two months because of scarcity of provisions and canoes where they are located and because of impedi-

ments in the way of seeking them elsewhere. It, therefore, would follow that troops would withdraw because of famine and that soldiers would desert.

17. These rich, influential, and industrous settlers will bring a great deal of money into the dominions of his Majesty which they are not willing for a foreign power to enjoy. Likewise there will come, as in fact they are actually desiring to come, people of all trades who will cause these Interior Province to flourish, there being among them many men instructed in the sciences of peace and of war by land and by sea ond conversant with the liberal and mechanical arts.

18. You must consider very carefully how many of the advantages to the crown will result if a port is opened for them. They will bring to these lands of the king many articles of commerce. Therefore, all the Interior Provinces—and especially these in the East—will be supplied with all necessities in a manner advantageous to the vassals.

19. This port opened and these lands flourishing, these unsettled coasts will be protected. Here, at any time, we might have an invasion by foreigners since it is said that its beautiful bays are suitable for the landing of vessels.

20. The large revenues which the import and export duties will bring to his Majesty at the said port will be sufficient to pay the large amounts expended from the royal treasury for the Interior Provinces. If they have a port through which to ship their bounteous crops and numerous live stock to Havana, they can supply the royal navy and can receive their reward from the products of their labor.

21. By means of this port the contraband trade which is said to be so prejudicial to the royal treasury in these regions will be stopped; for the people, having what they need in their own country, will not go to a foreign land to secure them fraudulently.

22. Having the above mentioned port and all necessaries in abundance, all communication with a foreign country can be cut off; for we are certain that these industrious people will supply the Indian nations and the royal troops with all the necessities so that their products and goods need not go out of the country to a foreign power nor, on the other hand, will it be necessary to apply to them for the said articles.

23. This port is indispensable so that through it the products of these vassals may be sold. Without it, we can not possibly immigrate; for [seeing] what may result from their endeavors, even the laziest will be encouraged to work.

24. If, perchance, the *consulado de Mexico* should object to the opening of this port as prejudicial to the interest of the crown, we beg you to interpose with your protection in order that they may either receive the products of the country or, if [this is impossible]

designate some company of Vera Cruz, Havana, or other point who may be allowed to receive them.

25. We do not expect the said *consulado* to offer any opposition to such great benefits as are promised from agriculture, industry, and commerce. On the contrary, we believe that the royal *consulado de Guadalajara* will protect us and thus carry out the charges of the king in articles 22, 23, and 24 of the royal *cédula* creating it.

NO. 9

THE COMMANDANT-GENERAL ADMITS REPUTABLE SPANISH CATHOLICS FROM LOUISIANA, IMMIGRATION REGULATIONS, 1806.[1]

1. Among the families of the citizens of Louisiana who may be introduced into that province, there must be included no negroes, mulattoes, or other kinds of servants who are not Catholics.

2. The settlements of applicants may be placed on the banks of the Guadalupe river, in one of several locations in the best places that can be chosen.

3. In the same place in which location is made, lands are to be assigned for farming, stock-raising, and for the construction of houses in proportion to the size of the family and the amount of property belonging to each head of a family.

4. They can introduce and cultivate all kinds of seed and plants except those that are not permitted [by law], such as tobacco; for, since it is under government monopoly, its cultivation, for the benefit of private individuals, is forbidden.

5. Even in case a harbor may be found at the mouth of the Guadalupe river or any nearby location, communication must not be carried on through it nor must the immigrants attempt to go out into the Gulf without the previous knowledge of the superior government.

6. In consideration of the fact that it is the intention of His Majesty to aid those unfortunate vassals who prefer his rule to that of any other, he will permit them to settle not only on the margin of the Guadalupe river, but, in case the desire to do so, at Béxar, the capital, at Bahía de Espíritu Santo, in any settlement of the neighboring province of Coahuila, in Nueva Viscaya, or in any province they may select in the viceroyalty of Mexico.

7. The post of Nacogdoches can not afford them equal security, convenience, or opportunity for development, they, therefore, ought not to present petitions for settlement in it. It must be remembered that to avoid the troubles which might come to those settling there,

---

[1]These regulations show that the commandant-general placed severe commercial restrictions upon all Louisiana emigrants and that he expected to grant them lands according to the size of their families and the amount of goods they possessed.

the permits mentioned in the previous article must not be granted them.

8. They must try to make their voyage and send you previous notice in order that, one after another, you may give the aid necessary for their establishment.

9. Since they are thus permitted to bring their equipments, their domestic utensils, tools, and other things belonging to their houses, buildings and machinery, any goods or manufactories of contraband goods any one of them might attempt to introduce would fall under the penalty of seizure.

10. To prove that they do not carry anything of the kind, they must submit to an examination of their goods and traveling equipment.

11. They must try to finish and conclude all business they may have in Louisiana before beginning their voyage, being reminded that, neither for this reason nor for any other, will they be given permission to return to that province, there remaining to them only the alternative of transacting their private business through the minister or consul of the nation, sending their letters or petitions through the mails. Copy made at Béxar, December 4, 1806.[2]

NO. 10

THE PRINCE OF THE PEACE DECIDES UPON A BUFFER AGAINST THE UNITED STATES, ROYAL ORDER DIVIDING THE INTERIOR PROVINCES INTO TWO COMMANDANCIES, 1804[1]

Most Excellent Sir, Don José Yturrigaray, Viceroy of New Spain,

In a letter of the 18th of the present month, the secretary of war, under the orders of His Majesty, wrote me as follows:

"The Field Marshals, Don Antonio Samper and Don Josef Navarro, Chiefs-of-Staff of Engineers and Artillery, in a letter of April 22nd last, explain that the General-in-Chief, the Prince of the Peace, has decided upon a new system of government for the Interior Provinces of North America and that, since the paper they included was a part of the plan, it was possible to begin the execution of the expedition.

The plan mentioned includes the following points:

1. Under existing conditions, it is well to divide the command of the Interior Provinces into two distinct governments under the names of Eastern and Western Interior Provinces. The first shall contain the Provinces of Texas and Coahuila, the Bolson de Mapimi, and the parts of Nuevo León and Santander situated between the Rio del Norte or Bravo and the Pillon river from the point where the last named river flows into the sea at Soto la Marina to its headquarters

---

[2]N. A.
[1]This order illustrates the determination of the supreme government to erect a buffer against aggression from the United States by colonizing Texas.

near Aldea de Labordores. From thence there shall be drawn a line to the northwest through the edge of the mountains to Saltillo and, passing through the Pueblo de Parras, it shall continue in a northerly direction until it strikes the Rio Bravo.

2. For the Western Division there will be left the Province of Sonora, Sinaloa, Nueva Viscaya, and Nuevo Mexico.

3. The new governor or commandant-general of the eastern division shall be appointed with the same powers and functions for his particular command as those held by the actual commandant-general of all the Interior Provinces.

4. There shall be elected a subordinate officer—a second in command—who, imbued with the same ideas and principles as the former, shall be able to aid or to take the place [of the said commandant-general].

5. For the present, there shall be formed provisionally a body of infantry taken from the regiments of New Spain and about two hundred men who wish to go as volunteers from the army of the Peninsula from among the soldiers who have served more than fifteen years and from those able-bodied retired soldiers who have not reached the age of fifty. One company of mounted artillery, with its officers also from the Peninsula, with some engineering officers and two aids for the governor, shall be formed.

6. Since the principal object is directed toward the establishment and development of the population of the Province of Texas by means of military colonists and militia, as it must be a buffer, and since there are not found in it sufficient supplies, these shall be collected in the province of Coahuila until the troops and colonists arrive. Meanwhile, the examination, the clearing and the distribution of the lands which are to be first settled shall be begun.

7. Since it is necessary to begin to settle along the coast, there shall be examined, with all possible care and attention, such places as may be suitable near the Rio Grande del Norte; and, to overcome such resistance as there may be on the part of the cannibal Indians, there shall be constructed boats and armed barges to enter the Rio Grande del Norte and the Colorado rivers, and the Bays of Espíritu Santo, San Bernardo and Galveston. To this end, the laborers and other necessary things shall be furnished by the governor of the Island of Cuba, the general of the department of marine at Havana, and the commandant-general of the Western Province with whom the commandant-general of the Eastern Province shall have the closest relations as well as with the viceroy of Mexico, touching all that may be conducive to the realization of his plans. It will be well to arrange that there shall be set apart two light vessels for [the transportation] of the mails, the introduction of colonists and their families, goods, ammunitions, and for other necessary purposes.

8. In proportion as the establishment and settlers continue increasing in the future, there shall be created a regiment of infantry and another of cavalry, a third part of whose officers and sergeants shall be promoted from the army of Spain and the other two parts from the troops of America and the *presidios* of the frontier which shall be organized one after another. There shall be formed likewise, another company of mounted artillery and, when circumstances demand it, there shall be named officials of the departments of the treasury, justice, parish priests and whatever else may be necessary for organization and good government in the new system.

Later, in a letter of the 22 of the same month [the secretary of war] advised me that his Majesty at the suggestion of the said General-in-Chief, the Prince of the Peace, had designed to name as the new governor and commandant-general of the Eastern Interior Provinces of North America, Colonel Don Pedro Grimarest, Commander of the Third Batallion of the Regiment of Infantry of Estremadura, with a salary of ten thousand *pesos*, and, as second in command, for the present, Lieutenant-Colonel, Don Luis Baccigalupi Sergeant Major of the Royal Engineers, who is to serve as commandant of engineers with a salary of two thousand *pesos* per year in addition to his present salary.

Aranjuez, May 30, 1804.
[Miguel Cayetano] Soler.

Viceroy of New Spain.

NO. 11

Description of Villa System of Colonization

Instructions for the Establishment of the New Villa of Pitic in the Province of Sonora, Approved by His Majesty and Ordered Adopted for Other Projected New Villas to be Established in this General Commandancy.[1]

Although by law VI, title VIII, book IV of the *Recopilación*, viceroy, *audiencias*, and governors are forbidden to grant the title of *ciudad* or *villa* or to exempt the *pueblos* of Spaniards or Indians from the jurisdiction of the principal capitals, this prohibition is limited to those that may already have been founded, since concerning new establishments and settlements, it is decreed that the provisions of other laws touching the subject are to be followed. Therefore, since law II, title III of the same book decrees that, after the country, province, and immediate location in which the new settlement is to be placed has been selected and its suitability and potential advantages have been investigated,

---

[1]This plan is especially interesting since it was the model for all settlements established in Texas between 1801 and 1821.

the governor in whose territory it may lie or be included shall decide whether it is to be a *ciudad, villa* or *lugar* and that, in conformity with this decision, its *cabildo* and officers shall be selected, therefore, exercising this prerogative and having in mind the extent of the district selected and the advantages which its lands offer when improved by irrigation and by the large irrigating ditches to be constructed for this purpose, you may declare the new settlement a *villa*, giving it the name it is to have and use for its designation and distinction.

2. In conformity with what is decreed in law VI, title V of the said book IV in regard to the *villas* of Spaniards which may be founded by agreement or contract and by law X touching those which, for want of a contractor, shall be established by private individuals who may agree to found them, there shall be granted to the *villa* in question four leagues of land, either square or rectangular, as may be demanded, for the best distribution of the lands, which shall be measured and marked out in order that its true limits may be known and recognized in order that no inconvenience may arise. Inasmuch, as it is more than five leagues from any other Spanish *villa, ciudad* or *lugar*, no injury can come to any private individuals or to any *pueblo* of Indians since Pueblo de los Seris is to remain within its boundary as a part or ward of the new settlement, subject to its jurisdiction and entitled to the privileges of enjoying, as citizens, all public and common advantages which the settlers shall have and which, up until this time, these natives have been denied because of their lack of application and intelligence there being reserved to them the right of selecting their *alcaldes* and *regidores* who shall exercise jurisdiction according to the provisions of laws XV and XVI, title III, book VI.

3. The *presidio* of San Miguel de Orcasitas[2] having been moved to Pitic in order that under its guard and protection the new settlement may be established in conformity with the provisions of article I and II, title XI of the *Nuevo Reglamento de Presidios*, dated September 10, 1772, and with article I of the old Reglamento of the Viceroy, Marqués de Casafuerte, dated April 20, 1729, which was ordered observed by royal decree of May 15, 1779, the royal jurisdiction of the new settlement, both civil and criminal, in first instance belongs [by right] to the captain or commandant. This jurisdiction he should exercise so long as the *presidio* remains at the point, with appeals to the royal *audiencia* of the district. But, since you have decided that the company shall be considered as detached in the new

---

[2] For the beginnings of the effort to control the Indians of this region by means of a *presidio* and the plea of Father Lissasoian for the formation of a settlement of Spaniards and people of caste with sufficient property to assure them a livelihood, on the ground that this was the strongest possible barrier against assaults from the enemy since "each individual was a post, each family a fortress, and each settlement a citadel," see *Informe*, [October 24, 1763], in A. G. I. S. *Guad.*, 103-3-11, April 14, 1763–December 14, 1764.

settlement and that, consequently, the use and exercise of the royal jurisdiction shall remain in the hands of the political governor of the province and in that of the *alcalde mayor* or commissioner who shall be named, it is necessary that the honor of this appointment shall fall upon a person of sufficient knowledge and instruction to ensure the development of the new settlement, to make the division of building lots and water privileges, and to follow exactly the heads of these instructions and other instructions which may in future be communicated to him.

4. For its better organization and government, in accordance with what is decreed in law X, title V, laws II and XIX, title XVII and laws I, II, and III of title X of book IV of the *Recopilación*, as soon as the number of the settlers shall reach the amount of thirty citizens, a *consejo, cabildo* or *ayuntamiento* shall be formed, composed of two ordinary *alcaldes*, six *regidores*, one *procurador sindico* or public agent, and one *mayordomo de propios* under whose charge shall be the economic government and the duty of provisioning the settlement and of keeping it clean and policed. The said officials shall be elected the first time by a vote of all the citizens and, thereafter, by the voting members of the *ayuntamiento*, in accordance with what the law provides in regard to this point. The report of election shall be sent annually to the political governor of the province in order that, his approval being given, the officers elect may take possession and enter into the use and exercise of their respective offices.

5. The ordinary *alcalde* by way of prevention and precaution, with the *alcalde mayor* or royal commissioner shall jointly exercise jurisdiction, civil and criminal, in first instance, with appeals to the royal *audiencia*, governor or *ayuntamiento* in the cases belonging to each by the laws of the kingdom set forth in law I, etc., of title III, book IV.

6. After the four leagues granted to the new settlement have been measured and marked off, the pastures, wood, water privileges, hunting, fishing, stone quarries, fruit trees, and other species of trees which it may produce shall be for the common benefit of the Spaniards and Indians settled in it and in the ward of Aldea de los Seris. So, likewise, shall be the pasture lands and reserve tracts, under law V etc., title XVII, book IV of the *Recopilación*, whatever may be the fruits planted there.

7. The citizens and natives shall share in the products of the woods, pastures, waters, and other advantages of the royal and vacant lands outside of the new settlement in common with the citizens and natives of the adjoining and neighboring settlement. This privilege and concessions shall last until the said lands shall be granted or alienated by his Majesty, in which case they shall conform to what is provided in the privileges granted to the new possessors or proprietors.

8. The place which may be considered most suitable for locating the new *villa* having been selected and marked off, the commissioners

shall take care in its establishment to see that all the houses and other buildings which shall be built from time to time, shall be constructed in conformity with the sketch or plan prepared by the special engineer, Don Manuel Mascaro;[3] and it shall be added to these instructions and municipal ordinances so that it may be kept in mind. Under this same plan, the streets shall run in a straight line as is best suited to facilitating traffic and communication of the citizens and settlers —their symmetry and regularity contributing to the beauty and cleanliness of the new settlement and to the healthfulness of those who may settle in it.

9. As the amount of land which each block is to occupy is indicated in the plan or sketch and as it is not easy to fix the size of the *solar* which shall be sufficient for each citizen, because of the difference there may be in the size of their families, and the revenue and ability of those who may determine to settle, there shall be left to the prudent judgment of the commissioner the power to grant the number of *varas* in a *solar* that he may consider each one needs for cultivating and for building in view of the size of the applicant's family, the amount of his property, and other just considerations. To this end, and in order that each may have what corresponds to his means, the commissioner may grant a whole, a half, a quarter, or an eighth of a block since these are the most suitable divisions for securing the **greatest possible uniformity in the buildings of the settlement.**

10. To avoid the complaints which might arise from an arbitrary distribution of town lots, because of the preference or advantages which might be given some over others, the division among the first settlers shall be made by lot, according to the law XI, title VII, book IV of the *Recopilación*.

11. The special engineer, Don Manuel Mascaro, having designated the place in which the new settlement is to be located, there shall be laid off in all four directions commons of sufficient size for the settlers to amuse themselves, to drive out their stock without damage, and where, as the settlement increases in the future, there may be lands to grant new settlers, so that they may build their houses and habitations according to the provisions of law VII, XIII, and XIV of said title VII, book IV.

12. In the same manner, he shall proceed to lay off and mark out the pasture lands or *prado boyal* which shall be sufficiently large to furnish abundant and suitable pasturage for the work animals and those which may be necessary for food for the new settlement, managing to select for this purpose good pasture lands but not those of the

---

[3]This plan has not been found. For instructions for laying off the first permanent settlement in Texas, see Austin, "The Municipal Government of San Fernando de Bexar, 1730–1800," in the *Quarterly of the Texas State Historical Association*, 1904–1905, VIII, 338–343 and map of Bexar, see Bolton, *Texas in the Middle Eighteenth Century*, 6–7. *Cf.* Sketch of the Alamo, post.

best quality for producing wheat or grain and vegetables for the food and subsistence of the settlers and their families as is required by laws VII and XIV, title VII, book IV of the *Recopilación*.

13. The laying off of the commons and pasture lands or *prado boyal* having been accomplished, the commissioner shall prepare a careful calculation of all the good and productive lands which can be irrigated by means of the irrigation ditch as well as the rest of the lands which have not this advantage but which may be considered suitable for planting crops in proper season and, dividing each into equal *suertes* of four hundred *varas* in length and two hundred in width, which is the amount a *fanega* of seed corn will plant, he shall ascertain the number of *suertes* of each kind there may be for distributing among the new settlers and those who may join them or increase their number in the future.

14. The *suertes* being thus divided and measured off, eight *suertes* of the best lands and those nearest the *pueblo* shall be set apart for municipal funds. The proceeds shall be managed by the *mayordomo* whom the *ayuntamiento* shall name, whose duty it shall be to render annual accounts—these to be examined and approved by the *ayuntamiento* after referring them to the *procurador* or agent so that he may make such notes or corrections as he may consider necessary and proper, under the supposition that its products shall be employed for the common benefit of all settlers under the regulations laid down for assuring its faithful management and legitimate expenditure. And, since there is, at present, no public fund with which to pay the expenses of this first breaking, sowing, and cultivating of crops, the settlers and citizens shall be obliged to work jointly either personally or with their servants, oxen, or stock in such equitable manner as the commissioner shall arrange; and he shall apportion the work in such a way that all shall participate in it equally without excepting any citizen or settler, remembering that this operation shall be limited to the first breaking, planting, and cultivating of crops. From their products, successive expenses shall be paid, the rest remaining to the benefit of the municipal fund to be expended for the public good as is designated by the laws of the kingdom.

15. The laying off and setting apart of the eight irrigable *suertes* reserved for municipal funds being accomplished, the remainder of the good lands in the district, both irrigable and non-irrigable, shall be left for the benefit of the settlers to whom they shall be allotted and granted as, from time to time, they may continue to settle. And since it is not possible to give a fixed rule as to the number of *suertes* which shall be distributed and granted to each settler, the power of regulating and granting whatever may be considered necessary, for the maintenance of each family shall be vested in the commissioner who shall keep in mind the number of persons composing the family, those in it who may be able to work, the tools and implements which

each one may have for doing the work, and, finally, their willingness to work since it is right that he who is industrious should be rewarded with a greater number of *suertes* than he who, through carelessness or lack of application, may leave those assigned him uncultivated. Therefore, the first distribution of lands among the settlers shall not exceed three *suertes* to each one, leaving the remainder to be divided among those who may be added to the settlement in the future, to the sons who may reach manhood, and those who by their industry and application shown in the cultivation of the first *suertes* distributed, have proved themselves worthy of receiving an increase; but these shall never exceed the number granted them in the beginning.

16. Since it is convenient that the number of *suertes* granted each one of the settlers shall be adjoining and contiguous, in order that, in this way, it will be possible to attend to their cultivation without the delay occasioned by one portion being separated from the other, the commissioner shall try to keep this in mind by arranging for the blocking of *suertes* as far as possible or, at least, by arranging for the least possible distance between the portions assigned. And, for the purpose of avoiding complaints which may arise because some lands are better than others, after it has been divided in the manner prescribed, he shall make the first distribution among the settlers by lot as is required for the distribution of town lots in article X of these instructions.

17. The commissioner under whose charge the new settlement shall be founded and the distribution of lands and town lots made, must prepare a book or *cuaderno* where the original records shall be kept. This shall be preserved in the archives of the settlement; and, after consulting it, he shall give to each settler a deed or *hijuela certificada* which shall briefly, clearly, and distinctly state the extent and boundaries of the town lot and the *suertes* which shall have been assigned to each of them. This instrument shall serve as a title of ownership for the settlers, for their children and descendants. To this end, they must be reminded that they must take care of said records and that, if they be lost, by any unavoidable accident, they may apply to the commissioner or to the *ayuntamiento* for a copy of said instruments which shall be placed in the archives for this purpose.

18. In the first steps of distribution, as well as in the issuance of the *hijuelas* or title-deeds which may be given to the settlers, the commissioner shall also set forth that the town lots and the lands are granted and bestowed in the name of his Majesty for ever and ever, by right of inheritance to them, to their children, and to their descendants, with the positive conditions that they are to keep arms and mounts and be ever ready to defend the place against the insults of such enemies as may attack it and to set out against them whenever commanded to do so, to construct and keep their houses and to reside with their families in the new settlement for at least the space of four

years—during which time they shall not have the right to alienate, mortgage, or encumber the lands and the lots which have been granted to them even though it should be for a pious purpose, to have in cultivation (within the space of two years) the lands which have been granted them and, at least, the houses on the lots assigned them started, under penalty of loss by all who may abandon them during this time to others more industrious. These conditions being fulfilled and a residence of four years in the settlement with one's family being completed, the settler shall acquire complete ownership of the lands and the lots which may have been assigned him and of the houses and other buildings which may have been erected thereon; and he shall, from that time forward, have the right to sell them and to do with them as he wishes just as with his private property, according to the provisions of law I, title XII, book IV of the *Recopilación*, but under the condition that he can never sell or alienate them to a church, to a monastery, to a priest, to an ecclesiastical community, or to any organization known as *manos muertes*, according to the provisions of law I of the same title and book, under penalty of loss of lands and buildings in case of such disobedience—the said property to be granted to others. Finally, within three months after the concession and distribution has been made to them, they shall be obliged to take possession of the town lots and lands which may have been assigned them and to plant the borders or confines either with fruit trees or trees of other species which may be useful for the support of the settlement, so that the place may enjoy a pleasant and agreeable arrangement and so that the settlers may take advantage of the fruits, timber, and wood which may be produced for their domestic use and for the utensils they are required to have in conformity with law XI of the said title and book.

19. Since irrigation is the principal means of fertilizing the lands and the one most conducive to the development of the settlement, the commissioner shall take particular pains in distributing the waters so that all the irrigable lands can enjoy the benefit, especially in the spring and summer seasons when it is most needed for assuring the crops. To this end, taking advantage of the skillful and intelligent settlers, he shall divide the land into districts or *heredamentos*, assigning to each one a flood-gate or channel leading from the main or principal ditch and carrying a sufficient quantity of water for its irrigation in the said seasons and at other times needed. By this means each settler will know the flood-gate and ditch with which he must irrigate his lands and that he must not take the water from another district nor in a greater quantity than should fall to his share. To this end, and in order that one may not receive an excess to the detriment of the districts located below him, it will be well for the flood-gates or *repartideros* to be joined to the main ditch by cement at the expense of the settlers themselves.

20. In order that these settlers may enjoy with equity and justice the benefits of the waters in proportion to the necessities of their respective crops, the *ayuntamiento* shall name annually an *alcalde* or *mandador* for each flood-gate under whose charge shall be the care of apportioning the water to the tracts comprised in the district to be irrigated, according to the need for this benefit, enumerating in the list which he shall make, the hours of the day or night in which each beneficiary shall irrigate his crops and, in order that, by the carelessness or laziness of the owner, those needing it shall not remain without irrigation and the crops be lost—so that in addition to his private loss there shall result also a common and public loss, due to a lack of provisions and supplies—it shall also be the duty of the *alcalde* or *mandador* of each flood-gate to have a *peon* or day laborer informed of the hour by day or night assigned for the irrigation of each piece of land or crop. Upon failure of its owner to do so, he shall see to its irrigation—there being assigned therefor by the commissioner or *justicia* the proper pay for the work which shall be given him promptly.

21. The repairs and cleaning which the principal ditch may need for its preservation shall be at the expense of all the settlers at the time fixed by the commissioner and *ayuntamiento*, each citizen aiding with a representative or by personal work, or, in lieu of this, with the amount of money which, upon division and equitable *pro rata*, shall be assigned to each for paying for and satisfying the *peons* and for the repair and cleaning of the ditches, flood-gates and channels assigned for the irrigation of the district or *heredamentos* into which the land is to be divided. It shall be under the charge of the land owners or *herederos* whose *suertes* and property shall be irrigated by them and among them shall be divided the expenses which may arise, prorating it according to the number of *suertes* each one may possess in the district or *heredamento*, it being the duty of the *cabildo* or *ayuntamiento*, in consultation with the commissioner, to determine the time at which, without injury to the crops, the said cleaning shall be made.

22. To avoid damages and prejudices which through the carelessness of the owners, cattle, horses, and small stock might make in the crops there shall be named annually, by the *ayuntamiento* two *alcaldes de campo*, one to serve by day and the other by night; and, like all public officials, they shall take oath before the *ayuntamiento* to perform their duties faithfully and well. Their testimony shall be taken unless sufficient proof shall be presented against them to justify the contrary. The two shall be obliged to watch by day and by night to see that stock do not cause any damage to the crops of the settlement and to catch those found causing any damage, to carry them to a *corral* belonging to the *ayuntamiento*, reporting the matter, and making complaint immediately to the *justicia*, so that, under his sworn statement,

a *sumaria* may be drawn up promptly, the damage which may have been done estimated, and the owner of the apprehended stock forced to pay for the damaged crops.

23. If obliging the owners to pay for the depreciation be not sufficient for preventing and avoiding damages which stock frequently cause in the crops, it will be necessary to follow this up by imposing some other moderate pecuniary penalty which must be collected without fail in all cases of contravention. He shall oblige them to watch their stock and to see that they do not again cause damage, and, since for the regulation of the said pecuniary penalty a detailed practical knowledge of the place, the ability of its inhabitants, and the value which the stock may have is necessary, this point shall be reserved for the decision of the *ayuntamiento*, in order that in conference with the commissioner, it shall fix and determine what ought to be imposed and demanded in case of contravention, taking care that the penalty imposed against those causing damage by night be greater because of the added difficulty of having them caught.

24. And, finally, it is peculiarly the prerogative of the *cabildos* or *ayuntamientos*, as the best informed as to what is best for the public they represent, to propose the measures which they may consider most useful and most conducive to the best management and economic and political government. These measures, after being approved by the superior authorities, shall become municipal ordinances to be observed as the particular laws of the settlement, in so far as they are not opposed to the general laws established by the king. The *ayuntamiento* of the new settlement shall enjoy the same privileges and, in exercising it, they shall proceed in accord with the commissioner in their preparation, they shall decide upon and draft the municipal ordinances which they may consider most necessary and proper, giving an account to their superior government so that being approved, they may have force and receive obedience.[4]

NO. 12

AN AMERICAN FRONSTIERSMAN DESIRES LAND IN TEXAS, PETITION OF DANIEL BOONE, 1806[1]

Sir,

Daniel Boone, a native of Carolina, a citizen of Opelousas for twelve years, and, at present, in this post, makes known to you, with the greatest respect, that I have come to this place with my family and goods because those lands have passed into the possession of the Anglo-Americans and it does not suit me to live under their laws. I

---

[4]*Missions and Colonization*, Vol. I, 853–868, Bancroft Library.
[1]This petition illustrates the strong desire of the Americans to secure lands in Texas. This seems to have been a national characteristic.

came to seek your protection in order that if you consider it well, you may order set apart for me a town lot and lands for farming—since this is my occupation.

Atascocito, June 11, 1806.

DANL. BOONE.

NO. 13

NATIVES AND EMIGRANTS FROM LOUISIANA FOUND THE VILLA OF TRINIDAD DE SALCEDO, CENSUS REPORT, 1806

Names	Place of Birth	Age	State	Occupation
[1] Don Berrnardo de Espallierr	New Orleans	36	Married	Farmer
His wife, Doña María Candida Grande	Nacogdoches	19	Married	
His son, José Berrnardo	Trinidad	2		
Another, Blas Felipe	Trinidad	1 mo.		
[2] Don Geronimo Herrn[ánde]s	Havana	29	Married	Farmer
His wife, Doña Isabel de Racal	Natchitoches	19	Married	
His son, José Silvestre	Nacogdoches	3		
Another, José Man^l.	Trinidad	1		
[3] Don Mig^l. Quin	Ireland	31	Bachelor	Farmer
[4] Don Juan Meguin	Ireland	35	Married	Farmer
His wife, Sara Burxer	United States	28	Married	
His son, José	Nacogdoches	3		
Another, Juan	Trinidad	15 mo.		
His daughter, María	Louisiana	6		
Another, Ana	Louisiana	4		
[5] José Quiroz	Illinois	28	Married	Farmer
His wife, Celesté Ruberson	United States	25	Married	
His son, José Angelico	Atascocito	18 mo.		
His daughter, Angelica	Opelousas	4		
[6] Carlos Trahan	Opelousas	30	Married	Farmer
His wife, Celeste Leesuhene	Opelousas	24	Married	
His son, Salanxe	Opelousas	7		
Another, Carlos	Opelousas	2		
His daughter, Celeste	Opelousas	10		
Another, Celesia	Opelousas	3		
[7] Santiago Fierr	Louisiana	27	Married	Carpenter
His wife, Anna Calaxan	Opelousas	19	Married	
His son, José Ignacio	Trinidad	14 mo.		
His daughter, Maria Loreto	Louisiana	4		
[8] Pedro Cruz	Adalisco	60	Married	Farmer
His wife, Juana Ma. Amador	Béxar	25	Married	
His son, José Antonio	Bahía	18	Bachelor	
Another, Estanislao	Béxar	7		
His daughter, María Sesaria	Béxar	9		
[9] José Borrego	Béxar	36	Married	Herdsman
His wife, Ma. Manuela Ramona	Béxar	20	Married	
His daughter, María Silesia	Trinidad	3		
[10] Juan Sii	United States	37	Bachelor	Farmer
[11] Feredicte Ecstozman	Germany	60	Married	Farmer
His wife, Catalina Bonete	United States	38	Married	
His son, Xorge	Louisiana	22	Bachelor	Farmer
Another, Enrrique	Louisiana	15	Bachelor	Farmer
Another, Juan	Louisiana	11	Bachelor	
Another, Pedro	Louisiana	8	Bachelor	
Another, José Anto.	Atascocito	2		
His daughter, Margarita	Louisiana	5		
[12] José Manl. Casanova	Béxar	39	Married	Farmer
His wife, María del Carmen	Orcoquisac	26	Married	

Former Residence	Date of Immigration	Residence	Property and Titles to Same	
Louisiana	February, 1804	This place	1 house and 2 lots, 60x60 *varas*, 1 *labor* of 3 *suertes*, 1 *sitio* for cattle. By first decree of governor.	
Nacogdoches	February, 1804	This place		
		This place		
		This place		4
Louisiana	Beginning 1808	This place	1 house and 2 lots, 60x60 *varas*, 1 *labor* of 2 *suertes*. By first decree of governor.	
Natchitoches	Beginning 1808	This place		
		This place		
		This place		4
Upper Louisiana	October, 1805	This place	1 house, 1 lot, 30x60 *varas*, 1 *suerte*. Property and stock on *sitio* belonging to public domain.	1
Upper Louisiana	December, 1805	This place	1 house with 2 lots, 60x60 *varas*, 1 *labor* with 4 *suertes*, 1 *sitio*. He has a ranch, 200 head of unbranded cattle, 60 horses. First decree of commission.	
Upper Louisiana	December, 1805	This place		
	December, 1805	This place		
	December, 1805	This place		
Upper Louisiana	December, 1805	This place		
Upper Louisiana	December, 1805	This place		6
Louisiana	March, 1808	This place	1 house with lot, 60x60 *varas*. Has 100 head of cattle and 30 head of horses on public lands.	
Louisiana	March, 1808	This place		
Louisiana	March, 1808	This place		
Louisiana	March, 1808	This place		4
Louisiana	March, 1808	This place	1 house and lot, 30x60 *varas*. Has about 100 head of cattle on public lands.	
Louisiana	March, 1808	This place		
Louisiana	March, 1808	This place		
		This place		
Louisiana	March, 1808	This place		
Louisiana	March, 1808	This place		6
Louisiana	June, 1806	This place	1 house and 2 lots, 60x60 *varas*, 1 *suerte*, planted this year, 17 head of cattle on public lands.	
Louisiana	June, 1806	This place		
	June, 1806	This place		
Louisiana	June, 1806	This place		4
Béxar	January, 1806	This place	1 house, 2 lots, 60x60 *varas*, 3 *suertes* cultivated land, 49 head of cattle on public land.	
Béxar	January, 1806	This place		
Béxar	January, 1806	This place		
Béxar	January, 1806	This place		
Béxar	January, 1806	This place		5
Béxar	January, 1805	This place	1 lot, 30x60 *varas*.	
Béxar	January, 1805	This place		
	January, 1805	This place		3
Louisiana	March, 1806	This place	1 house, 2 lots, 60x60 *varas*, 2 cows, 1 *suerte*, uncultivated.	1
Louisiana	March, 1806	This place	1 house, started, 1 lot 30x60 *varas*, 1 *suerte*, cleared but not cultivated.	
Louisiana	March, 1806	This place		
Louisiana	March, 1806	This place		
Louisiana	March, 1806	This place		
Louisiana	March, 1806	This place		
Louisiana	March, 1806	This place		
Louisiana	March, 1806	This place		
Louisiana	March, 1806	This place		8
Béxar	January, 1806	This place	1 house and 2 lots, 60x60 *varas*, 3 *suertes* cultivated land, about 16 head of unbranded cattle on public lands.	
Béxar	January, 1806	This place		2

[13] Dn. José Miguel de Sosa	Acambaro	31	Bachelor	Farmer	
[14] José Luis Durán	Béxar	30	Married	Farmer	
His wife, Guadalupe Travieso	Béxar	25	Married		
His son, Manuel	Béxar	8			
Another, Augustin	Béxar	7			
[15] José Manl. Lugo	Guadalaxara	34	Married	Farmer	
H s wife, Encarnación Pérez	Béxar	14	Married		
[16] Don Pedro Lartigue	France	53	Married	Farmer	
His son, Julian	New Orleans	18	Bachelor		
Another, Francisco	New Orleans	15	Bachelor		
[17] Vincente Micheli	Italy	45	Widower	Farmer	
His son	Italy	15	Bachelor	Farmer	
[18] Franco. Travieso	Béxar	50	Widower	Farmer	
His son, José Antonio	Béxar	5			
[19] Santiago McLoughlan	United States	52	Married	Farmer	
His wife, Martha Thompson	Louisiana	30	Married		
His daughter, Quecta	Louisiana	11			
Another, Rebeca	Louisiana	9			
[20] Enrique Seridan	Germany	54	Married	Farmer	
His wife, Christina Hench	Germany	54	Married	Farmer	
His son, Jacova	United States	21	Bachelor	Farmer	
Another, Juan	United States	15	Bachelor	Farmer	
His daughter, Isabel	United States	22	Single		
Another, Ana	United States	21	Single		
Another, Sara	United States	17	Single		
[21] Juan Lunn	Natchez	30	Married	Farmer	
His wife, Rebeca Cheridan	United States	24	Married		
[22] Don Hugo Coyle	Ireland	46	Bachelor	Surveyor	
[23] Zedo Charman	United States	63	Married	Farmer	
His wife, Betsy Clark	United States	54	Married		
[24] E'isha Nelson	United States	40	Married	Farmer	
His wife, Yhan Harman	United States	32	Married		
His daughter, Betsi	Louisiana	12	Single		
Another, Poyi	Louisiana	10	Single		
Another, Ana	Louisiana	8	Single		
Another, Sally	Nacogdoches	4			
Another, Patsy	Nacogdoches	2			
[25] Pedro Patterson	United States	29	Bachelor	Carpenter	
[26] Guillermo Burxer	United States	38	Bachelor	Stone-mason	
[27] Juan Malroni	Ireland	40	Bachelor	Farmer	
[28] Cilas Luci	United States	35	Bachelor	Farmer	
[29] Bautista Canaliano	Canada	34	Bachelor	Carpenter	
[30] Carrlos Dupon	Louisiana	35	Bachelor	Carpenter	

Acambaro	January, 1807	This place	1 house and lot, 30x60, 10 head of cattle, same of horse.	1
Béxar	January, 1806	This place	1 house and 2 lots, 3 *suertes* in cultivation, with 4 or 5 head of stock.	
Béxar	January, 1806	This place		
Béxar	January, 1806	This place		
Béxar	January, 1806	This place		4
Béxar	May, 1806	This place	1 lot with house started.	
Béxar	Beginning 1808	This place		2
Louisiana	Beginning 1806	This place	1 house, 2 lots, 60x60 *varas*, 1 ranch, about 140 head of cattle and 100 horses.	
Louisiana	Beginning 1806	This place		
Louisiana	Beginning 1806	This place		3
Nacogdoches	Beginning 1806	This place	1 house and lot, 30x60 *varas*, 1 ranch and 200 head of cattle and a drove of mares.	
Nacogdoches	Beginning 1806	This place		2
Béxar	January, 1806	This place	1 house, 2 lots, 60x60 *varas*, a ranch with about 40 head of cattle and a drove of mares.	
Béxar	January, 1806	This place		2
Louisiana	October, 1808	This place	As yet has no land, living on the ranch of Vincente.	
Louisiana	October, 1808	This place		
Louisiana	October, 1808	This place		
Louisiana	October, 1808	This place		4
Louisiana	December, 1805	This place	1 house and 2 lots, 60x60 *varas*, 3 *suertes* to put in cultivation, 1 ranch. Has 100 head of cattle and 12 horses with a drove of mares, and 3 mulatto slaves.	
Louisiana	December, 1805	This place		
Louisiana	December, 1805	This place		
Louisiana	December, 1805	This place		
Louisiana	December, 1805	This place		
Louisiana	December, 1805	This place		
Louisiana	December, 1805	This place		7
Nacogdoches	June, 1807	This place	1 house with 2 lots, 60x60 *varas*, 1 ranch and about 15 head of cattle.	2
Louisiana	December, 1805	This place		
?	December, 1805	This place	1 house and 2 lots, 60x60 *varas*, 2 *suertes* in cultivation, 50 head of cattle and about 80 horses.	1
Nacogdoches	March, 1807	On ranch	2 lots inclosed without house, 1 ranch well cultivated, 200 head of cattle, 6 horses, 1 slave, and 40 hogs.	
Nacogdoches	March, 1807	On ranch		2
Louisiana	March, 1807	This place	1 house on a well cultivated ranch, 50 head of cattle, 6 horses, and 60 head of hogs.	
Louisiana	March, 1807	This place		
Louisiana	March, 1807	This place		
Louisiana	March, 1807	This place		
Louisiana	March, 1807	This place		
Louisiana	March, 1807	This place		7
Nacogdoches	August, 1808	This place	Located on the lot and in the house abandoned by (?). Has 10 head of cattle and 15 horses.	1
Nacogdoches	August, 1808	This place	Companion of the writer.	1
Nacogdoches	Beginning 1807	This place	Living on ranch of Don Bernardo de Espallier and has no property.	1
Nacogdoches	Beginning 1807	This place	Living on ranch of Don Bernardo de Espallier and has no property.	1
Atascocito	End 1807	This place	Living on ranch of Benson.	1
Louisiana	Beginning 1807	This place	Living at home of Don Pedro Lartigue.	1

[91]

Villa Trinidad de Salcedo.

Antonio Saenz.

[OTHERS LOCATING PRIOR TO ABANDONMENT OF COLONIZATION PLAN 1809]

José Leal	At Trinidad.	1
Juan Macfale	At Trinidad.	1
Jaime Mirlan	At Trinidad.	1
Jose Giru	At Trinidad.	1
Luis Grande	At Trinidad.	1
Pedro Brase	At Trinidad.	1
Jacobo Dast	At Trinidad.	1
Joshua Ris	At Trinidad.	1
José Alderete	Deceased.	
Francisco Gomes	Deceased.	
José Anto. Esquibel	At Nacogdoches.	
Franco. Oranday	At Nacogdoches.	
Bernabe Trebiño	Retired.	
Andres Gonzales	Deceased	
Miguel Hernández	At Attakapas.	
María Ydlefonso Juárez	Expelled.	
Diego Samoro	Left.	
José Antonio Salinas	Left.	
Miguel Megui	Prisoner at Nacogdoches.	
Santiago Maconolte	Absent.	
Juan Dabis	Absent.	
Juan Carlos (alias *el Jamonero*)	Absent.	
Franco. Sancerman	Absent.	
Francisco Arduan	Attakapas.	
Santiago Fil	Absent.	
Enrique Paradiz	Absent.	
Mordic Richar	Not yet arrived.	
Geronimo Hernández	Living at Béxar.	
Remigo Bodr'o	Absent.	
Juan Erandrique	Expelled.	
Juan Oyales	Expelled.	
Yler Ducen	Absent.	
Salome Ducen	Absent.	
Pedro Engle	Deceased.	
Juan Rebies [Dribread]	Absent.	

Agregados

Genero Pon	At Trinidad.	1
Francisco Lacomba	At Trinidad.	1

[10]

October 6, 1809.

PEDRO LOPEZ PRIETO.

No. 14

NATIVE TEXANS AND MEXICANS FROM THE INTERIOR OF MEXICO FOUND
VILLA DE SAN MARCOS DE NEVE, 1807—CENSUS JULY 12, 1809[1]

	Classes	Names	Country	Age	State	Occupation	Whence	Date	Property	Total
1.	Settler	Dn. Felipe de la Portilla	Spain	41	Married	Stockman	Refugio	19 mo.	For Col. Dn. Cordero: Mares, 388; cattle, 300; horses, 20; mules, 200; *mesos*, 6; burros, 25	939
2.	Wife	Maria Igna. de la Garza	Mier	23	Married	Stockman	Refugio	19 mo.	1 lot on *plazn*, 30 *varas* wide, 60 deep; 1 ranch 12 leagues down the river where his servants and possessions are kept.	
3.	Children	José Calixto	Refugio	8			Refugio	19 mo.		
4.		Juan	Refugio	6			Refugio	19 mo.		
5.		Maria Dolores	Refugio	4			Refugio	19 mo.		
6.		José Franco	Refugio	2			Refugio	19 mo.		
7.		Maria Tomasa	Bexar	6 mo.			Béxar	19 mo.		
8.		Luciana	Refugio	1			Refugio	19 mo.		
9.		Maria Monica	Refugio	8 mo.			Refugio	19 mo.		
10.	Servant	Pedro Salasar	Refugio	50	Married	Herder	Refugio	19 mo.		
11.	Wife	Maria Igna. Salinas	Refugio	48	Married		Refugio	19 mo.		
12.	Servant	Maximo Salazar	Refugio	18	Bachelor	Herder	Refugio	19 mo.		
13.	Servant	Estanislao Salazar	Refugio	12	Bachelor	Herder	Refugio	19 mo.		
14.	Servant	Basilio Gómez	Refugio	26	Married	Herder	Refugio	19 mo.		
15.	Wife	Maria Guadalupe	Refugio	25	Married		Refugio	19 mo.		
16.	Servant	Santos Ernándes	Refugio	30	Married	Herder	Refugio	19 mo.		
17.	Wife	Juliana García	Refugio	25	Married		Refugio	19 mo.		
18.	Children	José Savas	Refugio	4			Refugio	19 mo.		
19.		Pedro José	Refugio	6 mo.			Refugio	19 mo.		
20.	Servant	Pedro Gómez	Refugio	20	Bachelor	Herder	Refugio	19 mo.		
21.	Servant	Franco. Gómez	Refugio	28	Bachelor	Herder	Refugio	19 mo.		
22.	Servant	José María Castañeda	Refugio	48	Married	Herder	Refugio	19 mo.		
23.	Wife	Jesús Salas	Refugio	30	Married		Refugio	19 mo.		
24.	Mother	Maria Greg\a.	Refugio	70	Widow		Refugio	19 mo.		
25.	Child	Maria Ignacia	Refugio	8			Refugio	19 mo.		
26.	Servant	José Eleuterio	Refugio	12	Bachelor	Herdsman	Refugio	19 mo.		
27.	Corporal	Jesús Solís	Refugio	41	Married	Stockman	Refugio	19 mo.	Cattle, 180; horses, 5; mules, 3 [His family in Refugio]	188
28.	Servant	Nepomuceno Mungia	Refugio	40	Married	Herdsman	Refugio	19 mo.		
29.	Settler	Mateo Gómez	Refugio	60	Married	Laborer	Refugio	19 mo.	Cows, 6; yokes of oxen, 2; horses, 3; 1 *solar*, 40 *varas* wide, 60 deep	13
30.	Wife	Maria Josefa	Refugio	25	Married		Refugio	19 mo.		

#	Role	Name	Origin	Age	Marital	Occupation	Dest.	Duration	Property
31.	Indian	María Rafela	Refugio	8			Refugio	19 mo.	
32.	Settler	Pedro Flores	Refugio	28	Married		Refugio	19 mo.	
33.	Wife	Rita de la Garza	Refugio	25	Married		Refugio	19 mo.	
34.	Children	José Felipe	Refugio	8	Married	Stockman	Refugio	19 mo.	Mares, 26; stock, 30; oxen, 2; horses, 6; mules, 12; *meso*, 1; 1 *solar* on plaza 67
35.		José Bernadino	Refugio	5			Refugio	19 mo.	
36.	Settler	Victorino Losoya	Béxar	40	Married	Carpenter	Béxar	19 mo.	Oxen, 6; horses, 2; 1 lot on *plaza*, with house 8
37.	Wife	Barbara Músquiz	Béxar	35	Married		Béxar	19 mo.	
38.	Children	Ma. Telésfora	Béxar	12	Maiden		Béxar	19 mo.	
39.		Ma. Matiana	Béxar	15	Maiden		Béxar	19 mo.	
40.	Servant	Salvador Belmúdez	Béxar	48	Bachelor	Herdsman	Béxar	19 mo.	Work-horses, 2 2
41.	Settler	Juan Soto	Nacogdoches	39	Married	Laborer	Béxar	19 mo.	Work-horses, 2; yoke of oxen, 2; 1 *solar* on *plaza*, with house 4
42.	Wife	Feliciana Rodríguez	Béxar	27	Married		Béxar	19 mo.	
43.	Children	José Tomas	Béxar	16	Bachelor	Laborer	Béxar	19 mo.	
44.		María Encarnación	Béxar	8			Béxar	19 mo.	
45.		José Soto	Béxar	6			Béxar	19 mo.	
46.		José Lorenzo	Béxar	1			Béxar	19 mo.	
47.	Servant	Cesario Sánchez	Béxar	28	Bachelor	Stockman	Béxar	19 mo.	Horses, 22; mules, 16; *meso*, 1; burros, 5; cattle, 160; 1 *solar* on *plaza* 204
48.	Settler	Juan Ramírez	Mier	35	Married		Béxar	19 mo.	
49.	Wife	Dolores de la Garza	Mier	30	Married		Béxar	19 mo.	
50.	Children	José Macedonia	Mier	9			Béxar	19 mo.	
51.		María Nicolasa	Mier	4			Béxar	19 mo.	
52.		María Salome	Mier	2			Béxar	19 mo.	
53.	Servant	Alexandro Peña	Mier	40	Bachelor	Herdsman	Béxar	19 mo.	
54.	Servant	Manuel Barcenas	Mier	25	Bachelor	Herdsman	Refugio	19 mo.	
55.	Servant	Jesús Baldes	Mier	16	Bachelor	Herdsman	Refugio	19 mo.	
56.	Settler	Franco. Farias	Mier	38	Widower	Stockman	Refugio	19 mo.	Cattle, 105; horses, 7; 1 *solar* on *plaza* 112
57.	Children	María Petra	Mier	13			Refugio	19 mo.	
58.		José Igno.	Mier	11			Refugio	19 mo.	
59.	Settler	Gil Gómez	Mier	35	Married	Stockman	Refugio	19 mo.	40 head branded stock, 4 horses, 8 mares 52
60.	Wife	Anta. Garza	Mier	22	Married		Refugio	19 mo.	
61.	Children	José Santiago	Mier	4			Refugio	19 mo.	
62.	Settler	José Sálinas	Béxar	32	Married	Stockman	Refugio	19 mo.	40 cattle, 13 horses, 3 mares, 97 sheep; 1 *solar* with house 153
63.	Wife	Margil Chirina	Béxar	28	Married		Refugio	19 mo.	
64.	Children	María Josefa	Béxar	14			Refugio	19 mo.	
65.		María Franca	Béxar	3			Refugio	19 mo.	
66.	Servant	Anto. Casias	Béxar	26	Bachelor	Herdsman	Refugio	19 mo.	
67.	Settler	Pedro Gallego	Boca de Leon	55	Married	Stockman	Refugio	19 mo.	45 cattle, 2 yoke of oxen, 5 horses; 1 *solar* with house 112
68.	Wife	María Michela	Boca de Leon	40	Married		Refugio	19 mo.	
69.	Child	Ma. de los Angeles	Boca de Leon	16			Refugio	19 mo.	
70.	Servant	Luis Villareal	Refugio	19	Bachelor	Herdsman	Refugio	19 mo.	

71. Settler	José Ma. Carillo	38	Married	Laborer	Boca de Leones	Refugio	19 mo.	16 head of cattle, 1 yoke of oxen. 20
72. Wife	[Torn]	32	Married		Boca de Leones	Refugio	19 mo.	2 horses; 1 *solar* with house
73. Children	[Torn]	15			Boca de Leones	Refugio	19 mo.	
74.	[Torn]	8			Boca de Leones	Refugio	19 mo.	
75.		2			Boca de Leon	Béxar	19 mo.	
76. Servant	Trinidad Montolla	31	Bachelor	Laborer	Béxar	Refugio	19 mo.	
77. Settler	Juan Almontes	58	Married	Stockman	Bahía	Bahía	19 mo.	2 droves of mares, 28 horses, 5 burros, 11 cattle, 3 yoke oxen; 1 *solar* with house 52
78. Servant	José María García	25	Bachelor	Herdsman	Camargo	Bahía	19 mo.	
79. Servant	María Prudencia	70	Widow		Béxar	Bahía	19 mo.	
80. Child	María Rita	6			Béxar	Bahía	19 mo.	
81.	Manuel Landa	70	Married	Herdsman	Camargo	Camargo	19 mo.	Has family in Camargo. He lives with Don Filipe, who brought him.
82.	José Estevan García	30	Bachelor	Teacher	Camargo	Camargo	6 mo.	

Villa de Sn. Marcos de Neve, July 12, 1809.

[1] The Spaniards of Villa de San Marcos and the settlers of Villa de Salcedo, listed in Appendix 13, represented practically the entire increase in the population of Texas from 1801–1809, when colonization work was temporarily abandoned.

NO. 15

NAPOLEON SEIZES THE SPANISH THRONE AND INCITES REBELLION IN THE COLONIES, 1808

Copy of the Instructions Given by the Usurper Joseph Napoleon to the Commissioner or Principal Agent Appointed by Him at Baltimore. [M. de Desmoland] and to Others who, Furnished with His orders, have Gone to Spanish America for the Purpose of Revolutionizing It.[1]

The object of these agents, for the present, is to aim only to show the Creoles of Spanish America and to persuade them to believe that His Imperial and Royal Majesty desires nothing but to free a people who have been enslaved for so many years and that he does not expect any return save the friendship of the natives and commerce through the harbors of both Americas.

To render them free and independent from Europe, His Majesty offers all the necessary assistance—that is, of troops and warlike stores, having come to an agreement, to this end, with the United States of America which is ready to accommodate him therewith.[2]

Being acquainted with the district in which he is located and also with the character of its inhabitants, each commissioner or agent-in-chief will know how to select suitable persons who will be capable of taking charge of the necessary details of persuading the people and of pointing out to them the advantages they will derive from throwing off the European yoke.

He will call their attention to the monies which will remain and circulate in the American provinces by stopping the immense sums which are constantly being sent to Spain; to the impetus which their commerce will receive when their ports are open to all foreign nations; to the advantages which will result from the freedom of agriculture and the cultivation of all those products which, at present, are prohibited by the Spanish government—for instance, that of saffron,

---

[1]Document No. 15 has been selected as making clear Napoleon's intentions concerning the Spanish Americas. From the records, it is quite evident that these ideas really originated with Napoleon and that Joseph was far from concurring in them. Villanueva, *Napoleon y la Independencia de América*, 245–6. In his *Memoirs* Adams, in 1810, says, "The emperor Napoleon, nearly a year since, declared himself ready and willing to acknowledge the independence of the Spanish colonies, if the people of the countries themselves desired it." II, 183.

[2]Villanueva claims that this was merely a wish of Napoleon and that he had probably never made any such agreement even with private citizens of the United States.

hemp, olives, vines, etc.; to the great advantages they will derive from the establishment of manufactories of every sort; and to the benefits and satisfaction to be enjoyed by other settlements through the abolition of monopolies in tobacco, gunpowder, stamped paper, etc.

To obtain all this with ease—since the people, for the greater part are ignorant—the agents, above everything else, ought to try to render themselves acceptable to the governors, the intendants, the sub-delegates, the parish priests, and the prelates. The agents shall spare no expense or other means of gaining their good will, especially that of the ecclesiastics, whom they are to persuade to consent to urge and persuade penitents, when they come to confession, that they stand in need of an independent government; that they must not loose so favorable an opportunity as the one which now presents itself and which is offered them by the Emperor Napoleon, making the people believe that he is sent by God to chastise the pride and tyranny of monarchs and that to resist God's will is a mortal sin, admitting of no pardon.

On every occasion, these agents shall call to the minds of the Creoles the opposition they experience from the Spaniards, the vile manner in which they are treated and the contempt to which they are exposed.

They will remind the Indians of the cruelties which the Spaniards employed in their conquests and the infamous punishments they inflicted upon the legitimate rulers, by dethroning them, by taking their lives, and by enslaving them. They shall call attention to the injustices which the Indians daily experience when petitioning for offices which are bestowed by the viceroy upon those who are more grasping or who pay more money.

They shall call their attention to the large number of Europeans in the province where they live. They shall point out the men of merit among the Creoles and the men who are employed in both the ecclesiastical and secular branches in the cases where the injustice is clear, bringing out the talents and merits of the Creoles as compared to the Europeans.

They will set before their eyes the difference between the United States and Spanish America, the comforts which the former enjoy, their progress in agriculture, commerce, and navigation, and their pleasure at being free from the European yoke and being left solely to their own patriotic and elective government. They will assure them that, once free from Spain, the Spanish American Dominions will become the legislatrix of Europe.

All agents, both principal and subordinate shall list the names of those who declare themselves friends and votaries of liberty, and the sub-agents are to transmit these lists to the principals, and they, in turn, to my envoy in the United State, for my information, in order that I may duly reward each person.

My agents will abstain from declaiming against the Inquisition and the ecclesiastical system, and, in their conversation, they shall rather insist upon the necessity for that holy tribunal and on the usefulness of the latter.

Upon the revolutionary standards or banners is to be inscribed the motto "Long live the Apostolic Catholic Religion, and perish unjust government."

Moreover, they will point out to the Indians how happy they will be when they shall become, once more, masters of their country and free from the tyrannical tributes which they pay to a foreign monarch.

Lastly, they shall tell the people that their monarch does not so much as live in his kingdom but that he is in the power of the restorer of liberty and the universal legislator, Napoleon. In a word, these agents, by all possible means must endeavor to show the people the advantage which will come to them from the proposed government.

The revolution having been thus prepared, and all the principal persons who are to take part in it, in every city and province, having been gained over, the subordinate agents must then be ready to come to an understanding as to the best time for the uprising, giving prompt advice to the sub-agents in order that the uprisings may take place at the various points agreed upon upon the same day and at the same hour,[3] this being a very material point and one which will greatly facilitate the enterprise. The principal agents, in every province in their districts and the sub-agents at the points assigned them, shall win over the servants of the governors, intendants, and other persons in power and, by means of them, shall poison such persons of the ruling class as may be considered hostile to the undertaking, this poisoning to precede the revolution in order that these obstacles may be removed.

The first point to be considered shall be to stop the remittances of treasures to the Peninsula. This may be effected easily by placing efficient agents at Vera Cruz and the other ports of the American continent, but principally at Vera Cruz where all the vessels arriving from Europe will be received and their officers and crews immediately confined in the fortresses and by preventing the departure of every vessel until everything shall have succeeded and the revolution be under way.

The agents are further instructed to direct their sub-agents to transmit to them frequently accounts of the progress of the revolution. They shall transmit them to the envoy in the United States through the channels indicated.

---

[3]The various revolutions throughout Spanish America really occurred almost simultaneously, as follows: Caracas, April 19, 1810; Buenos Ayres, May 25, 1810; New Grenada, July 3, 1810; Bogotá, July 20, 1810; Cartagena, August 18, 1810; Chili, September 18, 1810; Mexico, September 16, 1810; and Baton Rouge, September 26, 1810. Ward, *Mexico*, I, p. 101 and *American State Papers*, XV, 398.

For this purpose it will be proper to keep in readiness couriers to be sent overland to such points on the coast as may be thought suitable where vessels are always to be kept in readiness for any emergency.

[Signed] JOSEPH NAPOLEON.

To my Envoy.
 Desmoland.

Note.

For this purpose three additional vessels are being prepared at Baltimore. There are now four vessels frequenting the different points of the continent as the agents already know. By this means, they will continue to give information of what may occur. The points to which the vessels more especially are to resort are Nuevo Santander, and Tampico, in the Kingdom of Mexico; the coast of Comayagona, through Truxillo, in Guatamala; and the harbors of Perú, Cumaná, Rio de la Hacha, etc., for Cartagena, Santa Fé, Caracas, and the rest of the Mainland, whither two vessels frequently sail under the pretext of being smugglers from Jamaica.

From frequent advices received from Mexico, Desmoland gives assurance that the number of supporters already secured is immense and all these are of the first rank. He is very confident that the revolution will take place in that realm, that the success of the scheme is quite certain—and this will be the object of the whole undertaking. He, therefore, keeps ready a safe conveyance to bring advice to New Orleans where all necessary assistance is prepared. He thinks even these arrangements useless because of the promises of success held out by the large party in his favor, as well as by the supineness of the government which will take no decisive steps even when the crisis has arrived. He has also secured the co-operation of the powerful Indian governor of the Teypanes of San Juan and Santiago, Mexico and of the Provinces of Fascala and Tepecaca, which are on the direct road to Vera Cruz. By this means all the transportation of treasurers and all correspondence with Mexico will be cut off completely. He also has very encouraging reports from his agents in California while those from Lima are no less so. From the accounts he has received, Desmoland also calculates upon the principal officers of the army, especially on the garrison of Vera Cruz and the detachment at the Castle of Perote which he will soon have on his side. This is the point from which to cut off all correspondence between the whole kingdom and Vera Cruz. Finally, he flatters himself with the success of his future projects.[4]

---

[4]These instructions are undated but were copied from an original in the office of the secretary of the supreme *junta* in Venezuela and sent to the admiral of the Barbadoes, on May 31, 1810, as a precaution against the machinations of Napoleon. Copies of extracts from Walton, *An Exposé on the Dissensions of Spanish America*, Appendix B, pp. ii-vii, Bancroft Library. I also made use of a copy in Villanueva, *Napoleon y la Independencia de América*, 242-247.

NO. 16

THE COMMANDANT-GENERAL CLOSES THE DOOR TO FOREIGN IMMIGRANTS, THE COMMANDANT-GENERAL TO BONAVIA, JUNE 22, 1809[1]

Very Confidential.

Don Martin Garay, General Secretary of the Supreme Central Junta of Spain and the Indies, on March 1, communicated to me the following order:

"Certain information has been received from which it appears that the Emperor of the French, having lost the hope of overcoming the Spanish Americas through the ordinary means of seduction and deceit, has conceived the design of forcing the royal parents to embark for America with the object of dividing it into factions and of triumphing over it after it is thus divided.[2]

You are already aware and it is known to the whole world, that Charles IV voluntarily and freely abdicated in favor of his eldest son, the sworn heir, Ferdinand VII, who at once ascended the throne amidst the rejoicings, acclamations and well-founded hopes of his faithful vassals. [It is well known, too,] that all subsequent acts, protestations, and renunciations have been null because they have been the result of violence and the most tyrannical oppression. [It is known, also] that our king, Don Ferdinand VII, has been solemnly proclaimed in both continents; that, for his liberty, honor, and rights, as well as for the freedom, honor, and independence of the nation, the Spaniards have taken up arms and death alone can wrest these arms from them; that, consequently, our king, Don Ferdinand VII, alone is the sovereign of Spain and her colonies; and that as long as his unjust captivity continues and until his liberty be restored

---

[1]Document No. 17 established the fact that, although the commandant-general recognized the necessity for the formation of a buffer against the United States, he feared Napoleon too much to permit the entry of immigrants from a foreign country.

[2]This belief was widespread as the following quotation from the *Baltimore City Gazette and Daily Advertiser*, for April 14, 1809, will indicate:

London, January 5.—The vessel which conveyed General Dupont to France arrived at Gibraltar the 9th ult. on her way back to Cadiz. She brought intelligence respecting the deluded and wretched monarch, the late king of Spain, Charles IV. A person who accompanied Dupont on his voyage and was permitted to land at Marseilles, had several opportunities of seeing and conversing with Charles, who was in the city with the queen, the infant, Don Francisco, and the Prince of the Peace. The king was very earnest in his inquiries respecting the present state of affairs in Spain, which were minutely detailed to him; during which he often wept bitterly. It is positively stated that Charles and his suite were brought to Marseilles, preparatory to a voyage to Mexico, for which province he was to sail by the first convenient opportunity; and that when arrived, he was to assume the government of that country as an ally of France. Consequently one of the first acts of his government would be the separation of the people from the mother country.

in full splendor and grandeur, the supreme central governing *junta* of the kingdom of Spain and the Indies exercises sovereignty in his royal name throughout the dominions which compose the kingdoms of his Majesty. Consequently, even though the above mentioned rumor is not sufficiently authentic to deserve our unqualified credence, nevertheless, since the oppressor of our beloved king and our country is as skillful in planning the most unheard of and unjust projects as he is ruthless in the selection of means for carrying his plans into execution, the supreme central *junta* has thought it proper to give this information to you and to all officials of both Americas in order that you may avoid any possible surprise and in order that, if it should happen that our ambitious enemy should try such a project, you will have taken all effective measures, under the prudent reserve which your well known zeal in the service of our legitimate king and our country shall dictate, to prevent the landing of the royal parents or of any other person who is their representative in any port within the limits of that general commandancy upon any pretext whatever; for it is evident that such attempts are not authorized by our king, Don Ferdinand, since he is not free, nor by the supreme central *junta*. Therefore, it can only be for the purpose of introducing dissensions into these dominions and of preparing for their siezure or their separation from the Mother Country."

And I send you this order so that you may be informed and that, under the strictest caution, you may see to the exact fulfilment of the royal decision herein contained, with the understanding that, because of your earnest zeal in the just cause the nation defends, I do not doubt that you will not only proceed in the case with the proper vigor and force, but that you will take all precautionary measures you can to avoid a surprise both along the coast of Texas and across the frontier of Louisiana. To this interesting end, it is absolutely necessary that you should entirely close the door to the immigration of individuals who have lived in a foreign country, whatever may be the evidence they may submit to support their pretentions. It is also necessary that, carrying into execution the idea clearly conveyed in my previous orders concerning the apprehension of persons crossing the said frontier, you shall not permit, under any circumstances, the introduction of any person into the said province or consent to any communication through it, since you well know that, under the present conditions, no precaution is superfluous when the great number of deceitful enemies which the country already has within its confines is realized.

Chihuahua, June 22, 1809.
NEMESIO SALCEDO.

Bernardo Bonavía.

NO. 17

THE LOCAL AUTHORITIES FAVOR COLONIZATION AS A MEANS OF DEFENSE, BONAVIA'S IMMIGRATION REGULATIONS, 1809[1]

To be admitted into this province and into other provinces of the kingdom, persons from Louisiana must show before the consul at New Orleans:

1. That they were vassals of His Majesty during the time that Louisiana belonged to Spain. [They must also state] their religion, age, native country, condition, and employment or occupation, and the place in that province in which they were located. If foreigners, they must prove, in addition, the time they settled in that province and whether or not they have taken the oath of allegiance to the United States since it took possession.

2. That the personal belongings they possessed in that province have been converted into money or, that being impossible, into produce or goods—especially carpenter's, locksmith's, bricklayer's, and laborer's tools, such as axes, hoes, and plows.

3. That their removal to this province has been announced in that place for the purpose of settling up pending accounts and, likewise, that they do not honestly owe any person in that place.

4. [They must show] what has been their mode of life and customs as well as those of their families and slaves and shall prove that all are Roman Catholics.

All the preceding points must be fully established in writing before the consul who shall prepare an affidavit in legal form and deliver it to the interested party in order that he may present himself with it on the frontier to the commandant of the nearest Spanish post, who shall examine the four articles to see if they are satisfactory. In this event [the commandant] shall grant a passport to the capital in case this be desired. If unsatisfactory, he shall report to the government, enclosing the document—the applicant awaiting a reply.

The former vassals of his Majesty in the Province of Louisiana who shall present themselves with the proofs required by the above mentioned articles for the purpose of immigrating to this province or to any other province of this kingdom shall enjoy all the rights, privileges and exemptions of natives—in case they are Spaniards—and [all the rights] granted by the laws—if foreigners—provided they were vassals of his Majesty [in Louisiana]. All these persons

---

[1]These regulations illustrate the determination of the authorities in Texas to settle and develop the province through commercial concessions in the face of probable dangers from the United States and from Napoleon that had led the commandant-general to adopt an exclusive policy. They also show that Louisiana was the most favored region from which to secure the desired immigrants.

shall be located in such places as shall suit them save in Nacogdoches or Atascosito.

It shall, likewise, be understood that the immigrants shall be subject to the general laws and to the colonization laws, that they are to take the oath of allegiance to our sovereign, Ferdinand VII, to recognize, respect, and obey his Majesty, the supreme *junta*, etc., and that they shall not hold any communication with Louisiana across the frontier save by way of Vera Cruz, cutting off all relations with it. In case [this province] does not suit them they shall be allowed to select any other province or to return to their former residence under such precautions as the government shall think well to take.

Likewise, he who wishes to immigrate shall have the personal responsibility of securing beforehand all the information necessary and essential for his immigration, together with information in regard to the place he is to locate.

Those who immigrate shall bring an invoice, approved by the consul, in which he shall show what he brings with him, including his furniture and equipment.[2]

NO. 18

The Commandant-General Defends His Exclusive Policy, 1809.
The Commandant-General to the Governor of Texas, August 21, 1809[1]

The step which I have taken relative to closing the door to emigration from Louisiana to that province [Texas] must be understood by you as absolute along the frontier and the coast, applying to all persons, in conformity with the literal meaning of the order which I communicated to you under date of June 22 last. It is founded upon the necessity for removing every chance for direct or indirect communication with foreign territory, as has been expressed and repeatedly ordered by his Majesty, and in the realization of the fact that during the six years in which the said immigration has been permitted, no individual has entered who has not been prejudicial because of the lack of the qualities which are required to secure [legal] admission and these, likewise, are stated in royal orders.

I issue this reminder in reply to your letter of July 31 last, No. 66, adding that the faithful Spaniards who, in future, may desire to immigrate may do so by way of Vera Cruz, if the viceroy shall admit them, in which case he will indicate to them what he may consider proper in regard to their goods and the property they may possess in their actual dwelling place. In spite of the difficulties you

---
[2]*A. G. I. S. Guad.*, 104-2-25, June 14, 1809–September 20, 1809, Transc., U. of T.
[1]The commandant-general remained a firm adherent of this closed-door policy in spite of the protests of the local authorities.

mention, that of not being able to bring their money—since there is none in Louisiana—no saleable goods—since they are contraband—bills of exchange will supply the lack of money in the first case while the royal order of September 22, 1803, declares what may be done in the second case.

The charge which I gave you that you inform me of whatever inconsistencies you might have noted in my orders touching immigration in so far as they were essential and might lead to preventing the best service, I hope you will obey, since I desire notice of such inconsistencies as may appear in order that I may correct them, after thought and care, in obedience to royal orders.

August 21, 1809.
NEMESIO SALCEDO.

P. S. In the reports and records existing in that government through correspondence with this commandancy, you will find nothing touching Spanish emigrants from Louisiana except wholly prejudicial things which have come to us up until this time, and such noticeable disadvantages that any other province would have shown resentment the moment any person or persons, either by their own free will, or at the command of others, set foot in it—libertines, contraband traders, fugitives, and irreligious, restless persons—some pretenders still living in Louisiana or practically living there, such as Minor, Vidal, Despallier, De Clouet, Laussat, Bastrop, etc., etc. [They are] scoundrels, their purpose yet concealed, pretending as much love for this nation as hatred for the Republic. They make promises, present complaints, offer protestations and assurances; and, accustomed to the unwise and capricious liberality of our former government, which enriched them [through personal motives and not through merit] in goods, credit and fortunes they expect the same treatment, trying now just to be heard, so that they may be granted communication, and to be answered on any point whatever, in order that they may make their own deductions and support their own ideas—which are for the realization of their own private successes, etc. And, in general, they consider themselves necessary and act as if they were doing us a favor by the mere act of entering. They believe, with good foundation, that they will not be denied anything they want and become each time more troublesome and dangerous. I can do nothing less than to set this matter before you in perfect frankness in order that you may strictly carry out my orders in regard to expulsion, and exclusion of such people; for, in the end, they are not and will not be anything but crows to pick out our eyes.

No. 19

The Local Authorities Persist in Their Plans, Pardon for Contraband Traders.[1] July 29, 1810

When this government, oh, faithful settlers of Nacogdoches, is striving to recompense you for your labors and for the pains you have endured during a time of fears and forebodings, due to your critical situation and the neglect with which you have been treated since you were deprived of the necessities of life for your poor families because of the great distance to your settlement—[at this moment] I say, when the sure road to your happiness is being opened—and this must necessarily be through development and conservation by the wise and just government which, fortunately, controls us, at this day, in the name of our beloved king, Don Ferdinand VII, the best of monarchs, but one who is suffering through the iniquitous captivity of the greatest of tyrants—finally, I repeat, [at this very moment] when you are just ready to enjoy the results of the general inspection which we have just finished, when you have been explicitly assured of the ownership of your *solares* and when I have omitted no means of ensuring to you the continuance of the enjoyment of the fruits of your farming and stock lands without expense whatever, because of the great merits of your ancestors and of your own selves and in view of your interesting situations—at this moment, the happiest of your existence, I am feeling the disgust of knowing that there exists among you certain evil Spaniards who, with injury to that high name, have abandoned their country, their friends, and their relatives to live among foreigners—the most scandalous and the saddest of those ungrateful persons who, forgetting the sacred ties of our holy religion, have cast reproach upon it by their crimes and are leaving it forever to live delivered over completely to their vices. Do you not tremble when you consider the unhappy fate they prepare for themselves by the abandonment of their religion and their country? For you can not doubt that it will be fatal to them at the same time that it will be fortunate for you; for you will not have hidden, within your hearts, serpents, so venomous, that some day will be able to infect you with their deadly poison.

Therefore, have unlimited confidence in your wise superior government and in my weak abilities; [and believe] that shortly the day will come when those miserable fugitives will envy your situation, your riches, and the blessing of Heaven, which must fall upon your land and families, as a result of good conduct and the practice of your religion which you must consider the basis of all society. And those

---

[1]This proclamation illustrates the length to which the Texas authorities were willing to go in their efforts to hold the vacillating settlers of Texas to their allegiance to the Spanish crown and thus keep them in the province.

who now consider you unfortunate will look with admiration upon the rapid development which the wise measures and forethought of the supreme government must apportion out to you when, having conferred with your representatives in the *cortes*, it issues orders to this government for execution.

Overjoyed at the improvement of your condition, my heart can not resist the call of charity; and I venture to proclaim that, to the citizens of this province who have so shamelessly emigrated to Louisiana but have committed no other crimes than flight, even though, at the same time, they have taken stock with them, I offer pardon for their crimes in the name of the King, Don Ferdinand VII, on condition that they present themselves before the first day of the coming November in order that they may enter the bosom of their families, reoccupy their homes, and, particularly, that they may enjoy the blessings of our holy religion and the benefits of our government, with the understanding that this pardon does not extend to those who have committed greater crimes whose pardon exceeds my power. And I have no doubt that the superior government will approve this kind and beneficent step.

Calm the foreigners, then. Their permanent establishment in the province, in accordance with our laws, is assured, even though certain of them have no right to enjoy this blessing. Be relieved of your forebodings and take advantage of the paternal aid of the best and wisest of governments; and all of you realize fully that in return for this favor, you must live as faithful, submissive and obedient vassals to superior authorities and to your respective judges. Consider well that contraband trade will never make you prosper nor feed your families, but rather ruin them through the loss, in one day, of all the products of the savings of a long period.[2]

NO. 20

THE REGENCY PROVIDES FOR A BUFFER COLONY IN TEXAS, INSTRUCTIONS FOR DIVISION OF INTERIOR PROVINCES, MAY 1, 1811[1]

There was issued on May 1, last year, through the secretary of war *ad interim*, the following:

"Certain considerations of great weight have forced the Council of the Regency of Spain and the Indies, as a possible utility to the royal service, to again consider the project lately discussed for dividing the ten Interior Provinces of the kingdom of New Spain into two commandancies general of equal power, subject to the viceroyalty

---

[2]July 29, 1810, *Nacogdoches Borradores de Oficios*, January 4, 1810–January 15, 1811.
[1]The orders for the division of the Interior Provinces into the Eastern and Western districts marks the complete triumph of the local authorities of Texas over the commandant-general who was removed from office at this time.

and distinguished by the titles of Eastern and Western Interior Provinces. Consequently, it has decided that the division proposed by the king in 1804 and unfulfilled, because of unfavorable events which have succeeded each other since that time, shall be carried into effect at once, under the limitations that this day are fixed in regard to the viceroy, Don Francisco Xavier Venegas, one of which, in brief, is that he shall proceed, at once, to assume command *ad interim* of the two commandancies and shall be required to advise me immediately of the two officials who may be named and placed in command of them in order that the approval of the Regency may be given and the necessary royal commissions issued."

By order of the Regency, I communicate this to you for your guidance and in order that, on your part, you may render the most punctual and exact obedience to whatever orders the viceroy may give you on the subject. You shall, therefore, with all possible haste, equip the two commandants-general *ad interim* whom the superior power shall name. It seems natural that they should present themselves to you, if this be convenient; but, if not, they shall go with strong guards to the place which the viceroy shall name in private instructions. Your well known zeal for the royal service, your political and military knowledge, and your experience gained from a long command, as well as certain royal resolutions which I deem absolutely necessary, will guide you so that each of the commandants may be able to enter upon the discharge of his duties at once, pending the time when the viceroy shall give you the instructions he may think wise and proper for the division of the archives of the commandancy general.[2]

NO. 21

INSURGENT LEADERS PROMISE LANDS TO AMERICAN "FILIBUSTERS," GUTIÉRREZ TO HIS SOLDIERS, 1812[1]

Fellow Soldiers and Volunteers in the Mexican Cause,

I desire you to receive from me the tribute of my private feelings and, also, as the agent of my Mexican brethren, my warmest and most sincere thanks for the activity, zeal, readiness, and courage that you have shown in the obedience to those orders which you have received from your officers, acting under my command; and I flatter myself with the idea that the line of conduct which you have hitherto observed will be continued, to the discomfiture of tyrants, to the *emancipation* of the *Mexicans*, and to the complete success of the enterprise you have

---

[2]Secretary of War to Salcedo, November 22, 1812.
[1]Document No. 21 established the fact that, for a brief period, the slogan "Liberty" had become more popular than "Free Commerce" and that the idea of "Free Lands" was becoming common.

undertaken, which will crown your exertions with glory, honor, and fortune. The consolation of the justice of the cause which you support, of the fame and immortality which awaits your success, the idea that all the civilized nations of the world look on your actions with admiration and good will, the reflection that the future happiness or misery of a large portion of the habitable globe is now in your hands, will, I am certain, drive you on, and prove to your enemies and the enemies of liberty in every part of the world, that the spark which lighted the flame of independence in the northern part of America is not extinct in the bosoms of the descendants of those who fought, bled, and prevailed over tyrants; and will, at the same time establish beyond a possibility of a doubt, your individual right to that liberty, for the attainment of which for others, you have volunteered your lives, your property, and sacrificed all your social connections.

You are now, fellow-soldiers, in peaceable possession of one of the out-posts established by European tyranny, the more effectually to enslave the oppressed Mexicans. This possession has been obtained without bloodshed on your part because of the consciousness in the minds of the cowardly instruments of tyranny, that they never can prevail in arms against the brave, free, and independent citizens of the United States of America.

This pusillanimity of conduct in the engines of despotism has left in your power, in a weak and defenseless state, all the citizens of the post which you have gained. Your conduct to those citizens, has met my entire approbation. It has done honor to yourselves, as men and as soldiers; and, if continued, this will be more powerful than all the arms in the world—as it will conquer their minds and force them (should they ever feel a doubt) to declare that you are to them as friends, as brothers and as protectors against those who have held them enthralled for ages past, in the most ignominious bondage. From the information which I have received from different quarters, I flatter myself that your stay in this place will not be long—that your numbers will increase to a sufficient extent and enable you to seek the tyrants in their strongholds, and force them to acknowledge this long enslaved country as a free, sovereign and independent government. When this event takes place (and the time is not far distant) you are to look for the reward of your toils, dangers, sufferings and difficulties, in the enjoyment of all the rights of honored citizens of the Mexican republic, in the cultivation of those *lands*, *which I pledge myself will be assigned to every individual among you*, or in the pursuit of wealth and happiness, in such way as your inclination may point out to you. To those who desire it, the right of working or disposing of any mines of gold, silver, or whatsoever nature you may find will be given. The right of taming and disposing of the wild horses and mules which roam unclaimed over an immense tract of country, within the limits of the Mexican republic, will be common to all of you. The surplus of the property confiscated, as belonging to those who are inimical to the republican cause after the expenses of the expedition are paid, will be divided amongst you and those powerful and almost inestimable services which you will render, will further be rewarded from the public treasury of that government which you will have aided so materially in erecting.

JOSE BERNARDO GUITIERREZ.[2]

NO. 22

INSURGENTS, FRENCHMEN, AND AMERICANS CONTINUE AGGRESSIONS, ONIS TO THE COMMANDANT-GENERAL, AUGUST 20, 1813[1]

The French General, Humbert, well known in Europe for his bravery and his military ability—since it was he who commanded the noted expedition which was made against Ireland during the time of the French Republic—left here this week for New Orleans accompanied by various French officers and some Spaniards, among whom I suspect was the Frigate Captain, Don Antonio Mendosa, although this last is not positively known. The plan of France and of this government, who are fomenting the revolution in Mexico in an underhand way, is to send this general to Texas to direct the operations of the insurgent army under the orders of Toledo, who is to be the general-in-chief, deposing the leader, Bernardo Gutiérrez, on account of his ignorance and cruelty. General Humbert carries with him, as his chief-of-staff, another Frenchman, called Achard, a resolute man, and one of unusual ability and bravery who was formerly a captain in the French navy. As the last named gentleman has passed here as an extreme royalist and opposed to Bonaparte, he has approached me to propose to betray the entire insurgent army to our generals. I have praised this idea greatly as one worthy of the principles he has always shown. I have proposed to him that, as soon as there is an opportunity for doing so, he will communicate with you or with the chief of the army, resting assured that he will receive a generous recompense from the viceroy of Mexico in case the plan succeeds. I have not been willing to put myself to any trouble with him; for I do not believe his statement nor those of Ex-deputy Toledo, who made similar proposals to me before leaving for this expedition. But I think it very important that you be informed of the matter and that you also report it to the commander of his Majesty's troops with the instructions that, in case any of these persons communicate

---

[2]Niles' *Weekly Register*, 1812–1813, III, 104.

[1]Document No. 23 shows some of the obstacles in the way of carrying forward the development plans of the authorities in Texas. The very dangers against which the commandant-general had issued warnings were certainly imminent.

with you or with the said commander, you may both proceed with extreme caution, without trusting or distrusting their offers; for Toledo, as well as his companion, Picornel, and his Chief-of-staff, Achard, are prepared for forging papers, since he carries a passport bearing my signature and seal, a passport from the minister of France, and even one from the queen of England. And he may, perhaps, make use of them for some evil purpose. In any case, you may be sure that any person bearing a passport from me to travel in the interior is an impostor since the few I am issuing, with the greatest caution, are for Havana or Vera Cruz, and not under any consideration, for the interior.

NO. 23

The Cortes Grants Lands to Faithful Citizens and Soldiers
Decree cxiv, January 4, 1813.

For reducing royal and other lands to private ownership, allotments made to defenders of the country and to citizens who are not landowners.[1]

Believing that the reduction of the public lands to private ownership is one of the measures which the good of the people and the development of agriculture and industry most imperiously demand and, at the same time, desiring, by means of these lands, to provide additional funds for public necessities, as a reward for the worthy defenders of the country, and aid for the citizens who are not land owners, the general and special *cortes* decree:

1st. That all royal, free, and municipal lands, with and without timber, in Spain proper and its adjacent islands as well as in the provinces beyond the sea, except the necessary commons of the settlements, shall be reduced to private ownership, taking care that in case of municipal lands, annual rents shall be supplied in the most convenient manner, which the *cortes* shall approve upon the recommendation of the provincial deputations.

2nd. That, in whatever manner these lands shall be distributed, they shall be given in fee simple and with definite limits so that the owners may be able to enclose them (without obstructing streams, roads, public watering places, etc.) and to enjoy them freely and exclusively and to use them or to cultivate them to suit their own convenience, but they can never mortgage them or, at any time or under any title place them in mortmain.

---

[1]This decree marked a notable advance in the system of land distribution, taking it from the king's hands and placing it in charge of the *ayuntamientos* and provincial deputations created by the Constitution of 1812.

3d. That, in the jurisdiction of these lands, the citizens of the settlement in whose jurisdiction they lie and such persons as live on the royal lands shall be given the preference.

4th. That the provincial deputations shall propose to the *cortes*, through the regency, the time and the manner in which it will be most convenient to carry out this order in the respective provinces —according to the conditions of the country—and shall specify the lands that must be reserved for the towns so that the *cortes* may decide what is best for the territory.

5th. That this matter is called to the attention of the regency of the kingdom and of the two secretaries of the government in order that they may take action and inform the *cortes*, provided that recommendations of the provincial deputations be sent them.

6th. That, without detriment to what has been provided, half of the royal and free lands of the monarchy, excepting the commons, shall be reserved in order that these lands, or such part as may be considered necessary, may serve as a security for the payment of the national debt—giving preference to those which the citizens of the settlements to which the lands may belong may have against the nation—it being necessary among these debts to give preference to such as arose from money advanced for the national army or the loans for the war which the said citizens have carried on since May 1, 1808.

7th. That, in the transfer of this half of the royal and free lands reserved for the public debt, or such part as may be necessary to pledge, the citizens of the respective settlements and such persons as live on the royal domain shall have the preference in the purchase and from each shall be received, as payment at full value, receipts duly signed which they may hold by reason of said advance or loan and, in lieu of this, such legal national claims as they may possess.

8th. The said half of the royal and free lands shall include and contain such portion as may have already justly and legally been sold in some of the provinces for the expenses of the present war.

9th. That, from the remainder of the royal and free lands or arable municipal lands, there shall be given gratuitously one allotment of those best suited to cultivation, to each captain, first lieutenant, or second lieutenant who, due to advanced age, or disability resulting from military service, is retired with proper license without unfavorable comment and with legitimate proofs of good conduct; and the same shall be given to each sergeant, corporal, soldier, trumpeter, and bugler who, for the same reason or because he has served his time, obtains a final discharge without unfavorable comment, whether they be Spaniards or foreigners so long as there shall be lands of this class in the district in which they settle.

10th. That the allotments granted in each settlement to officers or to soldiers shall vary in size and quality, according to circumstances and to the amount of lands therein, trying, as far as possible, at least, to see that each allotment shall be large enough, if properly cultivated, to furnish sufficient for the maintenance of one individual.

11th. That the apportioning of these allotments shall be through the constitutional *ayuntamiento* of the settlements to which the lands belong as soon as the interested parties shall present the documents which show their faithful services and their discharges and no duties whatever being imposed, the *procuradores syndicos* first being heard briefly and in an administrative capacity.

12th. That the granting of these allotments which shall be called *premio patriótico*, shall not be extended, for the present, to any persons other than those who are serving or have served in the present war or in the settlement of actual disturbances in any of the provinces beyond the seas. But it includes captains, first lieutenants, second lieutenants, and soldiers who, having served in one or the other, have been retired without unfavorable comment and with legal discharges through having become crippled or disabled as a result of action in war and in no other manner.

13th. That there shall also be included those individuals not soldiers who, having served in expeditions or having, in some way, contributed to the national defense in this war or in the disturbances in America, have been injured, or who are disabled as a result of action in war.

14th. That these rewards shall be extended to the persons mentioned even though, because of their services and special deeds, they may enjoy other rewards.

15th. That, from the remainder of the said royal or free lands, there shall be given from those most suitable for cultivation, by lot, one time, and gratuitously, to each citizen of a settlement who has no lands and who shall ask for it an allotment according to the extent of the lands in such a manner that the total of the lands shall, in no case exceed the fourth part the royal and free lands; and, if these lands be not sufficient, the allotment shall be made from the arable municipal lands, in this case, placing upon them a redeemable tax equivalent to the rent of the same for the space of five years to the end of 1817, in order that there may be no diminution of municipal funds.

16th. If any of the beneficiaries named in the preceding article fail (for two consecutive years) to pay the tax—the allotment being municipal property, or held as municipal lands—it shall be granted to another more industrious citizen who has no lands.

17th. That the steps necessary for these concessions shall be taken by the *ayuntamiento* without any charges and the provincial deputations shall approve them.

18th. That all the allotments granted in conformity with articles IX, X, XI, XII, and XV shall likewise be in fee simple to the beneficiaries and their successors under the terms and with the powers expressed in Article II; but the owners of these allotments can not alienate them until after the expiration of four years from the time granted or mortgage them, or place them, at any time, in mortmain.

19th. Any of the beneficiaries named or their successors who shall build or erect a permanent building upon the said allotment shall be exempt from all contributions or tax upon the land or upon its products for eight years.

Cadiz, January 14, 1813.
FRANCISCO CISCAR, President.

NO. 24

A NEW COMMANDANT-GENERAL PROMISES COMMERCIAL CONCESSIONS, ARREDONDO TO THE PEOPLE OF TEXAS, SEPTEMBER 30, 1813.[1]

When it seemed that the precious dominions of our beloved monarch, Ferdinand VII, (may God guard him) were most exposed to the danger of being dominated by the tyrannical usurper, at that very moment, we saw spring into life at our feet new resources which the God of Battles plainly sent to our aid, in order that we should prevail over the enemies of God, of our king, and of our country.

This we have just seen accomplished in the glorious battle of the 18th of last August. This day, which we must keep forever in our memories, has proved [the fact] most convincingly both to the faithful vassals and to the rebels who occupied the province. To the first, because, through means of Divine aid and the wise arrangements of our most worthy commander-in-chief, they see themselves free from the tyrannical yoke which burdened them, and the second, because, foolishly believing themselves superior to all the rest of the world, they have received the condign punishment which they deserved, taking shameful flight and leaving the battlefield full of their dead. I would not have even believed it possible that they would have dared to face the brave troops of the king who in all ages have given proofs of the valor of the Spanish nation and who have never known how to do anything but to punish, to defeat, and to despise rebels and obstinate persons who oppose the rights of the king. And do you, for a moment, believe that this is the only victory we have gained during this period? No, believe what you can not understand; for it has been well established

---

[2]*Colecion de los Decretos y Ordenes que Han Expedidio las Cortes Generales y Extraordinarias*, III, 189–193.

[1]This proclamation shows that the new commandant-general of the Eastern Interior Provinces was in perfect accord with the development policy favored by the authorities of Texas.

that the wicked emperor of the French has been completely defeated in the neighborhood of Victoria by our brothers, under the command of the Duke of Ciudad Rodrigo, who, doubling upon the French, forced them to a shameful flight in which they lost a great number of their soldiers, all of their artillery, their ammunition, money, etc. And [believe also] that, in the *villa* of Revilla, the insurgents were attacked and destroyed by Acting Lieutenant-Colonel, Felipe de la Garza. In the jurisdiction of Refugio, likewise, [the insurgents] were defeated with great loss of life and the bandit chief, Marcelino García [was defeated] in Estremadua by Juan Gutiérrez, the captain of the regiment.

Faithful inhabitants, you need not doubt for a moment that you will find yourselves perfectly free and that, without the shadow of a doubt, you will enjoy the tranquility and peace that our wise government has always given us. But, if deaf to the voice of justice, you do not each of you force yourself to fulfill your duty as a faithful citizen, the labors which the government undertakes for our common happiness will be in vain and of no avail. Now, you have no apologies [for your foes]. Now, you will no longer be indulgent to them. Now, you are thoroughly convinced of the tyrannical way in which you have been treated by the rebels. And will you have among you, even with these examples in your own territory, any individual whatsoever who will dare to disturb good order and to snatch from your hands the rewards of your personal work?—depriving the wife of her husband's support, the child of its parent's care, the sister of her brother's loving companionship, substituting only devastation and ruin similar to that which has just been experienced in this province. No, I do not believe it, not even can I imagine it. Rather do I hope that, if fortunately there should be any individual so wicked and rebellious as to think of deceiving you and bringing upon you the evils I have just pictured, you will denounce him to this government, publicly or privately, to any person whatsoever of probity [if you do not wish your name to be known], in order that, through this channel, it may come to my knowledge and that the proper measures for punishing him may be taken so that the rights of the people may be respected.

I can not fail to make known to you (although you can not be ignorant of the fact) that to the general ruin which this province has suffered the clandestine contraband trade which certain evil doers of the province itself have carried on with foreigners through the post of Nacogdoches has contributed in no small degree, the oft-repeated orders which were issued by this government not having been sufficient to prevent it. So I hope that, in the future, you will cast from your memories for ever this abominable crime that you will not have the daring to buy from your enemies their despicable goods made by hands stained with the blood of their victims—your fathers, sons, brothers, friends, and compatriots—especially when our wise government, by every possible means, is seeking our happiness and is going to grant you shortly the benefit of the Port of Matagorda in order that, through it, this province may supply itself with every thing necessary for its comfortable subsistence—a thing which I believe will make you happy, especially if you dedicate yourselves to agriculture and other industries. And do you know how you should repay this beneficent decision?—with fidelity to the king, love for your country, and obedience to the legitimate authorities, each of you fulfilling the exact obligations of his station.

Headquarters at Bexar, September 30, 1813.

NO. 25

THE COMMANDANT-GENERAL EXPELS FOREIGN INVADERS BUT PARDONS MEXICAN INSURGENTS, GENERAL AMNESTY, OCTOBER 10, 1813[1]

I have considered the papers which you enclose in your letter of this date, sent by the natives of this province and of the *pueblo* of Nacogdoches, who are refugees in the Neutral Ground and who are seeking pardon in order that, with this safeguard, they may return to their old homes and live in peace in the bosoms of their families, enjoying the benefits and protection of the Spanish government. Therefore, believing them truly sorry for their mistakes, and wishing to prove to all the world that just as all the enemies of our beloved king, Don Ferdinand VII, are punished with sword in hand, so also is clemency extended to those who, through misunderstanding or other circumstances, have taken part in the rebellion, but, who, repenting of their sins, ask for pardon, I have decided to exercise the extensive powers vested in me and to grant, in the name of His Majesty (may God bless him) a general amnesty to all the inhabitants of the province, vassals of the Spanish government, who are refugees because of the crime of insurrection, who will present themselves at Nacogdoches, at Villa Salcedo, or at this capital within forty days, counting from the twentieth of this month, under the regulations and exceptions hereafter expressed:

1. Every person not expressly excepted in this amnesty shall be completely pardoned and can present himself, at once, without any hesitation, in the above mentioned places to the justices or to any person who may be in authority, who shall give information to the governor of this province of those who come to take advantage of this amnesty.

---

[1]Document No. 25 illustrates the vigor with which Arredondo acted in dealing with the invaders of Texas and the steps he took to win adherents to the Spanish king.

2. From the above mentioned regulations there shall be excepted, as not worthy of obtaining any consideration whatever, the accursed leaders, Bernardo Gutiérrez, José Alvarez Toledo, Francisco Arocha, Francisco Ruiz, Juan Beramendi, Vicente Travieso, and the infamous blood-thirsty Pedro Prado, who committed the atrocious crime of leading to the slaughter Colonel Don Simón de Herrera, Lieutenant-Colonel Don Manuel Salcedo, and the other helpless victims of the inhuman monsters who sacrificed them. . . .

3. The foreigners, Samuel Davenport, Bernardo Dortolan, and Pedro Girard are also excepted from this pardon—men ungrateful for the benefits the Spanish government has bestowed upon them, who abused the good faith under which they were admitted and who were recognized as vassals of the most pious and lovable Spanish monarch. These men and the infamous persons mentioned in article are proscribed; and, as such, any citizen may kill them with impunity, resting assured that the government, far from punishing them, will reward them as hereafter expressed.

4. Any person killing either of the two first mentioned bandits, Gutiérrez and Toledo, named in article 2, and proving death to be certain, shall be paid five hundred *pesos* reward, and if he shall present them alive to this government or to justices serving under it, he shall be given an additional recompense; and those doing this, with the others mentioned in articles 2 and 3, shall be given half the reward.

5. This amnesty embraces equally and under the same regulations foreign vassals of the king of Spain formerly living in this province who are refugees because of the revolution.

6. Any foreigner, whether or not a vassal of the Spanish government, who shall kill any of the bandits mentioned in articles 2 and 3 shall be paid five hundred *pesos* and admitted to this province if he be a Catholic, and in any other case, half this reward; and if he shall present any of the said leaders alive, he shall be given land in addition to the five hundred *pesos* mentioned in order that he may clear it and cultivate it with all the rights of proprietorship that a Spaniard could possess.

Bexar, October 10, 1813.

—Governor of the Province of Texas.

NO. 26

The Regency Determines to Colonize Texas, Minister of Foreign Relations to the Viceroy, 1813[1]

Among the different objects which this superior government has for a long time had in view when planning for and increasing the

---

[1] Document No. 27 shows that by this time the main interest of the government was fixed upon settling and developing Texas.

population of Texas with the greatest possible exertion, was the supreme object—barring that of securing its prosperity and development—of preserving its ancient limits and of placing an impenetrable or almost impassable barrier against the United States. This barrier they have tried to pass continuously; and, at times, they have succeeded in doing so, establishing themselves at points which offer the least resistance to contraband traders and the best advantages for the successful outcome of their combinations which have been formed for evil purposes. Unfortunately, there have intervened a thousand things and adverse circumstances which have brought to nought the arrangements and preparations for the accomplishment of the plans which have been considered. But it is a matter of great importance, as much for the benefit which those worthy and faithful inhabitants would enjoy through the execution of these plans—since it would render available to them all possible means for the betterment of their situation—as for assuring their political existence which, in the future, might be endangered or even annihilated by that neighboring power which believes it has a right to occupy that territory. Therefore, we, the Regency of the Kingdom, have taken this plan under consideration—and it certainly requires careful examination from all angles, especially, from a political view, as has been pointed out—and, lacking data and information which might contribute to the certain success of the operation in order that it might be carried out in the shortest length of time and with the least expense and risk—since the opinions which have been laid before the Regency have been very diverse and contradictory—the matter is placed entirely in your hands in order that you may take the measures you may consider opportune after consultation with the commandant-general of the Interior Provinces and after having first heard the Bishop of Nuevo León, who, since he has traveled in Texas, will probably be able to afford assistance from personal knowledge, as well as other persons whom you may consider in a position to give information concerning the matter and to clear up the question. You must consider as the prime object to be accomplished the increase of the population, the development of commerce, the creation of wealth, and the opening of the most direct and expeditious communication with other provinces, be it either by land or by sea. For this reason, establishments and settlements shall be made on the coast for the purpose of avoiding useless expense and in order that the persons locating shall suffer the least possible inconvenience and not be exposed to the diseases from which Europeans regularly suffer in this climate.

²Copy in Arredondo to the Governor of Texas, September 29, 1814.

NO. 27

THE CORTES ENCOURAGES AN AMERICAN TO INTRODUCE FOREIGN COLONISTS INTO TEXAS, DECREE OF NOVEMBER 29, 1813, PROVIDING THAT PLANS FOR THE SETTLEMENT AND CULTIVATION OF THE LANDS IN THE PROVINCE OF TEXAS BE RECEIVED AND APPROVED[1]

The *cortes* has thought well to decree:

That the project for the settlement and cultivation of lands in the Province of Texas proposed by Don Richard Raynal Keene shall be received and approved and that he shall be given ample and necessary aid for its execution as soon as possible because of the advantage which will result to the nation by its completion, with the following restrictions:

That the respective provincial deputation, together with the military commandant of the province, and Raynal Keene, shall select the site best suited for the location of the proposed settlement and shall grant the necessary land in conformity with the municipal laws which have not been abrogated;

That, in agreement with the same persons, it shall decide upon the lands which, in conformity with the constitution the decrees of the *cortes*—and especially that of January 4th of this year—shall be assigned each family as its personal property as well as those which, in justice and in conformity with the same laws, shall be given the said Keene for his services and as an indemnity for his expenditures, he being given as much aid as may be thought necessary for the successful execution of his project;

That, a plan or specific contract having been drawn up, the respective deputation shall furnish a legal and authentic copy to the *empresario* for the purpose mentioned and such others as the undertaking demands, proceeding with the prudence and precaution and in the manner which the political conditions of those countries require; and, lastly, that everything provided shall be understood and executed under the exact and unvariable conditions that follow:

First, that two thirds of the settlers must be Spaniards. For their assembling, Raynal Keene shall receive no aid whatever; but he shall not be restricted in regard to their origin or their point of embarkation, observing, however, the strictest precautions as to the emigration and entry of his settlers in order that the public tranquility and the project itself may not be injured. It is to be clearly understood that the departure of or emigration of the young men living in the Peninsula and in the adjacent islands who are subject to the draft during the present war shall be prohibited. The government will protect the

---

[1]By this decree, the *cortes* permitted an American to introduce foreigners of all nations, save the French, but provided that a definite plan of procedure should be mapped out.

Spaniards who desire to settle in the new establishment in Texas and those who may live in provinces where there is revolution.

Second, that the other third of the settlers shall be foreigners, necessarily Catholics, of any nation whatever, save the French who are definitely excluded. The settlers are to come from any region whatever save the Province of Louisiana alone, for its inhabitants are also excluded. The proposed settlers shall prove their religion by a document from the proper Spanish consul or ambassador.

Third, that there shall be sent at once to the *cortes*, through the executive, the plan and contract above described. . . . Finally, the *cortes* declares that the new settlers shall be exempt from the payment of tithes and duties on the products of the soil for the space of ten years. This shall be made known to the regency of the kingdom who shall make all the arrangements necessary for its execution. . . .

Given in San Fernando, November 29, 1813.[2]

NO. 28

THE KING OF SPAIN RELEASED BY NAPOLEON, ABROGATES THE CONSTITUTION OF 1812, MINISTER OF FOREIGN AFFAIRS TO ARREDONDO, MAY 24, 1814[1]

By the royal decree of the fourth of the present month, four copies of which I enclose to be published by order of the king in the territory under your command, the people will be informed of the great blessing with which Divine Providence has just rewarded all the efforts of the most loyal and valiant of all nations, by restoring to them their most beloved king after a long captivity. The wisdom of his Majesty has already ended the disputes and divisions which existed and which threatened to submerge the European provinces of the kingdom into the abyss of evils suffered by certain of the American provinces. The troubles of that section would also have ceased if the people could have been witnesses of the enthusiasm and the great joy with which their European brothers received his Majesty and, if, above all, they could have known his royal intentions towards his vassals of those provinces. Then the disturbances caused by the desolation of those provinces would have ended instantly, and then they would have been perfectly happy. His Majesty would have been no less so, but unfortunately he is not yet happy. Seated upon the

---

[2]*Publications Del Archivo General de la Nacion*, Director, Luis Obregon, Part IV, *Constitution de 1812 en Nueva España*, III, 135–136.

[1]This document is included in the Appendix since it offers a partial explanation of the failure of all development plans for Texas from 1814–1821. Upon reascending the throne, the king placed Texas upon exactly the same footing as that held at the beginning of the century. Even if the Spaniards had been fitted to cope with the difficulties of Indian defense and the development of a frontier country, they could have accomplished nothing under the *régime* described.

throne of his ancestors, he sees his oppressors condemned to humiliation and degradation. He sees the crown of France on the brow of its legitimate sovereign; and he enjoys the sublime spectacle presented by Europe, restored to peace, and turning astonished eyes upon it, realizes that the valor and the heroic constancy of the Spaniards are the prime cause of this wonderful thing. But, in the midst of such great causes for satisfaction, the mind of the king is troubled when he considers the revolutions which have broken out in certain provinces during his absence. His Majesty is firmly convinced that the provinces of the two hemispheres which comopose the monarchy can not prosper one without the other; and he has no less love for the vassals of the most remote section than he has for the residents of those nearest his home. Therefore, he has resolved to reform the evils which have been the motives or have served as a pretext for the revolutions. And, in order that he may proceed with a clear knowledge of conditions, he has asked for information from natives of those kingdoms who are esteemed therein and who, because of their reputation for impartiality, will give an account of the excesses which may have been committed by both parties. This information will be secured within a few days. And the truth being known, his Majesty will take his place among his children in Europe and America and will put an end to the discord which would never have existed among brothers if it had not been for the absence and imprisonment of their father. His Majesty will shortly issue an address to the natives and inhabitants of these provinces. Meanwhile, in the enclosed copy of the decree which he issued upon assuming the reins of government, His Majesty makes it evident that the pretended political constitution of the monarchy, promulgated in Cádiz on March 19, 1812, was the work of persons who had, from no province of the monarchy, the right to form it, and that those who were supposed to be deputies for America in that illegal *cortes* for the most part had been elected in Cádiz—the provinces they claimed ot represent having had no part in their selection and not having even been notified that this was to be done. To this fault of illegality is added that of an absolute lack of liberty in the deliberations held in the midst of tumult and threats of desperate men, a turbulent faction of which filled the galleries of the *cortes*, following the same system as that used in the revolutionary assemblies of France and with the same success—that of publishing a constitution under the false appearance of liberty, while, in fact, they destroyed the foundations of the monarchy, opened the doors for irreligion and awakened ideas whose inevitable consequence was war between those who, because of their vices or their perversity, have nothing and those who are enjoying the fruits of their honest labors, the incomes from the estates of their ancestors, or of the employment due them for services rendered. Such, in all ages, have been the results of popular revolutions and outbreaks, the hidden but true motives of the promoters thereof. None of these vices or of these terrible consequences of the said constitution were hidden from the good sense of the inhabitants of the Peninsulas; and in refusing to accept it, his Majesty has conformed to the general opinion personally ascertained during the long journey which has preceded his entry into the capital. Oh, that his Majesty might be able to travel among the vassals of America in the same way that he has traveled among the greater part of his vassals in Europe. His Majesty does not doubt that he would there find, as he has found in Spain, the true Spaniards of the times, prodigal with their splendid lives when honor is at stake and founding their honor upon the preservation of their religion, upon an unalterable fidelity to their legitimate sovereign, and upon their respect for the usages and customs of their ancestors.

At the time of making known his royal wishes, his Majesty has offered to his beloved vassals certain fundamental laws formed in consultation with the commanders of the European and American provinces. With regard to the approaching call of the *cortes* composed of deputies from a commission named for the purpose is now making plans although the call will be issued without delay. His Majesty desires that it be preceded by this decree in which he ratifies the contents of his royal decree of the fourth of the present month concerning the solid basis upon which the limited monarchy must be founded. And this is the only form of government suited to the natural inclinations of his Majesty and the only compatible with the progress of the century, the present customs, and the high ideals and noble character of the Spaniards. His Majesty does not doubt that this declaration, authorized by his royal signature, will preserve tranquility in the provinces not disturbed by revolution and he desires that it may reach those who are suffering from disturbances in order that, laying aside all rancor, preparation be made, as soon as the call for the *cortes* reaches them, to name deputies worthy of taking their seats among their European brethren; that, under the direction of the king, their common father, they may proceed to cure the wounds caused by the past calamities and, in the future, may prevent, as far as human prudence can, the evils which his Majesty and his vassals of both hemispheres have suffered.[2]

---

[2] N. A.

NO. 29

THE KING RE-ACCEPTS THE CONSTITUTION OF 1812, FERDINAND TO THE SPANISH PEOPLE, MARCH 10, 1820[1]

Spaniards,

When by your heroic exertions an end was put to the captivity in which I had been detained, by the most unheard of perfidy, I had scarcely set my foot on my native soil when all that I saw and learned tended to convince me, that the nation wished to see its ancient form of government restored: and this conviction determined me to comply with what appeared to be the almost general wish of the magnanimous people who, after having triumphantly contended against a foreign foe, dreaded the still more horrible contention of internal discord.

I did not fail to perceive, however, that the rapid progress of European civilization, the general diffusion of knowledge—even among the lower classes; the more frequent communication between the different countries of the globe, and the wonderful events which had been reserved for the present generation, had inspired ideas and wishes unknown to our ancestors and had created new and imperious wants; nor was it less obvious to me that it was indispensable to mould our political institutions in conformity with these elements, so as to establish between the people and the laws that harmony upon which the stability and repose of society depend.

But, while I was maturely deliberating with the solicitude peculiar to my paternal heart upon the changes to be introduced into our fundamental system of government those most suited to the national character and to the present condition of the various parts of the monarchy, and, at the same time, best adapted to the organization of an enlightened people; you expressed to me your anxious desire for the re-establishment of the constitution which, amidst the clash of hostile arms, was promulgated at Cádiz in the year 1812, at a period when, to the admiration of the world, you were fighting for the liberty of your country. I have attended to your wishes, and, as a tender father have consented to that which my children think conducive to their happiness. I have sworn to that constitution for which you were sighing, and I will ever be its firmest supporter. I have already taken the necessary measures for the early convocation of the *cortes*. United with your representatives, I shall then rejoice in assisting in the great work of the national prosperity.

Spaniards: your glory is the only ambition of my heart. My soul desires only to see you united round the throne in peace and

---

[1] By this decree, the king restored the Constitution of 1812 and made it possible for the people to undertake colonization work once more. He was forced to this action by a rebellion among the troops he planned to send to America to quell the insurrection there.

harmony. Trust, then, to your king, who addresses you with the sincere feelings inspired by the circumstances in which you are placed at this moment and with a deep sense of the exalted duties imposed upon him by Providence. Your happiness from this day forward will depend in a great measure upon yourselves. Beware of being misled by delusive appearances of immense benefits, which frequently prevent the attainment of substantial ones. Avoid the effervescence of the passions, which too often transform into enemies those who ought to live as brothers, united by affection, as they are by religion, language and habits. Repel the artfully disguised, perfidious insinuations of those who envy your condition. Let us follow openly, myself the first, the path of the constitution, and, holding out to Europe an example of wisdom, order, and perfect moderation, at a crisis which, in other nations, has been attended with tears and misfortunes, let us draw down admiration and reverence upon the Spanish name, at the same time that we establish for ages our own happiness and glory.

Palace of Madrid, 10th of March, 1820.   FERDINAND.[2]

NO. 30

AN AMERICAN "FILIBUSTER" PROMISES LANDS TO THE "PRESIDENT OF THE REPUBLIC OF TEXAS," LONG TO RIPLEY, JUNE 23, 1820[1]

Republic of Texas,
Headquarters Mina,
June 23, 1820,

To Major El. W. Ripley,
   Sir:,

I do myself the honor to announce to you that, having resigned the office, you have been elected president of the republic of Texas, by the supreme council thereof, convened conformable to the constitution; and as president ex-officio generalissimo of the armies and navies thereof. Should you accept of the appointment, the government have determined that a grant shall be made to you of twenty miles square of land, to be located on any unappropriated lands in tracts of 1280 acres each; and in addition thereto, the annual allowance of $25,000 out of the treasury of the Republic. The government of the

---

[2]Translation, *British and Foreign State Papers*, 1819–1820, VII, 280–81.

[1]This document shows that the invaders of the province of Texas realized as fully as did its defenders that the lands of the region furnished the surest and most acceptable means for the payment of officials for the new Republic planned. The scheme did not succeed, because the authorities were soon able to capture the filibusters and to send them to Mexico City.

republic will await with anxiety your determination. With high consideration, your obedient servant,

JAMES LONG,
Commander-in-chief of the forces.[2]

NO. 31

THE CORTES INSISTS UPON THE DISTRIBUTION OF LANDS, DECREE FOR THE DISTRIBUTION OF CROWN AND PUEBLO LANDS, NOVEMBER 8, 1820[1]

For the purpose of promoting and stimulating, as far as possible, the distribution of crown and *pueblo* lands in the manner prescribed by the general and extraordinary decree of January 4, 1813, and in order to carry out the distribution of the same for the benefit of the people and meritorius soldiers, the *cortes* has decreed:

1st. That each *pueblo* of the monarchy shall form, in the time prescribed by the provincial deputations, a detailed statement of all unoccupied lands within its jurisdiction, whether belonging to the crown or to the *pueblos*. This list shall contain, first, the measurements or boundaries of the said land; second, the title which the *pueblo* has to it; third, its use; fourth, its capacity; fifth, its quality; sixth, its improvements; seventh, its market value; eighth, its liabilities; ninth, its products—whether considered as *pueblo* or unoccupied lands; tenth, the mode of dividing as prescribed by the decree of January 4—in the division of the lands, those who actually occupy these lands being given the preference; eleventh, the claims of the retired and discharged soldiers and those disabled in battle that may have been presented and the manner of rewarding them with the fourth part of the crown lands as prescribed by the decree of January 4 or by allotments of municipal lands or the municipal lands without the payment of a tax; and, finally, what remains of both kinds for those who may present claims in the future.

3d. That reports in the case of unoccupied crown lands shall be prepared with the assistance of agents of the public credit in the provinces or of the sub-delegates in the *pueblos*.

4th. That the lists prepared shall be sent to the provincial deputation, who shall have them corrected whenever not in conformity with the decree of January 4 and with what is herein prescribed.

5th. That if the reports should be in proper form, or as soon as they shall be corrected, the provincial deputations shall send them

---

[2]*The Galveston News*, August 8, 1896.
[1]The *cortes* led in the Liberal movement which the king had accepted reluctantly and sought to carry forward the plans for the distribution of lands which they had outlined in 1813.

with their recommendations, through the proper secretary, to the government for its approval.

6th. That, for the examination of these lists, the provincial deputations shall be authorized to secure the aid of the necessary persons who shall be accompanied by the agent and accountant of credits when the reports concern royal lands.

7th. That the reports being returned by the government with its approval to the provincial deputations and by them sent to the *ayuntamientos* who shall proceed to fix the tax due the public treasury, and the allotments to individuals, the secretary of the *ayuntamiento* shall give to each one a statement of what has been done in order that it may serve as a title deed.

9th. That all towns shall prepare report similar to those prescribed in article 2 and everything shall be done as required in the case of royal lands, except the intervention of the department of public credit, which is not necessary in this case.

10th. That, before proceeding to the distribution of these lands, the *ayuntamientos* shall call all persons who have a claim to them by annuity, mortgage, or other obligation accepted as giving title, to receive such portions thereof as may be necessary to extinguish their claims. If the creditor should be deceased, matters shall be arranged as provided in the said decree of January 4.

11th. That the detailed reports which shall be prepared in connection with these transactions shall be sent to the respective provincial deputations and, with their recommendations, when in proper form, shall be forwarded for the approval of the government.

12th. That the tax which, according to the decree of January 4, shall be placed on these lands, shall be fixed by the respective provincial deputations in view of the detailed reports of the *ayuntamientos;* but it shall not exceed two per cent of the capital value when assigned as a donation to citizens not already freeholders, or three per cent when held by persons of wealth or ability.

13th. That in order to save the towns from new assessments or exactions, the transfer, whether of royal or *pueblo* lands, which have been made up to this time both to our troops and to our enemies during the past war of invasion, shall be held valid even though all requisites may not have been complied with, except in the case of a demand for the invested value against any party concerned. But, if the transfer was made with enormous loss, the purchaser shall be forced to acknowledge the duty accruing to the public treasury, if they were royal lands, or to the *pueblo*, if they were municipal lands.

14th. That when the soil belongs to a private individual, the timber to the *pueblo* or to the king, or when the soil belongs to the *pueblo* or to the king and the timber to private individuals, the person who desires to become a sole proprietor shall include in the purchase price the tax spoken of in the previous article in favor of the public treasury or of the *pueblos* as the case may be.

15th, and lastly, that the government is authorized, under the conditions added to the decree of January 4, 1813, above mentioned, to distribute the royal and *pueblo* lands of the monarchy. All of which I communicate to you by order of the *cortes* in order that, notice having been given to his Majesty, he shall arrange for its execution.

God guard you many years,
Madrid, November 8, 1820.
ANTONIO DIAZ DEL MORAL, Secretary to the Deputies.
JOSE MARIA COUTOU, Secretary to the Deputies.[2]

NO. 32

THE KING AND THE CORTES OFFER FOREIGNERS AN ASYLUM IN SPANISH TERRITORY, DECREE, SEPTEMBER 28, 1820[1]

After having observed all the formalities prescribed by the constitution, the *cortes* has decreed the following:

Article 1, Spanish territory is an inviolable asylum for the persons of all foreigners and properties belonging to them, whether they reside in Spain or beyond its borders, so long as they respect the political monarchy and the laws which govern her subjects.

Art. 2. Asylum for the person shall be understood as not prejudicing the treaties existing with the powers; but, since political opinions can not be comprehended in these treaties, it shall be declared that those residing in Spain and persecuted for their political opinions shall not be delivered to the governments unless they are guilty of the crimes named in the treaties.

Art. 3. The persons comprehended in the previous article and their property shall enjoy the same protection that the laws provide for Spaniards.

Art. 4., Neither through pretext of reprisal in time of war or for any other motive whatever can the said properties be confiscated, sequestered, or seized unless they belong to the governments that are at war with the Spanish nation or their allies.

---

[2]*Decretos de las Córtes*, VI, 345–347.

[1]A comparison of this decree with the instructions for the exclusion of foreigners, Appendix I, shows that the authorities had now completely reversed their policy concerning the treatment of foreigners. In Texas, of course, the fact that the United States definitely abandoned all claim to Texas under the Onis Treaty must have made the change in policy much easier than had the province still been a bone of contention. Although passed several months before Moses Austin's arrival in Texas, the old policy was still in force; for news traveled slowly in those days. In fact, the change was not known until after Austin's petition had been acted upon and he and his colonists had been admitted as Spanish vassals from Louisiana.

This the *cortes* refers to his Majesty in order that he may give his approval.

Madrid, September 28, 1820.
EL CONDE DE TORENO, President.[2]
JUAN MANUEL SUBRIE, Secretary for the Deputies,
ANTONIO DIAZ DEL MORAL, Secretary for the Deputies.

NO. 33

MOSES AUSTIN ASKS TO BE ALLOWED TO INTRODUCE LOUISIANIANS INTO TEXAS, AUSTIN TO THE GOVERNOR OF TEXAS, DECEMBER 26, 1820

Governor and Political Chief,

Moses Austin, a native of the state of Connecticut in the United States of America and a resident of Missouri, with due respect, sets forth and declares that, being a vassal of His Catholic Majesty when the Province of Louisiana was turned over to the French nation, and, later sold to the United States—as the credentials I have presented to your Excellency show—saw himself forced to remain there without making an attempt to immigrate so that he might not lose his property and possessions. These added to his love for his family detained him; but, upon learning of the establishment of the political constitution of the Spanish monarchy and because the removal of immigrants was not forbidden, he has come with the purpose of asking the requisite permission to settle in this province under your command in the place best suited for the cultivation of cotton, wheat, sugar cane, corn, etc.—for which reason he needs to select a suitable place from his knowledge of the requisites.

At the same time he presents himself as the agent of three hundred families who, with the same purpose in view, are desirous of seeing the intention of his Majesty fulfilled, since, at the same time the transfer of the said province, he permitted the entry of those vassals who voluntarily desired to establish themselves in any part of his dominions and also as the agent of a great number of families (including your petitioner's) who, at that time as well as subsequently desired to immigrate, without being able to do so because of impediments from the commanders of these provinces.

Therefore, the said families who, through your petitioner, beg permission for their removal, bind themselves to bring credentials and testimonials proving their good character and conduct. All of them,

---

[2]*Decretos de las Cortes*, VI, 152. In addition the cortes soon passed a most liberal colonization law, "Decree of the Cortes of Spain for the Colonization of Spaniards and Foreigners in the Spanish Colonies, June 27, 1821," in *British Foreign and State Papers*, 1820–1821, Vol. VIII, 1303–1308. This law, however, did not apply in Texas because of the establishment of independence. It probably did lead the Mexicans to adopt a liberal policy, especially in the case of the Americans who had aided them in throwing off Spanish yoke.

or the greater part of them have property. Those without it are industrious. As soon as they are settled, they bind themselves by oath to take up their arms in defense of the Spanish government either against the Indians, filibusters, or any other enemy that may plan hostilities—coming upon call and obeying the orders given them. For this reason, I respectfully ask that you will deign to take whatever action you may think just—in case you have the authority, or, in case you have not, to send it to the proper person with such information as you may think just and may consider necessary. I will appreciate this kindness.

Béxar, December 26, 1820.[1]

NO. 34

CONDITION OF TEXAS IN 1820[1]

I.

NOTES ON THE SETTLEMENTS IN TEXAS

1.

Numbers

"In 1820 the settlements of Texas were exclusively confined to the towns of Bexar and La Bahía, the former containing 800 and the

---

[1]A. P. In preparing this petition, Austin had an able assistant in Baron de Bastrop. Favorable action followed in an astonishingly short time as the following letter to the commandant-general will show:

It will be very expedient to grant the permission asked for by Moses Austin for the removal and settlement in the Province of Texas of the three hundred families who declare that they are desirous of so doing as soon as possible under the conditions fixed in the petition which he presented to the governor of the province for this purpose, the original of which you transmitted in your letter of the 16th of this month. It would be well also if, in addition to the first and most important conditions of being Catholics or agreeing to become so before they enter Spanish territory and that of proving their character and good conduct as is offered in the said petition, they would take the required oath to be obedient to the government in all things, to take up arms in its defense against all classes of enemies whatsoever, to be faithful to the king, and to defend the political constitution of the Spanish monarchy. Very flattering hopes may then be entertained that the province will receive a noticeable development in the branches of agriculture, industry, and the arts through the new inventions they shall bring with them. Monterrey [January 17, 1821.] A. P.

[1]This Appendix, made up of information obtained from Austin's Map of Texas [1829?], notes of other individuals, and a census of Béxar for 1820, shows that in spite of the need for development and the interest shown in the question by many Spaniards, nothing was done prior to the arrival of Moses Austin, December, 1820.

latter 600 inhabitants, and to the margins of the Sabine near the road leading from Natchitoches, where about ten families were settled.[2] Nacogdoches was at that time totally abandoned.[3]

2.

Westward Expansion

"A gentleman who had occasion to visit the capital of Texas states that on his departure from Nacogdoches he found the American settlements to continue for about fifteen miles on the great road leading to the seat of government—and to his astonishment on his return (which was in a month), he met the advanced posts of those settlements at least seventy miles in the interior! However, these settlements were the first habitations of men he had seen in traveling a distance of nearly five hundred miles. The old Louisiana road through the country is still discernible, though there is not the least sign of the abode of a civilized being after the traveler passes the American improvements until he arrives in St. Antonio. But the most important fact respecting Texas which has come to our knowledge is that a concession of the immediate country at the *mouth* of the great river Colorado has actually been made to a gentleman of the West, by the Spanish authorities, on condition that he will cultivate the lands and bring with him a certain number of families.

"The Colorado empties into the Bay of St. Bernard, and, at the contemplated spot will afford a fine harbor. A town, upon an extensive plan, is to be laid out, which will enjoy the advantage of a port of entry, agreeably to a late order of the cortes establishing a port at the 'mouth of the Colorado.' This recalls to our mind the assertion of the late Mr. Sampson, of New Orleans, who, in speaking some years ago of the outlets of the Bravo and Colorado, pronounced them amongst the most eligible site in North America for large commercial cities."—*St. Louis Enquirer.*

[2]The names of the heads of families thus informally located have not been ascertained with certainty. Tradition declares that between 1800 and 1820 the following heads of families came in: Matthew Earl, [?] Ward, Jesse Walling, A. G. Walling, Lewis Halloway, Nathan Davis, Jonathan Anderson, Jonas Harrison, Raymond Daly, and John Ayres. Information furnished by Reverend George W. Crockett, of Nacogdoches, who has collected some interesting facts concerning the history of that section.

[3]*Daily National Intelligencer*, June 24, 1821. Thus was fulfilled the prophecy of Gutiérrez, who, as early as 1812, had "observed a strong desire among the people of the United States to go to Mexico." He declared that many children had been placed under special teachers, so that they might be taught the Spanish language. He even believed that, should immigration be permitted, "over a million would flock there."—*Diary*, 21, State Archives.

II.

CENSUS OF BEXAR

CITY OF BEXAR, JURISDICTION OF THE PROVINCE OF TEXAS, INTENDENCY OF SAN LUIS POTOSI, JANUARY, 1820

Parishes, 1; vicarages on a fixed basis, none; missions, 3; farms, none; abandoned ranches, none; independent ranches, none; dwellings, none.

Age	Single men	Single women	Married men	Married Women	Widowers	Widows	Total
To 7 yrs.	176	191	----	----	----	---	
7 to 16	241	218	----	1	----	----	
16 to 25	81	83	16	58	1	----	
25 to 40	50	26	76	160	2	68	
40 to 50	12	6	47	37	7	38	
50 on up	10	2	68	36	7	83	
Totals	570	526	207	292	17	202	1814
	1096		499		219		
Grand total			1814				

DIVISION INTO NATIONALITIES

Nationality	To 7 yrs.		7–16		16–25		25–40		40–50		50		Total	
	M	W	M	W	M	W	M	W	M	W	M	W	M	W
Europeans	----	----	----	----	----	----	1	----	----	----	----	----	1	----
Spaniards	102	108	134	127	73	87	73	144	37	41	47	71	466	578
Mestizos	74	80	97	90	44	74	55	125	26	40	33	30	329	439
Negroes	----	----	----	----	----	----	----	----	1	----	----	----	1	----

DIVISION INTO CLASSES

Curates	1	Farmers	110
Vicars	0	Miners	0
Sacristans	0	Merchants	3
Clergy	0	Artisans	33
Retainers of the Crusade	0	Mine Operators	0
Nobles of Castille	0	Day Laborers	108
Lawyers	0	Doctors	0
Students	0	Surgeons	0
Employes of Royal Treasury	1	Druggists	0
Retired with Military Rights	1	Barbers and Bleeders	0
Secretaries	1	Schoolmasters	1
Court Employees	0		

RELIGIOUS AND PHILANTHROPIC INSTITUTIONS[3]

SUMMARY

Total number of persons shown	1814
Religiosos	1
Religiosas	0
Colleges, convents, etc.	0
Houses of correction and prisons	0

[Notes Appended]

1. Among the number of artisans and handicraftsmen named above there are: Fourteen shoemakers, four tailors, four carpenters, six blacksmiths, two masons, four silversmiths, and one foreman.

2. In this vicinity there are no other occupations than that of farming. A person incapable of farming engages in hunting bear and deer. The crops that are cultivated are confined to corn, wheat, and cane. There are no manufactories or mule trains. Likewise, there are no miners.

3. The number of cattle upon which the settlement can count at present is small and cannot be given in detail because they have left their pastures. There are no sheep left except about seventy head— and about thirty goats. There are no brood mares and the number of domestic horses amounts to only sixty.

Béxar, January 1, 1820.

ANTON⁰· MARTINEZ.

---

[3][Merely a form showing that none existed.]

BIBLIOGRAPHY

In this study of the struggle between various nations and factions for the possession of Texas during an epoch-making but sadly neglected period, the manuscripts and maps in the Austin Papers and the Béxar Archives, in the Library of the University of Texas, and the supplementary Nacogdoches Archives, at the State Library, at Austin, have been the chief sources of information. These three collections are particularly rich in materials for Texas history for the first quarter of the nineteenth century. From them alone it has been possible to secure practically all the information needed. However, other collections have furnished details that have filled in several gaps in the story and added a few important items of which no hint appeared in the three sources upon which chief reliance was placed. Among these collections may be named:

Records of the General Land Office, Austin.
Documents in the García Library, University of Texas.
Transcripts of documents in the Bancroft Library, Berkeley, Calif.
Transcripts from French Archives, Paris; *El Archivo General de México*, Mexico City, and *El Archivo General de Indias*, Seville, Spain.

Besides these unprinted manuscript sources, documents of printed manuscripts have been used, as follows:

Adams, John Quincy, *Memoirs of*, Philadelphia, 1875, IV–V.
American Historical Review, New York, 1904–1911, V, VI, IX, XV, and XVI.
American State Papers, Washington, 1832, Lands, I–IV, VIII; Foreign Relations, III–IV.
Austin, Stephen F., *Translation of the Laws, Orders, and Contracts of Colonization, from January, 1821, up to the Present Time, by Virtue of which Colonel Stephen F. Austin Has Introduced and Settled Foreign Immigrants in Texas*, San Felipe de Austin, November, 1829.
British and Foreign State Papers, London, 1830, I, V, VII, VIII.
"British Correspondence Concerning Texas," *Southwestern Historical Review*, Austin, 1915–1916, XIX.

Claiborne, W. C. C., *Official Letter Books* (Rowland, Dunbar, Ed.), Jackson, Miss., Deparment of State Archives, 1917.
Clay, The Honorable Henry, *Life and Speeches of* (Mallory, Daniel, Ed.), Hartford, 1883.
Colección de los Decretos y Ordenes Que Han Expedido Las Cortes Generales y Extraordinarios, Madrid, 1820, II–III, VI–VII.
Correspondence de Napoleon 1er., Publiée par Ordre D' L'Empereur Napoleon III, Paris, 1858, XVI–XVII, XX, XXII.
Coxe, William, *Espagne Sous la Maison de Bourbon*, Paris, 1827, VI.
Hernández y Dávolos, J. E., *Colección de Documentos Para la Historia de la Guerra de Independencia de México*, México, 1882, VI.
Houck, Louis, *The Spanish Régime in Missouri*, Chicago, 1909, I–II.
Jefferson, Thomas, *The Writings of* (Beigh, A. E., Ed.), Washington, 1907.
Keene, Richard Raynal, *Memoria Presentada A. S. M. C. El Señor Don Fernando VII, Sobre El Asunto De Fomentar La Poblacion y Cultivo En Los Terrenos Baldiós En Las Provincia Internas Del Reyno De México*, Madrid, 1815.
Martens, George Friederich von, *Noveau Receul de Traités*, Gottengeu, 1816, I.
Memoria Politico-Instructiva Envidada de Philadelphia en Agosto 1821. A Los Gefes Independentes del Anahuac, Philadelphia and Mexico, 1822.
Moza, Francisco de la, *Codígo de Colonización y Terrenos Baldios de la Republica Mexicana*, Mexico, 1825.
Niles' *Weekly Register*, Baltimore, 1812–1820, II, IV, X, XI, XII.
Public Documents Printed by Order of the Senate of the United States, Second Session, Twenty-eighth Congress, Washington, 1845, Documents 389, and Senate Report First Session, No. 150.
Recopilación de Leyes de los Reynos de India, Madrid, 1681, IV, VII, IX, XXVIII.
Rios, Juan Miguel de los, *Código Español del Reinado Intruso de Napoleón Bonaparte*, Madrid, 1845.
Robertson, James Alexander, *Louisiana under the Rule of Spain, France and the United States*, Cleveland, 1911, I.
Treaties, Conventions, and International Acts, Protocols, and Agreements between the United States of America and Other Powers, 1776–1909 (Compiled by William Malloy), Washington, 1910, II.

Valuable information has also been secured from certain secondary publications. Among the most helpful may be named:

Alamán, Lucas, *Historia de Méjico*, Méjico, 1852.

Austin, Mattie Alice, "The Municipal Government of San Fernando de Béxar, 1730–1800,"*The Quarterly of the Texas State Historiacal Association*, Austin, 1904–1905, VIII.
Bancroft, Hubert Howe, *History of Mexico*, San Francisco, 1886, IV; *History of North Mexican States and Texas*, San Francisco, 1889, II.
Barbé-Marbois, François, *La Histoire de la Louisiana*, Paris, 1829.
Bolton, Herbert Eugene, *Texas in the Middle Eighteenth Century*, Berkeley, 1915; *Guide to the Materials for the History of the United States in the Principal Archives of Mexico*, Washington, 1913.
Brown, John Henry, *History of Texas*, St. Louis, 1892, I.
Burlage, John, and Hollingsworth, J. B., *Abstracts of Valid Land Claims Compiled from the Records of the General Land Office and Court of Claims of the State of Texas*, Austin, 1859.
Cavo, Andres, *Las Tres Siglas de Méjico*, Méjico, 1852.
Chapman, Charles E., *Catalogue of Materials in the Archivo General de Indias for the History of the Pacific Coast and the American Southwest*, Berkeley, 1917.
Cox Isaac Joslin, *Exploration of the Louisiana Frontier, 1803–1806*, Washington, 1905; *The Early Exploration of the Louisiana Frontier*, Cincinnati, 1906; "Monroe and the Early Mexican Revolutionary Agents," *Annual Report of the American Historical Association*, Washington, 1911; *The West Florida Controversy, 1789–1813*, Baltimore, 1918.
Duvallon, [Berquin-Duvallon] (Ed), *Vue de la Colonie Espagnole Du Mississippi ou Des Provinces de Louisiane et Florida Occidentale*, Paris, 1803.
Filisola, Vicente, *Memoria Para la Historia de Guerra de Tejas*, Mexico, 1848.
Foote, Henry Stuart, *Texas and the Texans*, Philadelphia, 1848, I–II.
Fortier, Alcée, *History of Louisiana*, Paris, 1904, I–II.
Fuller, Robert Bruce, *The Purchase of Florida*, Cleveland, 1906.
Garrison, George P., *Texas*, New York, 1903.
Gayarré, Charles Etienne Arthur, *History of Louisiana*, New York, 1854, IV.
Hartmann and Millard, *Le Texas où Notice Historique sur la Champ D'Asile*, Paris, 1819.
Hecke, J. Val., *Reise durch die Vereinigten Staaten von Nord-Amerika*, Berlin, 1820–1821, I–II.
Hume, Martin, *Modern Spain*, New York, 1900.
Kapp, Friederick, *The Life of William von Steuben*, New York, 1859.
Kennedy, William, *Texas, The Rise and Progress of the Republic of Texas*, London, 1844, I, II.
Martin, Francis Xavier, *The History of Louisiana*, New Orleans, 1822.

Navarro, José Antonio, *Apuntes Historicos Interesantes de San Antonio de Béxar*, San Antonio, 1869.
Obregón, Luis Gonzales, *Publicaciones del Archivo General de la Nacion*, IV; *La Constitucion de 1812 en Nueva España*, Mexico, 1912.
Ogg, Frederick Austin, *The Opening of the Mississippi*, New York, 1904.
Oman, Charles W., *The Peninsula War, 1807–1808*, Oxford, 1902.
Parker, David W., *Calendar of Papers in Washington Archives relating to the Territories of the United States* (to 1783), Washington, 1911.
Phelps, Albert, *Louisiana*, Boston and New York, 1905.
Portillo, Esteban L., *Apuntes para la Historia Antigua de Coahuila y Texas*, Saltillo, 1886.
Priestley, H. I., *José de Gálvez, Visitador-General de New Spain, 1763–1771*, Berkeley, 1916.
Reeves, Jesse Siddal, *The Napoleonic Exiles in America*, Baltimore, 1905.
Robertson, William Spence, *Rise of the Spanish American Republics as Told in the Lives of Their Liberators*, New York and London, 1918.
Roosevelt, Theodore, *Winning of the West*, New York and London, 1897–1898, IV.
Schoolcraft, H. R., *Travels in the Central Portion of the Mississippi Valley*, New York, 1825
Smith, Ashbel, *Reminiscences of the Texas Republic*, Galveston, 1876.
Sparks, Jared, *American Biography*, New York, 1848–1849, XXIII.
Thrall, Homer S., *A Pictorial History of Texas*, St. Louis, 1879.
Treat, Payson Jackson, *The National Land System*, New York, 1910; *The Independence of the South American Republics*, Philadelphia, 1903.
Viles, Jonas, "Population and Extent of Settlement in Missouri before 1804," *Missouri Historical Review*, Columbia, Mo., 1911, V.
Villanueva, Carlos A., *La Monarquia en América, Fernando y Los Nuevos Estados*, Paris, 1912; *Historia de Diplomacia: Napolean y la Yndependencia de América*, Paris, 1912.
Violette, Eugene Morrow, *History of Missouri*, Boston, New York, Chicago, 1918.
Ward, *Mexico*, London, 1829.
Winsor, Justin, *The Westward Movement*, Boston, 1897.
Wortham, Louis J., *From Wilderness to Commonwealth*, Fort Worth, 1924, V.

INDEX

Acadians, 10, 12, 17.
Adams, Calvin, 167.
Agriculture, 28, 32, 36, 52, 79, 81, 198, 219, 235, 246, 248, 257, 275, 276, 279, 303–305; distaste of Spaniards of Texas for, 65; encouragement of by Napoleon, 323–324; resources of Texas, 77.
Aguaverde, 252, 283.
Alabamas, 74, 114, 215; admitted to Texas, 76; hostility to Americans, 30.
Alamo de Parras, 215.
Aldrete, José, 102, 323.
Alleghany Mountains, barrier to Americans, 10.
Almonte, Juan, 323.
Alvarado, José, 201.
Amador, Juana María, 314.
Amblemont, Dr., 211.
Americans, activities of, 43, 225–226; admitted to Louisiana, 13, 21, 22, 32; aggressions of, 216–218; aid insurgents of Mexico, 249, 256; barrier against, 39, 219; defense of by Salcedo, 194; exclusion from Texas, 92, 116; filibusters, 237; hostility of French, 28; hostility of Indians, 30; hostility of Spanish, 36–39, 43, 50, 54, 92, 216; land hunger, 257; number in Texas, 57, 193.
Anderson, Jonathan, 355.
Andreton, John, 110.
Anti, Juan Bautista, 108.
Apalaches, 74.
Apodaca, Juan Ruiz de, 254.
Appendix,
Aranames, 304.
Aranda, Conde de, 12.
Arcos, 194, 257.
Arduán, Francisco, 178, 323.
Aresmendi, Alferes, 247.
Arkansas, Post of, 50.
Aroberson, Martin, 58.
Arocha, Francisco, 323.
Arrambide, Juan Ignacio de, 104.
Arredondo, Joaquín de, 230, 234, 236, 237, 238, 246–249, 250, 258, 271, 282; colonization plans, 253–254.
Arsenaux, Pedro, 89.
Artisans, favored as colonists, 221.
Ashley, Robert, 74.
Atascocito, 89, 90, 119, 136, 140, 199, 283.
Attakapas, 89, 90, 91, 112, 209; Acadians at, 10, 12.
Audrain, Pedro, 27–28.
Aury, Luis, 256–266.
Austin, Moses, 32–34, 142, 284–286, 301, 354–356.
Austin, Stephen F., 9, 185, 286.
Avres, John, 366.
Ayuntamiento, 279, 283.
Azana, Miguel José de, 183.

Baca, Antonio, 304.
Baccigalupi, Luis, 83, 314.
Bahía, 66, 82, 125, 199, 224–225, 230, 249–254, 271, 285, 203–304, 311, 313, 358.
Baldes, Jesus, 323.
Balentín, Andres, 299.
Baltimore, 184, 185, 195, 255, 326.
Bandera Pass, 251–252.
Barbie, José, 299.

Barcenas, Manuel, 323.
Barker, Eugene C., 6.
Barnett, Timoteo, 178.
Barr, William, 56, 75, 84, 85, 89, 298, 301.
Barr and Davenport, 121.
Barrataria, 248.
Barre, William de la, 12.
Bart, Francisco, 300.
Basily, Juan de, 63.
Bastrop, Felipe Enrique Nerí, Baron de, 95, 97, 115, 121, 151, 174, 249, 284, 331; colonization, 31, 32, 35, 96–98; Indian trade, 98; objectionable to Spaniards, 272.
Baton Rouge, 77, 78, 122, 307; colony proposed, 14; revolution, 186–191.
Baume, José de la, 249–250, 299, 302.
Bayonne, Cession of, 128.
Bayou Pierre, 73, 180, 199, 214, 249.
Bebe, Guillermo, 299.
Belmont, Francis, 175, 183.
Belmudez, Salvador, 313.
Benoist, See Venua.
Beloxis, 215.
Benua, See Venua.
Beramendi, Juan, 343.
Berlin, 197.
Bermudez, Francisco, 162.
Béxar, 62, 64, 65, 66, 71, 81, 82, 89, 94, 104, 105, 119, 111, 114, 120, 123, 125, 130, 136, 191, 193, 199, 201, 206, 207, 213, 214, 217, 224, 226, 230–232, 238, 251–263, 271, 283, 303, 304, 311, 356, 358, archives, 114, 141; census, 67, 180; road, 94; settlements on road, 65; trade, 141, 142; trading house, 115; troops and settlers from Orcoquisac and Adaes, 66.
Biens, [Bin] [Juan], 298.
Blanco, 257.
Bodoya, Manuel, 177.
Bodro, Remegeo, 145.
Bolton. H. E., 6, 8.
Bonaparte, Joseph, 128, 184.
Bonavía, Bernardoo, 149, 152, 155–158, 160–161, 167, 170, 173–174, 176, 182–183, 186, 191–192, 234, 328.
Bonet, Catalena, 314.
Boone, Daniel, 5, 38, 109, 111, 151, 322.
Boquilla de Piedras, 256.
Born, Francisco, 300.
Borrego, José, 314.
Bosie, Francisco, 74.
Bosque, Pedro, 299.
Boston, 260.
Bouquer, Juan, 298.
Bouquet, Nicolas, 119.
Bowles, 42.
Boyle, Carlos, 53.
Brady, Fray Juan, 77, 82, 83, 307.
Bray, Pedro, 121, 123.
Brazos de Santiago, 209.
Brazos River, 218, 248, 283; proposed settlement on, 94.
Brirns, Santiago, 300.
Bron, Juan, 298.
Bruin, Bryan, 14.
Bruno, Miguel, 300.
Bryan, James, 142.
Bucareli, abandonment of, 66.
Buges, 141.

364　　　　　　　　　　　　Index

Bullett, Judge, 142.
Burgess, William, See Burxer.
Burr, Aaron, 86, 117, 122, 127, 187.
Burxer, Guillermo, 142, 146, 196, 314, See Burgess, William.
Butler, William, 16.

Cabello, Domingo, 296.
Cádiz, 278.
Calaxan, Anna, 314.
Californias, 262.
Calleja, Felix, 208, 234.
Calvert, Juan, 297.
Camino Real, 93, 103, 121, 125.
Campeche, 52, 137.
Canada, 56, 79, 197, 308.
Canadians, settlers in Louisiana, 11, 12.
Cana'iano, Bautiste, 124, 314.
Canary Islanders, 74, 272, 308.
Canel, Nicholas Urbano Carlos, 73.
Cañon de San Sabá, 251.
Cape Girardeau, 38, 141.
Capuran, José, 299.
Carr, Enrique, 201.
Carillo, José Ma., 323.
Carrasco, Pedro Nolasco, 102.
Carlos, Juan, 178.
Carmen, María, 314.
Carondelet, Baron de, 31, 35, 60, 95, 305; favors French settlers, 28, 30, 34, 35.
Carthegena, 130.
Casa Calvo, Marqués de, 51, 78, 85–90, 95, 96, 106.
Casanova, Jose Manuel, 102, 314.
Casis Lillia Mary, 6
Cashily, John, See Casili, 113.
Casias, Anto., 323.
Casili, Juan Carlos, 113.
Castañeda, José María, 323.
Catholics, 13, 15, 16, 17, 18, 30, 35, 36, 195, 198, 221, 227, 235, 241, 242, 257, 289, 311, 329,
Chabus, Francisco, 63.
Charles III, 10, 12, 39, 52.
Charles IV, 83, 128, 327; excludes Americans from Louisiana, 40.
Champ d'Asile le, 260–261.
Charman, Zedo, 120, 123, 314.
Cheridan, Rebecca, 314.
Cherokees, 30, 123.
Chickasaw Indians. 123.
Chirino, Margil, 323.
Christen, Santiago, 299.
Choctaws, 48, 49, 74, 76, 96, 124, 215.
Chote, David, 113.
Cidre, Juan. 178.
Claiborne, W. C. C., 68. 92, 127, 245.
C'aimorgan, Santiago, 167.
Clark, Betsy, 314.
Clark, Daniel, 72.
Clay, Henry, 264, 277.
Clouet, Brogné de, 89, 90, 97, 109, 111, 120, 141, 331; objectional character of, 172.
Coahuila, 61, 64, 65, 71, 82, 84, 107, 117, 139.
Coasatis, 114, 123.
Cocos, 304.
Colorado River, 84, 218, 283, 313, 356.
Comanches, 47, 48, 50, 66, 114, 215, 217, 218, 224, 252, 283.
Commandant-General, 183, 185, 191. 192, 203, 209, 213, 214, 217, 224, 234, 327.
Commerce, 28, 209, 231, 232, 234, 235, 279.
Concepción Mission. 271.
Conilt, Santiago, 56, 298.

Constitution, 1912, 236, 243, 244, 278; abrogated, 347; re-enacted, 349–350.
Contraband trade, 49, 50, 52, 53, 63, 71, 76, 80, 81, 82, 90, 107, 108, 115, 121, 136, 137, 143, 144, 198, 237, 249, 283, 332–333, 341.
Cordero, Antonio, 47, 92, 93, 94, 95, 97, 98, 102, 106, 108, 113, 114, 118, 121, 123, 124, 125, 128, 132, 133, 140, 143, 145, 164, 202, 214; defense plans, 133, 158, 168; instructed to remain in Texas, 149; recalled to Coahuila, 179.
Cork, Guillermo, 112.
Cornel, Antonio, 183.
Cortes, Juan, 177.
Cortes, Spanish, 205, 217, 234, 243, 255, 278, 279, 280, 347, 348; colonization plans of, 234, 241, 345–346.
Council of the Indies, 185, 244–245.
Coyle, Hugo, 73, 102, 121.
Cro, See Crow.
Croix, Cabellero de, 93; powers of, 8.
Creoles. 129, 234, 257, 323.
Crow, Hare, 55.
Crow, José Miguel, 123, 184, 298.
Cruz, Pedro, 102.
Cuatro Cienegas, 93.
Cuba, 280.
Cujanes, 304.
Cu'ebra Island, 136.
Curon, Juan, 72, 306–307.

D' Alvimar, 197; Napoleonic appointee, 130.
Daly, Raymond, 355.
Dannequien, Louis, 110.
Darbonne, Jose, 108.
D'Arges, Pierre Wouves de, 7, 18, 22.
Davenport, Samuel, 55, 117, 215, 227, 235, 297, 301–302, 343.
Dav's, Juan, 165, See Debis.
Davis, Nathan, 355.
Debis, Juan, 140, 298, 300.
Debua, Antonio, 300.
De Lassus, Duhault de, 27, 28.
Dallette, Tomás, 144.
Deserters, American, in Texas, 182; disposition of, 116, 169.
Desgraviers, Francisco Marceau, 111.
Desmoland, 130, 185, 323.
Despallier, Bernardo Martin, 60, 78, 83, 88, 102, 226, 235, 242, 305–306; colonization plans of, 307–311; objectional character of, 172.
Despallier, Estevan, 72.
Diles, José, 250.
Dill, Santiago, 56, 198, 297.
Do'eo, Pedro, 299.
Dominguez, Christobal, 204, 214, 236.
Dorst, Jacob, 193.
Dortolan, Bernardo, 197, 198, 299.
Dorvan. Manuel. 106.
Doyle, Martin, 58.
Dribread. John, 141.
Dubuc. Julien, 30.
Duforest. Juan Valentine, 63–64.
Dumelan, 184.
Dunn, W. E., 6.
Dupon, Carlos, 314.
Duran. José Luis, 102, 314; land granted to, 104.
Dutch colonists, 23, 31.
Duxen, Sa'ome, 140.

Earl, Mathew, 355.
Ecrleastics, favor desired by Napoleon, 324.

Index

Ecstozman, Feredicte, 104, 314.
Eluterio, José, 323.
Elguezabal, Juan Bautista de, 48, 49, 61, 93, 303–305.
Eliot, Santiago, 298.
Engle, Pedro, 178, 299.
England, policy of, 28, 42, 44, 50, 56, 58, 190, 223–226, 243, 262, 263, 266–269; relations with France, 28, 51, 54; relations with Spain, 35, 42, 63, 92, 127; relations with United States, 323.
Ernández, Santos, 323.
Erondreque, Juan, 144.
Esmiete, Serafina, 145.
Espallier, Bernardo de, See Despallier.
Espíritu Santo Bay, 84, 228, 304.
Espoz y Mina, 278.
Esquibel, José Antonio, 178.
Estevan, Pedro, 135.
Europe, diplomacy of, 281–282; immigration to Louisiana, 27; to Texas, 57; international relations, 259.
Eválvez, Juan, 11.
Farías, Francisco, 323.
Fatio, Felipe, 258, 261.
Fear, John, 104, 110, See Fierr.
Feliciano, Acadians at, 12.
Ferdinand VII, 128, 232, 234, 327–328, 332, 340, 342, 346–350; relations with Napoleon, 243, 2444–245.
Ferrold, Santiago, 64.
Fierr, John, See Fear.
Fier·, Santiago, See Fier·.
Fil, Santiago, 178.
Filihol, Juan, 113.
Fitzgerald, Patricio, 178.
Fitzgerald, William, 16.
Flanders, 27.
Flores, Pedro, 323.
Flogny, Pedro, 135.
Floridas, 211, 234, 264, 269; policy of England, 42; of United States, 90, 276; revolution, 186–187.
Folch, Vicente, 127, 147, 190.
Fontan, Juan, 298.
Fonten, Louis, 178.
Fooey, Benjamin, 31.
Foreigners, 185–191; aggressions of, 50, 203, 220, 221, 226, 233, 235, 236, 248; exc·uded from Texas, 9, 10, 26, 44, 183, 191, 195 342–343, 395,; in Texas, 55, 77; in Spanish Dominions, 285, 353. .
Foronda, Valentin, 147.
Fort Pitt, 19, 20.
France, immigration from to Louisiana, 26. 28, 308; Indian policy, 45; relations with England, 28; with Spain, 21, 43, 54, 187, 194, 208, 210, 218, 220, 221, 237, 276, 336; with United States, 28.
French, in Louisiana, 20, 26, 28, 186, 190, 193, 195.
Frio River, settlement on, 99, 179, 224–225.
Frio River, 251.
Fur trade,, 94, 120.

Gachupines, 229.
Gallego, Pedro, 323.
Galliopolis, 27, 28.
Galveston, 255, 260, 261, 265, 269, 313.
Ga'veston Bay, 84, 275.
Gálvez, Conde de, 12, 43, 93.
Gañon, María Louisa, 302.
García, José María, 323.
García, José María, 323.
García, Juliana, 323.
Gardner, Guillermo, 110.
Gardoquí, Diego, 13, 14, 16, 17, 18, 21, 23, 25.

Carner, Patricio, 110.
Garnier, Juan, 89.
Garza, Antonia, 323.
Garza, Dolores de la, 323.
Garza, María Ygnacio de la, 323.
Garza, Rita de la, 323.
Gayoso, Manuel de, 35, 85.
Genet, 29.
Germans, 197, 242; colonists, 11, 12, 18, 23, 27, 31, 79, 219, 220, 273–275, 308; French influence on in Louisiana, 185.
German Coast, 10.
Girard, Pedro, 343.
Giru, José, 178.
Glass, Anthony, 122.
Goceazochea, Manuel, 124.
Godoy, Manuel, 36, 83, 84; colonization plans, 312–314.
Goguet, Estevan, 299.
Gómez, Basilio, 323.
Gómez, Francisco, 178, 325.
Gómez, Gil, 323.
Gómez, Mateo, 323.
Gómez, Pedro, 323.
Gonzales, Andres, 178.
Grande, Lous, 177.
Grande, María Candida, 314.
Greenville, Treaty of, 33.
Grimarest, Pedro, 83, 84, 88, 153, 155, 167, 238, 242, 314.
Guadalupe, María, 323.
Guadalupe River, 81, 87, 89, 121, 252, 265, 283; advantages for settlement, 81, 94, 251, 260, 311.
Guadiana, José María, 55, 57.
Guapasces, 123.
Guelete, Alexo., 73.
Guelete, Guillermo, 300.
Guitan, Manuel Alvarez, 72.
Guitérrez, José Bernardo, 222, 226, 228, 229, 232, 233, 248, 269, 334–336.

Hackett, C. W., 6.
Halloway, Lewis, 355.
Harmon, Yhan, 314.
Harrison, Jonas, 355.
Havana, 80, 87; 130, 253.
Hecke, J. Val., 273–275.
Hench, Christian, 314.
Hernández, Geronimo, 102, 314.
Hernández, José, 177.
Herrera, Pedro Miguel, 120, 178.
Herrera, Simón, 116, 117, 128, 203, 233; arrest of, 207–208, 231; defense plans, 169.
Hesser Christian, 72, 73, 198, 249.
Hidalgo, Miguel de, 131, 202, 208, 230.
Hinson, José, 198.
Houston, [?] See Austin, Moses.
Holland, settlers from, 27.
Holly, Mary Austin, 258.
Houck, Louis, 11, 21.
Hubbard, Amos, 114, 123.
Huerta de Jesus, Father, 198, 212, 213.
Hughes, Daniel, 174.
Huguet, Francisco, 177.
Humbert, 233, 258, 259, 336.

Illinois, 18, 28.
Illinois River, French settlers on, 27; Americans westward, 5, 7.
Immigration, plans, 101, 122, 151, 172, 177, ; regulations, 134, 162.
Independence, declaration, 270.
Indians, 30, 43, 45, 50, 54, 55, 70, 74, 75, 76, 85, 96. 114, 123, 176 214–216, 217, 248, 252, 272, 282, 295, 305, 325; hostile to Americans, 257.

Inquisition, 15.
Insurgents, 233–235, 245–248, 262–263, 268, 342–343; congress, 240.
Interior Provinces, 8, 14, 16, 17, 182, 196, 205, 234, 240, 251, 252, 253, 254, 261, 268, 269, 310, 312–314, 333–334; division of, 83, 209–210, 221; French agents, 184.
Irish, 57, 197, 241, 242, 249.
Irrigation, 65, 304.
Islas Negras, 197.
Italians, 11, 12, 192.

Jamaica, 182.
Janson, Edward, 113.
Jay, Treaty, 30.
Jefferson, Thomas, 266–267.
Jernigham, Henry, 11.
Johnson, Isaac, 119.
Jones, Daniel Colman, 110.
Johnston, Guillermo, 296.

Karankawas, 304.
Keene, Richard Raynal, 127, 241–242, 345–346.
Kemper, Reuben, 190.
Kentuckians, 14, 17, 21, 38, 258, 259.
King, David, 110.
Koasatis, 76, 215.
Korkens, David, 300.
Kuerke, Enrique, 196, 198.

Labastida, Ignacio de, 103.
Lacomba, Francisco, 178.
Lafitte, Pablo, 73, 74.
Lafon, Bartolomé, 250.
Laforçada, Juan, 299.
Laguardia, Bautista, 177.
Lalemand, Charles, 260.
L'Amis de Lois, 222.
Lands, attraction of in Texas, 187, 220, 229, 257; laws, 259, 279–280, 337–340; prices, 107.
Landres, José Nicolas, 110.
Langlois, Agustin, 108.
La Pita Road, 257.
Laredo, 202, 250.
Larrua, Miguel del, 123, 134, 163.
Lartigue, Julien, 124.
Lartigue, Pedro, 104, 122, 146, 226.
Las Casas, 207, 216.
Lassus, 38, 69, 331.
Latour, Lacarriére, 250.
Laviña, Pedro, 300.
Layssard, Valentin, 48, 49, 60, 61, 72, 75, 306.
Lead Mines, 32.
Leal, José, 178.
Leathem, John, 178.
Le Conte, Juan Bautista, 108.
Lee Matias, 109.
Lepin, Estevan, 299.
Lestigue, Pedro, 165.
Leseuhne, Celeste, 314.
Lipans, 66, 215, 252, 283.
Loid, John, 178.
Long, James, 269, 270–271, 286, 351.
Longueville, Pedro, 55, 151.
Lorenzo, José, 232.
Losoya, Victoriano, 323.
Louisiana, 10, 39, 56, 231, 235, 256, 257, 295, 301,; discontent of settlers of 61–63, 73, 77, 78, 110; Lower Louisiana, 12, 32, 36, 39; Upper Louisiana, 32, 33, 35, 36, 39; Napoleonic agents, 67, 214; trade, 71, 216, 220, 247; transfer, 7, 58, 65–68, 79, 189; 307–308.

Low Countries, 26.
Luci, Silas, 124, 314.
Lucobichi, José, 178.
Lugo, José Manuel, 146, 314.
Lunn, Juan, 102, 124.

McFallen, Juan, 297.
McFarlan, Juan, 165, 190, 250.
McFarrel, Juan, 55.
McLaughlin, Santiago, 11, 107, 314.
McKoy, Simón, 101.
McNulty, Santiago, 124.
Macarty, Augustin, 16.
Maconilt, Juan, 298.
Macoy, Francisco, 300.
Madison, James, 68, 127, 229.
Magee, Agustus, 183, 233.
Magee, Juan, 102, 141, 165, 196.
Maison Rouge, 29.
Malroni, Juan, 124, 314.
Maquin, Juan, 314.
Marchan, Juan Eugenio, 112, 167.
Martínez, Antonio, 258, 271, 272, 282.
Martínez, Francisco, 177.
Martínez, Melchor, 177.
Maryland, 11.
Masmela, Apolinar, 246.
Matagorda, 114, 137, 217, 242, 252, 256; port of, 81, 82, 159, 183, 238, 283, 342.
Maton, Francisco, 177.
Mayeyes, 304.
Maynes, Father, 194, 197.
Mechanics, 36, 220, 221.
Medina, battle of, 233, 236, 340.
Medina River, 251, 283.
Melaclon, James, 109.
Menchaca, José, 314.
Mequin, Juan, 314.
Mercantel, Francisco, 109.
Merlan, James, 178.
Michamps, Eugenio, 134.
Michela, María, 323.
Micheli, Vicente, 194, 314.
Millan, Florenço, 63.
Mims, Juan Felipe, 177.
Mina, Xavier, 245, 255–256.
Mine A Burton, 34.
Minor, Juan, 85, 86, 172, 331.
Minorca, 262.
Miranda, 93, 117.
Miró, Estevan, 14, 15, 17, 19, 20, 21, 56.
Mississippi River, 29, 30, 40, 43, 52.
Mission lands, 237, 283; mission on Brazos, proposed, 215.
Mobile, 187, 190.
Molinar, Antonio, 119.
Monroe, James, 275, 276.
Montolla, Trinidad, 223.
Moore, Sara, 143.
Mora, José María, 104.
Moral, Miguel del, 58, 50.
Morasen, Carlos, 151.
Morel, José, 300.
Morfil, Eduardo, 55.
Moreau, General, 127.
Morgan, George, 18, 20–22.
Morphi, Diego, 197, 219–222, 248.
Morvan, Francisco, 300.
Munguia, Nepomuceno, 323.
Muñoz, Manuel, 47, 55.
Musquiz, Barbara, 323.

Nacogdoches, 55, 57, 62, 63, 65, 66, 67, 71, 72, 73, 76, 86, 89, 91, 94, 105, 194, 203, 207, 213, 214, 215, 222, 227, 228, 229, 235, 283, 300, 301, 302, 303–304, 306, 307, 332, 342, 356; American

Index

troops at, 18; census, 180, 267, 297; condition at, 198; contraband trade, 67; defense, 50, 51, 65, 92, 182; fair at, 205, 246; foreigners at, 57; immigrants, 90; immigrants to Louisiana, 108; road, settlements on, 65; settlement, 82; settlement of, 105.
Nadakas, 215.
Napoleon, 39, 84, 87, 129, 147–148, 203, 204, 208, 210–213, 218, 219, 220, 233–234, 237, 243, 295, 305; agents, 162; aggressions, 68, 80, 126, 127, 128–129, 147, 161, 175, 185–186, 189, 325; emissary to United States, 184, 242, 323–326.
Nash, Ira, ordered to leave, 167.
Natchez, 13, 31, 49, 77, 248, 269.
Natchitoches, 55, 63, 74, 77, 115, 194, 212, 214, 219, 226, 237, 246, 247, 248, 249, 269.
Nava, Pedro, 41, 42, 48, 51, 78, 93, 302.
Navarro, José María, 222.
Neches, 250.
Negroes, 13, 20, 32, 36.
Nelson, Elisha, 120, 123, 314.
Nes, Juan, 123.
Neutral Ground, 117, 129, 183, 211, 224, 227, 342.
Neve, Philipe de, 56, 93, 110, 296.
New Madrid, 19, 20, 28, 29, 30, 35, 38, 257.
New Mexico, 26.
New Orleans, 10, 13, 27, 30, 32, 65, 82, 85, 140, 185, 186, 193, 203, 211, 227, 248, 306.
New York, 3, 16, 222.
Nicolas, Juan, 300.
Norfolk, French agents at, 184.
Nolan, Philip, 53, 54, 60, 74, 151.
Norman, Hilda, 6.
Norrain, Batista Juan, 177.
Norris, Edmund, 73, 120, 123.
Northern Indians, 47.
Nueces River, proposal for settlement on, 106, 124, 125.
Nueva Bourbon, 27.
Nueva, Feliciana, 201.
Nueva Jaén, 99.
Nueva Viscaya, 61, 63, 71, 117, 139; open to settlers, 82.
Nuevo León, 107, 116; Bishop of, 77, 143, 240, 344.
Nuevo, Santander, 106, 107.
Numans, Guillermo, 300.

Oconor, Juan, 298.
O'Fallen, Benjamin, 269.
Ohio, settlers from for Louisiana, 14, 254; immigrants from, 29.
Ohio River, 275.
Olivares, Francisco, 73.
Olivero, Joseph, 119.
Onís, 175, 182, 184, 185, 193, 260, 269, 273–274, 336–337; treaty, 276.
Opelousas, 10, 12, 91, 109, 201, 226, 269.
Oranday, Francisco, 178.
Orcoquisac, 66, 84, 85, 88, 89, 90, 91, 92, 107, 108, 111, 122; proposal to settle Louisiana families, 89.
Orkokisas Indians, 114.
Ortis, Miguel, 140.
Ortis, Tadeo, 222.
Osage Indians, 966.
Ottoman Porte, attitude toward Spanish revolution in Spanish America, 262.
Ouachita, 29, 30, 35, 72, 87, 95, 112, 185, 257.

Padilla, Juan Antonio, 272–273.
Pallou, Guillermo, 299.

Parat, Louis, 120.
Pared, Antonio, 297.
Pascagoulas, 114, 124.
Palafox, Viıla de, 202, 252, 253.
Paso de Tomas, 66.6
Paulas, Pedro, 23.
Patterson, Pedro, 141, 146, 314.
Pecan Point, 269.
Pensacola, 186, 187, 190.
Pennsylvania, 18.
Peña, Alexandro, 323.
Pérez, Encarnación, 314, 323.
Philadelphia, 27, 28, 32, 38, 184, 211, 219, 222, 233, 260.
Pifermo, Juan Ignacio, 300.
Pike, 256.
Pittsburg, 56.
Plaquemines, 12.
Platt, Jonathan Hale, 178.
Poinsett, Joel, 219.
Pointe Coupee, 10.
Poles, 219–220.
Pon, Nicolas, 299.
Porras, Marín de, 77.
Portilla, 124, 125, 323.
Poston, Henry, 141.
Prado, Pedro, 343.
Presidios, 45, 47, 167, 215, 221, 251, 283, 314.
Priestley, H. I., 6.
Pridomo, Francisco, 299.
Pridomo, Sebastian, 300.
Protestants, 13, 35, 37, 81, 194, 195, 196, 230, 235.
Puelles, Father, 153.
Puesto de Arkansas, 32.
Punta Cortada, 62

Quinn, Miguel, 102, 142, 165, 196, 214, 304.
Querque, Enrique, 297.
Querque, Reimundo, 297.
Quiros, José, 146, 314.

Ramírez, José Antonio, 106, 179.
Ramírez, Juan, 323.
Ramona, Manuela María, 314.
Ramos de Arispe, Miguel, 209–210.
Rapides, 55, 61, 78, 226, 306, 307.
Rascal, Isabel, 314.
Rechar, Mordecai, 178.
Rechard, Estevan, 112.
Recopilación de Indias, 295.
Red River, 257, 276.
Rees, Joshua, 121, 123, 298.
Refugio, 125; mission of, 282, 304.
Regency, 185, 220, 237–241, 333–334.
Religious tolerance, 15, 20, 22, 23, 36, 37.
Reliquet, Luis, 299.
Reveque, Lorenzo, 55, 151.
Revolution, 44, 182, 184, 219, 266.
Rhea, John, 189.
Richmond, 32.
Rio Grande, presidio, 25; river, 84, 202, 225–228, 250, 253, 258, 265, 275, 313.
Ripley, Major El. W., 350.
Ris, See Rees.
Robin, C. C., 87.
Robinson, John, 221, 2448.
Robinson, John H., 264.
Rochelle, 56.
Rodríguez, Feliciana, 323.
Ronells, John, 110
Roquier, Francisco, 113.
Rosa, Francisco de la, 136–139, 157, 163.
Rosales, Juan, 298.
Rosario, 304.
Rubeson, Celeste, 314.
Ruíz, Francisco, 343.
Rumanola, Carlos, 134.
Russia, 281, 262–263, 276.

Saabedra, 175.
Sabine River, 39, 76, 86, 114, 184, 225, 248, 263.
Sais, Pedro Antonio, 201.
Salas, Jesus, 323.
Salazar, Estanislao, 323.
Salazar, Maximo, 323.
Salazar, Pedro, 323.
Sa'cedo, Juan Manuel, 75, 96.
Salcedo, Manuel María de, 133, 134, 145, 153, 160, 168, 169, 176, 179,, 182, 183, 191, 204, 207, 214, 217, 223, 227, 233, 343.
Salcedo, Nemesio, 58, 61, 71, 75, 83, 84, 86, 88, 95, 106, 107, 113, 114, 116, 118, 119, 124, 128, 130, 222, 234, 303, 328.
Salcedo, Villa de, 95, 102, 104, 111, 112, 121, 140, 144, 150, 182, 191, 193, 194, 196, 197, 203, 224, 225, 230, 248, 314–315, 342.
Salie, Carlos, 105.
Salinas, José, 323.
Salinas, José Antonio, 178.
Salinas, María Ignacia, 323.
Somora, Diego, 178.
Sancerman, Francisco, 176.
San Andres de Nava, 93, 102.
San Antonio, 67, 282.
Saint Genevieve, 11, 38.
St. Louis, 11, 12, 33, 38.
St. Petersburg, 259.
St. Vrain, James Ceran Delassus, 29.
San Bernardo Bay, 88, 108, 137, 358.
Sánchez, Cesario, 323.
San Fernando de Béxar, 103.
San Juan, mission of, 102.
San Idlefonso, treaty of, 60.
San Marcos de Neve, 54, 124, 125, 126, 180, 199, 224, 323; fort on, 238; river, 124, 125, 218, 283.
San Martin de Tesmaluca, 201.
San Pedro de Pitic, 103.
San Sabá, 283.
Santa Fé, 130, 252.
Santo Domingo, 84, 130.
Sarnac, Juan, 56, 299.
Schoolcraft, Henry Rowe, 34.
Seridan, Enrique, 102, 114.
Seridan, Rebecca, 102.
Si, Juan, See Sy.
Sibley, Dr. John, 122, 212.
Sims, Rafael, 298.
Slaves, 88, 96, 136, 143, 144.
Solis, Jesus, 323.
Sonora, 103.
Smith, Dennis, 255.
Solana, Joachin Domingo, 11.
Solivello, Miguel, 122.
Sosa, Father, 144.
Soto, José, 323.
Soto, Juan, 323.
Spahn, Guillermo, 77.
Spain, weakness, 39, 148; Indian policy, 30, 44, 94; international relations, 33, 39, 40, 41, 43, 44, 77, 83, 84, 85, 87, 95, 116, 117, 132 192, 2660, 318; settlers from 24, 242.
Steele, Andrew, 189.
Steuben, Baron von, 23–26.
Stock, 50, 52, 53, 54, 56, 57, 106, 115, 205, 246, 303, 304.
Suel, Guillermo, 298.
Swiss, 273–274.
Switzerland, 27.
Sy, Juan, 104, 134, 1666.

Tacoma, Gabriel, 121.
Tampico, 238, 248, 254, 256.
Tancahuas, 117, 215, 252.
Tardiveau, Bartholomé, 26, 28.
Tarp, Roberto, 300.
Tatishoff, 281.
Tawakanas, 114, 224.
Tawehash, 50, 224.
Taylor, [Joseph], 214.
Tecier, José, 300.
Tecier, Pedro, 300.
Tennessee, 258–259.
Tessier, Carlos, 313–314.
Texas, census, 55, 67, 99–100, 192, 203, 236, 247, 286, 303–305; colonization, 61, 86, 88, 95, 98, 106, 107, 113, 114, 1716, 62, 64, 67, 71, 83, 140, 191, 237, 308, 308–311, 313–314, 343; foreign designs upon, 5, 7, 39, 42, 69, 70, 83, 130, 142, 156, 182, 186, 192, 208, 209, 219, 224, 225, 250, 251, 270, 271, 276, 281; trade, 65, 115, 185, 205, 215, 222, 235, 246, 265, 266, 275, 305.
Thomas, Benjamin, 110.
Thompson, Martha, 314.
Tilsit, 184.
Tinsas, 75, 90, 114.
Tlascaltecas, 271–272.
Toledo, José Alvarez de, 210, 233, 248, 343.
Tortuga, 283.
Travieso, Franciscoo, 102, 314.
Travieso, Guadalupe, 314.
Travieso, Vicente,
Treviño, Bernabé, 178.
Trinity River, 66, 73, 766, 866, 87, 88, 89, 93, 94, 111, 218, 260, 274, 283.
Trudeau, Felix, 63.
Turreau, General, 184.

Ugarte, Joaquín, 70, 866, 90, 93, 300.
Ugarte, Juan, 65, 66.
United States, objection to rule of in Louisiana, 306; policy, 88, 195, 219, 223, 229, 236, 262, 295; relations with Spain, 182, 212, 223, 262, 263, 263, 318.

Va'ency, treaty of, 243.
Valero, San Antonio de, 304.
Valle, François, 34.
Vechan, Rosa Francisco, 133.
Venua, María Magdalena, 107, 110.
Venua, Sebastian, 109.
Vera Cruz, 52, 73, 78, 80, 87, 88, 201, 231, 249, 253, 325, 325, 330.
Verán, Andres, 119.
Victoria, General, 256.
Vidal, José, 62, 65, 137, 138, 148, 331.
Vienna, Court of, 259.
Villereal, Luis, 321.
Vil!as, 103, 314–322.
Virginia, land grants in, 38.

Walker, Juan Pedro, 63.
Walling, A. G., 355.
Walling, Jesse, 355.
Warnett, Juan Francisco, Baron de, 111.
Washington City, 184.
Welche, Nicole, 65–66.
Wellington, 242.
West, Guillermo, 123.
West, relations with Spain, 22.
Wilkinson, James, 18–22, 33, 34, 117, 175, 195, 227, 249, 285.
Willett, Germain, 120.
Williams, Guillermo, 62.
Williams, John, 256.
Winkler, E. W.., 6.

Yanso, Guillermo, 123.
Yrujo, Marqués de, 34, 281.
Yucante, Crisostome, 51, 300.

Zambrano, Juan José, 208, 214, 233.
Zambrano, Manuel, 251.
Zerban, Federico, 142.